"Far too many Christians are ignorant or misinformed about church history. Far too many church history textbooks don't help matters because they are too dense, too dry, and/or too distorted! Fortunately, this is not the case with this excellent resource from Steve McKinion and Benjamin Quinn. They offer a compelling, sympathetic, and (not for nothing) readable narrative that covers many of the eras and figures that are the least familiar to contemporary Christians."

—**Nathan A. Finn**, professor of faith and culture, North Greenville University

"Church history is the story of God's people reading the Scripture, confessing Christ, and engaging a broader culture. McKinion and Quinn provide great insights into each aspect of this story since the first century. The readability and insightful interactions with select primary sources allow the voices of the church's past to guide the narrative."

—**Jason K. Lee**, professor of theological studies, Cedarville University

"The church today is undergoing significant changes, making this an ideal time to reflect on our shared history. McKinion and Quinn offer more than a simple recounting of past events; they present a thoughtful synthesis of key theological themes and historical insights that is sure to edify anyone seeking a spiritually enriching overview of the Great Tradition. This book would make an excellent textbook for a church history course, and I am confident it will rekindle a love for Christ's church in readers."

—**Stephen O. Presley**, director of education and engagement and senior fellow for religion and public life, Center for Religion, Culture, and Democracy

CHRISTIAN
History

VOLUME 1

VOLUME 1

CHRISTIAN *History*

From the Apostolic Fathers to the Eve of the Reformation

STEVEN A. MCKINION
AND BENJAMIN T. QUINN

Christian History, Volume 1: From the Apostolic Fathers to the Eve of the Reformation

Published by B&H Academic®
Brentwood, Tennessee

ISBN: 978-1-0877-3611-2

DEWEY: 270.1
SUBHD: CHURCH HISTORY--30-600, EARLY CHURCH \ CHURCH HISTORY--600-1500, MIDDLE AGES \ CHRISTIANITY

Cover design by Gearbox. Cover images by Shutterstock.

Printed in China
31 30 29 28 27 26 RRD 1 2 3 4 5 6 7 8 9 10

CONTENTS

INTRODUCTION

The Great Tradition

So then, brothers and sisters, stand firm and hold to the traditions you were taught, whether by what we said or what we wrote.

Now we command you, brothers and sisters, in the name of our Lord Jesus Christ, to keep away from every brother or sister who is idle and does not live according to the tradition received from us.

—The Apostle Paul, 2 Thess 2:15 and 3:6

Tradition is a multifaceted term that refers to the content of the Christian faith handed down from one generation of believers to another, as well as the practices by which that faith is passed on. The earliest Christians, or followers of "the Way" of Jesus, a label often applied to the early Christ followers (e.g., Acts 9:2), cultivated diverse practices, languages, customs, and beliefs to express the faith. There is no pure age in Christian history where everyone who claimed to be a Christian articulated every aspect of their faith in the same manner, worshipped the same way, or even saw one another as within the same community of faith. Diverse "Christian" communities interpreted the gospel of Jesus Christ in unique and sometimes incompatible ways. The diversity of contemporary Christian practice is nothing new.

Amid this diversity, however, there was a unified confession, a gospel, that Jesus Christ delivered to the apostles and that they in turn passed along to their congregations. That gospel proclaimed that Jesus of Nazareth is the Christ from the Hebrew Scriptures. From the beginning, the apostles received from the crucified and risen Lord the gospel that envisions him as the fulfillment of the Scriptures, the Law, Prophets, and Writings, or what we know today as the Old Testament.

The most well-known definition of the Great Tradition can be found in Vincent of Lérins's *Commonitorium*. Written in the fifth century to distinguish true Christian teaching from heresy, the *Commonitorium* defines the Great Tradition as "that faith which has been believed everywhere, always, by all [those in the church]."[1] While the dictum does not identify the specific content of the Great Tradition, it is a valuable reminder that there is a community of faith that holds in common the beliefs and practices of the true gospel of Jesus Christ. The history of the church is the history of the people of God trying to live out and pass along the common faith of Jesus Christ according to Scripture.

The content of the Great Tradition is not a simple list of acceptable truth claims and practices. Instead, it is the message of Scripture, both the Old Testament and the New Testament, interpreted and applied in history. There is a single unchanging gospel but innumerable ways to live that gospel within community. The history of the church is the history of the proclamation of the gospel of Jesus Christ. For two thousand years, Christians have received, preserved, and passed on these core beliefs and practices, while fellowshipping with Jesus and one another to make disciples of all nations.

Christians recognize that some beliefs and practices are outside the Great Tradition. Through conflict, councils, and creeds, they debate the faith they hold in common and distinguish that faith from errant interpretations of the gospel, also known as heresy. By observing those conflicts and the resulting confessions, we can identify four characteristics of the church's Great Tradition. First, the Great Tradition is scriptural. The Christian faith is rooted in the Hebrew Bible and the writings of the apostles, which we know as the Old and New Testaments. These inspired Scriptures, interpreted rightly, are the ultimate source of Christian faith. Second, the Great Tradition is Christological, centered on Jesus Christ as the Son of God. As the Son, Jesus is the revelation of God by whom God reconciles humanity to himself. Third, the Great Tradition is liturgical, which means it preserved and passed along the gospel within the church's prayers, songs,

[1] Vincent of Lérins, *Commonitorium* 2.6, https://www.newadvent.org/fathers/3506.htm.

sermons, and ordinances/sacraments (baptism and the Lord's Supper). Finally, the Great Tradition is moral or ethical. Apostolic Christianity is more than doctrinal fidelity; it is also fidelity to a way of life found in Jesus and the Scriptures. The Great Commandment to love God and neighbor is the lived essence of the Christian gospel. Affirmation of the truth of the gospel goes hand in hand with practicing the Christian ethic. Throughout the two volumes of this Chistian history, we will trace the ways in which the church of Jesus Christ has attempted to faithfully preserve and live out the gospel of Jesus Christ contained in Scripture.

The Great Tradition Is Scriptural

The first identifying characteristic of the Great Tradition is the unwavering commitment to Holy Scripture as the source of the Christian faith. Christianity is rooted in the texts of the Bible. The church was birthed out of a Jewish context: Its Lord is Jewish; its apostles were Jewish; and its scriptures were Jewish. Thus, the first "Bible" of the first Christians was the Old Testament Scriptures. During his earthly ministry and after his resurrection, Jesus taught his disciples that the entire Old Testament (Law, Prophets, and Writings) are about him (John 5:6 and Luke 24:27, 44–45; Matt 16:16 has an implied reference to Psalm 2), consequently giving a new hermeneutic for how to read the Jewish Scriptures. While the point will be developed in chapter 3, suffice it to say here that very early in the life of the church, Christians began to read Paul's letters, the Gospel accounts, and other apostolic letters in the worship service alongside the Old Testament as Christian Scripture (see 2 Pet 3:15–16).

The Great Tradition is founded on the faith "that was delivered to the saints once for all" (Jude 3) through the teaching of the apostles, who learned it from the risen Jesus. The deposit of faith is the gospel of Jesus according to the apostles, locating the foundation for Christianity in the prophetic and apostolic texts.

Apostolic Christianity contrasts with other so-called Christianities, such as Docetic, Ebionite, gnostic, and Judaistic Christianities, in their reliance on the Scriptures of the Old and New Testaments as authoritative texts.[2] Other "Christianities," such as Arianism,

[2] See Bart Ehrman, *Lost Christianities: The Battle for Scripture and the Faith We Never Knew* (Oxford University Press, 2005). Ehrman's descriptions of these various alternatives to apostolic Christianity are helpful, even while his assessment of the rejection of these articulations of Christianity is less so.

Pelagianism, and monophysitism, sought to base their beliefs on Scripture, but their interpretations were determined to be inconsistent with the overall message of the biblical faith and were jettisoned, usually after considerable debate and controversy.[3] The process of debating these controversies often resulted in the calling of ecumenical councils, where the competing sides presented the biblical evidence for their interpretations. Orthodox Christians based their faith and practice on Scripture.

When the second-century pastor and theologian Irenaeus of Lyons wrote against various heresies known collectively as Gnosticism (see ch. 3), he identified their fundamental error to be appealing to sources other than the apostolic understanding of the Old Testament, such as a "secret" personal revelation and special oral traditions. Irenaeus's handbook for Christian preachers, *Demonstration of the Apostolic Preaching*, explains how the Hebrew Scriptures along with the apostolic writings describe the true gospel of Jesus Christ. The *Demonstration* was Irenaeus's effort to show that orthodox Christianity is derived from both the Old Testament and the writings of the apostles. He meticulously details how Christians reading the Old Testament can see the Christian gospel clearly. Irenaeus provides exegesis of important texts that tell the story of the gospel and argues that true Christianity rests on the written text of Scripture, which was inspired by the Holy Spirit.

Even in their early confessions and creeds, Christians described the church as "one holy, apostolic, and catholic church." The catholic (meaning universal) church is only the true church when its faith in Jesus Christ is that of the apostles, which is contained in the Scriptures of the Old and New Testaments.

The Church's Great Tradition Is Christological

As we consider the common faith of Christians throughout the history of the church, a second characteristic of the Great Tradition is the person of Jesus Christ as the Son of God. The Gospels narrate different understandings of Jesus's identity among the various groups of people who interacted with him. These groups include the religious leaders, the crowds of unnamed people, his disciples, and the Roman political leaders, among others. The people composing the crowds understood Jesus in different ways (Mark 6:2–3;

[3] See John Behr, *The Way to Nicaea* (St. Valdimir's Press, 2001); and Khalid Anatolios, *Retrieving Nicaea: The Development and Meaning of Trinitarian Theology* (Baker Academic, 2018).

John 6:14; John 7:12). The unclean spirits interpreted Jesus to be someone else still (Mark 3:11). As an example of his interaction with the disciples, a crucial episode between Jesus and Peter illustrates this point. Jesus asks him, "Who do people say that the Son of Man is?" Peter responded that some people believed Jesus to be Jeremiah and others John the Baptist resurrected. Jesus then asks, "Who do you say I am?" Peter answered, "You are the Messiah, the Son of the living God" (Matt 16:13–16). Jesus acknowledges that Peter's answer is the correct one: Jesus is rightly identified as the Messiah prophesied in the Old Testament and identified as the Son of God in passages such as Ps 2:7. Jesus further states that Peter did not learn this from "flesh and blood" (i.e., humans), but from God the Father. Peter arrives at this conclusion by revelation, not by rationality. We learn from the encounter between Peter and Jesus, as well as these others that the orthodox faith is this Christological confession: the belief that Jesus is the promised Christ of the Old Testament.

The Great Tradition proclaims the message of the New Testament, namely that God is Father, Son, and Holy Spirit and that the Son was incarnate and given the name Jesus, as he would save his people from their sins. Jesus Christ reveals God to human beings and provides for their salvation because he *is* God and *is* their salvation. The God who created humanity and promised salvation has come to fulfill that promise. In Jesus Christ, God is "with us" (Matt 1:23; Luke 1:32, 35), and those who have seen him have seen the Father (John 14:9). All who believe in him will have eternal life (John 3:16). God also makes his presence and salvation known by the Holy Spirit. The first and unequivocal commitment to Jesus Christ as the revelation and salvation of God is not in dispute among the earliest Christians. For this reason, much of Christian theology has centered on the identity of Jesus Christ as both God and human.

Outside of the Great Tradition, there are groups, such as the Docetists and Ebionites, who will be discussed further in chapter 3, that denied the deity of Jesus. The former group (of which there was a variety) denied that Jesus of Nazareth was actually God incarnate. Likewise, the Ebionites believed that Jesus was an obedient human prophet but not God in the flesh. Both perspectives in various iterations are outside of the Great Tradition of the church. Jesus is the cornerstone and foundation of the church (Matt 21:42; Acts 4:11; Eph 2:20; 1 Pet 2:6–7). He builds his church (Matt 16:18), and the church is his body (Eph 1:22–23). Thus, the church is founded on Jesus Christ and the Holy Spirit. The church is a spiritual community participating both in the life and mission of God.

The Great Tradition Is Liturgical

Some years ago, I (Benjamin) attended a New England Episcopal service one Sunday morning with a family friend. I didn't realize beforehand that the two presiding ministers were actively and publicly engaged in a lifestyle contrary to the teaching of Scripture. Despite my disappointment, I was struck by the liturgy. From the prayers to the Scripture readings and recitations of both the Apostles' and Nicene Creeds, the gospel of Jesus was clearly articulated. As I reflected on the service, I prayed the church would continue to observe this historic liturgy that includes prayers of prior saints, Scripture readings, and the ancient creeds, as this may be the only assurance that the gospel is preserved and promoted among that congregation.

God's people are a liturgical community. Throughout the Pentateuch, Moses instructs Israel about worship, from the design of the space to the attitude of the worshipper. Through the prophets, God judges Israel for idolatry and worship in which they "approach me with their speeches to honor me with lip-service, yet their hearts are far from me, and human rules direct their worship of me" (Isa 29:13). Worship gatherings past to present have centered around Scripture, prayer, and sacrament (or ordinance) which distinguish the Christian church from other corporate gatherings, religious or nonreligious. For our purposes in identifying "liturgical" as an essential element of the Great Tradition, we will give special consideration to worship (or liturgy), sacrament, and the gathered community.

Many modern-day Christians might use a phrase such as "order of service" to describe what takes place during a Sunday morning worship service. "Liturgy" (*liturgia* in Latin) is the historic term for "order of service," which simply means the customary order in which public worship is conducted. This term has enjoyed a revival in recent days through the work of James K. A. Smith and others, wherein liturgy is applied to all of life, an intentional rhythm that prioritizes those daily habits and rituals that are important for a flourishing life (work, rest, silence, community, exercise, meditation, etc.).[4] By submitting oneself to daily liturgy, one is then formed by the routine. The fact is liturgy is operative in our lives whether we recognize it or not. The important thing is to become critically aware of these liturgies, then reform them in accord with the love and wisdom of Jesus Christ.

---

[4] For a helpful summation, see James K. A. Smith, *You Are What You Love: The Spiritual Power of Habit* (Brazos, 2016).

The same is true in Christian worship services regardless of denomination or tradition. Some traditions, such as Eastern Orthodoxy, are especially attentive to a traditional liturgy in corporate worship, for the shape of the service serves as a journey toward God climaxing in the Eucharist (Lord's Supper).[5] Others, such as Pentecostalism, are less rigid in the order of service, preferring flexibility and lack of structure to allow the Spirit of God to work freely among the people. And many other examples exist between these two.

In early Christianity, we have only a few examples of a precise weekly liturgy, but there are several general examples of the elements included in corporate worship. In his first letter (officially called an "apology") to the emperor, Justin Martyr (c. 110–165) provides a detailed illustration of what typically took place during an early second-century Christian worship service. In the context of describing a newly baptized convert, Justin describes the common elements of a worship service beginning with communion or the Lord's Supper:

> But we, after we have thus washed him who has been convinced and has assented to our teaching, bring him to the place where those who are called brethren are assembled, in order **that we may offer hearty prayers in common for ourselves and for the baptized**. . . . There is then brought to the [presiding one] of the brethren **bread and a cup of wine mixed with water**; and he taking them, gives praise and **glory to the Father of the universe, through the name of the Son and of the Holy Ghost**, and offers thanks at considerable length for our being counted worthy to receive these things at His hands. . . . And when the [presiding one] has given thanks . . . those who are called by us deacons give to each of those present to **partake of the bread and wine** mixed with water over which the thanksgiving was pronounced. . . . **And this food is called among us *Eucharistia***, of which no one is allowed to partake but the man who believes that the things which we teach are true, and who has been washed with the washing that is for the remission of sins, and unto regeneration, and **who is so living as Christ has enjoined.**[6]

Justin goes on describing the church in language similar to Acts 2:42–47:

---

[5] Cf. Vassilios Papavassiliou, *Journey to the Kingdom: An Insider's Look at the Liturgy and Beliefs of the Eastern Orthodox Church* (Paraclete, 2012).

[6] Justin Martyr, *The First Apology* 65–66, in *The Apostolic Fathers with Justin Martyr and Irenaeus*, vol. 1 of *The Ante-Nicene Fathers*, ed. Alexander Roberts and James Donaldson (Christian Literature Company, 1885), 185–86.

> And the wealthy among us help the needy; and we always keep together; and for all things wherewith we are supplied, we bless the Maker of all through His Son Jesus Christ, and through the Holy Ghost. And **on the day called Sunday, all who live in cities or in the country gather together to one place, and the memoirs of the Apostles or the writings of the prophets are read, as long as time permits; then, when the reader has ceased, the [presiding one] verbally instructs, and exhorts to the imitation of these good things. Then we all rise together and pray**. . . . And they who are well to do, and willing, give what each thinks fit; and what is collected is deposited with the [presiding one], who succours the orphans and widows, and those who, through sickness or any other cause, are in want, and those who are in bonds, and the strangers sojourning among us, and in a word takes care of all who are in need.[7]

As underscored by the bolded sections, the above illustrates well the core elements of Christian worship from the time of the early church up to the present. For more than twenty centuries, God's people have gathered across the globe for regular weekly meetings centered around the following:

- the celebration of baptism and the Lord's Supper (Eucharist);
- remembering the remission of sins and regeneration in Jesus (i.e., the gospel);
- joining together in prayer;
- reading aloud the Scriptures;
- hearing the Scriptures explained along with the exhortation to live accordingly;
- tithing, or providing for the poor, widows, orphans, and strangers;
- regular gatherings and special occasions for worship.

These represent the distinctives of the Christian church, and to remove any of these from worship is to undermine the church's very purpose and practice. Liturgy thus represents an integral part of the Great Tradition, as it distinguishes the gathered people of God from other corporate assemblies. Moreover, the liturgy not only speaks to the activities incorporated into Christian worship, but it also has a formative effect on God's people for the promotion of godliness and the preservation of doctrine. The Latin phrase *Lex orandi, lex credenda* (loosely translated "the law of prayer is the law of faith") speaks to the preserving

---

[7] Justin Martyr, *The First Apology of Justin* 65.67 (*ANF* 1:1:185).

nature of Christian liturgy. The church's confessions made in worship and prayer serve to preserve and maintain the church's faith as that which is to be handed down to future saints.

In between the time of Arius and the current era, as we will argue, some within the church veered off course with respect to proper Christian leadership and doctrine, though the Great Tradition was preserved in the church's liturgy as it was handed down from generation to generation.

The Great Tradition Is Moral

Returning to the point that liturgy also promotes godliness, the moral/ethical dimension of the Christian faith serves as our fourth component of the Great Tradition. Laced throughout the quote above from Justin's *First Apology* is the emphasis and expectation that God's people are called to, as Eugene Peterson writes, a "life of congruence."[8]

Congruence concerns the consistency between a Christian's confession of Christ and his or her way of life. This means that the lives of God's people—especially the clergy—should align with the way of Jesus, who calls his followers to love God and others above all things. Acts 9:2 refers to the followers of Jesus as the people of "the Way," whom Saul (later Paul) sought to persecute. In his defense to the people of Jerusalem in Acts 22, Paul admits that he "persecuted this Way to death, arresting and putting both men and women in jail" (22:4). Then, in Acts 24:14–16, Paul identifies himself as one who follows the Way, stating, "I worship the God of my ancestors according to the Way, which they call a sect, believing everything that is in accordance with the law and written in the prophets. I have a hope in God, which these men themselves also accept, that there will be a resurrection, both of the righteous and the unrighteous. I always strive to have a clear conscience toward God and men."

Paul's defense recognizes both a doctrinal and moral commitment as one who now follows the way of Christ. His defense as recorded in Acts aligns with his exhortation in 2 Thessalonians 2 and 3, in which he speaks twice of the "tradition" (*paradosis*) of the apostles, first concerning proper doctrine (2:15), then of proper conduct of life when he writes, "Now we command you, brothers and sisters, in the name of our Lord Jesus Christ, to keep away from every brother or sister who is idle and does not live according to the *tradition* received from us. For you yourselves know how you should imitate us" (3:6–7a, emphasis added).

---

[8] Eugene Peterson, *Christ Plays in Ten Thousand Places* (Eerdmans, 2008), 330.

This way of life modeled and taught by Paul and the other apostles is the way of holiness, which they learned from Jesus, the embodiment of holiness. Holiness—corporate and individual, public and private—is part of the legacy of God's people, who are called to be holy as God is holy (1 Pet 1:15). At least, it should be. While there are countless examples of so-called Christian men and women committing all sorts of evil, the Great Commandment to love God and neighbor remains, and it serves as a standard set by Jesus against which all Christians and Christian activity is measured. The command of love has also informed the church's practice for centuries on public matters, such as participation in politics, the arts, military service, marriage, care for the vulnerable (such as orphans, widows, the unborn, and the poor), and education, as well as more private matters, such as spirituality, liturgical practices, and communal living.

We may thus summarize this distinctive of the Great Tradition as God's people who, filled with the Holy Spirit, are compelled by the life and teachings of Christ and the apostles to be a holy people, walking in the way of Christ, in all piety and love for God and neighbor. Christians both past and present may disagree on the wisest expression of neighborly love in particular times and places, but the call to holiness and high moral standards remains part of what it means to be the people of God.

Recommended Reading

Papavassiliou, Vassilios. *Journey to the Kingdom: An Insider's Look at the Liturgy and Beliefs of the Eastern Orthodox Church*. Paraclete, 2012.

Peterson, Eugene. *Christ Plays in Ten Thousand Places*. Eerdmans, 2008.

Smith, James K. A. *You Are What You Love: The Spiritual Power of Habit*. Brazos, 2016.

—— Chapter 1 ——

Apostolic Christianity

Peter and Pentecost

Following the ascension of Jesus, the apostle Peter became the leader of the disciples. Jesus had instructed the disciples to remain in Jerusalem and wait for a gift from the Father, namely that they would "receive power when the Holy Spirit has come upon you, and you will be my witnesses in Jerusalem, in all Judea and Samaria, and to the ends of the earth" (Acts 1:8). Upon returning to Jerusalem, they devoted themselves to prayer along with other believers, including Jesus's mother and his siblings (Acts 1:12–14).

During this time, Peter led the disciples in selecting Matthias, a fellow witness of the ministry and resurrection of Christ, who would take the place of Judas, the betrayer of Jesus. This is the last mention of Matthias in the Bible, but his inclusion in the Twelve signals the importance of apostolic eyewitness in the passing down of the faith delivered once and for all to the saints.

About fifty days after Jesus's death and resurrection,[1] on the day of Pentecost, Luke reports that the sound of a mighty rushing wind filled the house where the disciples and

[1] See Justo González, *Acts: The Gospel of the Spirit* (Orbis, 2001), 33; and John Barton and John Muddiman, *The Oxford Bible Commentary* (Oxford University Press, 2007), 131.

their friends were staying. It divided like tongues of fire resting on each one of them, and they were all "filled with the Holy Spirit and began to speak in different tongues, as the Spirit enabled them" (Acts 2:1–4).

Peter then stood up and proclaimed to the Jews and other residents of Jerusalem that what they were witnessing was not a display of drunkenness, but rather the fulfillment of the prophecy from Joel 2:28–32a, which states:

> After this
> I will pour out my Spirit on all humanity;
> then your sons and your daughters will prophesy,
> your old men will have dreams,
> and your young men will see visions.
> I will even pour out my Spirit
> on the male and female slaves in those days.
> I will display wonders
> in the heavens and on the earth:
> blood, fire, and columns of smoke.
> The sun will be turned to darkness
> and the moon to blood
> before the great and terrible day of the Lord comes.
> Then everyone who calls
> on the name of the Lord will be saved.

Peter continued by claiming that Jesus of Nazareth, who performed signs and wonders in their midst, who was killed at the hands of lawless men according to the plan and foreknowledge of God, who was raised from the dead, who was loosed from the pangs of death as prophesied by the prophet David, was and is the Messiah. "Therefore," Peter concluded, "let all the house of Israel know with certainty that God has made this Jesus, whom you crucified, both Lord and Messiah" (Acts 2:36).

Upon hearing this message, the crowd asked Peter and the other apostles how they should respond. Peter instructed them that the proper response was to repent and be baptized in the name of Jesus Christ, for the forgiveness of sins and the assurance of receiving the gift of the Holy Spirit. Around 3,000 people responded to Peter's message and were baptized that day, and as these new believers continued in fellowship, worship, and service, their numbers continued to grow.

Peter's sermon at Pentecost is important for us to consider at this stage in the story for at least four reasons. First, immediately following Jesus's ascension, Peter takes up the mantle of leadership among Jesus's followers. But Peter's approach is not one of establishing his own new way among the disciples. Rather, he passes on what he had received, the offensive and culturally subversive yet gentle and life-giving gospel of Jesus.

Second, Peter connects his message about Jesus to the familiar message of the Hebrew scriptures, citing both Joel and the Psalms. This is particularly important as it reinforces Jesus's teaching that his message and ministry are in continuity with the Law and Prophets, not in contradiction to them. While there is a newness to the new covenant, there is an oldness to it as well, a continuity reaching back to Gen 1:1, "In the beginning, God," and connects to the Gospel of John's opening line that also begins with "In the beginning." God's promise in Gen 3:15, as well as his promises to Abraham, Moses, David, and the prophets, have been fulfilled in the person and work of Christ and given to Christ's followers, known as the church, through the Spirit of Christ. The fulfillment of the Old Testament in the person of Jesus Christ signals that the tradition of the apostles, even from Peter's first sermon, is in continuity with the Hebrew scriptures and inextricably linked to the person and work of Jesus, who is the Messiah.

Third, Peter's sermon underscores the essential role of the Holy Spirit in the spread of the gospel and in God creating a new people for himself. Whereas the Holy Spirit had previously worked through the prophets of God and among other men and women in various ways as pleased the Lord, now the Holy Spirit will dwell within those who believe in Jesus and are born again into his family and kingdom.

Finally, recalling Jesus's final words in Matt 28:18–20 and Acts 1:8, the Great Commission calls disciples of Jesus to carry the gospel of Jesus to "Jerusalem, Judea, Samaria and to the ends of the earth." Before Peter begins his sermon, Luke informs the reader that "now there were Jews staying in Jerusalem, devout people from every nation under heaven" (Acts 2:5). From the beginning of this Spirit-filled ministry, the audience is the nations of the earth, though at this point in the story it is primarily Jewish. But soon, the Lord will remind Peter that the Gentiles should also hear the gospel (Acts 10), and he will call Saul to a ministry especially for the Gentiles.

People of the Way

As the book of Acts continues, the apostles continue to proclaim the gospel and perform miracles, but we also see that these early believers encountered persecution from the very beginning.[2] In Acts 3 Peter and John are brought before the Jewish leaders who demanded that they cease speaking or teaching in the name of Jesus. But the apostles continued to preach Christ, and as the number of believers increased, so did the persecution of these early believers, culminating with the stoning of Stephen after he gave a detailed explanation of the gospel before the Jewish leaders in Acts 7. This account also mentions the young Saul, the persecutor of Christians, who was present and apparently approved of Stephen's stoning.

Acts 9:2 specifically mentions that Saul sought out men and women who "belonged to the Way" for his persecution efforts against Christians. More than twenty years later, speaking to the people in Jerusalem following his arrest, Paul (also known as Saul) spoke of his former life, when he "persecuted this Way to the death, arresting and putting both men and women in jail" (22:4).[3] Yet now he speaks as Paul the apostle, missionary to the Gentiles, and a leader of the Way.

The introduction to this volume discussed the moral component of the Great Tradition, but Acts's multiple references to the Way show that it was not simply a list of dos and do nots for Christian behavior. The Way was a way of life, including a mindset (Phil 2:5), for early Christians, who reduced their faith neither to mere doctrine nor to a set of rules. Rather, the Way was a holistic framework for living a holy life before man and God—the God of Abraham, Isaac, Jacob, Joseph, Moses, David, the prophets, and Jesus—in his world. The language of "Way" is thus inextricably linked to Old Testament imagery (cf. Deut 10:12–22; Psalms 1, 119; Proverbs 1–9; and other examples from the Prophets), as well as to Jesus himself, whom John identifies as "the way, the truth, and the life" (John 14:6).

With respect to life and doctrine, the Way points us back to the four strands of the Great Tradition presented in the introduction. The Way *is* the "faith that was delivered to the saints once for all" (Jude 3) and the tradition of the apostles concerning both doctrine and manner of life (2 Thess 2:15; 3:6). The people of the Way represented something different than that exhibited by other first-century religious leaders. This Way of life confessed the good news of the resurrected Jesus, called sinners to repentance, and baptized in the

---

[2] Craig S. Keener, *Acts: An Exegetical Commentary*, vol. 2, *3:1–14:28* (Baker Academic 2013), 1626–27.

[3] See timeline in F. F. Bruce, *Paul: Apostle of the Heart Set Free* (Eerdmans, 2000), 475.

name of the Father, Son and Holy Spirit. Moreover, the people of the Way worshiped in Spirit and truth, from the inside out, seeking complete congruence between confession, inner/spiritual posture before God and others, and external actions.

Before long, Christians began to consider the relationship between Christ and everything, including food, the calendar (time), architecture (space and places of worship), sports, politics, military engagement, work, and so on. Christianity was far more than the promise of heaven (or insurance against hell). The way of Christ demanded all of one's life, thus the New Testament letters and other early Christian writings are packed with both Christian doctrine (orthodoxy) and Christian ethics (orthopraxy). The two cannot be divorced, for Christian character flows from the gospel of Christ.

The Didache

While most of what we know about how first-century Christians lived and worshipped comes from the books of the New Testament, they are not the only sources of this information. Although much is unknown about the Didache (or The Teaching of the Twelve Apostles), including precise date and authorship, though an earlier date of c. 50 seems most likely, the Didache was an early Christian manual for worship and ethics. The intended audience is also uncertain, but it was certainly influential. While early Christians did not include it alongside Scripture, some ancient authors, such as Athanasius, claimed that the Didache should be read by new believers.

With strong overtones of both the Hebrew Scriptures and the teachings of Jesus, the Didache begins with the language of two ways, "There are two ways, one of life and one of death; and great is the difference between the two ways. This is the way of life: 'First you shall love God who made you, secondly, your neighbor as yourself; and whatever you would not like done to you, do not do to another.'"[4] The opening two verses sound familiar notes from Psalms (especially 1 and 119) and the Great Commandment to love God and neighbor above all, and they echo Acts's identification of early Christians as people of the Way, as this Way reflects the way of Wisdom, who is Jesus (1 Cor 1:24), and the Sermon on the Mount (Matt 5–7). The following four chapters detail various sins that Christians should avoid, as well as attitudes and behaviors that Christians should adopt. These chapters

---

[4] From Michael W. Holmes, ed. and trans., *The Apostolic Fathers: Greek Texts and English Translations*, 3rd ed. (Baker Academic, 2007), 334–37.

reaffirm the early Christians' concern with maintaining a way of life that was consistent with their claims to be followers of Jesus Christ. However, this was not just an ethical handbook for Christians; it also contained concrete instructions concerning church practice, such as baptism, the administration of the Eucharist, the day the gathering should take place, and the election of deacons and bishops.

Chapter seven of the Didache speaks to the practice of baptism, which is to be administered in the name of the Father, Son, and Holy Spirit as commanded in Matt 28:19–20. The baptism was to take place in a stream with cold, running water, though still or warm water was sufficient if cold, running water wasn't available. Immersion seems assumed, but the chapter notes that if sufficient water wasn't unavailable, pouring over the head three times was sufficient. This chapter also encourages the person being baptized, the person administering baptism, as well as anyone else in the church who was able, to fast for one or two days before baptism.

> On the Lord's own day gather together and break bread and give thanks, having first confessed your sins so that your sacrifice may be pure. But let no one who has a quarrel with a companion join you until they have been reconciled, so that your sacrifice may not be defiled.
>
> ———
>
> The Didache

In chapters 9 and 10, the author of the Didache speaks to the administration of the Eucharist. Prayers were to be offered before receiving both the cup and the bread. Based upon the command in Matt 7:6 to "not give what is holy to dogs," only those who had been baptized were allowed to partake of the Lord's Supper. Finally, after those who received the bread and wine were filled, another prayer of thanksgiving was made.

In other areas to note, chapter 14 commands that believers are to gather on Sunday, the Lord's Day. This represented a departure from Jewish practice of gathering on the Sabbath. Chapter 15 speaks briefly of the electing of bishops and deacons to serve the congregation in prophecy and teaching. The manual offers little in the way of a theology of baptism, Eucharist, or a full-throated ecclesiology. Rather, it is most concerned with the character of those leading and participating and the respectful manner with which the gathering of believers and observance of the sacraments are carried out.

This early handbook for morals and church practice enjoyed broad influence among early Christians, and it alerts us to what was important to these first communities of Christ followers. The Didache shows that early Christians, as they followed the way of Christ, were concerned with both believing and behaving rightly, whether it was in their daily lives or in the structure of their worship services.

Good News for the Gentiles

We referenced above Paul's conversion from persecuting the people of the Way to becoming a leader of the Way in Acts 9. In Acts 13, Paul and Barnabas were sent out by the church in Antioch for the work of the Lord. After their message was rejected by the Jews in Antioch of Pisidia, Paul and Barnabas replied,

> It was necessary that the word of God be spoken to you first. Since you reject it and judge yourselves unworthy of eternal life, we are turning to the Gentiles. For this is what the Lord has commanded us:
>
> I have made you
> a light for the Gentiles
> to bring salvation
> to the ends of the earth. (Acts 13:46b–47)

The Gentiles rejoiced when they heard this and "the word of the Lord spread through the whole region" (Acts 13:49). Through a vision and conversation with Cornelius, the Lord also made clear to Peter that the gospel was for both Jew and Gentile. Peter's subsequent ministry, however, would be directed primarily to the Jews, while Paul's ministry would be primarily directed toward the Gentiles. Paul's ministry to the Gentiles is reaffirmed in his letter to the Romans, where he writes, "Yet I have written you quite boldly on some points to remind you of them again, because of the grace God gave me to be a minister of Christ Jesus to the Gentiles. He gave me the priestly duty of proclaiming the gospel of God, so that the Gentiles might become an offering acceptable to God, sanctified by the Holy Spirit" (Rom 15:15–16 NIV).

But Paul's ministry came at great cost. Five times he was whipped by the Jews; three times he was beaten with rods. He was stoned, shipwrecked three times, and in constant danger (2 Cor 11:24). He was arrested at least three times (Acts 16:19–23; cf. 21:31; 2 Tim 1:8). Yet, even from prison he tells the Philippians that he desires to know the fellowship of Christ's sufferings (Phil 3:10) and exhorts them to "Rejoice in the Lord always. I will say it again: Rejoice!" (Phil 4:4).

Despite the sufferings, this ministry would yield the fruit of some fourteen new churches across two continents with some 7,500 Christians by the end of the century.[5] Of course, the total number of Christians in the first century is not solely from Paul's ministry, but the impact of his fervor and faithfulness is immeasurable. Moreover, thirteen of Paul's letters are recognized by all Christians (Roman Catholic, Orthodox, and Protestant) as Christian Scripture.

But what happened amidst the blended family of Jews and Gentiles? The history of Christianity, regardless of the narrator, is overwhelmingly a Gentile story. So what happened to the Jewish voice and influence in the story?

The Blended Family

While Paul is remembered as the apostle to the Gentiles, Peter's ministry remained more focused on the Jews. The blending of these different cultures into the new family of God was not always easy. Acts 15 tells of the deliberation about whether Gentiles should be circumcised. Jews from Judea were teaching the brothers that "unless you are circumcised according to the custom prescribed by Moses, you cannot be saved" (Acts 15:1). After some debate, Paul and Barnabas were sent by the church up to Jerusalem to discuss the matter with the apostles and the elders. Upon consideration, Peter reminded them how God had used his words to deliver the gospel to the Gentiles and had seen fit to give them the Holy Spirit without any distinction. Peter challenged the brothers, therefore, not to place a yoke around the neck of the Gentiles. Paul and Barnabas shared what signs and wonders God had done among the Gentiles, and James supported their testimony with words from the prophets.

This gathering of apostles and church leaders decided to send a letter to the brothers and sisters "among the Gentiles in Antioch, Syria, and Cilicia," stating that nothing was required of them beyond abstaining from "food offered to idols, from blood, from eating anything that has been strangled, and from sexual immorality" (Acts 15:22–29). However, cultural differences centered around Jewish ceremonial law remained among Jews and Gentiles that made the blending of these families a difficult undertaking.

---

[5] The precise number of Christians in the early centuries is notoriously difficult to calculate. For sociological studies and estimates, see the following: Rodney Stark, *The Rise of Christianity: A Sociologist Reconsiders History* (Princeton University Press, 1996); and Philip Jenkins, "How Many Christians?," Patheos, September 22, 2017, https://www.patheos.com/blogs/anxiousbench/2017/09/how-many-christians/.

Galatians 2 speaks to the struggles of acclimating to the blended traditions of Jews and Gentiles, even among the apostles. In this passage, Paul confronts Peter over inconsistent behavior. Peter was enjoying a meal with Gentiles until a group of Jews arrived. Peter then withdrew from the table and separated himself from the Gentiles because "he feared those from the circumcision party" (Gal 2:12). Paul would have none of this and opposed Peter to his face in front of the others. Paul argued, "If you, who are a Jew, live like a Gentile and not like a Jew, how can you compel Gentiles to live like Jews?" (Gal 2:14). The Galatians struggled with accepting Gentile believers who had not been circumcised, and even Peter was caught up in their discrimination. Paul's admonition shows that despite their differences, all believers, whether Jew or Gentile, were part of God's new creation (Gal 6:15) and should live their lives accordingly.

For the earliest Christians, whether they were from a Jewish or Gentile background, congruence of word and deed was central. Followers of Christ were expected to "walk" (Eph 4:1; 5:2; Col 1:10) in a manner worthy of the gospel they proclaimed, despite external or internal tensions that arose as a result. Early Christians were by no means perfect at this, as the letters of the New Testament attest. But the message of hope in the risen Christ continued to spread among Jews and Gentiles alike, and the church grew exponentially.

Externally, the commitment to worship the God who is Father, Son, and Spirit earned Christians no favors with the Jewish authorities who viewed the Christians' worship of Jesus as incompatible with Jewish monotheism. Christians were seen less as Jewish followers of the way of Christ and more as their own separate religion. Roman officials continued to view Christianity as a subset of Judaism, which was widely accepted, but they were still wary of the growth and influence of this sect that rejected the Roman gods. Moreover, the Christian command to "love your neighbor" (Matt 22:39) compelled them to care for the sick, the poor, and widows in ways that were countercultural, which both helped the church continue to grow and alarmed the Roman officials. However, amid the church's growth, the surrounding Jewish and Roman cultures would experience their own conflict, which would help distinguish the newly emerging Christian faith from the Jewish religion.

Destruction of the Temple

The definitive break between the emerging Christian faith and the Jewish religion was precipitated by several events. In AD 66, a Jewish revolt broke out against the Roman procurator Gessius Florus in response to his execution of some 3,600 Jewish citizens after not receiving enough taxes from the temple. This rebellion had been brewing for decades and would come to be known as the First Jewish Revolt. In response to this revolt, the newly appointed general, Titus, initiated his plan to attack Jerusalem strategically near the time of Passover, when many pilgrims were in the city, stressing the supply chain of food. By August, a weak and starved Jewish population was overtaken by the Romans. The final blow was the destruction of the Jewish temple, a flexing of Roman muscle meant to do irreparable damage to the Jewish psyche. This loss of the temple is still mourned by Jews today. Rome marked its victory by erecting the Arch of Titus in AD 81 at the entrance of the Roman Forum.

Image 1.1. *Arch of Titus*

Almost seventy years later, the Second Jewish Revolt (sometimes called the Third Jewish-Roman War), ultimately fell short as well. The effort was led by Simon Bar Kokhba, a messianic figure who promised restoration in Israel. Any independence enjoyed by Bar Kokhba's group was short-lived as the emperor Hadrian sought to uproot Judaism, barring the Jews entirely from Jerusalem. This expulsion from Jerusalem resulted in a further scattering of the Jewish people.

Following the destruction of the temple in AD 70, the Christian voice quickly began to lose its Jewish accent. Christianity was emerging as its own faith with its own practices, prayers, and culture. Theological differences began to make Christianity as distinct from Judaism as well.[6] Mark Noll writes, "Before [AD 70], Christianity was emerging in a definitively Jewish context. After that time, Christianity rapidly became its own distinct religion."[7]

As the religious distance grew between Jews and Christians, so too did the relational distance. Michael Holmes notes that "the years following AD 70 are marked by a sense of increasing distance between Judaism and Christianity. . . . the forcefulness of Ignatius's (c.35–c.108) denunciation of those who 'profess Jesus Christ' yet continue 'to practice Judaism' alerts us to the permeability of the boundaries between congregation and synagogue on a local level. . . . Judaism and Christianity are following diverging trajectories, and the legacy of suspicion and hostility from these early decades would be, regrettably, long-lived."[8]

Both Judaism and Christianity were forever marked by the destruction of the temple in AD 70. While the Jews sought to recover and regroup in the decades following, Christianity moved forward proclaiming the gospel of Jesus, establishing churches and church practices, and eventually formulating creedal statements and recognizing a set of authoritative texts now known as the New Testament.[9]

---

[6] Michael Kruger lists four theological categories that created tension: (1) Christians claimed Jesus was the Messiah, who shared the identity of Yahweh; (2) they claimed they were the true sons of Abraham; (3) they did not require Gentile Christians to submit to Jewish ceremonial law; and (4) they criticized the relevance of the temple. Michael J. Kruger, *Christianity at the Crossroads: How the Second Century Shaped the Future of the Church* (InterVarsity, 2018), 14.

[7] Mark A. Noll, *Turning Points: Decisive Moments in the History of Christianity*, 3rd ed. (Baker Academic, 2012), 45.

[8] Holmes, *Apostolic Fathers*, 10–11 (from the introduction).

[9] Noll notes a similar pattern with his emphasis on episcopate, canon, and creed as the chief "vehicles" upon which the church traveled in the early centuries. Noll, *Turning Points*, 45.

Handoff: Apostles to Early Christians

With the death of the apostle John near the turn of the second century, the handoff between the original apostolic torchbearers and the next generation of Christian leaders was official. Some seventy years earlier, Jesus declared that upon "this rock" (Greek *petra*, a play on words while speaking to the apostle Peter) he would build his church. Moreover, Jesus also declared to Peter that he would be given the keys of the kingdom "and whatever you bind on earth will have been bound in heaven, and whatever you loose on earth will have been loosed in heaven" (Matt 16:18–19).

No lack of ink has been spilled over the centuries insisting on various interpretations of this passage—a matter we will return to in later chapters. But for now, who serves as the rock and who holds the keys after the death of the apostles?

Apostolic Fathers Overview

"The Apostolic Fathers" is the designation given to the people whose writings influenced early Christians, though these writings were not ultimately recognized as Scripture. The earliest of the writings among the corpus of the Apostolic Fathers may have overlapped with the writings of some portions of the New Testament. And certain writings, the Didache for example, were at times cited alongside Scripture. Ultimately, these writings and the people associated with them had significant influence on early Christian communities, but their authority was not on the same level as the apostles', and they were not included in the canon of Scripture. These texts also provide an important window into the conversations and priorities of early Christians—their struggles and questions as well as their passions and purpose.

The collection of the Apostolic Fathers includes the following:

Apostolic Fathers	
Name	**Date**
1 Clement	96
2 Clement	100/150

Ignatius's seven letters: *To the Ephesians* *To the Magnesians* *To the Trallians* *To the Romans* *To the Philadelphians* *To the Smyrnaeans* *To Polycarp*	117
Polycarp, *To the Philippians*	115/135
Martyrdom of Polycarp	155–180
Didache	100
Epistle of Barnabas	97/135?
Shepherd of Hermas	100–155
Commandments (Mandates)	100–155
Visions	100–155
Epistle to Diognetus	117–310
Fragments of Papias	130

The general consensus among scholars is that this collection is quite arbitrary, lacking any overall coherence. However, this seeming lack of consistency does not mean that these works represent different understandings of the Christian faith. Rather, as Michael Holmes suggests, "we should accept the lack of coherence for what it is: testimony to the vigorous diversity characteristic of early Christianity at this time in history. In this way the documents can be appreciated for what they are—evidence of the actual issues and concerns with which early Christian believers struggled in their efforts to integrate faith and life."[10] From a bird's-eye view, there are at least four distinctives to consider from the corpus of the Apostolic Fathers.

---

[10] Holmes, *Apostolic Fathers*, 6. See also Clayton N. Jefford, *Reading the Apostolic Fathers: A Student's Introduction* (Baker Academic, 2012).

First, the majority of the collection is written in the familiar form of letter or epistle. Epistles were already familiar to early Christians not merely as a culturally common form of communication, but as a common way for leaders of the church (such as the apostles) to communicate. But epistles tend to be "occasional" writings, meaning they are written for a specific occasion, whether celebratory, disciplinary, or devotional. We see this in the New Testament letters; Paul's letter to the Philippians, for instance, is not less than an impassioned thank you letter for their ongoing support of his ministry. First Corinthians, on the other hand, is far more corrective and disciplinary in nature.

We see similar variety among the letters of the Apostolic Fathers. First Clement is written in excellent Greek by a competent rhetorician, a carefully constructed essay arguing for order in the church. Ignatius's letters, by contrast, are, as Richard Norris argues, "hasty, personal, and, even allowing for their occasional imitation of the 'Asian' style in rhetoric, thoroughly breathless and inelegant."[11] These stylistic differences showcase the diversity that existed among the early church fathers. We will say more about Clement and Ignatius and their writings below.

Second, the texts of the Apostolic Fathers are a personal and passionate collection of material. The Martyrdom of Polycarp comes to mind first in this respect. Polycarp, bishop of Smyrna, was likely a disciple of the apostle John, and Irenaeus of Lyons was likely a disciple of Polycarp. This work tells the story of Polycarp's more than eighty years of dedication to Christ and the church and his unwavering commitment to Christ in the face of death. Polycarp's testimony provides personal and passionate detail that makes the experiences of early Christians come alive to contemporary readers, pulling us into their world as a persecuted religious minority with a Spirit-empowered momentum that was well on its way to changing the world.

Third, the Apostolic Fathers present a posture of preservation by early Christians, as opposed to a posture of progressivism that sought to change their underlying convictions. In other words, Clement, Ignatius, Barnabas, Polycarp, and the other writings seem to be most concerned with *preserving* that which was received from Jesus and the apostles, a message that is in continuity with the Old Testament. They wanted the gospel to advance in

---

[11] Richard A. Norris Jr., "The Apostolic and Sub-Apostolic Writings: The New Testament and the Apostolic Fathers," in *The Cambridge History of Early Christian Literature*, ed. Frances Young, Lewis Ayres, and Andrew Louth (Cambridge University Press, 2004), 14.

time and space, but they were not interested in Christianity 2.0 or anything that differed in essence from the Great Tradition established by Jesus and the apostles.

Fourth, despite the posture of preservation, the Apostolic Fathers illustrate a variety of examples where the language surrounding certain issues is still under development for early Christians, signaling that the young movement is barely out of its infancy, if at all. For example, concerns related to how to read the Bible (especially regarding the relationship of the Old Testament to the teachings of Jesus and the apostles), church structure and authority, Jewish-Christian relations, and various matters of doctrine and daily living are just a few of the areas where the language is under development as observed in the corpus of the Apostolic Fathers.

With the passing of the original apostles, the vacuum of leadership and authority had to be filled. This mantle of leadership would be passed on to those who apprenticed under the apostles or were their close associates. But did the second generation of leadership carry the same weight of authority as the original apostles of Jesus? What is the relationship between apostolic authority and that of pastors and deacons in the various congregations that continue to spread around the Mediterranean? Did the apostles plainly prescribe a polity for the churches, and if so, what is it? These kinds of questions remained unanswered around the turn of the century, but church leaders, such as Clement of Rome and Ignatius of Antioch, offered needed direction for the churches, and their extant writings give valuable insight into the beliefs, practices, and leadership of the early church.

First and Second Clement

Church tradition identifies Clement, the bishop of Rome (c. 35–c. 100) and the third person to hold the office of bishop (or "pope" of Rome) after the apostle Peter, as the author of 1 Clement, though he is not explicitly named as its author. The date of the letter is also uncertain but may have been as early as c. 70 or as late as c. 96. The letter is carefully crafted in excellent Greek, well organized, and poignant in purpose and provides one of the earliest and clearest examples, apart from the New Testament, of how Christians were to live.

The letter is sent from "the church of God that sojourns in Rome to the church of God that sojourns in Corinth." This opening line of the letter highlights both its communal voice, being from the church in Rome rather than simply from Clement, and the sojourner or pilgrim mentality of these early Christians. This understanding reveals a sense of the early Christians being *in* Rome and Corinth, but not *of* Rome or Corinth, as they had doubtless learned from the apostles to be *in* but not *of* the world (i.e., John 15:19; 17:14–16).

The letter can be divided into two parts: "general moral considerations applicable to the situation at Corinth (1–38) and practical suggestions to solve the problem (39–65)."[12] Indeed, the first half of the letter is saturated with the call to true Christian living, with special emphasis on humility, obedience to Christ and church leaders, and unity among church members. Moreover, the author assumes much about his audience's knowledge of the Old Testament as he repeatedly draws on Old Testament characters and stories to illustrate his call to humility, obedience, and so on.

> We write these things, dear friends, not only to admonish you, but also to remind ourselves. For we are in the same arena, and the same contest awaits us. Therefore let us abandon empty and futile thoughts, and let us conform to the glorious and holy rule of our tradition.
>
> ———
>
> 1 Clement 7.1-2

Clement also reminds his readers of more recent noble examples of those who followed Jesus even to death, including Peter and Paul, as well as two women, Danaids and Dircae. During Clement's lifetime Christians had endured intense persecution, which included imprisonment, torture, and execution, at the hands of the Roman emperor Nero. Persecution will be the focus of the following chapter, but endurance in the midst of suffering was a theme of Christian writings from the earliest days. Clement writes that despite their terrible tortures and suffering, "they safely reached the goal in the race of faith and received a noble reward, their physical weakness notwithstanding." To die a martyr's death was considered by early Christians among the greatest gifts one might receive and a guarantee of one's admission into the kingdom of God. In the decades to come, however, the unhealthy pursuit of martyrdom became an issue of its own that had to be addressed by Christian leaders.

Additionally, the theme of obedience features strongly throughout the letter. In the first half, the heaviest accent is on obedience to God and his will. The emphasis on obedience is also seen in the multiple references to the "fear" of God and Christ, which ties thoroughly into the Old Testament's ethical imagery for living before God in his world. And this theme of obedience pivots naturally from one's relationship with God to one's relationship with

---

[12] Everett Ferguson, *Church History*, vol. 1, *From Christ to Pre-Reformation* (Zondervan, 2005), 53.

church leaders. Clement writes, "Let us fear the Lord Jesus Christ, whose blood was given for us. Let us respect our leaders; let us honor the older men; let us instruct the young with instruction that leads to the fear of God. Let us guide our women toward that which is good" (21.6).

The second half of the letter (39–65) turns toward practical solutions for the church in Corinth, beginning with *order*. In chapter 40, the author carries an Ecclesiastes-type tone, arguing for a proper order for all things at proper times and seasons. This emphasis on order extends to matters of worship and offering as observed in the order of the Levitical system. From the beginning, Christians were concerned with the order of the church. Just as Paul left Titus in Crete to bring order to the church there (Titus 1:5), so the Apostolic Fathers were concerned with the organization of the church's worship and practice. First Clement illustrates the beginning of a long road of liturgical development within Christianity. The author then pivots toward the order of authority from Jesus (sent from God) to the apostles to bishops and deacons in the church. Notice the logic of authority in chapter 42:

> The Apostles received the gospel for us from the Lord Jesus Christ; Jesus the Christ was sent forth from God. So then Christ is from God, and the Apostles are from Christ. Both, therefore, came of the will of God in good order. Having therefore received their orders and being fully assured by the resurrection of our Lord Jesus Christ and full of faith in the word of God, they went forth with the firm assurance that the Holy Spirit gives, preaching the good news that the kingdom of God was about to come. So, preaching both in the country and in the towns, they appointed their first fruits, when they had tested them by the Spirit, to be bishops and deacons for the future believers. And this was no new thing they did, for indeed something had been written about bishops and deacons many years ago; for somewhere thus says the scripture: "I will appoint their bishops in righteousness and their deacons in faith."[13]

Near the end of the letter in chapter 63, the author offers a parting reminder about unity and obedience to church leaders. He writes, "Therefore it is right for us, having studied so many and such great examples, to bow the neck and, adopting the attitude of obedience, to submit to those who are the leaders of our souls, so that by ceasing from this futile dissension we may attain the goal that is truly set before us, free from all blame" (63.1).

---

[13] Holmes, *Apostolic Fathers*, 101.

The letter known as 2 Clement is also addressed to the church at Corinth but is almost certainly not written by Clement and is actually not a letter but a sermon. The date of the letter is also uncertain, ranging from c. 100–140. Nevertheless, its status among the church fathers remains.

At least three characteristics of 2 Clement deserve mention. First, the sermon-like style serves as an exhortation to "sincere, heartfelt repentance" (9.8) and moral living that accords with the Christian life. Like 1 Clement, the author of 2 Clement is deeply concerned with moral living among the Christian communities as befits followers of Jesus. The Christian life begins with repentance, a dominant and reoccurring theme in the letter.

Second, the author stresses the Christians' transient relationship to this world in view of the kingdom of God and eternal life to come. The author writes in 5.1, "Therefore, brothers and sisters, let us turn away from life as transient residents in this world and do the will of the one who called us, and let us not be afraid to depart from this world." This language finds some continuity with New Testament language and imagery, but it doesn't share as robust a view of missional living in "this world" as the New Testament authors or 1 Clement. He goes on to say, "Moreover you know, brothers and sisters, that our stay in this world of the flesh is insignificant and transitory, but the promise of Christ is great and marvelous: rest in the coming kingdom and eternal life!" (5.5). This passage is instructive for the future-directed mindset of this author and of early Christians. And, indeed, Christians of every age are encouraged to be ever ready for the "day of the Lord" and the glorious return of Christ, though we may resist the emphasis of life in the flesh being "insignificant."

Third, 2 Clement is framed with the metaphor of competition. First in 7.1–6, then closing in 20.2, the author exhorts, "Let us have faith, brothers and sisters! We are competing in the contest of a living God and are being trained by the present life in order that we may be crowned in the life to come." Lightfoot suggested that this competition imagery may indicate that the author was writing or preaching from a site of well-known competitions.[14] Corinth, for example, was home of the Isthmian games, a biannual event in honor of

---

[14] J. B. Lightfoot, *The Apostolic Fathers*, part 1, *S. Clement of Rome*, 2nd ed., 2 vols. (repr., Baker Academic, 1981), 197. Lightfoot writes, "The allusion to the athletic games, and presumably to the Isthmian festival, is couched in language which is quite natural if addressed to Corinthians, but not so if spoken elsewhere. When the preacher refers to the crowds that 'land' to take part in the games . . . without any mention of the port, we are naturally led to suppose that the homily was delivered in the neighbourhood of the place where these combatants landed. Otherwise we should expect [*eis ton Isthmon*], or [*eis Korinthon*], or some explanatory addition of the kind."

Poseidon, the Greek god of the sea. The Isthmian games were considered second only to the Olympic games. It is speculative, of course, if this competition imagery informs us on the location of the author, but it is clear that early, insightful Christian authors employed athletic metaphors, as the apostle Paul was fond of doing, to illustrate and motivate Christians "toward the prize" of Christ (1 Cor 9:24.)

First and Second Clement represent some of the earliest examples outside of the New Testament of both the motivation for and the expectation that Christians were to live as citizens of the eternal kingdom of God while living as temporary citizens of an earthly kingdom. These works display continuity with the teachings of the apostles but also reveal how language concerning the authority of bishops was developing in the early church.

Ignatius of Antioch

Ignatius (c. 35–c. 107) was bishop of Antioch in Syria at the turn of the second century. Little is known about Ignatius's life apart from his arrest and execution at the hand of the Roman emperor Trajan (98–117). Trajan expanded the Roman Empire farther than it had known before and as far as it would ever know. To the west, Trajan's rule was only halted by the ocean but reached far east to the western edges of Arabia. From the northern borders of Britannia to the Mediterranean coasts of Spain and North Africa, Roman rule was vast. Trajan's persecution of Christians will be discussed further in chapter 2, but our focus will be on the seven letters that Ignatius wrote en route to Rome, where tradition tells us he was martyred at the Roman amphitheater.

Trajan was not the hot-headed executioner of Christians that Nero had been, for Nero, who ruled from AD 54–68, was known for his brutality toward Christians. Both Peter and Paul were almost certainly executed under Nero. The exact number of Christians killed under Nero is uncertain, though Tacitus referred to a "vast multitude" (*Annals* 15.44) who were arrested and executed following the Great Fire of Rome in AD 64. Those who followed Nero were not as severe in their persecution of Christians, including Trajan, who came to power in AD 98 and seemed generally unconcerned with the new religion so long as its adherents did not cause trouble. But despite Trajan's relative tolerance, Ignatius was arrested and carried to Rome for execution. Seven letters were written by Ignatius on his journey to Rome, all of which are broadly recognized as authentic. They are included in the corpus of the Apostolic Fathers and join Clement's letters as the most influential writings in the collection.

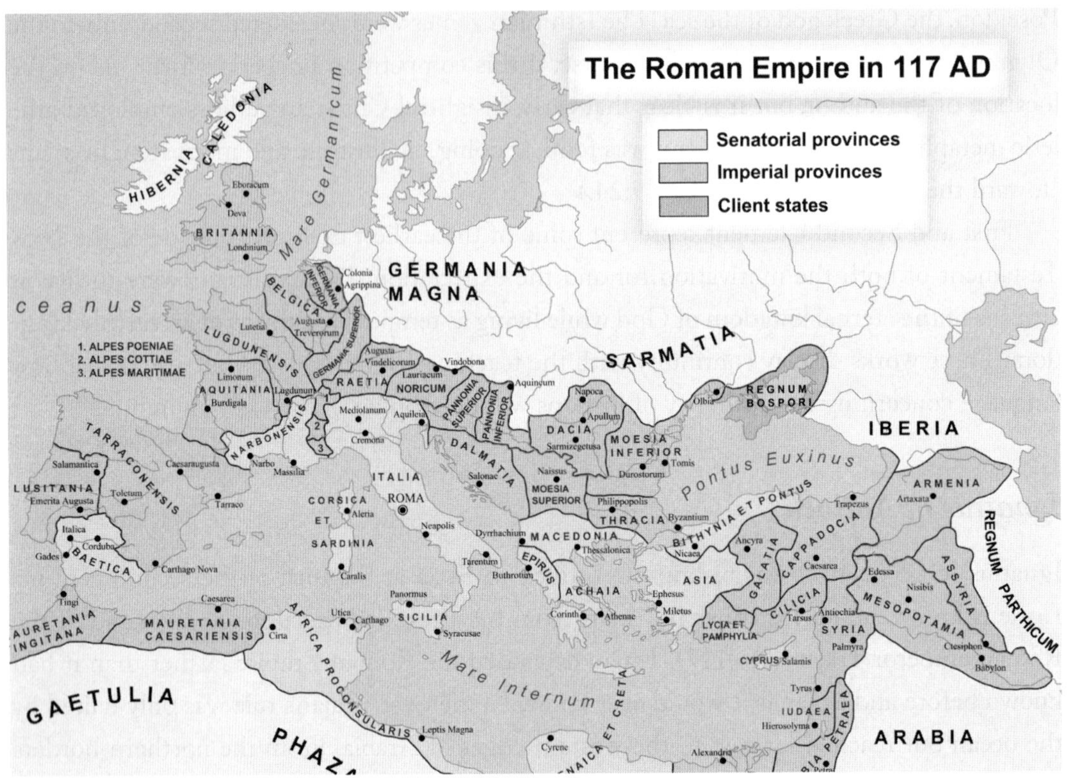

Image 1.2. *The maximum extent of the Roman Empire.*

The date of Ignatius's letters is uncertain, but the most common consent suggests that Ignatius was martyred around the mid-point of Trajan's rule (c. 107) as reported by the fourth-century historian Eusebius, though some have suggested Ignatius's martyrdom, and thus letter writing, to have occurred later, during Hadrian's reign (117–138).[15] Additionally, Eusebius describes the order of the letters as follows: Smyrnaeans, Polycarp, Ephesians, Magnesians, Philadelphians, and Trallians.[16]

[15] Holmes, *Apostolic Fathers*, 170; Eusebius, discussing the time of Trajan's rule, said "During this period . . . Ignatius, who is still famous now among many . . . was sent to the city of Rome to become food for wild beasts, for bearing witness to Christ." Eusebius, *The History of the Church*, trans. Jeremy M. Schott (University of California Press, 2019), 159.

[16] Philip Schaff and Henry Wace, eds., *Nicene and Post-Nicene Fathers*, Series 2 (Hendrickson, 1890), 166.

Content and Character of the Letters

Ignatius's letters carry quite a different style and tone from 1 Clement's smooth and sophisticated style. Ignatius's writings are punchy and poignant, packed with the passion of a bishop who understands he is moving toward martyrdom and who is most concerned with a parting exhortation to the churches (whom he refers to as his children) to right love for God and others and order in the church.

Ignatius is clearly familiar with at least some of the New Testament books and letters, and his style feels quite Pauline at points. Major themes include unity versus division in the church, authority of church leaders, a noteworthy emphasis on the voice of the congregation with respect to leadership (also seen in 1 Clement), issued with a tender pastoral tone.

Among the many noteworthy themes found in Ignatius's seven letters, we highlight the following four. First is Ignatius's pastoral, even fatherly, tone to the churches. Ignatius's salutations all begin the same way, "Ignatius the Image-bearer to the church." The language in each of his salutations is warm and pastoral, like that of Paul, Peter, John, and others of the New Testament letters. His writing shows readers a shepherd concerned for the sheep with respect to right doctrine, unity within the body, and a manner of life that befits Christ. And not just for one church: Ignatius stresses over the health of many churches in various cities, and he desires that they pray for one another. As he writes in his *To the Romans*, "Remember in your prayers the church in Syria, which has God for its shepherd in my place. Jesus Christ alone will be its bishop—as will your love" (9.1–2). This pastoral care for churches across geographical regions reveals Ignatius's desire that Christians remain unified as the gospel continues to spread.

Second, and perhaps best known, is Ignatius's emphasis on the order of authority in the churches. A theme that Ignatius returns to time and again is the authority of the bishop and the importance of obedience to him. One such example is found in *To the Ephesians* 6.1–2. The final sentence of chapter 5 reads, "Let us, therefore, be careful not to oppose the bishop, in order that we may be obedient to God." Ignatius continues: "Furthermore, the more anyone observes that the bishop is silent, the more one should fear him. For everyone whom the Master of the house sends to manage his own house we must welcome as we would the one who sent him. It is obvious, therefore, that *we must regard the bishop as the Lord himself.*"[17]

[17] Holmes, *Apostolic Fathers*, 187. Italics added for emphasis.

Further, in his letter *To the Magnesians*, Ignatius offers the following three-fold structure for church leadership: "Be eager to do everything in godly harmony, the bishop presiding in the place of God and the presbyters in the place of the council of the Apostles and the deacons, who are especially dear to me, since they have been entrusted with the ministry of Jesus Christ" (6.1). And, in *To the Trallians*, he states, "It is essential, therefore, that you continue your current practice and do nothing without the bishop, but be subject also to the council of the presbyters as to the Apostles of Jesus Christ. . . . Furthermore, it is necessary that those who are deacons of the mysteries of Jesus Christ please everyone in every respect. For they are not merely deacons of food and drink but ministers of God's church" (2.2–3).

In these letters, Ignatius outlines what will become the standard structure for ecclesial leadership for the next 1500 years. Michael Holmes argues that while the Pauline approach appears to be a two-fold leadership structure (elders and deacons), Ignatius reapplies the vocabulary, with bishops, as the senior leaders; the presbyters or elders, functioning like an apostolic council (though they did not carry the same authority as the apostles themselves); and deacons.

Third, Ignatius's letters exhibit trinitarian themes in keeping with the Great Tradition as discussed in the introduction to this volume. While the theological grammar for articulating the relationship between Father, Son, and Spirit continued to develop for another 250 plus years, the default accent of Ignatius is trinitarian. Here is one example from his letter to the Ephesians: "You covered up your ears in order to avoid receiving the things being sown by them, because you are stones of a temple, prepared beforehand for the building of God the Father, hoisted up to the heights by the crane of Jesus Christ, which is the cross, using as a rope the Holy Spirit; your faith is what lifts you up, and love is the way that leads up to God" (9.1b).

> Be eager, therefore, to be firmly grounded in the precepts of the Lord and the apostles, in order that 'in whatever you do, you may prosper,' physically and spiritually, in faith and love, in the Son and the Father and in the Spirit . . .
>
> ———
>
> Ignatius, *Letter to the Magnesians 13:1*

The salutation of Ignatius's letter to the Philadelphians also employs a strong trinitarian understanding, especially regarding the unified operations of Father, Son, and Spirit in the appointing of leadership in the church. Also noteworthy is Ignatius's clear recognition of Jesus's full humanity and divinity (i.e., *To the Ephesians* 7.2; 18.2; *To the Magnesians* 11; 13.2) as well as his emphasis on remaining in agreement with apostolic teaching (*To the Ephesians* 11.2).

Finally, Ignatius has high expectations for proper moral conduct among Christians. His default is to couch moral exhortations in the context of obedience to the bishop with language that promotes harmony among the brethren, love as the chief manner of life, congruence of word and deed, and a teleological approach to life. Ignatius utilizes the two-ways imagery in his letter to the Magnesians when he writes, "Seeing then that all things have an end, two things together lie before us, death and life, and everyone will go to his own place. For just as there are two coinages, the one of God and the other of the world, and each of them has its own stamp impressed upon it, so the unbelievers bear the stamp of this world, but the faithful in love bear the stamp of God the Father through Jesus Christ, whose life is not in us unless we voluntarily choose to die into his suffering" (5.1–2).

Polycarp

Polycarp (c. 69–c. 155), bishop of Smyrna (modern-day Izmir in western Turkey), was one of the most prominent Christian leaders in the early to mid-second century. One of Ignatius's seven letters was addressed to him, the only one written to an individual. Further, we have a letter written by Polycarp to the Philippians as well as an inspiring and emotional account of Polycarp's martyrdom. Thus, as Phillip Schaff observes, Polycarp serves as the "connecting link between the apostolic and post-apostolic ages" because of his discipleship under the apostle John and his training of Irenaeus.[18]

Little is known about Polycarp's life apart from what is recorded in *The Martyrdom of Polycarp*, a letter written by Christians in Smyrna in the mid- to late second century that was also chronicled in book 4 of Eusebius's early fourth century work *Ecclesiastical History*. He was widely respected for his piety and leadership as bishop of Smyrna, and he is remembered for traveling to Rome to meet with Bishop Anicetus about the date and annual recognition of Easter. But most prominently, Polycarp is remembered for the account of his death at the hands of governing officials.

> Let us serve him (*Jesus*) with fear and all reverence, just as he himself has commanded, as did the apostles, who preached the gospel to us, and the prophets, who announced in advance the coming of our Lord.
>
> ———
>
> *The Letter of Polycarp to the Philippians 6:3*

[18] Phillip Schaff, *History of the Christian Church*, vol. 2 (Eerdmans, 1910), 51.

Polycarp's martyrdom is the first surviving account of a Christian martyr outside the New Testament. The account was recorded by the church at Smyrna and addressed to the church in Philomelium, as well as to "all the communities of the holy and catholic church sojourning in every place." The recording of the event was intended to be broadcast to encourage Christians far and wide. While the pursuit and inappropriate celebration of martyrdom soon became a problem for the church to address, Polycarp's death is a remarkable testimony of faithfulness and confidence in the Lord.

As Jeffrey Bingham says concerning Polycarp's martyrdom, "He was passive and compliant in his arrest, even setting a table of refreshment for the arresting officials. He prayed two hours for all those he knew personally and for the church spread throughout the world before he was taken to the stadium."[19] Upon entering the stadium, Polycarp was given the customary opportunity to swear the oath to Caesar and revile Christ, and he would be released. He replied, "For eighty-six years I have been his servant, and he has done me no wrong. How can I blaspheme my King who saved me?" (9.3).[20]

The story continues with the crowd's angry response to Polycarp's confession of Christ and their call to have him burned alive. Following his prayer of thanksgiving, the fire was lit to burn Polycarp alive. But the author records a miracle that the fire did not touch Polycarp's body: "For the fire, taking the shape of an arch, like the sail of a ship filled by the wind, completely surrounded the body of the martyr; and it was there in the middle, not like flesh burning but like bread baking or like gold and silver being refined in a furnace. For we also perceived a very fragrant aroma, as if it were the scent of incense or some other precious spice" (15.2). Thus, he was killed with the sword by the executioner.

The death of Polycarp provides an example of one of the central features of early Christianity: persecution. Whether it was at the hands of Jewish leaders or the Roman government, persecution was a common thread running through the first few centuries of the history of the church. The following chapter will examine the impact that persecution had on the spread of the gospel and the growth of the early church.

---

[19] D. Jeffrey Bingham, *Pocket History of the Church* (InterVarsity, 2002), 29.

[20] *Mart. Pol.* 9.3, in Holmes, *The Apostolic Fathers*, 232.

Recommended Reading

Barton, John, and John Muddiman. *The Oxford Bible Commentary*. Oxford University Press, 2007.

Bass, D. Butler. *A People's History of Christianity: The Other Side of the Story*. HarperCollins, 2009.

Bingham, D. Jeffrey. *Pocket History of the Church*. InterVarsity, 2002.

Bruce, F. F. *Paul: Apostle of the Heart Set Free*. Eerdmans, 2000.

Eusebius. *The History of the Church*. Translated by Jeremy M. Schott. University of California Press, 2019.

Ferguson, Everett. *Church History*. Vol. 1, *From Christ to Pre-Reformation*. Zondervan, 2005.

González, Justo. *Acts: The Gospel of the Spirit*. Orbis, 2001.

Holmes, Michael W., ed. and trans. *The Apostolic Fathers: Greek Texts and English Translations*. 3rd ed. Baker Academic, 2007.

Jefford, Clayton N. *Reading the Apostolic Fathers: A Student's Introduction*. Baker Academic, 2012.

Kruger, Michael J. *Christianity at the Crossroads: How the Second Century Shaped the Future of the Church*. InterVarsity, 2018.

Lightfoot, J. B. *The Apostolic Fathers*. Part 1, *S. Clement of Rome*. 2nd ed. 2 vols. Reprint, Baker, 1981.

MacCulloch, Diarmaid. *Christianity: The First Three Thousand Years*. Penguin, 2011.

Noll, Mark A. *Turning Points: Decisive Moments in the History of Christianity*. 3rd ed. Baker Academic, 2012.

Norris, Richard A., Jr. "The Apostolic and Sub-Apostolic Writings: The New Testament and the Apostolic Fathers." In *The Cambridge History of Early Christian Literature*, edited by Frances Young, Lewis Ayres, and Andrew Louth. Cambridge University Press, 2004.

Pliny the Younger. *Letters*. Vol. 2, *Books 8–10, Panegyricus*, translated by Betty Radice. Loeb Classical Library. Harvard University Press, 1969.

Schaff, Phillip. *History of the Christian Church*. Vol. 2. Eerdmans, 1910.

— Chapter 2 —

Persecution and Resilience in the Ancient Church

The book of Acts describes the spread of the gospel of Jesus beyond Jerusalem into the surrounding Judean countryside, Samaria, and ultimately to the faraway city of Rome (1:8). As Jewish authorities pressured Christians in Jerusalem, they moved to other cities and towns. However, as the church began to spread within Jewish communities, religious leaders forced Jewish Christians out of the synagogues and temple worship entirely.

The apostle Paul's missionary journeys took him to cities throughout the Roman Empire, where he often first proclaimed the gospel of Jesus in Jewish synagogues. He reasoned with the leaders of these Jewish communities, trying to convince them that Jesus was the promised Messiah. Paul saw some success in his evangelism in the synagogues but also experienced conflict and persecution. Jewish religious leaders opposed Paul's message of Jesus and often appealed to local Roman authorities for assistance in stopping the spread of Christianity. Ironically, Paul also appealed to the Roman authorities for protection from persecution by these Jewish leaders, resulting in his transport to Rome and the proclamation of the gospel in the capital of the empire.

By the end of the first century, the chasm between Jews who embraced the apostles' message of Jesus as the Christ and those who rejected that message became greater. However, even as the two religious groups distinguished between themselves, the Romans continued to view Christians as a sect of Judaism into the second and third centuries. While Christians initially faced persecution primarily from religious leaders within Judaism, by the end of the first century, the Roman state sporadically and periodically persecuted the church as well. Christians were essentially free of any state persecution early because Christianity was considered a part of Judaism by the authorities. Judaism was a legal religious sect in the Roman Empire, providing its adherents with some legal protections and freedoms. As Christians increasingly distinguished themselves from Judaism, they lost those protections, becoming viewed as a group operating outside of Roman society.

The Earliest Roman Persecution: Nero

The first persecution of Christians by Roman authorities was under Emperor Nero. During the reign of Nero, Christians faced one of the earliest and most brutal waves of persecution in the history of the church. Nero ascended to power in AD 54 at age sixteen. Initially, his reign saw a degree of stability and prosperity. However, as Nero's rule increased, his behavior became increasingly erratic and authoritarian as evidenced by political intrigue, corruption, and a desire for personal glorification. In the year AD 64, a devastating fire swept through Rome, destroying large portions of the city. While the exact cause of the fire remains uncertain, Nero faced widespread public outrage and suspicion that he had orchestrated the blaze. Seeking a scapegoat to deflect blame, Nero targeted the growing Christian community, which Romans already viewed with suspicion due to its distinct beliefs and practices. The Roman historian Tacitus writes, "Nero set up as culprits and punished with the utmost refinement of cruelty a class hated for their abominations, who are commonly called Christians."[1]

Christians suffered various forms of torture, including crucifixion, burning alive, and being torn apart by wild animals in the arena. Roman authorities arrested, tortured, and executed Christians in public spectacles designed to instill fear and deter others from embracing the faith. One of the most notable aspects of Nero's persecution was the martyrdom of the apostles Peter and Paul. Tradition holds that both apostles suffered martyrdom in Rome during this time. Peter was said to have been crucified upside down while Paul was beheaded. Later Christians looked back on their deaths and found comfort as they also

[1] Tacitus, *Annals* 15.44, in *The Annals: Books 13–16*, trans. John Jackson, rev. John Yardley, Loeb Classical Library 322 (Harvard University Press, 1937), 282–87.

faced persecution. In fact, the Greek word for martyr means "witness." The death of the apostles was a witness to the gospel of Jesus Christ, the crucified and risen Lord.

The courage and resilience displayed by the martyrs became a powerful testimony to the truth of the Christian message, attracting many to the faith. Amid persecution, the early church also experienced periods of growth and expansion. Christians remembered the martyrs in their worship services, and martyrdom became a vital part of Christian identity and practice. Nero's persecution set a precedent for later waves of persecution against Christians in the Roman Empire. While subsequent emperors would vary in their attitudes toward Christianity, the persecution under Nero established a pattern of state-sponsored violence and oppression that would continue for centuries.

Vespasian's Effort to Restore Order

Emperor Vespasian, who reigned from AD 69 to 79, is often celebrated for his efforts to restore stability to the empire, strengthen the economy, and bring peace after a period of chaos and civil wars known as the "Year of the Four Emperors." His reign was also marked by periods of persecution against Christians, though the extent and severity of these persecutions were not as great as the persecutions under later emperors.

It is unclear why Vespasian began to persecute Christians. Officials likely targeted Christians for reasons similar to those under other emperors. Christianity was viewed with suspicion by many in the Roman Empire due to its monotheistic beliefs, refusal to participate in traditional religious practices, and perceived threat to the social and political order. Additionally, Christians were often scapegoated during times of crisis or unrest, as the Romans saw them as outsiders who refused to honor the Roman gods and the emperor. In his work *Octavius*, the Christian apologist Minucius Felix described accusations against Christians that undermined the unity and health of Roman society. These accusations ranged from refusal to participate in civic life to participation in incestuous relationships. Officials sometimes targeted Christians for their perceived association with political dissidents or social unrest. As social decay and threats from outsiders increased in the empire, efforts to bring unity through Roman civil religion likewise increased. These efforts were at odds with Christian practices, creating more reasons for persecution.

The persecution of Christians under Vespasian was not as widespread or systematic as under some later emperors. Nevertheless, Christians were forced to practice their faith discreetly in those areas where persecution persisted. Facing persecution did strengthen the resolve and solidarity of the Christian community, as believers stood firm in their faith despite the risks. The persecution underscores the challenges faced by believers in the Roman Empire and the resilience of the Christian community in the face of persecution.

Domitian Seeks the Favor of the Roman "Gods"

Emperor Domitian, who ruled the Roman Empire from AD 81 to 96, is remembered for his authoritarian rule and intolerance toward dissent. The Domitian persecution began in AD 95 after the emperor levied a tax on all inhabitants that would support the cult of Jupiter. The emperor's persecution of Christians was not because of their religion *per se*. However, it was nonetheless religious because they refused to pay this tax. After all, it violated their commitment to worship Jesus alone as their God. The religious character of the tax led to the punishment of Christians by the empire. The apostle John suffered exile to the island of Patmos, where he had visions of heaven and perhaps wrote the book of Revelation during this persecution.

The Roman historian Suetonius makes mention of this persecution, claiming Christians were executed for the crime of "atheism," a term frequently applied to Christians because of their unwillingness to worship the Roman gods, not because they did not believe in any god. Tacitus likewise mentions the punishment of Christians for being "superstitious." Again, the charge is that Christians worshiped a strange god rather than the gods of the Romans. Their superstitions would ostensibly put them outside Roman civil religion, endangering society's fabric.

His reign saw a resurgence of persecution against Christians, marked by widespread violence and oppression. Domitian ascended to the throne following the death of his brother Titus, and he sought to consolidate his power through strict authoritarian rule. Domitian's regime emphasized traditional Roman values and a desire to enforce conformity to imperial authority. The Roman Empire was a religious society with a strong history of civil religion. Due to military and political setbacks, Domitian appealed to the Roman gods for favor, like Roman emperors before and after. These appeals typically came with a renewed emphasis on the need for Roman citizens to participate in religious activities, such as making offerings at local pagan temples. Regardless of the sincerity of religious commitment, the emperors took seriously the role a common, civil religion played in strengthening the social fabric.

Domitian desired to maintain social order. In the Roman Empire, a shared civil religion among the population was a major way to do so. Christians rejected the pagan religion of the empire, refusing to participate in the public rituals, such as sacrifice and participation in temple rites. Christians worshipped only one God and therefore were unwilling to engage in activities deemed idolatry. After all, the first commandment is, "You shall have no other gods before me" (Exod 20:3 NIV). Romans viewed this unwillingness to practice the Roman civil religion as a challenge to the imperial religion threatening the cultural stability of the empire. Under Domitian, Roman officials targeted Christian leaders and prominent members of the community, seeking to eliminate any potential sources of resistance.

Persecution of Christians Spreads Under Trajan

In the early second century, Pliny the Younger became governor of the region called Bithynia-Pontus. Pliny's father had been an important member of Roman society, affording Pliny opportunities for education and travel. Despite these opportunities, Pliny was unfamiliar with Christianity until he encountered accusations from local citizens that some Christians were causing unrest. Unsure how to handle this religious and cultural dispute, Pliny wrote Emperor Trajan (AD 98–117) to ask what he should do. In his correspondence with the emperor, Pliny mentioned that this group who called themselves Christians worshipped Jesus as God. Pliny referred to this religion as a superstition spreading throughout the region in rural areas as well as cities. Christianity was so successful in many areas that pagan temples were rarely used, and the marketplace for animals used as sacrifices to the gods dried up, reminiscent of the silversmith's anger at the apostle Paul in Acts 19, when the gospel's progress meant fewer people buying idols for pagan worship.

Trajan responded that Pliny should not seek out Christians to punish them simply for being Christian. There was too much important state business to spend time hunting for Christians. However, because cultural stability is important, if someone were to accuse another person of being a Christian, Pliny was to have them questioned and offered a chance to worship the Roman gods. This was a way to resolve the conflict without unnecessary punishment. If the accused was willing to offer worship to the gods of Rome, the problem was solved. If, however, they refuse to do their duty to offer a sacrifice, then they were to be put to death as a sacrifice themselves.

Trajan's response to the growing number of Christians and the disruption that growth meant for parts of the empire was to leave the punishment of Christians to local officials, avoiding widespread and direct persecution by the empire. However, this passive persecution could tacitly encourage accusations against Christians, thereby creating a climate of fear of punishment and persecution. While the breadth of the persecution was less than that of later emperors, the effects on the churches whose leaders and members suffered were not.

Marcus Aurelius Persecutes Christians

Under the reign of the emperor Marcus Aurelius, who ruled from AD 161 to 180, a somewhat different form of persecution broke out, as Christians were the objects of persecution precisely because they were Christians. Marcus viewed Christianity as a rival philosophy and way of life to his own philosophy of Stoicism. The emperor also attributed the empire's military demise and an unusual number of natural disasters to the growth of the Christian religion. Whereas Stoicism made citizens productive members of society, Christianity made people useless within society. Consequently, he ordered that Christians be persecuted to end the growth of the religion, if not eradicate it. The theologian and apologist Justin Martyr (c. 110–165) was the most well-known martyr during this persecution, but thousands of nameless Christians also suffered for their refusal to worship pagan gods and give up their faith.

Septimius Severus Asserts the Empire's Authority in Religion

Septimius Severus (ruled 193–211) was the next in a line of emperors to persecute Christians in an effort to strengthen the fabric of Roman society. Severus was deeply committed to traditional Roman religion and saw Christianity as a threat to the stability of the empire. Perpetua and Felicity, whose story will be discussed later in this chapter, were put to death during the reign of Septimius Severus.

Severus's persecution of the church was widespread. As before, Christians were arrested, imprisoned, tortured, and even executed for their refusal to renounce their faith or offer sacrifices to the Roman gods. In addition to the typical efforts to punish Christian leaders, Severus banned conversion to Christianity and prohibited all Christian gatherings, effectively criminalizing the practice of the faith.

The Apologists

During the second century, at the same time Christians were enduring persecution, Christian writers responded to critics with texts known as *apologies*. Several Christian theologians also wrote texts defending the Christian faith. These apologists each addressed accusations and criticisms leveled against Christianity by its opponents. Second century apologists include Justin Martyr, *First* and *Second Apology*; Tatian, *Address to the Greeks*; Theophilus, *To Autolycus*; Athenagoras, *The Resurrection of the Dead* and *A Plea for the Christians*; and Aristides, *Apology*.

Unlike polemical texts, which were written to confront theological opponents, apologetical texts were written to address particular challenges to Christian faith or practice, both to justify Christianity to non-Christians and to teach Christians the faith. Christians label these writings "apologies," not because the authors are apologizing for being Christians, but because they are justifying their beliefs and practices. An "apology" is an explanation and defense of one's position. These "apologies" were often directed at specific opponents, such as religious leaders, philosophers, or political authorities, and sought to present Christianity favorably and refute charges of atheism, immorality, and disloyalty to the state. These apologetic works engaged with the philosophical and theological arguments of pagan critics, demonstrating the rationality and coherence of Christian beliefs.

Critics of Christianity focused on several topics, to which the apologists responded. One topic was Christian monotheism. Greek and Roman religions promoted belief in multiple gods. This polytheism was one reason Christians refused to participate in pagan sacrifices. In response to this criticism, Theophilus argued that the order of the universe makes sense only if a single God designed and created everything that exists in the material world. A pantheon of gods would make creation irrational. The only rational position is monotheism.

Another criticism of Christianity by pagan writers was the recent arrival of the Christian religion. Roman critics argued that Christianity could not be the one true religion—or even one true religion among others—because it only recently arose. The apologists countered by arguing that the Christian faith was derived from the message delivered to Abraham and Moses, thus predating both Judaism and paganism. Justin Martyr went so far as to say that whatever true statements could be found in the writings of philosophers like Plato and Socrates were plagiarized from the Old Testament, which is Christian Scripture. It was important to the apologists that Christianity was more ancient than the pagan religion.

Pagan critics of Christianity also ridiculed the most important doctrine of the Christian faith: the bodily resurrection from the dead. Resurrection confounded Roman writers. The apostle Paul acknowledged that it was foolishness to the Greeks. One argument Theophilus used was the changing of the seasons. Each spring, for example, nature is "made new." God made a world that demonstrates a type of resurrection; there is no reason to believe that he could not raise a human body from the dead.

The apologists turned the tables on their critics by arguing for both the superiority of Jesus to the Roman gods and the superiority of Christian morality to that of the Romans. Regarding the contrast of Jesus to the Roman gods, Athenagoras points out that the gods behave in reprehensible ways; they are guilty of rape, murder, and deception. Jesus Christ loves people and came to serve them and give them life. The contrast is significant. Regarding morality, each of the apologists argue that Christians live exemplary lives. Christians obey the law, pray for their rulers (even the ones who persecute them), do not practice abortion or infanticide, and do not even attend the theater. Christian morality is superior to pagan morality.

Even if the Roman rulers and critics of Christianity are not willing to adopt the religion, they should at least leave the Christians to live their lives in peace. After all, Christians are useful members of society who help the poor and love their neighbors. Christians are not criminals, so they should not be treated as such.

During his trial, Justin Martyr defended the Christian faith by arguing that Christians were law-abiding citizens who posed no threat to the Roman state. He portrays Christians as virtuous and upright citizens. If the Romans valued morality and an upright life, they should applaud Christians rather than punish them. Justin celebrates the martyrs, presenting their willingness to die for their faith as a powerful testimony to the truth of Christianity. Devotion was likewise a Roman virtue. The Christian devotion to Jesus should demonstrate to the Romans that Christians were virtuous and sincere. While Roman culture was committed to traditional virtues and norms, Christians claimed an even longer tradition of virtue, evidenced in the Old Testament. The Romans should not only accept Christians in the empire; they should embrace the gospel of Jesus for themselves.

Early Christian Martyrologies

Martyrologies were collections of accounts detailing the lives and deaths of Christian martyrs. Notable examples of early Christian martyrologies include the Martyrdom of Polycarp, the *Acts of the Scillitan Martyrs*, and the *Martyrdom of Perpetua and Felicity*. These accounts provide vivid and moving portrayals of the courage and faithfulness of early Christian martyrs, inspiring generations of believers with their testimonies. These accounts served multiple purposes within the early Christian community. First, the written accounts of martyrdom inspired and encouraged believers facing persecution by highlighting the courage of martyrs who willingly sacrificed their lives for their faith. They also enabled Christians to commemorate those who suffered martyrdom as a witness to the gospel of Jesus Christ. Second, martyrologies reinforced the Christian community's identity and solidarity by commemorating martyrs' sacrifices and celebrating their witness to the truth of the gospel. Christians revered martyrs as heroes of the faith, and their stories helped to forge a sense of shared identity and purpose among believers. Finally, martyr stories served as a form of resistance to persecution by affirming the legitimacy of Christian beliefs and practices in the face of Roman opposition.

In the *Martyrdom of Polycarp*, the author describes the Roman proconsul's threat to burn Polycarp alive if he does not recant his faith in Jesus. Polycarp responds, "You threaten me with fire that burns for an hour and then will go out after just a little while. You do not know about the fire of the judgment to come, the fire of eternal punishment reserved for the ungodly."[2] Once the fire was lit, the executioner stabbed Polycarp to ensure he was dead. The narrative states that a dove flew out of his chest and so much blood flowed from his body that it put out the fire! Such stories of faith in the face of death were inspirational to other Christians who faced persecution. Within the Great Tradition, this willingness to suffer and die for the faith, rehearsing Jesus's own suffering and death, is a consistent witness to the truth of the Christian faith.

The *Martyrdom of Perpetua and Felicity* is a moving and well-documented account of Christian martyrdom from the early church. It offers insights into the courage, faith, and solidarity of early Christians facing persecution. Perpetua and Felicity were Christian women living in the North African city of Carthage (modern-day Tunisia) in the early third century. Perpetua was a young noblewoman, while Felicity was Perpetua's slave. They were both new Christians preparing for baptism into the church. New Christian converts underwent a time of teaching or catechizing in the faith before their baptism. These new Christians were called catechumens.

In 203, Roman officials arrested Perpetua, Felicity, and several other Christians for their refusal to renounce their faith and offer sacrifices to the Roman gods. Despite being pregnant at the time of her arrest, Felicity was also imprisoned along with Perpetua, who had an infant son, and others. During their imprisonment, Perpetua kept a diary, recounting their experiences and the events leading up to their martyrdom. The diary, known as the *Passion of Saints Perpetua and Felicity*, provides a detailed account of their faith, struggles,

[2] *Martyrdom of Polycarp*, 11.2, in Michael W. Holmes, ed. and trans., *The Apostolic Fathers: Greek Texts and English Translations*, 3rd ed. (Baker Academic, 2007), 239.

and eventual martyrdom. Perpetua and Felicity faced several trials and tribulations during their imprisonment, including attempts by their families to persuade them to renounce their faith. Perpetua refused to deny Christ despite her father's pleas. Both Perpetua and Felicity experienced vivid visions and dreams during their imprisonment, which they interpreted as signs of their impending martyrdom and their entrance into eternal life. These spiritual experiences strengthened their resolve and provided comfort and assurance in the face of suffering. In the *Passion of Saints Perpetua and Felicity*, we read when the executioner sought to execute her by decapitation, he failed in his first attempt, causing immeasurable pain. Perpetua then helped him finish the job herself.

Felicity was allowed to give birth before her execution. As she cried out due to the pains of childbirth, her captors asked how she expected to face the beasts in the arena. Felicity responded that Jesus would be present with her in her suffering and cause her to endure death for his sake. Despite the horrific death that awaited her, Felicity served as a faithful witness for others who were facing persecution, whether they were slaves or, in other cases, philosophers and theologians. Within the Great Tradition, Perpetua and Felicity serve as lasting witnesses to encourage Christians to fidelity to Christ in the face of even the greatest of threats. Eternal life is the hope of the martyr.

> The day of their victory dawned, and they marched from the prison to the amphitheatre, joyously, as if going to heaven, their faces radiant; and if by chance they trembled, it was from joy and not from fear.
>
> ———
>
> *The Passion of Perpetua and Felicity*

Conclusion

Many Roman critics considered Christians to be part of a "secret society," working in the shadows and posing a potential threat to the towns and cities in which they lived.[3] This understanding of Christianity by the Romans contributed to the imperial persecution of Christians. The Christian apologist Marcus Minucius Felix (d. 250) addressed the accusation that Christians represented a shadowy threat to society in his work, *Octavius*. The text is a debate over the merits of Christianity between Octavius, a Christian, and Caecilius, a

[3] For greater detail, see Robert L. Wilken, *The Christians as the Romans Saw Them* (Yale University Press, 1984), 44–47.

pagan Roman. Caecilius views the Christians' worship practices with suspicion because they often worship in secret. He states, "For why do they endeavour with such pains to conceal and to cloak whatever they worship, since honourable things always rejoice in publicity, while crimes are kept secret?" While *Octavius* presents a fictional conversation, it highlights the accusations made against the Christians and shows the antagonistic relationship between Christianity and Roman society.

The Roman Empire was a religious society with its own state religion. Pagan priests led prayers at the opening of official government offices, citizens offered sacrifices to the Roman gods, and emperors appealed to the ancient religious practices to encourage people to be productive members of society. There was no identifiable separation of religious adherence and loyalty to the empire. Roman citizens went to temples where priests offered sacrifices to the Roman gods, asking for protection and favor. While Roman religious commitments were not personal, those commitments were sincere and pervasive in society. Government meetings would open with invocations. New businesses might open with prayers of blessing from priests. The gods were gods of all the Romans, merely by birth or citizenship. Christianity's insistence that Jesus is Lord would ultimately put Christians in the crosshairs of Roman authorities. Persecutions in the first century were primarily due to local conflicts and not political policy opposing Christians or Christianity. However, over time, persecution became increasingly common in the Roman Empire as subsequent emperors sought to solidify their authority and quell any groups who would oppose their rule. Christians experienced persecution on and off for the next two centuries, with intense periods of suffering interrupting times of relative calm. Christianity expanded throughout the empire during the second and third centuries despite this occasional persecution, leading Tertullian of Carthage to state, "The blood of the martyrs is the seed of the church."[4]

Roman persecution was initially localized and limited. Eventually, that would change.

Recommended Reading

Barton, John, and John Muddiman. *The Oxford Bible Commentary*. Oxford University Press, 2007.

[4] Tertullian, *Apology* 50.13, in *Latin Christianity: Its Founder, Tertullian*, vol. 3 of *The Ante-Nicene Fathers*, ed. Alexander Roberts and James Donaldson, trans. S. Thelwall (Christian Literature Company, 1885), 55.

Bass, D. Butler. *A People's History of Christianity: The Other Side of the Story*. HarperCollins, 2009.

Bingham, D. Jeffrey. *Pocket History of the Church*. InterVarsity, 2002.

Bruce, F. F. *Paul: Apostle of the Heart Set Free*. Eerdmans, 2000.

Dulles, Avery. *A History of Apologetics*. 2nd ed. Ignatius, 2005

Eusebius. *The History of the Church*. Translated by Jeremy M. Schott. University of California Press, 2019.

Ferguson, Everett. Church History. Vol. 1, *From Christ to Pre-Reformation*. Zondervan, 2005.

González, Justo. *Acts: The Gospel of the Spirit*. Orbis, 2001.

Holmes, Michael W., ed. and trans. *The Apostolic Fathers: Greek Texts and English Translations*. 3rd ed. Baker Academic, 2007.

Jefford, Clayton N. *Reading the Apostolic Fathers: A Student's Introduction*. Baker Academic, 2012.

Kruger, Michael J. *Christianity at the Crossroads: How the Second Century Shaped the Future of the Church*. InterVarsity, 2018.

Lightfoot, J. B. *The Apostolic Fathers*. Part 1, *S. Clement of Rome*. 2nd ed. 2 vols. Reprint, Baker, 1981.

MacCulloch, Diarmaid. *Christianity: The First Three Thousand Years*. Penguin, 2011.

Noll, Mark A. *Turning Points: Decisive Moments in the History of Christianity*. 3rd ed. Baker Academic, 2012.

Norris, Richard A., Jr. "The Apostolic and Sub-Apostolic Writings: The New Testament and the Apostolic Fathers." In *The Cambridge History of Early Christian Literature*. Edited by Frances Young, Lewis Ayres, and Andrew Louth. Cambridge University Press, 2004.

Pliny the Younger. *Letters*. Vol. 2, *Books 8–10, Panegyricus*. Translated by Betty Radice. Loeb Classical Library. Harvard University Press, 1969.

Schaff, Phillip. *History of the Christian Church*. Vol. 2. Eerdmans, 1910.

—— Chapter 3 ——

Competing Christianities

While Christianity expanded in the second century, it also grappled with a surge of internal theological debates and conflicts. These disputes, often complex, shaped the core of Christian identity and paved the way for the diverse landscape of later Christianity. It is easy to think that Christianity existed as a monolithic religion without internal challenges, but there were many groups all identifying themselves as part of the Christian church. Rather than imagining a pristine era of Christian belief and practice in the second century and beyond, we find various groups claiming to have the correct version of Christianity. These groups each claimed the title "Christian," but there were key differences among them. The most important difference was whether or not they remained faithful to the message of the apostles that was handed down in the churches they planted.[1] Some churches held to the apostolic faith while other churches preached a novel version of Christian doctrine that was contrary to the gospel. The apostle Paul had warned about false teachers who preached a false gospel. Second century theologians recognized the importance of heeding his warning.

Apostolic Christians held to the teaching of the apostles that Jesus of Nazareth is the Christ of the Old Testament. This faith is contained in the writings of the New Testament and the practices of those churches that embraced it. Jesus explained himself to the apostles,

---

[1] See Bart D. Ehrman, *Lost Christianities: The Battles for Scripture and the Faiths We Never Knew* (Oxford University Press, 2003).

and they passed that explanation and teaching along to those who accepted it. Already in the New Testament, some groups claim to be Christian but teach a gospel different than the apostles. Paul discusses this at length in the New Testament book of Galatians. We also see this in the book of 1 John, in which the author speaks of "those who have gone out from us" but were never really "of us."

In the second century, pastors and theologians in apostolic Christian churches regularly found themselves needing to address heresies, or explanations of the gospel and practices within Christian churches that were inconsistent with the apostolic faith. The word "heresy" comes from the Greek word describing a division or schism. A group that separates itself is a heresy. In Christian theology, a heresy refers to a doctrine that is not orthodox, separating those who hold it from the true, apostolic faith. Orthodox Christians developed objective and reliable ways to distinguish between orthodox teaching and heresy. The faith handed down from the apostles was found in the preaching of the church, in the ordinances or sacraments of the church, and in the various rules of faith. Christians preserved the faith they had received and handed down that faith to others.

The source of the Christian faith is the Bible. Christians have always had Scripture. Initially, it was the Hebrew Scriptures. In Luke 24, Jesus tells his disciples that the Hebrew Scriptures are about him: "These are my words that I spoke to you while I was still with you—that everything written about me in the Law of Moses, the Prophets, and the Psalms must be fulfilled" (v. 44). These Scriptures promised his death, his resurrection on the third day, and the proclamation of God's forgiveness of sins: "This is what is written: The Messiah will suffer and rise from the dead on the third day, and repentance for the forgiveness of sins will be preached in his name to all nations, beginning at Jerusalem" (Luke 24:46–47).

When Paul and the other Christian missionaries in Acts traveled to cities and towns where synagogues existed, they often went to those places first to proclaim that Jesus was the Christ of the Scriptures (e.g., Acts 13). Some in the synagogues believed, and others did not. Those who did believe gathered together to read those Scriptures afresh in the light of Jesus being the promised king. The apostolic message of Jesus as the Christ of the Jewish Scriptures was the gospel message. Eventually, as the apostles preached that message throughout the empire, there was a growing need to write down the justification for that claim. Initially, Paul wrote letters to churches explaining the gospel message by claiming Jesus was the Old Testament Christ (see 1 Corinthians 15). Peter likewise wrote down the message he had been preaching so his hearers could remember the gospel message more clearly and more easily pass that message along to others (see 2 Pet 1:16–21).

Additionally, the Gospel accounts of Jesus's life, ministry, and teaching demonstrated that Jesus was the Christ, the Son of God, so that people might believe that message and receive eternal life (John 20). These writings contained the apostolic message of Jesus Christ as Lord and Savior. Eventually, though quite early, these writings were read alongside the Old Testament as Christian Scripture.

Theological debates in the early church served several essential functions. In particular, they played a crucial role in defining the boundaries of orthodoxy within the Christian community. As the religion spread throughout the empire, diverse theological perspectives emerged, leading to disputes over such key doctrinal issues as the apocalyptic nature of Jesus's life, the Trinity, and the relation of faith to works. Christian theologians, such as Irenaeus of Lyons and Origen of Alexandria, wrote treatises against heresies. Irenaeus's *Against Heresies* and Origen's *On First Principles* served to teach orthodox Christian theology and explain why various heresies were unacceptable. Moreover, the debates sparked by these disagreements yielded the creeds, confessions, and theological treatises in which apostolic Christians formulated language to convey the right beliefs and reject heterodox teachings.

For example, Christological disputes in the second century resulted in the need for a clear and concise summary of the faith that excluded identifiable heresies, such as Ebionism, Docetism, Arianism, and others. Theologians formulated the rule of faith, which affirmed that Jesus was both fully divine and fully human while in no way falling into the various heretical errors that had putatively threatened to distort an accurate understanding of Jesus's identity. As theological terms and constructs were clarified and worked out, these early debates reconciled different theological idioms with one another and, more crucially, united belief within the religion's ranks and erected a framework of Christian identity within which cultural and geographical differences could be subsumed (if not overcome). Theological debates of the early centuries also helped foster the budding intellectual life of the Christian community. In wrestling with complex theological questions, theologians drew on various philosophical, rhetorical, and exegetical tools to compile and articulate their views and defend their positions.

The development of Christian theology during the second century occurred within the rich cultural and intellectual milieu of the Greco-Roman world. Christians preached the message of reconciliation to God through faith in Jesus Christ to those who had differing conceptions of cosmology, divine realities, and cultural expressions of religious practice. The Jews to whom Christians proclaimed Jesus as Christ understood the major figures and background of Christianity in the Old Testament. But the Greco-Roman world did not.

Christians developed ways of preaching and practicing Christianity that spoke to their various contexts. Theological formation also happened in these same contexts.

Preaching Jesus as Christ in a Jewish Context

As noted above, the earliest Christians had a written Scripture, the Hebrew Bible. These texts were the basis of their understanding of Jesus of Nazareth as the Christ, the Son of the living God. Jesus did not come to proclaim a new faith but the fulfillment of the faith in the Jewish Scriptures. While the church had various writings from the apostles, their "Scriptures" were the Old Testament writings. Early Christians interpreted the Hebrew Bible through the lens of messianic expectation, identifying Jesus of Nazareth as the long-awaited Christ foretold by the prophets. The Hebrew Scriptures provided a rich tapestry of messianic prophecies and typological patterns that early Christians interpreted as fulfilled in Jesus. Jewish beliefs about the coming kingdom of God and the resurrection of the dead shaped early Christian beliefs about the end times and the ultimate destiny of humanity. The apocalyptic imagery and prophetic visions of the Hebrew Scriptures provided a framework for understanding the eschatological dimensions of Christian theology. Justin Martyr's *Dialogue with Trypho* is an example of the ways Christians contrasted their reading of the Old Testament with the Jewish reading. Justin not only laid claim to the Hebrew Scriptures but demonstrated how Jesus of Nazareth was the Christ promised in them.

Jewish theological concepts, such as monotheism, covenant, and redemption, informed early Christian understandings of God's nature, his relationship with humanity, and the redemptive work of Christ. The monotheistic worldview of Judaism provided the foundation for early Christian beliefs about the oneness and sovereignty of God. Early Christians affirmed the Jewish confession of faith in one God while also elaborating upon the triune nature of the Godhead as Father, Son, and Holy Spirit. Jewish concepts of the covenantal relationship between God and his people influenced early Christian understandings of salvation history and the role of Jesus as the mediator of a new covenant. Early Christian theologians, such as Paul and the author of Hebrews, interpreted the death and resurrection of Jesus in light of the fulfillment of God's covenant promises. As early as the Pentateuch, or the first five books of the Old Testament, the Scriptures promised a "new covenant." Jesus's life, death, and resurrection fulfilled the new covenant, in which all nations would find blessing through faith in Christ.

Early Christian polemics against Judaism emerged as a response to theological disputes and conflicts between the nascent Christian movement and the Jewish religious authorities of the time. These polemical engagements were characterized by theological debates, textual interpretations, and accusations against Judaism, often reflecting the growing divergence between Christianity and Judaism in the first few centuries of Christianity's history.

Early Christian polemics frequently centered around the concept of supersessionism, which posited that Christianity had superseded or fulfilled the promises and covenantal relationship between God and Israel as expressed in the Hebrew Scriptures. Christians argued that the advent of Jesus Christ and the establishment of the new covenant rendered the Mosaic law obsolete, and that God had rejected the Jewish people due to their rejection of Jesus as the Messiah. Once again, Justin argued that Christians are the rightful heirs of the Old Testament because Jesus fulfills the promises found in them.

Early Christian polemicists often depicted the Jewish people as spiritually blind and obstinate in their rejection of Jesus and his teachings. They cited passages from the New Testament, such as Rom 11:25, to argue that God had temporarily hardened the hearts of the Jews to facilitate the spread of the gospel among the Gentiles. This portrayal of Jewish blindness served to justify the Christian mission to the Gentiles and to assert the superiority of Christianity over Judaism.

Early Christian polemics frequently criticized Judaism for its perceived emphasis on legalistic observance of the Mosaic law and ritual practices. Christians argued that Judaism's focus on external rituals and ceremonies had obscured the spiritual essence of religion and hindered the Jewish people from recognizing the true spiritual fulfillment found in Jesus Christ. This criticism of legalism and ritualism contributed to developing a distinctive Christian identity centered around faith in Christ rather than adherence to religious laws.

Early Christian writings, including the New Testament epistles and the works of church fathers such as Justin Martyr and Origen, contain polemical passages that denounce Judaism and its adherents. These texts often employ hostile language and negative stereotypes to characterize Jews, portraying them as adversaries of the Christian faith and deserving of divine punishment for their rejection of Jesus as the Christ of the Old Testament. The fathers speak this way of Judaism because of the promised judgment in the Old Testament prophets. Throughout the Old Testament, God is said to be angry with Israel, promising judgment because of their idolatry. Because Israel rejected the promised Christ, early Christians believed the Jews were deserving of God's judgment. These theologians were not anti-Semitic or anti-Jewish. Instead, they were opposed to Judaism, believing it to be in opposition to the gospel of Jesus.

Early Christian polemics against Judaism happened within the broader historical context of the first few centuries. The rise of Christianity as a distinct religious movement within the Roman Empire coincided with increasing tensions between Jews and Gentiles, as well as with the persecution of Christians by Jewish and Roman authorities. These sociopolitical dynamics contributed to the formulation of polemical arguments and the perpetuation of negative attitudes toward Judaism within the early Christian community.

Preaching Jesus in a Greco-Roman Context

Greco-Roman philosophy provided conceptual frameworks and philosophical vocabulary for articulating Christian beliefs. Plato's metaphysical ideas, Aristotle's logic, and Stoic ethics all contributed to the development of Christian theological language. Early Christian theologians, such as Justin Martyr and Origen, drew upon Platonic metaphysics to expound upon concepts such as the soul's preexistence and the eternal nature of God. Aristotelian logic provided Christian theologians with categories to use in translating the Christian faith to a pagan audience. Stoic ethical principles, such as the pursuit of virtue and the endurance of suffering, resonated with early Christian notions of moral integrity and true faith. The Stoic emphasis on self-discipline and detachment from worldly pleasures appears within Christian ascetic practices and ethical teachings. It is important to note, however, that Christians did not merely adopt the Greek philosophy prevalent in the culture. Adolf von Harnack, in his *History of Dogma*, popularized the notion that the pristine gospel of Jesus and the apostles was "hellenized" through its encounter with Hellenistic Greek thought. Harnack's view was the consensus for a century, but recent scholarship has noted this conclusion is no longer warranted.[2] Rather than hellenizing Christianity, theologians instead Christianized Greek thought. It is more appropriate to recognize that in the formation of Christian theology, theologians utilized the language of Greek philosophy without embracing the underlying meaning. Instead, Christian theologians maintained the Great Tradition and resisted syncretism between the Bible and Hellenistic philosophy. The Great Tradition stands in contrast to Hellenism.

---

[2] For more, see Robert L. Wilken, *The Spirit of Early Christian Thought: Seeking the Face of God* (Yale University Press, 2003).

The Greco-Roman literary and rhetorical tradition provided early Christians with rhetorical tools and literary genres for articulating their theological beliefs and defending their faith against intellectual challenges. Early Christian apologists, such as Justin Martyr and Tertullian, employed Greco-Roman rhetorical techniques and philosophical arguments to defend Christian beliefs against accusations of atheism, immorality, and sedition. These apologetic writings reflect a sophisticated engagement with the cultural and intellectual currents of the time. Greco-Roman rhetorical conventions, such as allegory and typology, influenced early Christian homiletic literature, shaping how biblical texts were interpreted and preached. Figures such as Origen and Clement of Alexandria employed allegorical interpretation to uncover hidden spiritual meanings within the biblical text. Allegory considers elements within a text to be symbolic of some other reality. An example from the New Testament is Paul's reading of Genesis about Sarah and Hagar in Galatians. Paul concludes that the two women represent those who are free from the law and those who are slaves to it. Typology considers elements within a text to typify or signify other realities. Adam, for example, is a "type" of Christ rather than a symbol of Christ. By signifying Christ, Adam points the reader toward the reality of the Christ who was to come.

Orthodoxy and Heresy in Second- and Third-Century Christianity

Historians have debated for some time whether orthodoxy preceded heresy or whether orthodoxy arose in response to heresy. While the development of doctrines emerges over time, Christians in the second century already had a faith handed down ("traditioned") from the apostles. This faith "once for all delivered" is the orthodox, apostolic teaching. The content of this orthodox faith, found in the Old Testament and in the apostolic writings of the New Testament, was summarized in the rule of faith. However, theological formation continued in response to teaching that was inconsistent with this biblical Christianity. Intense theological debates and controversies marked the second and third centuries of Christianity as the early Christian community grappled with questions of doctrine, authority, and orthodoxy. The need to delineate the apostolic teaching of Jesus as Messiah from other expressions of "Christian" understandings of Jesus was of great importance. Groups such as the Docetists, Ebionites, Gnostics, and others rejected the orthodox teachings. Christians who followed the teaching of the apostles sought ways to express that faith and distinguish it from false interpretations. The term used for the apostolic understanding of Jesus is "orthodoxy." Orthodoxy, from the Greek words *orthos*, meaning "right," and *doxa*, meaning "worship," refers to the beliefs and practices considered true and correct within a particular religious tradition. In second- and third-century Christianity, Christians defined orthodoxy in relation to several critical criteria.

First, orthodoxy was grounded in the apostolic tradition, which consisted of the teachings and practices handed down from the apostles to subsequent generations of Christians. Early Christian writers, such as Ignatius of Antioch and Irenaeus of Lyons, emphasized the importance of apostolic succession and fidelity to the teachings of the apostles as a mark of orthodoxy. Apostolic succession was not, in the ancient church, merely a succession of office but rather a succession of teaching. The faith that was handed down (literally, *traditioned*) from the apostles to their successors was the "right" or "true" faith.

Christian theologians defined this apostolic faith in relation to the authority of Scripture, which initially meant the Old Testament but came to include the writings of the New Testament. Early Christians appealed to the Scriptures as the only authoritative source of doctrine and used them to refute heretical teachings and practices. While differences persisted over which apostolic texts, including gospel accounts of Jesus's life and ministry, should be read and taught in worship, apostolic Christianity universally considered written texts the basis of their life and practice. These apostolic churches also looked to summarize the scriptural and apostolic faith with creedal formulations and confessions. These statements of faith are called the rule of faith. The language of various rules differs slightly, but they all serve the same purpose of delineating the apostolic faith from other "Christianities." The development of creeds, such as the Apostles' Creed and the Nicene Creed, expanded these earlier rules of faith and provided concise summaries of orthodox Christian belief. These creeds served as doctrinal standards against which theological innovations and deviations could be measured. While Christians developed theological language to express their faith, they never wanted to introduce novelty into the gospel.

Alternative Understandings of Christianity

Christianity begins and ends with the answer Jesus posed to his disciples in Matthew 16:13, "Who do you say that I am?" The essence of the rule of faith was the confession of Jesus Christ as Lord. Fundamentally, Christianity is about trusting and following Jesus, so his identity is paramount to the proper worship of God. As Jesus explains in Matthew 16, because he is the scriptural Christ, he must suffer and die, be buried, and be raised from the dead for the salvation of those who receive him. Interpretations of Jesus that are inconsistent with, or other than, his identity as the Son of God described in the Old Testament are not apostolic Christianity. Christians rejected other so-called Christian messages besides the teaching of the apostles because they did not lead to the proper worship of God.

Understanding Jesus as the scriptural Christ means confessing two realities. First, Jesus is the Son of God. He is unique from creatures and has a divine origin, divine life, and union with God the Father. Because of his divine origin, he is not a creature but God. Christians recognized an impenetrable ontological divide between God as Creator and his creation, meaning that only God is uncreated. Everything else that exists was created by the one true God, who has come to be present in his creation in the incarnation of Jesus Christ (John 1:1–18). Having made all things out of nothing, God is "other than" all other things ontologically. Because Jesus is the Son of God, he is "other than" all created things. He is the agent of creation, not a part of it.

Second, apostolic Christians recognized that through the virgin birth, the Son of God became human. The human reality of Christ's existence is just as essential to his identity as the divine reality. The incarnation of the Son of God was the means of his becoming present with his creation and the means of him saving fallen, sinful human beings. His life, death, burial, and resurrection from the dead was a genuine human existence that brought salvation to the world. Jesus Christ is God reconciling the world to himself.

Because both realities are necessary, Christians needed to avoid articulations of the gospel, which trended toward one in opposition to the other. A gospel that highlighted the divine reality of Christ but neglected the human reality did not adequately provide for the salvation of human beings. Likewise, a gospel in which believers affirm Jesus's human reality without fully confessing his divine reality does not allow God's personal and real presence in creation or union with human beings. In both instances, there is no salvation for human beings nor reconciliation with God. To paraphrase Gregory of Nazianzus, "That which the Son has not assumed he has not saved." In the incarnation, the divine Son took on humanity to redeem it. If he did not become fully human, then humanity has no salvation. When theologians ventured too far toward in one extreme or the other, there was a need to address those extremes. Each of the heresies we see in the ancient church was, at their core, an expression of one of the realities of Jesus to the neglect of the other. Regardless of other deviations from apostolic Christianity, the fundamental problem with each of these heresies is how they answer the question, Who is Jesus of Nazareth? The problem was not one of power or prominence but one of proclamation. Despite the emergence of competing answers to that question, those who followed the teachings of the apostles that Jesus was the scriptural Christ opposed alternative presentations.

Docetism

One second-century heresy was Docetism. The term "Docetism" is derived from the Greek word *dokeō*, meaning "to seem" or "to appear." Docetism originated as a response to questions about the nature of Jesus Christ's humanity and suffering. It gained traction in early Christological debates and theological controversies, particularly concerning the relationship between the divine and human in Christ. The Docetists posited that Jesus Christ only appeared to be human and that his physical body was an illusion or "appearance." According to Docetism, Jesus's humanity was not genuine, and his sufferings, death, and resurrection were only apparent. Docetists believed that Christ's divine nature was unaffected by his human experiences and that he transcended the limitations of human existence.

Prominent proponents of Docetism included various gnostic and proto-gnostic groups within early Christianity. Influenced by dualistic and ascetic philosophies, these groups held Docetic views as part of their broader theological frameworks. Docetism found adherents among certain Christian sects and communities, particularly those that emphasized the spiritual over the material and sought to elevate the divine nature of Christ above his human attributes. Docetism denied the scriptural teaching concerning the full humanity and divinity of Jesus Christ. First John addresses those who reject the humanity of Jesus, saying, "Every spirit that acknowledges that Jesus Christ has come in the flesh is from God" (1 John 4:2). The church fathers, such as Ignatius of Antioch, Irenaeus of Lyons, and Tertullian of Carthage, criticized Docetism, arguing that it undermined orthodox Christology and compromised the reality of Christ's incarnation and salvific work. Docetism was ultimately condemned as heretical by the apostolic church.

Docetism catalyzed ongoing debates about the relationship between the divine and human in Christ, particularly in subsequent Christological controversies. Its rejection of the full reality of Christ's humanity anticipated later debates about the nature of Christ's personhood, the hypostatic union, and the communication of attributes within the Chalcedonian formulation of Christology.

Ebionism

Ebionite Christology was another theological perspective in early Christianity that emerged in the first century. The Ebionites were a Jewish-Christian sect that adhered to a distinct understanding of the person of Jesus Christ, rejecting the gospel of the apostles that, as the Son of God, Jesus of Nazareth was divine. They also rejected the doctrine of Jesus's preexistence. They believed that Jesus was a human prophet God chose, but they denied that he was divine. Instead, they regarded him as only a human Jewish Christ and king. The Ebionites maintained strict observance of Jewish law and customs. They insisted on circumcision, dietary laws, and adherence to the Sabbath. This adherence to Jewish practices was central to their identity and distinguished them from other Christian groups. The Ebionites rejected the teachings of the apostle Paul, viewing him as an apostate from authentic Judaism. They did not accept his letters as authoritative Scripture and held views contrary to Paul's teachings on topics such as salvation by grace through faith. Ebionite Christology espoused a form of adoptionism, which posited that Jesus became the Son of God by adoption at his baptism or some other event in his life rather than by nature. This view emphasized Jesus's exemplary life and obedience to God rather than his divine nature. The Ebionites accepted a written Gospel known as the Hebrew Gospel, likely a revised edition of the Gospel of Matthew. Ebionite Christology represented a unique synthesis of Jewish and Christian beliefs but was ultimately marginalized within early Christianity as the orthodox understanding of Jesus's nature and role became more firmly established. Despite their rejection of apostolic Christianity, the Ebionites persisted for some time, with remnants of their community surviving into the early medieval period.

Gnosticism

During the second and third centuries of Christianity, the early church encountered a variety of heterodox beliefs and movements, chief among them being Gnosticism. Gnosticism traces its roots to various sources, including Jewish mysticism, Hellenistic philosophy, and Christian theology. The term "Gnosticism" itself is derived from the Greek word *gnosis*, meaning "knowledge," reflecting the movement's emphasis on esoteric spiritual knowledge as the key to salvation. Gnostic teachings emerged in diverse forms and variations across different regions, and the term itself refers to several groups with similar understandings of the identity of Jesus Christ. In 1945, researchers discovered a gnostic library at Nag Hammadi in Egypt, giving scholars greater insight into gnostic belief and practice.

Gnosticism posits a radical dualism between the material world, seen as corrupt and inferior, and the spiritual realm, viewed as divine and transcendent. This dualistic cosmology often leads to a denigration of the material world and a focus on escaping its confines through spiritual enlightenment. Central to gnostic belief is that salvation comes through secret knowledge (gnosis) revealed to a select few. This knowledge involves understanding the divine origins of the soul, the nature of the divine realm, and the path to liberation from the material world. Gnosticism often posits the existence of a lesser deity known as the demiurge, who is responsible for creating the material world but is ignorant of the higher spiritual realms. The demiurge was a flawed and imperfect creator, distinct from the supreme divine being. Gnostic systems frequently feature a variety of divine beings or aeons, including a transcendent God or "pleroma," as well as intermediary figures, such as the divine Sophia or Christ. These figures play critical roles in the process of salvation and the restoration of the divine order.

Adoptionism

Adoptionism, or dynamic monarchianism, was a Christological view that emerged in the second century. Dynamic monarchianism posits that Jesus was a human being who was adopted to be the Son of God. For that reason, the doctrine is sometimes called adoptionism. Adoptionists believed that Jesus Christ was a purely human figure who was "adopted" or "elevated" to divine status by God at some point during his life, often at his baptism. According to adoptionism, Jesus became the Son of God through his faithful obedience and moral perfection rather than being inherently divine.

Prominent proponents of adoptionism included figures such as Theodotus of Byzantium and Paul of Samosata. Theodotus, a Christian thinker in Rome during the late second century, is often regarded as one of the earliest proponents of adoptionism. Paul of Samosata, a bishop of Antioch in the early third century, espoused adoptionist views, leading to his rejection by the church.

Adoptionism faced opposition from orthodox Christian leaders and theologians who maintained traditional beliefs about the nature of Jesus Christ's divinity and humanity. Church fathers such as Tertullian and Origen criticized adoptionism, arguing that it undermined orthodox Christology and compromised the doctrine of the Trinity. Despite its condemnation as heretical, adoptionism left a lasting impact on the development of Christian theology and doctrine. Its emphasis on Jesus's humanity and his exaltation by God contributed to ongoing debates about the nature of Christ's personhood and the relationship between his divine and human natures. Adoptionism prompted theological reflection on the significance of Jesus's baptism and the role of divine agency in his earthly ministry. Furthermore, adoptionism's rejection of the preexistence of Christ and its emphasis on his moral perfection as the basis for divine sonship anticipated later Christological controversies, particularly those surrounding Arianism and Nestorianism in the fourth and fifth centuries. Adoptionism served as a precursor to subsequent debates about the nature of Christ's incarnation, his relationship to God the Father, and the implications of his humanity for Christian soteriology.

Modalism, or Modalistic Monarchianism

Modalistic monarchianism, also known as Sabellianism or modalism, was a Christological view that emerged in the second century. Modalists maintained that the Father, Son, and Holy Spirit were not distinct persons within the Godhead but somewhat different "modes" or manifestations of the same divine essence. According to modalism, God manifested himself in different ways throughout history, first as the Father in the Old Testament, then as the Son in the incarnation of Jesus Christ, and finally as the Holy Spirit in the church's life.

Modalists emphasized the unity and indivisibility of the Godhead, rejecting the idea of three separate persons within the Trinity. Prominent proponents of modalistic monarchianism included figures such as Sabellius, Noetus, and Praxeas. Sabellius, a Christian theologian in Rome during the third century, is often regarded as the leading proponent of moralistic monarchianism. Noetus, a Christian teacher in Smyrna during the late second century, also espoused modalistic views, leading to his condemnation by orthodox Christian authorities. Modalistic monarchianism faced opposition from orthodox Christian leaders and theologians who maintained traditional beliefs about the Trinity and the personhood of the Father, Son, and Holy Spirit. Church fathers such as Tertullian and Hippolytus criticized modalism, arguing that it undermined orthodox trinitarian doctrine and compromised the distinction between the Father and the Son. Modalistic monarchianism was ultimately condemned as heretical by the mainstream Christian church. The controversy regarding modalism was a precursor to subsequent Christological and trinitarian controversies, particularly those surrounding Arianism and Nicene orthodoxy in the fourth century. Its rejection of the distinct personhood of the Father, Son, and Holy Spirit anticipated later debates about the one being of the Trinity, known as the consubstantiality of the divine persons, along with the eternal generation of the Son and the procession of the Holy Spirit. Tertullian wrote his famous *Against Praxeas* to defend the doctrine of Father, Son, and Holy Spirit as distinct divine persons against modalism.

Montanism

Montanism was a Christian movement that emerged in the second century founded by a prophet named Montanus. It originated in Phrygia, a region in Asia Minor (modern-day Turkey), and gained followers primarily in the Eastern Mediterranean and North Africa. Montanism emphasized prophecy, asceticism, and strict moral discipline as a way of life to enable Christians to endure persecution and remain faithful to Jesus. Montanus himself claimed to be the mouthpiece of the Holy Spirit, delivering new revelations and prophecies. He and two female prophets, Priscilla and Maximilla, purportedly received ecstatic messages from the Spirit, which they believed superseded traditional Christian teachings. These prophetic utterances were seen as authoritative by Montanists, often leading to tensions with churches and pastors who believed Scripture to be the revelation of God. Many of these prophetic utterances centered on the belief that Christians were living in the "end times." Montanist prophets called on their followers to prepare for the imminent second coming of Jesus. Montanists believed they represented a restoration of the true faith soon to establish the New Jerusalem. The persecutions fulfilled Jesus's promise of trials and tribulations in the "last days."

In response to the falling away of many Christians under the weight of persecution and the threat of death, Montanists advocated for rigorous ascetic practices, including fasting, celibacy, and withdrawal from worldly pursuits. They adopted strict moral codes and emphasized personal holiness and purity. Because they viewed themselves as a remnant of faithful believers, they committed to lives that reflected God's coming kingdom. Strict asceticism, eschewing worldly pleasures and pursuits such as marriage, was necessary because the world's end was soon to come. Why participate in the activities of this world when the next world was imminent?

Montanism emerged as a reaction against what its followers perceived as the growing institutionalization and compromise of the early Christian church. Montanists criticized the clergy for their perceived laxity and sought to restore the charismatic spontaneity and purity of the apostolic era. As a result, they faced opposition from the more established churches, mainly from ecclesiastical authorities, who viewed its prophetic claims as heretical and disruptive. Several church councils, including the Council of Hierapolis and the Council of Iconium, condemned Montanism as a false teaching.

Tertullian of Carthage eventually converted to Montanism, which occurred later in his life, likely in the early third century. Montanism appealed to Tertullian for several reasons.

First, the Montanists were rigorous in their morality. As a fervent believer in the need for personal holiness and purity, he resonated with the movement's emphasis on fasting, celibacy, and moral rigor. Second, Tertullian found the acceptance of the ongoing manifestation of spiritual gifts and the inspiration of the Holy Spirit appealing. The movement's charismatic fervor and claim to represent a purer, more authentic expression of Christianity appealed to him. Third, Tertullian shared Montanism's eschatological outlook, believing in the imminent return of Christ and the expectation of divine judgment on those persecuting Christians. Montanism's emphasis on the "end times" resonated with Tertullian's belief in the urgency of repentance and preparation for the coming kingdom of God.

Tertullian's conversion to Montanism marked a departure from mainstream Christianity and led to his eventual excommunication from the church. Despite this, he wrote prolifically to defend Montanist beliefs and practices, becoming one of its most prominent advocates. Tertullian's involvement in Montanism underscores the diversity of early Christian thought and the complex interplay of theological perspectives within the early church. While a sincere conviction in its principles may have driven his conversion to Montanism, it reflects his time's broader theological debates and controversies.

Conclusion

As Christianity spread throughout the Roman Empire, doctrinal innovations prompted the need for Christians to refine their theological language to defend against false teaching. These heresies threatened to divide Christians from one another, undermining the message of love and the unity of the church. Apostolic Christians would need to continue to refine their theological language and doctrines to help Christians remain faithful to orthodox Christianity. The true faith could be found in the church's worship and the rule of faith. But further development was needed. The faith received from the apostles, practiced in the churches, and handed down to the next generation is the Great Tradition.

Recommended Reading

Athenagoras. *A Plea for the Christians*. In *The Apostolic Fathers with Justin Martyr and Irenaeus*. Edited by Alexander Roberts and James Donaldson. Eerdmans, 1975.

Barnard, Leslie William. *Justin Martyr: His Life and Thought*. Cambridge University Press, 1967.

Edwards, Mark J. *Apologetics in the Roman Empire: Pagans, Jews, and Christians.* Oxford University Press, 1999.

Grant, Robert M. *Greek Apologists of the Second Century.* Westminster Press, 1988.

Justin Martyr. *The Dialogue with Trypho.* Translated by Thomas B. Falls. The Catholic University of America Press, 2003.

Justin Martyr. *The First Apology.* Translated by Leslie William Barnard. Paulist Press, 1997.

Minucius Felix. *Octavius.* Translated by Gerald H. Rendall. Heinemann, 1931.

Osborn, Eric. *Justin Martyr.* Mohr Siebeck, 1973.

Paget, James Carleton. *The Epistle of Barnabas: Outlook and Background.* Mohr Siebeck, 1994.

Parsons, Michael. *Justin Martyr and the Apologetic Tradition.* Brill, 1995.

Pelikan, Jaroslav. *The Emergence of the Catholic Tradition (100–600).* University of Chicago Press, 1971.

Richardson, Cyril C. *Early Christian Fathers.* Macmillan, 1953.

Tatian. *Address to the Greeks.* In *Ante-Nicene Fathers*, vol. 2, *Fathers of the Second Century.* Edited by Alexander Roberts and James Donaldson. Eerdmans, 1975.

Theophilus of Antioch. *To Autolycus.* Translated by Robert M. Grant. Clarendon, 1970.

Wilken, Robert Louis. *The Christians as the Romans Saw Them.* Yale University Press, 1984.

Young, Frances M. *The Making of the Creeds.* SCM Press, 1991.

—— Chapter 4 ——

Preserving the Great Tradition

Christian theologians of the second century responded to heresy by leaning into the church's Bible as the source of Christian orthodoxy. This meant identifying the canon of Scripture that contained the Christian gospel. Christians had circulated several writings of the apostles that preached the gospel, but churches differed with one another about which ones were inspired Scripture. They also identified a rule or guide for reading Scripture rightly. The early Christian understanding of the rule of faith, as discussed in the previous chapter, referred to a summary of essential Christian beliefs or doctrines that served as a standard for orthodoxy and a guide for interpreting Scripture. It functioned as a foundational creedal statement or summary of the core teachings of Christianity, providing a framework for understanding the faith and guarding against heresy. It was seen as a faithful expression of the apostolic tradition, embodying the teachings received directly from Jesus and transmitted by the apostles to their successors primarily through the baptismal formula found in Matt 28:18–20.

The rule of faith encompassed fundamental Christian beliefs, such as the Trinity (the belief in one God existing in three persons: Father, Son, and Holy Spirit), the deity of Christ, the incarnation, the atonement, the resurrection, and the final judgment. It affirmed the core tenets of the Christian faith that distinguished it from other religions or sects. While theologians had different specific ways of expressing the rule of faith, the fundamental message remained the same. One example of the rule of faith is found in Irenaeus of Lyons:

> God, the Father, not made, not material, invisible; one God, the creator of all things: this is the first point of our faith. The second point is: The Word of God, Son of God, Christ Jesus our Lord, who was manifested to the prophets according to the form of their prophesying and according to the method of the dispensation of the Father: through whom all things were made; who also at the end of the times, to complete and gather up all things, was made man among men, visible and tangible, in order to abolish death and show forth life and produce a community of union between God and man. And the third point is: The Holy Spirit, through whom the prophets prophesied, and the fathers learned the things of God, and the righteous were led forth into the way of righteousness; and who in the end of the times was poured out in a new way upon mankind in all the earth, renewing man unto God.[1]

The rule of faith provided a unifying standard for the diverse Christian communities scattered across different regions and cultures. It ensured doctrinal consistency and helped maintain unity among believers by establishing common ground for faith and practice. The rule of faith also served as a hermeneutical tool for interpreting Scripture and discerning the authentic teachings of Christianity from false interpretations or heresies. It guided Christians in understanding the meaning of biblical passages in light of the broader doctrinal framework of the faith.

The rule helped Christians combat heresy and preserve orthodoxy within the early Christian community. It provided a criterion for evaluating theological innovations or deviations from established doctrine, enabling the church to identify and refute false teachings that threatened the integrity of the faith. Examples of early Christian formulations of the rule of faith include the Apostles' Creed, the Nicene Creed, and the rule of faith articulated by early church fathers, such as Irenaeus of Lyons and Tertullian. These creeds and doctrinal statements crystallized the essential beliefs of Christianity and provided a firm foundation for the development of Christian theology and doctrine in subsequent centuries.

Defining Scripture

Christians always had a Bible. In Luke 24, Jesus reminded his disciples that they were to understand him according to the Law, the Prophets, and the Writings, by which he meant

[1] Irenaeus of Lyons, *Demonstration of the Apostolic Preaching*, sections 6–7, trans. Joseph P. Smith, in *Ancient Christian Writers*, vol. 16 (Newman, 1952), 42–43.

the Scriptures of the Old Testament. The canon of truth or rule of faith ensured reading those Scriptures rightly, as the apostles learned from Christ. Eventually, the apostolic preaching of Jesus, of whom the Old Testament Scriptures were about, also took on written form. As the apostles themselves wrote texts and as their followers captured their teaching in gospel writings, Christians began to read those texts as Scripture as well. In earliest Christianity, the churches began to determine which writings captured the apostolic faith of Christ according to the Old and New Testament and which did not. While it took work for Christians to make this determination, it became clear quite early what writings were Scripture. While some differences existed for more than a century, eventually Christians agreed on the writings of the New Testament Scriptures.

Books believed to have been written by apostles or closely associated with apostolic figures had priority. The Gospels of Matthew, Mark, Luke, and John circulated as a subcollection. This "Fourfold" Gospel captured the message Jesus gave to his apostles. Letters written by the apostles Peter and Paul also circulated among churches. This criterion emphasized the direct connection between the writings and the authoritative teaching of Jesus and his apostles. The theological content of a book plays a crucial role in its inclusion in the canon. Books that upheld orthodox doctrine accurately conveyed the teachings of Jesus and his apostles and contributed to the spiritual edification of the Christian community. The book's antiquity and widespread usage within the early Christian community were paramount. Books that churches read in worship, were cited by early Christian writers, and were included in early Christian manuscripts were more likely to be considered canonical.

The process of defining the New Testament collection of texts was gradual and varied among different Christian communities and regions. By the second and third centuries, specific canonical lists emerged as Christian churches identified which apostolic texts were authoritative Scripture and which were not. The Muratorian Fragment, dating from the late second century, is one of the earliest known lists of New Testament books. It contains a list of accepted books, including the Four Gospels, Acts, Pauline Epistles, and several other letters. It also mentions disputed, or noncanonical, writings, indicating ongoing debates about specific books. The Gospel of Thomas, a gnostic text, was popular among some groups. This Gospel, like the other noncanonical Gospels, contained stories about Jesus and sayings purportedly from him. But these Gospels did not present Jesus as the Christ of the Old Testament. The canonical Gospels all situate Jesus within the message of the Old Testament. The third-century theologian Origen compiled a list of canonical books based on their widespread acceptance and usage within the early Christian community. His list included most books now part of the New Testament, although he acknowledged disagreement among Christians regarding some writings. Some Christians would have included some of the Apostolic Fathers among accepted New Testament writings. The Shepherd of Hermas and the Epistle of Barnabas were popular. Eventually, Christians recognized these texts as handing down the apostolic preaching but not being the source of that gospel. Second Peter, James, and the book of Revelation were disputed for a long time before the church acknowledged them to be Scripture. Eusebius of Caesarea, writing in the early fourth century, provides one of the earliest comprehensive lists of New Testament books in his *Ecclesiastical History*. He categorizes books into three groups: universally accepted, disputed, and rejected. This list closely aligns with the modern New Testament canon.

Apostolic Succession and Ecclesiastical Authority in Second- and Third-Century Christianity

In the second and third centuries of Christianity, apostolic succession and ecclesiastical authority were pivotal in shaping the early Christian community's organizational structure and theological identity. The notion of apostolic succession emerged from the belief that Christian churches maintained the gospel of the apostles and passed down that faith to their successors. There are two prevailing interpretations of the early Christian notion of apostolic succession. First is the idea that the church's bishops possess the authority of the apostles through the ecclesiastical office. With this view, succession is ecclesial; bishops occupy the office of the apostles as their successors. Second is the interpretation that the bishops are successors to the apostles, having received their gospel and been given the responsibility to preserve and pass it along. With this interpretation, the church does not possess apostolic authority by virtue of office but by virtue of maintaining the Great Tradition of scriptural Christianity.

In the late first century, Clement of Rome provided one of the earliest references to apostolic succession in his First Epistle to the Corinthians. Clement emphasized the importance of order and authority within the church, affirming the role of bishops as successors to the apostles.

Ignatius of Antioch, writing in the early second century, stressed the importance of episcopal authority and unity within the church. In his letters to various Christian communities,

Ignatius emphasized the role of bishops as guardians of apostolic tradition and urged Christians to submit to their authority.

Irenaeus of Lyons, writing in the late second century, provided a systematic defense of apostolic succession in his seminal work *Against Heresies*. Irenaeus argued that the apostles' teachings were faithfully preserved and transmitted through the preaching of the gospel articulated in the rule of faith. When Irenaeus appealed to the bishops as the successors of the apostles, he stated, "It is possible, then, for everyone in every church, who may wish to know the truth, to contemplate the Tradition of the Apostles which has been made known to us throughout the whole world. And we are in a position to enumerate those who were instituted bishops by the Apostles and their successors down to our own times, men who neither knew nor taught anything like what these heretics rave about."[2] Irenaeus calls the church's message the "Tradition of the Apostles." The church receives the gospel message from those to whom it was entrusted and deliver that to others.

Tertullian, writing in the early third century, likewise affirmed the importance of apostolic succession as handing down of the apostolic message, not holding the apostolic office. He states, "[The apostles] founded churches in every city, from which all the other churches, one after another, derived the tradition of the faith, and the seeds of doctrine, and are every day deriving them, that they may become churches. Indeed, it is on this account only that they will be able to deem themselves apostolic." Apostolic churches are those which hold to the "tradition of the faith."[3] Tertullian goes on to argue that the legitimacy of Christian doctrine and practice depended on its adherence to the apostolic tradition in the church's baptismal practices and the rule of faith.

The idea of apostolic succession as receiving the apostolic message and passing that message along eventually gave way to apostolic succession as the basis of ecclesiastical governance, theological formulation, and liturgical practice. In the early church, however, theologians such as Irenaeus, Tertullian, and others stood against the heretics by appealing to the teaching of the apostles, which could be found in all true churches. Heterodox congregations had abandoned the message of the apostles, holding to doctrines that did not come from them.

---

[2] Irenaeus of Lyons, *Against Heresies* 3.3.1, in *The Ante-Nicene Fathers*, vol. 1, ed. Alexander Roberts and James Donaldson, trans. Alexander Roberts and William Rambaut (Hendrickson, 1994), 415.

[3] Tertullian, *On the Prescription of Heretics* 20, in *Ante-Nicene Fathers*, vol. 3, ed. Alexander Roberts and James Donaldson, trans. Peter Holmes (Hendrickson, 1994), 258.

Developing Church Structure

As Christianity continued to grow, the church needed to develop an organizational structure which would assist in making disciples of Jesus through teaching the Scriptures and practicing the biblical gospel. This development culminated in the emergence in many places of an episcopacy and hierarchical structure. In the decades following the death and resurrection of Jesus Christ, the early Christian community operated primarily through informal networks of leadership, with local congregations guided by a plurality of elders or overseers (presbyters or bishops). These leaders provided pastoral care, administered sacraments, and exercised spiritual oversight within their communities. However, as the Christian movement grew and spread throughout the Roman Empire, the need for more structured and centralized forms of leadership became increasingly evident.

By the late second century, a shift toward a monarchical episcopacy began. A single overseer (Greek: *episkopos*) emerged as the primary leader and authority figure within a local Christian community. This transition marked a departure from the earlier model of collegial leadership among multiple pastors and signaled the emergence of a more hierarchical structure of church governance. Alongside the development of monarchical episcopacy came the concept of episcopal succession, which emphasized the continuity of leadership within the church through the ordination and consecration of bishops by their predecessors. Episcopal succession legitimized the bishop's authority and was meant to ensure the continuity of the teaching of the apostles within the church. With the rise of monarchical episcopacy, the authority of bishops became increasingly centralized within their respective dioceses or regions. Bishops exercised oversight over individual congregations and a network of churches within their jurisdiction, coordinating liturgical practices, doctrinal teaching, and disciplinary matters. In theory, a single overseer who held the church's other leaders to account would ensure biblical fidelity. However, this did not always happen. While many churches within the Great Tradition practiced a hierarchical form of church government, episcopal polity itself is not considered part of the Great Tradition. Church government exists to serve the purpose of evangelism and discipleship. As later departures from a hierarchical government show, theological reflection, spiritual formation, and fidelity to Christ can and does happen where the Bible is preached, the church's ordinances are practiced, and the Spirit of God is present, regardless of polity.

The second and third centuries also witnessed the convening of church councils, often called synods, to address theological controversies, clarify doctrinal issues, and establish norms of church practice and discipline. These gatherings brought bishops and church leaders from various regions to deliberate on theological significance and ecclesiastical governance. Typically, these synods were regional gatherings of likeminded Christians, who were in association with one another already. There are dozens of known synods and perhaps many more that met without leaving behind a record.

The first recorded church council or synod was the Council of Jerusalem in Acts 15. At the council, the church's leaders debated whether or not Gentile Christians were expected to adopt Jewish practices. The council determined it should not be expected of these new believers, though they should respect those Jewish believers who wished to maintain their practices.

Other synods in the second and third centuries gathered to address Montanism, quartodecimanism, and even whether or not clergy should marry. Often, councils meeting in different regions had different conclusions. One example is quartodecimanism, which is the practice of celebrating Easter on the fourteenth day of the Jewish month of Nisan, which was traditionally the day of the Passover. Some churches held Easter on the Sunday following Passover, while others celebrated on that day, regardless of which day of the week it fell. A synod in Asia Minor affirmed quartodecimanism while one in Rome condemned it. These regional gatherings persistent even after the First Ecumenical Council, in which leaders from all regions were invited to address questions that applied to all churches.

The Role of Tradition in Christianity in the Second and Third Centuries

During the second and third centuries of Christianity, tradition played a crucial role in shaping the early Christian community's identity, theology, and practices. Tradition comes from the Latin word *traditio*, meaning "to hand down." Tradition refers to transmitting beliefs, teachings, practices, and customs from one generation to the next within a religious or cultural community. In the context of early Christianity, tradition encompassed a broad range of elements, including oral teachings, liturgical practices, theological interpretations, and ecclesiastical structures. The message of Jesus Christ preached by the apostles is the content of Christian tradition. Jesus taught his apostles the message of the Old Testament, which he fulfilled, then instructed them to preach that message to all nations "beginning at Jerusalem" (Luke 24:47). The apostles preached that gospel and planted Christian communities throughout Jerusalem, Judea, Samaria, and much of the Roman Empire.

Christian baptism is a visible witness of this tradition. As new believers entered the church through baptism, they professed the apostolic tradition of Jesus Christ. The church's liturgy, prayers, and celebration of communion likewise "handed down" the apostolic gospel. Church leaders, such as bishops, elders, pastors, and deacons, function to preserve and pass along the apostolic tradition by preaching the scriptural Christ. Christian tradition was not a supplemental message to the Scriptures but the authoritative understanding of how to read and understand the Scriptures. The church's "tradition" was articulated in the canon of truth or rule of faith, exemplifying the church's way of expressing the gospel of Jesus. In other words, the church preserves and preaches the same message they formerly heard in the beginning. Remaining faithful to that message was the priority of the church. Churches maintained that tradition through preaching the Bible and practicing baptism and the Lord's Supper. The message of the gospel and Christian practice are derived from the apostles and handed down in the church to others.

Theologians and Teachers

Irenaeus of Lyons (c. 130–202)

Irenaeus was bishop in the city of Lyons, in Gaul, which is modern-day France. His works include *Against Heresies*, in which he refutes gnostic teachings and defends orthodox Christian doctrine, and *Demonstration of the Apostolic Preaching*, in which he explains the gospel of Jesus Christ in accordance with the Old Testament. Irenaeus was a theologian, pastor, and defender of orthodoxy in the early Christian church. As bishop of Lyons, he was responsible for pastoring the local Christian community and providing leadership in matters of faith and doctrine. Irenaeus also served as a mediator and peacemaker within the church, seeking to reconcile theological disputes and maintain unity among believers.

> If He was not born, neither did he die; and if He did not die, neither was he raised from the dead, death is not conquered, nor its kingdom destroyed; and if death is not conquered, how are we to ascend to life?
>
> ---
>
> Irenaeus, *Demonstration of the Apostolic Preaching*

Irenaeus's *Against Heresies* is one of the earliest and most comprehensive defenses of orthodox Christian doctrine against heresy. Irenaeus vigorously refutes gnostic teachings and other deviations from the apostolic faith, affirming the authority of Scripture, the apostolic tradition, and the role of the church in preserving the truth. This work is the first technical work of systematic theology in the ancient church. Irenaeus developed the concept of recapitulation (*anakephalaiōsis*) as a central theme in his theology. He taught that Christ, as the new Adam, recapitulated or summed up humanity in himself, undoing the effects of Adam's sin and restoring humanity to communion with God. Key biblical texts for Irenaeus were Romans 5 and 1 Corinthians 15. In the former text, the Bible clearly states that Jesus is the second Adam, replacing disobedience and death with obedience and life. In the latter passage, Paul explains that Jesus has come to redeem humanity: "The first man was from the earth, a man of dust; the second man is from heaven. Like the man of dust, so are those who are of the dust; like the man of heaven, so are those who are of heaven. And just as we have borne the image of the man of dust, we will also bear the image of the man of heaven" (1 Cor 15:47–49). This theological motif of recapitulation influenced later Christian thinkers, such as Athanasius of Alexandria and Cyril of Alexandria.

Irenaeus's writings provide essential insights into early Christian ecclesiology, emphasizing the church's unity and catholicity. He affirmed the authority of the apostolic reading of the Old Testament. The church is responsible for maintaining doctrinal orthodoxy and preserving the apostolic preaching of Jesus Christ. Irenaeus's ecclesiological teachings contributed to developing the church's hierarchical structure.

Clement of Alexandria (c. 150–215)

Clement of Alexandria, also known as Titus Flavius Clemens, was a prominent Christian theologian and philosopher who lived in the late second and early third centuries AD. He was born around AD 150, likely in Athens or Alexandria, Egypt. Clement received a classical education in philosophy and rhetoric before converting to Christianity. He became a disciple of Pantaenus, who served as the head of the Catechetical School of Alexandria, also known as the Didascalium, and whom Clement eventually succeeded.

Unlike other "schools" of thought in antiquity, like the Antiochene "school" of theology or Neoplatonic "school" of philosophy, the Catechetical School was an actual institute of learning. At the Alexandrian school, theology was taught alongside philosophy, math, and science. Despite its multidisciplinary lectures, the purpose of the school was instruction in the Christian faith. Clement, for example, would lecture on philosophy to pagans in an effort to transition to the gospel message. Other disciplines served the ultimate purpose of evangelism and Christian discipleship.

Clement of Alexandria was a prolific writer, and several of his works have survived. Three of his writings are the most significant. *Stromateis* (*Miscellanies*) is a collection of theological statements covering various topics, including ethics, philosophy, biblical interpretation, and Christian doctrine. It reflects Clement's eclectic approach to knowledge, drawing on Christian and pagan sources to present a comprehensive Christian worldview. *Protrepticus* (*Exhortation to the Greeks*) is a work in which Clement addresses pagan readers, urging them to abandon their false gods and embrace the truth of Christianity. He argues that Christianity offers a superior philosophy and way of life compared to the philosophical systems of the Greeks. Finally, *Paedagogus* (*The Educator*) is a treatise that provides practical guidance for Christian living, addressing moral behavior, household management, and spiritual growth. Clement emphasizes the importance of ethical conduct and spiritual discipline for Christian discipleship.

> Let none of you worship the sun; rather let him yearn for the maker of the sun. Let no one deify the universe; rather let him seek after the creator of the universe.
>
> ———
>
> Clement of Alexandria,
> *Exhortation to the Greeks*

The goal of the Christian life is loving God and loving others, for which *The Educator* offers practical instruction, like avoiding gluttony and drunkenness along with overindulgence in any behaviors. Christians are to be modest, because wearing expensive clothing and jewelry could be harmful to those who are poor. He rejects both celibacy and sexual promiscuity, restricting sexual activity to marriage. Christians should avoid using the public baths at times when members of the opposite sex are most likely to be there bathing. Clement says that Christians should be sensitive to how their dress or behavior might be interpreted by non-Christians. Both men and women should avoid wearing makeup or clothing that would focus on outer beauty rather than the beauty of the soul. Clement also rejects the use of certain instruments, such as drums, in worship because those instruments are used by soldiers going into war. He prefers that the only "instruments" in worship are the voices of the church, offering praise through singing.

Clement of Alexandria was both a theologian and an educator. As the head of the Catechetical School of Alexandria, he trained future Christian leaders and defended the faith against philosophical and theological challenges. Clement's writings were essential for instructing and edifying believers, guiding doctrine, ethics, and spiritual formation. He sought to integrate the Christian faith with Greek philosophy, viewing philosophy as a preparatory discipline for the reception of Christian truth. His writings reflect an engagement with Greek and Christian sources, demonstrating the compatibility of reason and revelation. Clement emphasized the importance of ethical living and spiritual growth in the Christian life. His practical guidance on moral behavior and spiritual discipline influenced subsequent Christian writers and theologians, shaping the tradition of Christian ethics. Through his apologetic works, such as the *Exhortation to the Greeks*, Clement defended Christianity against pagan criticisms and presented it as a rational and morally superior alternative to pagan religion and philosophy. His efforts helped to legitimize Christianity within the intellectual and cultural context of the Roman Empire.

Tertullian of Carthage (c. 155–240)

Quintus Septimius Florens Tertullianus, commonly known as Tertullian, was a prolific North African theologian and apologist who was the first theologian to write in Latin. His theological contributions laid the groundwork for later formulations of trinitarian doctrine within the Christian tradition. He used the language of God as a triad to express the threefold nature of God as one divine essence. His triadic language helped Christian theologians develop a doctrinal grammar for God as one Being, three Persons. Tertullian distinguished between the "economic" Trinity, which pertains to God's activities in salvation history, and the "ontological" Trinity, which refers to the eternal relationships within the Godhead. He explored the eternal generation of the Son from the Father and the procession of the Holy Spirit, emphasizing their inseparable yet distinct identities. Tertullian employed analogies and illustrations, such as the sun, its rays, and its heat, to elucidate the relationship between the Father, Son, and Holy Spirit. These analogies helped clarify the distinction between the persons of the Trinity while illustrating their unity in essence.

In his work *De praescriptione haereticorum* (*On the Prescription of Heretics*), Tertullian contends that heresy is a deviation from the truth, which implies that orthodoxy must necessarily exist first as the foundation from which heresy departs. He writes, "That which is first is true, and that which is later is adulterated." For Tertullian, the Christian faith, handed down through the apostles and safeguarded by the church, constitutes the original and authentic teaching of Christ. Heretical doctrines, by contrast, arise later as distortions of this original truth, often motivated by human curiosity or philosophical speculation rather than divine revelation.

Tertullian's argument rests on the premise that the apostolic tradition is both public and verifiable, preserved in the succession of bishops and the teachings of the universal church. He dismisses heretical claims to hidden knowledge or esoteric teachings, emphasizing that the genuine gospel was openly proclaimed by Christ and his apostles. This emphasis on the chronological and doctrinal priority of orthodoxy underpins Tertullian's "prescription" against heretics, a legal metaphor implying that heretics have no standing to interpret Scripture since they operate outside the apostolic tradition. By asserting that orthodoxy predates heresy, Tertullian not only defends the legitimacy of the church's teachings but also provides a framework for identifying and rejecting theological errors.

Tertullian demonstrated his theological commitments in his *Against Praxeas*. Praxeas had embraced modalistic monarchianism, representing a departure from this concept of God. In his work *De praescriptione haereticorum* (*On the Prescription of Heretics*), Tertullian articulates a central argument for the primacy of orthodoxy over heresy by emphasizing the chronological and doctrinal precedence of apostolic teaching. Written around AD 200, this treatise is a defense of the authority of the church's tradition against the claims of heretical groups. Tertullian asserts that heresies are corruptions or distortions of the original truth handed down by the apostles. In chapter 7, he identifies philosophy as the seedbed of heresies, stating that "heresies are themselves instigated by philosophy," which gives rise to the speculative doctrines of heretical systems, such as the Valentinian theory of aeons and other metaphysical constructs. He describes heresy as the "first-born of philosophy," underscoring its derivative nature and its deviation from the authentic teaching of the church.

Throughout the treatise, Tertullian's argument hinges on the claim that truth necessarily precedes falsehood; heresy could not exist without the original orthodoxy from which it diverges. By grounding the authority of orthodoxy in its continuity with apostolic tradition, Tertullian seeks to invalidate the legitimacy of heretical teachings. He argues that the truth of the church's teachings is demonstrated by their direct lineage from Christ and the apostles, whereas heresies emerge later as distortions. This framework not only defends the church's teaching authority but also asserts that heretical doctrines, by virtue of their novelty, lack the authenticity and authority inherent in apostolic tradition. Tertullian's reasoning thus establishes a foundational argument for the precedence and primacy of orthodoxy in the face of heretical challenges.

Tertullian wrote against the gnostics, particularly Valentinus. In the polemical *Against the Valentinians*, he claims that the gnostic views of cosmology, humanity, Christ, and salvation contradict the apostolic faith and is outside of the Great Tradition. As we saw in chapter 3, gnostic cosmology dissolved the Creator-creation distinction, conceiving of a descending hierarchy of divinity in which all created beings emanate from God in lesser states of divine being. We also discussed that Gnosticism taught that human beings were a mixture of an immaterial spirit and a material body. The immaterial spirit was good while the material body was evil. Tertullian argued that even the material world, because it was created by God, was good and beautiful. Finally, we learned that gnostics preached salvation by knowledge of a secret truth passed down orally rather than in the text of Scripture. By making salvation purely intellectual, the gnostics denied the salvation of the entire human being. Tertullian, like Irenaeus before him, sees salvation in terms of the bodily resurrection from the dead in which the believer inherits eternal life, meaning both spiritual and physical life.

Despite his defense of Christian doctrine, later in life, Tertullian joined the Montanists, a sect of legalists who believed the end of the world was near. However, his participation in Montanism does not diminish his earlier theological contributions in explaining the Christian doctrines of God, Christ, and salvation.

Tertullian, one of the most influential Christian writers of the second and third centuries, emerged as a formidable apologist during a period of intense persecution. His apologetic writings defended Christianity against its critics and offered encouragement to believers facing persecution. His writings concerning the persecutions include his *Apology*, *To the Martyrs*, and the letter *To Scapula*. The persecution faced by Christians in the Roman Empire shaped the content and character of these apologies. He defended the faith against accusations of atheism, immorality, and disloyalty to the state, arguing that Christians were law-abiding citizens who posed no threat to the empire. Like Justin Martyr, Tertullian focused his defense of Christianity against the Roman attacks on the Christian's sincere belief in a true and personal God, the deep and abiding moral virtue of Christians, and the antiquity of Christian tradition from the beginning. His appeal to the Old Testament Scriptures as the foundation for Christianity countered the Roman argument that Christianity was a novel religion founded by a traveling preacher whose radical ideas and followers led to his public execution. In the same vein as other early apologists, Tertullian argued that Christianity was intellectually honest and morally justifiable.

Origen of Alexandria (c. 185–c. 253)

Origen of Alexandria was born to Christian parents and received an extensive education in Christian and secular subjects. Origen's father, Leonides, was martyred during the persecution under Emperor Septimius Severus. When his father was arrested, Origen attempted to turn himself in for martyrdom as well, but his mother hid his clothes to prevent him from going since he refused to leave the house naked. Following his father's death, Origen joined the Catechetical School of Alexandria, eventually becoming a teacher there. While his career was spent teaching in the Catechetical School and writing to strengthen the church, Origen was a controversial figure, especially after his death, as we shall see. Origen's theological system did not always distinguish between the received Christian theology and the speculative theology in which he often engaged. Three hundred years after his death, Origen was condemned because of his speculations about eternal human souls and the universal redemption of all of creation.

Origen's literary output was vast and influential. *On First Principles* is Origen's systematic theology, much like Irenaeus's *Against Heresies*. Origen organizes his theology by the rule of faith, which he provides at the beginning of the book. The first part of the book is the teaching of the church, while later chapters contain his more speculative theology. These later theological reflections are the application of the church's teaching to other pressing theological and philosophical questions. In the first section, Origen addresses topics such as the triune God, the nature of God, creation, the incarnation, salvation, and the world's end. He especially contributed to the development of trinitarian theology, articulating the relationship between the Father, Son, and Holy Spirit and affirming their unity in essence while also recognizing their distinct roles. Origen's emphasis on Jesus as the eternally begotten Son of God, whose relationship with the Father is ontological and eternal, helped the church develop trinitarian language and grammar against later challenges to apostolic Christianity. Origen explored the eternal generation of the Son from the Father and the procession of the Holy Spirit from the Father and the Son. He understood these relationships as intrinsic to the divine nature, highlighting the eternal coexistence and mutual interdependence of the three persons of the Trinity.

Origen also responded to the attack on Christianity by the pagan philosopher Celsus, who had criticized Christian teaching. In his *Against Celsus*, Origen defends Christianity against Celsus's arguments, presenting a reasoned defense of Christian doctrine and ethics. Celsus attacked Christian doctrines as not worthy of belief because "truth comes by way of the Greek mind." He was especially dismissive of the incarnation and the virgin birth, which he believed to be irrational. Celsus also dismissed Christianity because most believers were uneducated, poor, and from marginal communities in society. Origen addressed Celsus's criticisms of trinitarian theology and presented reasoned arguments for the coherence and rationality of Christian belief. He also defended Christians as productive members of society and good neighbors even to those who persecuted them. While Celsus dismissed Christians as weak, Origen argued that their weakness was their greatest strength.

> And may God and His Only-begotten Son the Word be with us, to enable us effectively to refute the falsehoods which Celsus has published under the delusive title of *A True Discourse*, and at the same time to unfold the truths of Christianity with such fullness as our purpose requires.
>
> Origen, *Against Celsus*

Origen believed the Bible had multiple layers of meaning and that the interpreter of Scripture was to seek deeper spiritual truths through allegorical interpretation. Thus, he produced many commentaries on biblical books to uncover deeper spiritual meanings within the biblical text and to provide practical guidance for Christian living. Origen's extensive commentaries on biblical texts, such as the Gospel of John and the Pauline Epistles, contain numerous reflections on trinitarian themes. Origen's exegetical methods influenced later Christian theologians and shaped the development of biblical hermeneutics. One example of his interpretation of the Bible is his reading of the parable of the good Samaritan in Luke 10:25–37. Origen interprets the story as an allegory of Christ's work. The donkey which carries the injured man in the story represents Christ's body, the inn to which he is carried represents the church, and the good Samaritan himself represents Jesus. A similar example of how he searched for deeper spiritual meaning in the text can be found in his reading of 1 Samuel 28, where the appearing of the prophet Samuel from Hades is a picture of Jesus's resurrection from the dead.

Besides his contributions as a theologian and biblical interpreter, Origen was also an educator. He was the head of the Catechetical School of Alexandria, where he taught theology, philosophy, and biblical studies to Christian and pagan students. Origen's teachings and writings influenced Christian thought and doctrine during his lifetime. Gregory Thaumaturgus describes Origen's pedagogy in an *Oration and Panegyric to Origen*. He writes that Origen sought to teach anyone willing to study, whether Christian or not. He began with the fundamental assumptions of the Greek philosophers who were read and accepted by the intellectual in the culture of the day. Origen used the teachings of the philosophers and poets as a bridge to the gospel of Jesus. He identified places where the Greek thinkers affirmed truths embraced by Christians, such as eternal Wisdom. Origen then explained how the Christian understanding of Wisdom was different than the Greek understanding. His method was very similar to that of the apostle Paul in Acts 17. It was important, Gregory notes, that Origen's Christian students read the philosophers so they might better explain Christian theology to those who followed them.

Conclusion

The second century was a time of dramatic theological formation. Theologians faced the rise of several heresies and schismatic groups who threatened the unity of church and the Christian gospel. Christians in the Great Tradition were those who embraced the biblical faith handed down from the apostles. Pastors and teachers such as Irenaeus, Clement, Tertullian, and Origen contributed to the development of Christian doctrine as a polemic against heresies and instruction for believers. Their contributions led to the preservation of the gospel and the spread of the church, as we will see in the next chapter.

Recommended Reading

Behr, John. *Irenaeus of Lyons: Identifying Christianity*. Oxford University Press, 2013.

Behr, John. *Origen: On First Principles*. Oxford University Press, 2017.

Brown, Peter. *The Body and Society: Men, Women, and Sexual Renunciation in Early Christianity*. Columbia University Press, 1988.

Dunn, Geoffrey D. *Tertullian*. Routledge, 2004.

Ferguson, Everett. *Backgrounds of Early Christianity*. 3rd ed. Eerdmans, 2003.

Frend, W. H. C. *The Rise of Christianity*. Fortress, 1984.

Grant, Robert M. *Greek Apologists of the Second Century*. Westminster Press, 1988.

Grant, Robert M. *Irenaeus of Lyons*. Routledge, 1997.

Hanson, R. P. C. *Allegory and Event: A Study of the Sources and Significance of Origen's Interpretation of Scripture*. Westminster John Knox Press, 2002.

Kannengiesser, Charles. *Handbook of Patristic Exegesis: The Bible in Early Christianity*. Brill, 2004.

Kelly, J. N. D. *Early Christian Doctrines*. 5th ed. HarperOne, 1978.

Lyman, Rebecca. *The Early Christian Controversy on the Trinity*. Oxford University Press, 1997.

Martens, Peter W. *Origen and Scripture: The Contours of the Exegetical Life*. Oxford University Press, 2012.

Osborn, Eric. *The Emergence of Christian Theology*. Cambridge University Press, 1993.

Osborn, Eric. *Irenaeus of Lyons*. Cambridge University Press, 2001.

Osborn, Eric. *Tertullian, First Theologian of the West*. Cambridge University Press, 1997.

Pelikan, Jaroslav. *The Emergence of the Catholic Tradition (100–600)*. University of Chicago Press, 1971.

Richardson, Cyril C. *Early Christian Fathers*. Macmillan, 1953.

Stead, G. C. *Philosophy in Christian Antiquity*. Cambridge University Press, 1994.

Trigg, Joseph Wilson. *Origen: The Bible and Philosophy in the Third-Century Church*. John Knox Press, 1983.

Wilken, Robert Louis. *The Christians as the Romans Saw Them*. Yale University Press, 1984.

Young, Frances M. *From Nicaea to Chalcedon: A Guide to the Literature and Its Background*. 2nd ed. Baker Academic, 2010.

Young, Frances M., Lewis Ayres, and Andrew Louth, eds. *The Cambridge History of Early Christian Literature*. Cambridge University Press, 2004.

Chapter 5

The Spread of the Church

Jesus's thirty-three years of life and ministry hardly stretched more than fifty miles beyond his birthplace in Bethlehem. In fact, his three years of ministry were confined roughly to thirty miles. In the sixty-five years following Jesus's ascension, the apostles' ministry and mission expanded well beyond Jesus's fifty-mile radius. They travelled as far north and west as Rome and as far south and east as the southern part of India. And, while the apostles' reach was remarkable for their time, it was still only a fraction of the globe.

So, how far did the missionary efforts of the church reach by the end of the third century? What were the challenges, successes, and failures of the church during this time? Who were the Christians and Christian communities involved in such efforts? Moreover, how did Christians relate to the broader community and culture?

The Spread of the Gospel

By the end of the third century, Christianity had spread as far west as Britain and Spain, quickly approaching Ireland, and as far east as India. Syria, Greece, Italy, Egypt, and North Africa were also heavily impacted by the spread of the gospel. Philip Jenkins estimates the total Christian population of the early centuries as follows:

150—40,000
200—218,000
250—1.17 million[1]

The leading Christian centers during the first three centuries were the urban areas of Rome, Carthage, Alexandria, Jerusalem, Ephesus, and Antioch, and each were also connected to groups of Christians in nearby rural areas.[2] Precise numbers of the total Christian population by 300 are far from certain, but less than a century later, it would be the dominant religion of the empire, both in policy and in numbers.

Mission Efforts Among Early Christians

A common assumption about early Christianity is that constant persecution kept Christians on the move, thus spreading the faith around the known world. While Christianity was illegal until the early fourth century, persecution was consistent but not constant in the first three centuries of the church. Eusebius, writing in the middle of the fourth century, could speak of those in the second century who received the faith as follows:

> They, seeing as they were fitting disciples of such great men, laid another course upon the foundations of the churches that had been founded by the apostles in every place, further intensifying the Preaching and sowing the salvific seeds of the heavenly kingdom widely throughout the whole inhabited world. For indeed, many of the disciples at that time had their souls struck by the Divine Logos with a deep desire for philosophy, and first fulfilled the salvific command to distribute their property to the needy, and then went out on journeys to perform the work of evangelists, aspiring to proclaim the report of faith to those everywhere who had not heard it and to provide the written text of the Divine Gospels. Once they had established foundations of the faith in foreign places they appointed shepherds and selected others along with them . . .[3]

---

[1] Philip Jenkins, "How Many Christians?," Patheos, September 22, 2017, https://www.patheos.com/blogs/anxiousbench/2017/09/how-many-christians/.

[2] Jenkins, "How Many Christians?"

[3] Eusebius, *The History of the Church*, trans. Jeremy M. Schott (University of California Press, 2019), 163.

From the beginning, the church was a missionary movement, consciously obeying the command of Christ to go and make disciples of all nations (Matt 28:19–20). It was not merely the fleeing of persecution which spread the faith. The message of Christ motivated the church to proclaim their Lord to a world in need of redemption and communities in need of neighborly love. They possessed a burning conviction that their tidings were of "incomparable significance for the whole of the human race."[4] As they went, they appointed shepherds for the churches, cared for those in need, and shared the written texts of Scripture.

While many faithfully took up the missionary's task, three especially come to mind:

1. Pantaenus (c. 120–c. 200) led the catechetical school of Alexandria and was a major influence on Clement of Alexandria. On the eve of the third century, he traveled as far as India to spread the faith. Upon arrival he found that the Gospel of Matthew had arrived sometime before him in Hebrew. Eusebius claimed it was brought by the apostle Bartholomew.[5] Mark, the author of the Second Gospel, was said to have been the first evangelist in Alexandria, and within a century the Egyptian city commissioned Pantaenus across the globe as their own missionary.[6]
2. Gregory Thaumaturgus (c. 210–c. 260), after an elite classical education, was converted to Christianity under the tutelage of Origen of Alexandria. Gregory, whose name meant "wonderworker," later travelled as a missionary to Pontus and Cappadocia, performing miracles and evangelizing.[7] Gregory of Nyssa wrote a biography of Gregory Thaumaturgus,

> There are other marvels of the great Gregory preserved in memory to this time which we have not set down in writing out of consideration for unbelieving ears, lest people be harmed because they think the truth in the extraordinariness of the accounts to be a lie.
>
> ---
>
> Gregory, Bishop of Nyssa,
> *On the Life and Wonders of Our Father Among the Saints, Gregory the Wonderworker*

[4] Stephen Neill and Owen Chadwick, *A History of Christian Missions*, 2nd ed., Penguin History of the Church 6 (Penguin, 1990), 35.

[5] Eusebius, *History of the Church*, 247–48.

[6] Saint Jerome, *On Illustrious Men*, Fathers of the Church (Catholic University of America Press, 1999), 59.

[7] Everett Ferguson, *Church History*, vol. 1, *From Christ to Pre-Reformation* (Zondervan, 2005), 174.

and the wonderworker gained a reputation of wisdom and piety in life. In his missionary endeavors, "he won the multitude over by proclamation, because vision coincided with hearing and the tokens of divine power illumined it through both. For his word amazed the hearing as his mighty deeds with the sick amazed the eyes."[8]

3. Gregory the Illuminator (c. 239–c. 330) went to Armenia to share the faith, and the nation subsequently became "the first . . . on earth to accept Christianity as its established religion."[9] King Tiridates the Great's conversion occurred c. 301 after Gregory healed him of lycanthropy, an illness that came upon the king after he'd ordered the murder of a group of Christian women from Rome. The king granted Gregory authority to establish the Christian church across Armenia, even tearing down pagan temples. Gregory also established Christian schools across Armenia, especially for those preparing for priesthood.

Each of these men were motivated to share the gospel with those who had not yet believed, and this motivation drove them far from home. But these missionary motives in the second and third centuries were not the only cause in the spread of the church.

In the World, Not of the World—Carrying the Mission Forward

Discerning how to be in and not of the world, especially as Christians relocated to new places and cultures, brought its own set of challenges. In his *Introducing Christian Mission Today*, Michael W. Goheen describes the character and mindset of early church Christianity as follows:

1. They continued the mission of Jesus, thus living in the newly inaugurated kingdom;
2. They understood themselves as resident aliens (*paroikoi*) in the Roman Empire;[10]
3. They found their identity and citizenship in the kingdom of God;
4. They were fundamentally different, unassimilated, and thus at odds with the prevalent way of life.[11]

[8] Saint Gregory Thaumaturgus, *Life and Works*, Fathers of the Church (Catholic University of America Press, 1998), 61.

[9] Nick Needham, *2000 Years of Christ's Power*, vol. 1, *The Age of the Early Church Fathers* (Christian Focus, 2016), 158.

[10] Goheen also includes the language of "third race."

[11] Michael W. Goheen, *Introducing Christian Mission Today* (InterVarsity, 2014), 122.

We find this a helpful general outline of early Christian character and cultural posture, especially for the ordinary Christians of the day. These four characteristics can be summarized by the unique relationship shared by Christians and their hope in and submission to the kingdom of God.

Additionally, historian Stephen O. Presley has recently argued that early Christian cultural engagement may best be understood as "a posture of cultural sanctification," and he uses the Epistle to Diognetus as a window into the everyday cultural mindset of early Christians. Presley explains cultural sanctification, urging that "from the time of the Apostles to the rise of Constantine, the church was engaged in a slow and steady process of living faithfully and seeking sanctification both personally and corporately in ways that transform the culture."[12] Hear the language from the Epistle to Diognetus, an anonymously written early second-century defense of the faith describing the everyday conduct of early Christians:

> For Christians are not distinguished from the rest of humanity by country, language, or custom. . . . But while they live in both Greek and barbarian cities, as each one's lot was cast, and follow the local customs in dress and food and other aspects of life, at the same time they demonstrate the remarkable and admittedly unusual character of their own citizenship. They live in their own countries, but only as aliens; they participate in everything as citizens, and endure everything as foreigners. . . . They marry like everyone else, and have children, but they do not expose their offspring. They share their food but not their wives. They are "in the flesh," but they do not live "according to the flesh." They live on earth, but their citizenship is in heaven. They obey the established laws; indeed, in their private lives they transcend the laws. They love everyone, and by everyone they are persecuted. They are unknown, yet they are condemned; they are put to death, yet they are brought to life. They are poor, yet they make many rich; they are in need of everything, yet they abound in everything. . . .
>
> In a word, what the soul is to the body, Christians are to the world. . . . The soul dwells in the body, but is not of the body; likewise, Christians dwell in the world, but are not of the world.[13]

---

[12] Stephen O. Presley, *Cultural Sanctification: Engaging the World Like the Early Church* (Eerdmans, 2024), 20.

[13] As quoted in Presley, *Cultural Sanctification*, 14–15.

While specific questions about how to be in but not of the world persisted, this description of early Christians is a beautiful portrayal of their loyalty to the kingdom of Christ without neglecting their citizenship on earth, especially their neighborliness.

Power of the Congregation

As we've argued previously, the call to upright moral conduct is an irreducible element of the Great Tradition of the faith. While early Christian communities were far from perfect—one only needs to survey the letters of the New Testament to see this was the case—there was a shared expectation of love for Christ and charity toward others that permeated the people of God. Moreover, early Christians quickly recognized incongruence between the way of life of ordinary citizens and the way of Christ. Henry Chadwick elaborates on this point:

> Nevertheless, the Christian mission was not directed merely at centres of power. It was consciously aimed at the common people, and the ideals of simplicity and humility were never far from the minds of those who had to propagate their faith. The missionaries took it for granted that the gospel corresponded to the needs of mortal men and women, and that they must communicate with ordinary people in direct colloquial language. They wrote hymns and songs for the illiterate to sing, and, in a world that was acutely conscious of rank and class, the separate strata of which were distinguished not only by manner and speech but also by forms of address and clothes, the Christians deliberately set out to treat the poor with dignity and without condescension.[14]

Early Christians thus understood that their call to Christ included a call to love the common folk, the blue-collar and the poor, as much as to the influential. Whether through song or common forms of speech, they prioritized sharing the gospel of Jesus in word and deed to those barely acknowledged by the rest of society.

Kingdom Mindset

In his well-known "Lord's Prayer," Jesus taught his followers to pray, "Your kingdom come, your will be done, on earth as it is in heaven." So how did early Christians do this? For

---

[14] Henry Chadwick, *The Early Church* (Penguin, 1993), 72.

centuries, Christians have endured criticism for their indifference to cultural and political circumstances. For example, Celsus, the second century philosopher and critic of Christianity, wrote against the lack of Christian civic and political engagement, saying, "For if all were to do the same as you, there would be nothing to prevent [the emperor from] being left in utter solitude and desertion, and the affairs of the earth would fall into the hands of the wildest and most lawless barbarians."[15]

Christians likely deserved a reputation of indifference toward the broader political landscape. This was due in large part to the "outsider" nature of Christianity before Constantine, mixed with sporadic persecution. While this changed, Christians were more occupied with right worship and right living before God and neighbor than about local governmental appointments. In other words, their focus was more ecclesial and communal, and less municipal.

As Chadwick further notes, "The paradox of the church was that it was a religious revolutionary movement, yet without a conscious political ideology; it aimed at the capture of society throughout all its strata but was at the same time characteristic for its indifference to the possession of power in this world."[16]

This is not to say that Christians never spoke to political or public square matters as discussed in the previous chapter concerning the apologists. Indeed, on important apologetic and moral matters, Christian leaders spoke as they believed best for the Christian community. As John the Baptist was imprisoned for confronting Herod's sin of stealing his brother's wife, so too were there early Christians who, though first concerned with the matters of doctrine and the church, raised their voices in opposition to false accusations against Christians (e.g., Justin Martyr) and immoral practices of culture in general or political leaders in particular (e.g., Ambrose confronting the emperor).

But, while Christianity remained illegal, the community of faith turned inward first in an effort "to seek to lead a quiet life, to mind your own business, and to work with your own hands, as we commanded you, so that you may behave properly in the presence of outsiders and not be dependent on anyone" (1 Thess 4:11–12). These quiet, though public, means of living out the kingdom on earth as in heaven included social action, such as care for the poor, widows, and orphans.

---

[15] Alexander Roberts and James Donaldson, eds., *Ante-Nicene Fathers: The Writings of the Fathers down to A.D. 325*, vol. 4, *Book VIII* (Hendrickson, 1885), 665.

[16] Chadwick, *Early Church*, 69.

Care for the Poor, Widows, and Orphans

Jesus said, "blessed are you who are poor, for the kingdom of God is yours" (Luke 6:20). This passage, and others like it, were the motivation for early Christian concern for the poor and afflicted from the beginning. Even among the early detractors of Christianity, one finds amazement at how Christians cared not only for their own people, but even for non-Christians. The fourth-century emperor Julian the Apostate begrudgingly acknowledged the charity of early Christians when he wrote, "For it is disgraceful that, when no Jew ever has to beg, and the impious Galileans support not only their own poor but ours as well, all men see our people lack aid from us."[17] This faith wasn't a mere set of beliefs, nor was it simply a matter for Sunday only. Followers of the Great Tradition strove to live in accord with Scripture's teaching: to live congruent with the message of the gospel of Christ that begins with the double-love of God and neighbor.

Stephen Presley explains, "The early church did not simply think in terms of distinctiveness and purity; it also turned outward in active mercy and compassion. The very work of social reform and positive social change amounted to a positive good. Its high standards of purity marked it as a community bent on serving and caring for the least of those inside and outside their community."[18] As the tradition spread and interfaced with the world, Christians attended to the impoverished and the poor, who were largely invisible to society.[19] Immersed in the biblical teaching, Christians sought to live out the spirit of what it taught: "If anyone has this world's goods and sees a fellow believer in need but withholds compassion from him—how does God's love reside in him?" (1 John 3:17).

One manifestation of this came through the fourth century Cappadocian Father Basil of Caesarea, who led the effort to create hospitals seeking to care for those who were neglected, poor, and injured. Basil advocated for families, magistrates, and the church to attend to hurting neighbors, and he gave of his own time and resources to assist where he could.[20] In addition to hospital buildings, Basil encouraged the training of medical professionals to care for patients and to mitigate against the cultural stigma surrounding the sick, and he

---

[17] Julian, *The Works of Emperor Julian*, trans. W. C. Wright, Loeb Classical Library (Harvard University Press, 1953), 69–70.

[18] Presley, *Cultural Sanctification*, 135.

[19] Robert L. Wilken, *The First Thousand Years: A Global History of Christianity* (Yale University Press, 2012), 157.

[20] Wilken, *First Thousand Years*, 156.

stressed an overall concern for the sick and dying. Robert L. Wilken observes that given the rise of such cultural phenomena as hospitals led by Christians, "the Church was no longer a private institution; its affairs were now interwoven with the life of the society."[21] The church was not merely a community set apart from the world but was also a community that cared for the hurting and vulnerable in the world. Truly, as the Epistle to Diognetus suggests, the church was becoming the soul of the world.

Concerning women, "Christians were the first group in the history of the world to value women of all life choices and circumstances, whether single, married with children, married and childless, or widowed."[22] This posture signaled a resistance of Greco-Roman cultural norms concerning women, most of which were bound up with one's socioeconomic status and the levels of convenience versus inconvenience that accompanied one's situation in society. The New Testament's inclusion of women as the first witnesses of the resurrection; as congregational leaders, even if informally; and as disciple makers alongside the men are but a few ways in which the Scriptures attest to the high value of women by Christians (e.g., Matt 28:1–10; Acts 16:11–15; 18:25–27; Rom 16:1).

Widows and orphans were of particular concern for early Christians as those representing the most vulnerable in society. The Old Testament book of Ruth sets up well the posture of Christians toward widows, a point Paul elaborates on further in 1 Tim 5:1–16. Concerning both widows and orphans, James's link between "pure and undefiled religion" and the care for "orphans and widows in their distress" perhaps best underscores this point. As is urged in the influential second-century Christian work Shepherd of Hermas, "Hear now what follow upon these; to minister to widows, to visit the orphans and the needy, to ransom the servants of God from their afflictions, to be hospitable (for in hospitality benevolence from time to time has a place)."[23]

Conclusion

Early Christians were thus committed not merely to doctrinal fidelity and liturgical unity on Sundays; they sought to demonstrate love for God and neighbor in the world in how they cared for one another, how they cared for their neighbors whether Christian or not,

---

[21] Wilken, 160.

[22] Nadya Williams, *Cultural Christians in the Early Church* (Zondervan, 2023), 93–94.

[23] Roberts and Donaldson, eds., *Ante-Nicene Fathers: The Writings of the Fathers down to A.D. 325*, 25.

and how they cared for the poor, sick, widowed, and orphaned. Fully expectant of cultural dissonance between their way of life and the world's, the disposition of early Christians was not one of "run and hide" nor of "take up and fight" against the cultural powers. Rather, there was a humble and committed posture of modeling the way of Jesus in the world while not of the world.

Recommended Reading

Chadwick, Henry. *The Early Church*. Penguin, 1993.

Eusebius. *The History of the Church*. Translated by Jeremy M. Schott. University of California Press, 2019.

Goheen, Michael W. *Introducing Christian Mission Today*. InterVarsity, 2014.

Gonzalez, Justo L. *The Story of Christianity*. Vol. 1, *The Early Church to the Reformation*. HarperOne, 2010.

Haykin, Michael A. G. *Rediscovering the Church Fathers: Who They Were and How They Shaped the Church*. Crossway, 2011.

Needham, Nick. *2000 Years of Christ's Power*. Vol. 1, *The Age of the Early Church Fathers*. Christian Focus, 2016.

Neill, Stephen, and Owen Chadwick. *A History of Christian Missions*. 2nd ed. Penguin History of the Church 6. Penguin, 1990.

Norris, Richard A. *The Christological Controversy*. Sources of Early Christian Thought. Fortress, 1980.

Rousseau, Jean-Jacques. *The Social Contract*. Translated by Maurice Cranston. Penguin, 1968.

Saint Gregory Thaumaturgus. *Life and Works*. Fathers of the Church. Catholic University of America Press, 1998

Saint Jerome. *On Illustrious Men*. Fathers of the Church. Catholic University of America Press, 1999.

Tertullian. *Christian and Pagan in the Roman Empire*. Translated by Robert Sider. Catholic University of America Press, 2001.

Wilken, Robert L. *The First Thousand Years: A Global History of Christianity*. Yale University, 2012.

— Chapter 6 —

Persecution Intensifies in the Third Century

Imperial persecution of Christians intensified and became increasingly widespread in the third century. Emperors responded to imperial concerns by demanding greater conformity to the pagan cult through participation in the civil religion. Because Christians refused to worship gods other than the Triune God of the Bible, they were viewed with suspicion and targeted with persecution, including arrest, imprisonment, and execution.

The First Empire-Wide Persecution Under Emperor Decius

The periodic and mostly regional persecution of Christians in the first and second centuries gave way to the first empire-wide, intentional persecution of followers of Jesus under Emperor Decius (249–251). This persecution began in AD 250 in an effort to bring religious unity to the empire. The decline of the Roman Empire in the second century under Marcus Aurelius continued in the third century. Sedition by opposition groups within the empire coincided with successful attacks from neighboring groups that eroded the stability of the empire. Decius believed that only a return to the values and culture of ancient Rome could restore the ancient glories of Rome. As Christianity was experiencing a period of growth and increased influence in the empire, Decius perceived them to be a danger to his plans of restoring the empire to its previous place of power and glory that required a revival of classical religion.

Decius instructed that every resident of the empire should make at least an annual offering of sacrifice to the Roman gods at a local temple. To help ensure compliance with this edict, those who participated in the sacrifice would obtain a certificate (Latin, *libellus*) as a receipt for their sacrifice. If someone was found without a certificate as proof of their sacrificial offering, they would be required to immediately go to a priest and offer a sacrifice. Those who refused, particularly Christians, would be imprisoned or put to death. One well-known martyr was Origen of Alexandria, who refused to worship at the temple and was tortured, eventually dying from the punishment he received.

In an interesting twist, some Christians would purchase a certificate from a non-Christian who would make an offering on their behalf. Those Christians could argue that they did not personally worship the Roman gods while still avoiding arrest. Cyprian of Carthage described this practice in his *On the Lapsed*, arguing that the practice made persecution even worse for those who refused to obtain a certificate. Buying a receipt as proof of sacrifice was participation in the Roman cult just as personally offering sacrifice was. When Decius died, the persecution ended, but the consequences of the persecution remained for the church. Hundreds or thousands of Christians had made sacrifice to the pagan gods under threat of imprisonment or death. How churches responded to those who repented of their sin and wanted to return to the church was a controversy, as we will see later in the section on the Novatianist controversy.

Valerian Promotes Traditional Roman Values

After a brief respite, Emperor Valerian (253–260) reignited the persecution of the church throughout the empire. Several vital figures emerged during the persecution of Christians under Valerian, including notable Christian leaders, such as Cyprian of Carthage, Sixtus II of Rome, and Lawrence of Rome. These leaders played crucial roles in providing pastoral care and support to persecuted believers. Cyprian became a central figure in the church's response to persecution and its aftermath. In particular, he helped lead the church's reflection on how to address Christians who denied the faith under threat of death but repented of that decision when the persecution ended.

Diocletian's Attempt to Unify the Empire Through Religion (284–305)

While Christians were trying to pick up the pieces following Decius's persecution, the Roman Empire continued its steady decline in terms of power and peace. Some blamed a Roman government of shared power between the Senate and the emperor for failing to achieve stability and achieve peace throughout the empire. Diocletian ruled Rome from 284 until his abdication in 305. When Diocletian became emperor, he ended the current form of shared government with the senate and other nobles, replacing it with a single ruler. All power would be centralized in the hands of the emperor without a legislative body to interfere. He also believed, as Decius had, that restoration of Roman civil religion was necessary to establish peace. Diocletian's commitment to religion does not have to be seen as a personal commitment to faith, but as a commitment to a common civil religion in the empire. Civil religion unifies society. Diocletian was convinced that allowing religious practice outside a universally held religion would cause divisions, weakening society. Moreover, civil religion serves the positive purpose of giving people a standard set of values and affirmations, which can create a sense of shared destiny. To allow Christianity to persist in opposition to Roman paganism would only cause further social decay.

Consequently, in 303, Diocletian issued an order calling for the empire-wide persecution of Christianity. Christians were no longer allowed to gather. Officials destroyed their churches, imprisoned anyone claiming to be a Christian, and confiscated and burned all copies of the Bible. When these measures did not quickly eradicate Christianity, Diocletian then ordered that all Christians be arrested and executed if they refused to recant. The executions were ruthless, and many Christians were fed to wild animals.

When Diocletian's reign ended in 305, the era of Roman imperial persecution of Christians came to an end for all practical purposes. A Roman civil religion remained the official religion of the empire. However, Emperor Galerius would soon grant Christians an official reprieve when, in the year 311, he allowed Christians to worship unless they were a direct threat to the peace of the empire. While opposition to Christianity remained in portions of the empire, Christians could now expect to worship without fear. Two years later, Emperor Constantine issued the Edict of Milan, which legalized Christianity and granted true freedom of worship in the Roman Empire, putting an official end to over three centuries of the persecution of Christians at the hands of the Roman government. However, these stories of persecution became an important component of early Christianity, and writers such as Eusebius of Caesarea would ensure that the legacy of these martyrs would be passed down to the ensuing generations.

Christianity was no longer a persecuted minority religion within the Roman Empire but was now an officially recognized and supported religion. Christian writers began to reflect on the previous centuries, seeking to make sense of the struggle against the imperial persecution of Christians. How were Christians to think about the Christian faith when their religion was now accepted by the government that until recently sought to stamp it out? How might Christians understand the past while shaping the present and future practice of orthodox Christianity? The fruit of this reflection can be found in Eusebius's interpretation of the Roman persecution of Christians.

Cyprian of Carthage (210–58)

Cyprian of Carthage was a prominent figure in the Christian church during the third century. His leadership and writings offer valuable insights into Christians' challenges during intense persecution at the hand of the Roman emperors Decius and Valerian. Cyprian was born around 200 in North Africa and received a classical education before converting to Christianity. He quickly rose to prominence in the Christian community and was ordained as bishop of Carthage in 248. Cyprian faced persecution from outside the church and heresy within the church. Cyprian was concerned that Christians were too easily attracted to the entertainment of the world, such as the gladiator contests. He addressed this temptation in his work written to his friend Donatus, calling Christians to a life of prayer and faithfulness. During a time when Cyprian had fled persecution, he wrote a treatise entitled *On the Unity of the Catholic Church*, in which he rejected schismatics, such as the Novatianists, who had separated from those churches they believed to be led by improper pastors. Cyprian wrote, "[T]he church is one, though it is spread far and wide by its ever-increasing fruitfulness. There are many rays of the sun, but one light. . . . You cannot separate a ray of light from the sun, because its unity does not allow division."[1] He encouraged his flock to resist the pressure to renounce Christ, even when facing severe persecution. Cyprian went into hiding to avoid arrest because he believed that he was of better service to his church alive than as a martyr. Although separated from his congregation, he was able to continue to

---

[1] Cyprian of Carthage, *On the Unity of the Church* 5, in *The Ante-Nicene Fathers*, vol. 5, ed. Alexander Roberts and James Donaldson, trans. Robert Ernest Wallis (Hendrickson, 1994), 423.

provide pastoral guidance and encouragement to them through his letters and other writings. Eventually, though, Cyprian was captured and executed for his faith.

Cyprian directly addressed the Novatianist schism, which emerged in the third century. The Novatianist controversy came to a head during the Decian persecution in the mid-third century, when many Christians faced the choice of renouncing their faith or facing martyrdom. Some Christians chose to offer sacrifices to pagan gods or obtain fraudulent certificates claiming they had sacrificed to avoid persecution. After the persecution ended, the question arose as to whether the church should readmit those who denied the faith under duress.

Novatian, a Roman priest, became the leader of a movement advocating for a strict stance on readmission to the church for those who had renounced their faith under persecution. Novatian and his followers, known as Novatianists, argued that those who had lapsed could not be readmitted to the church under any circumstances, even if they sincerely repented. He based his position on the belief that the church should maintain its purity and integrity by excluding those who had committed apostasy.

On the other hand, Cyprian advocated for a more lenient approach to the lapsed, emphasizing the importance of forgiveness and reconciliation within the Christian community. He argued that the church should readmit those who acquiesced under persecution to sincere repentance and a time of penance. Cyprian's position was grounded in his understanding of the church as a community of sinners needing God's mercy and grace. Cyprian convened synods in Carthage to address the issue, advocating for a compassionate approach to the lapsed.

Cyprian addressed the issue of those who offered sacrifice in several of his writings, most notably in his treatise *On the Lapsed.* This work reflects Cyprian's pastoral concerns and theological convictions regarding the reconciliation of those who had renounced their faith under persecution. In this work, Cyprian begins by acknowledging the severity of the persecution faced by Christians and the challenges it posed to their faith.

Cyprian's approach to the lapsed was grounded in his understanding of the church as a community of sinners needing God's mercy and grace. Cyprian's famous statement, "If the church is not your mother, then God is not your father," found in chapter 6 of his treatise *On the Unity of the Church*, encapsulates his understanding of the intimate relationship between Christian believers and the church as the spiritual mother who nurtures and guides them in their faith journey. This treatise was written around the middle of the third century and addresses various aspects of ecclesiology, emphasizing the importance of unity within the church and the role of the bishop as a unifying figure. He emphasizes the role of the church as a mediator of forgiveness and reconciliation, entrusted with the ministry of healing and restoration. Cyprian's pastoral theology reflects his belief in the efficacy of the sacraments. At the time, Christians universally accepted the two sacraments of baptism and the Lord's Supper, or the Eucharist. Cyprian was no exception. Along with other Christians, Cyprian taught that the sacraments (also called ordinances) were ecclesial practices which strengthened the faith of those who participated in them. Only the true church was able to perform true sacraments. Heretics and schismatics do not have the right to baptize or offer the Lord's Supper to believers. Cyprian's commitment to the church's sacraments meant that Christians practice unity and witness to the one church through the proper administration of the sacraments/ordinances.

> He cannot have God as a father who does not have the Church as a mother.
>
> ---
>
> Cyprian,
> *On the Unity of the Church*

This view of the sacraments shaped his response to the lapsed. Cyprian also acknowledges the need for discipline within the church, particularly in cases where the lapsed demonstrate insincerity or lack of remorse. He warns against a lax approach to readmission, advocating for a careful and discerning process that ensures the integrity of the church and upholds its moral standards.

One way to understand Cyprian's rejection of Novatianist ecclesiology is to consider the church a network of interconnected believers united by the Spirit of God. The gospel is the common confession that believers share. The church is then a community of fellow believers in union and fellowship. The Novatianists, as schismatics, had broken the fellowship by denying the validity of the other Christian churches. Cyprian believed that such sectarian behavior separated them from the gospel of Jesus Christ.

In his work *On the Lapsed*, Cyprian emphasizes the church's essential role as the believer's spiritual parent. He draws upon the imagery of motherhood to convey the idea that just as a biological mother provides care, nourishment, and protection to her children, so too the church provides spiritual care, sustenance, and guidance to its members. Furthermore, Cyprian underscores the inseparable connection between the believer's relationship with the church and their relationship with God. He suggests that one cannot claim a relationship with God as their Father without recognizing and acknowledging their relationship with the church as their mother. For Cyprian, the church mediates the grace and love of God to believers, serving as the visible manifestation of God's presence and care in the world. Therefore, to reject or neglect the church is to reject or neglect one's relationship with God.

From a theological perspective, Cyprian highlights the importance of ecclesial identity and community in the Christian life. It underscores the idea that salvation is not an individualistic or isolated experience, but a communal and relational reality mediated through the church. By affirming the church as the spiritual mother of believers, Cyprian emphasizes the interconnectedness of believers within the body of Christ and the mutual responsibility they share for one another's spiritual well-being. Schismatics such as the Novatianists undermine the spiritual well-being of Christians by separating them from the true church and orthodox preaching.

Some Effects of Persecution on Christian Life and Practice

Along with external disagreements, the Roman persecutions sparked intense internal debates and theological shifts within Christian communities. The concept of the baptism of blood emerged as a theological response to the Roman persecutions, particularly during periods of intense martyrdom. The question was particularly important in relation to new Christians who had not yet been baptized as a believer. In the early church, baptism typically followed a long period of instruction called the catechumenate, from the word "catechize," meaning "teach." These not-yet-baptized Christians were called catechumens. As baptism was an essential step in identifying with Christ and the church, what was one to think of a catechumen who was martyred before their baptism? Cyprian of Carthage proposed two ways of being "baptized." One baptism was water baptism. However, if a new Christian was martyred before they could be baptized with water, they were said to be baptized by blood.

Writing to a fellow Christian named Jubaianus, Cyprian says, "[Catechumens who have suffered martyrdom] are not deprived of the sacrament of baptism. Rather, they are baptized with the most glorious and greatest baptism of blood, concerning which the Lord said that he had another baptism with which he himself was to be baptized."[2] Along with Cyprian, other early Christians, such as Tertullian and Cyril of Jerusalem, supported the concept of the baptism of blood.

---

[2] Cyprian of Carthage, *Epistle LXXII:22*, in *Fathers of the Third Century: Hippolytus, Cyprian, Caius, Novatian, Appendix*, vol. 5 of *The Ante-Nicene Fathers*, ed. Alexander Roberts and James Donaldson, trans. Robert Ernest Wallis (Christian Literature Company, 1886), 384.

Christians grappled with issues of apostasy, leadership, and the role of the laity, leading to the development of new theological perspectives and ecclesiastical structures. Persecution prompted intense theological reflection on the nature of suffering and redemption within the Christian tradition. Christians grappled with questions of why God allowed his followers to endure persecution and how to reconcile suffering with the promise of redemption through Christ. Various theological responses emerged to address these questions. Christians emphasized the redemptive value of suffering and portrayed martyrs as exemplars of virtue and courage. Drawing on Jesus's own suffering and death, others emphasized Christ's solidarity with the suffering of humanity and the promise of future vindication for believers. Irenaeus remarked about the martyrs that they "were zealous in the imitation of Christ." Christians were reminded of Jesus's own words to his disciples: "Whenever you are arrested and brought to trial, do not worry beforehand about what to say. Just say whatever is given you at the time, for it is not you speaking, but the Holy Spirit" (Mark 13:11 NIV). The debates on suffering and redemption reshaped Christian identity, emphasizing the centrality of martyrdom and endurance in the Christian life. Christians venerated the martyrs as heroes of the faith whose suffering and sacrifice were powerful witnesses to the gospel's transformative power. At the same time, Christians faced the danger of zealous believers seeking out martyrdom through volunteering to be arrested and executed. If martyrs receive a great crown of honor, why not seek it out? Cyprian states that self-martyrdom is not true martyrdom.

Most often the authorities persecuted the church by targeting the leadership. Pastors and other church leaders were the first to be arrested. As persecution became more widespread and intense, authorities began targeting anyone who was a Christian, first outlawing conversion to Christianity and then outlawing Christianity altogether. Despite these attacks, Christianity continued to grow in the empire.

Eusebius of Caesarea's Interpretation of the Roman Persecution of Christians

Eusebius of Caesarea, often called the "father of church history," provides valuable insights into the history of Christianity, including the Roman persecution of Christians.[3] Eusebius

---

[3] Eusebius of Caesarea, *Church History* 4, in *Eusebius: Church History, Life of Constantine the Great, and Oration in Praise of Constantine*, vol. 1 of *Nicene and Post-Nicene Fathers*, Second Series, ed. Philip Schaff and Henry Wace, trans. Arthur Cushman McGiffert (Christian Literature Company, 1890), 176–214.

sought to highlight the faithfulness of Christians in the face of persecution, memorializing those who both preached and practiced the biblical gospel. Eusebius's understanding of Roman persecution shaped the early Christian narrative of God's faithful preservation of Christianity despite assaults against it by evil Roman emperors.

Eusebius lived during a tumultuous period in Roman history, marked by intermittent periods of persecution against Christians. Roman emperors often instigated persecution because they viewed Christianity as a threat to the empire's traditional religious and social order. Eusebius witnessed firsthand the persecution of Christians under Emperor Diocletian, which culminated in the Great Persecution of 303–11. Following the end of persecution and the legalization of Christianity under Constantine, Eusebius occupies an essential position concerning the emperor.

Eusebius provides a detailed account of the persecution of Christians, chronicling the sufferings endured by believers and the triumph of faith amidst adversity. He catalogs the various edicts and decrees issued by Roman emperors against Christians and the heroic acts of the martyrs. He views persecution as a test of faith and a means of purifying the Christian community. He portrays martyrs as exemplary figures who willingly endured suffering and death for the sake of Christ, thereby earning a place of honor in the annals of Christian history. Eusebius emphasizes the role of divine providence in guiding and protecting the church during times of persecution, highlighting the ultimate triumph of faith over persecution.

> How many there were who fought for the truth of God's word, during these storms, even to the suffering of tortures and shedding of blood.
>
> ---
>
> Eusebius of Caesarea,
> *Ecclesiastical History*

In addition to chronicling the persecution of Christians, Eusebius offers a defense of Christianity against its critics. He argues that the sufferings endured by martyrs serve as a powerful testimony to the truth of the Christian faith, demonstrating the transformative power of Christ's teachings in the lives of believers. Eusebius presents Christianity as a rational and morally upright religion, contrasting it with the decadence and moral bankruptcy of pagan society.

Eusebius's interpretation of Roman persecution reflects his belief in the providential guidance of God in the affairs of history. He views persecution as a temporary setback in the progress of Christianity, ultimately leading to the triumph of the church over its adversaries. Eusebius's persecution narrative contributes to the broader theme of divine providence in

Christian history, underscoring the belief that God works all things together for the good of those who love him. Eusebius characterizes the Roman persecution of Christians as a test of faith, a means of purifying the church, and a testimony to the transformative power of Christianity. His *Ecclesiastical History* offers valuable insights into the challenges and triumphs of the early Christian community in the face of persecution.

Conclusion

The phenomenon of Christian martyrdom not only shaped how Romans viewed Christians and Christianity. The willingness of Christians to face torture and death rather than renounce their faith challenged the authority of the Roman state and its methods of control. The martyrs demonstrated that the state's power was ultimately limited in the face of unwavering faith and conviction. This erosion of Roman authority contributed to a sense of uncertainty and insecurity among the ruling elite. The spectacle of Christian martyrdom left a lasting impression on Roman society, prompting widespread admiration and curiosity among elites and commoners. The courage and resilience displayed by martyrs captured the imagination of many Romans, challenging their preconceived notions about Christianity and its followers. Christians retold and circulated the stories of the faithful martyrs, contributing to the growing popularity of Christianity within the empire.

Initially viewed with suspicion and disdain as a secretive and subversive sect, Christians gradually gained respect and admiration as their willingness to suffer for their faith became widely known. The example of martyrs challenged stereotypes and misconceptions about Christians, leading many Romans to reassess their attitudes toward the faith. The courage and conviction of martyrs served as a powerful witness to the truth of the gospel, leading to the conversion of many Romans to Christianity.

Christians' refusal to participate in state-sponsored religious rituals and to pledge allegiance to the emperor as a deity posed a direct challenge to the authority of the state. The persecution of Christians became a contentious issue for Roman authorities, leading to debates and disagreements over the appropriate response to the growing influence of Christianity.

While the church continued to grow through the third century, the effects of repeated seasons of empire-wide persecution took its toll on the church. Christian leaders were weary of facing imprisonment and death. Church members who lost loved ones to the persecution resented those who apostatized under threat of arrest. Schismatic groups divided churches from one another. But despite the seemingly insurmountable struggles, the gospel prevailed. Christians remained faithful to the Christian truth. People continued to embrace the good news of Jesus. The faith once for all delivered continued to be handed down from one generation to the next. God's people found strength in the power and presence of God in their lives, choosing faithfulness to their God rather than acceptance by the Roman authorities. And when persecution finally came to an end, the Great Tradition of theological fidelity, liturgical witness, and ethical commitment remained.

Recommended Reading

Boyarin, Daniel. *Dying for God: Martyrdom and the Making of Christianity and Judaism.* Stanford University Press, 1999.

Brent, Allen. *Cyprian and Roman Carthage.* Cambridge University Press, 2010.

Cyprian of Carthage. *The Lapsed; The Unity of the Catholic Church.* Translated by Maurice Bévenot. Paulist, 1957.

Cyprian of Carthage. *The Letters of St. Cyprian of Carthage.* Translated by G. W. Clarke. 4 vols. Newman, 1984–1989.

Dunn, Geoffrey D. *Cyprian and the Bishops of Rome: Questions of Papal Primacy in the Early Church.* St. Paul's, 2007.

Eusebius of Caesarea. *The History of the Church.* Translated by G. A. Williamson. Penguin Classics, 1989.

Frend, W. H. C. *Martyrdom and Persecution in the Early Church: A Study of a Conflict from the Maccabees to Donatus.* Basil Blackwell, 1965.

Frend, W. H. C. *The Donatist Church: A Movement of Protest in Roman North Africa.* Clarendon, 1952.

Galli, Mark. *Persecuted: The Global Assault on Christians.* Baker, 2013.

Hoffmann, R. Joseph. *Marcion, On the Restitution of Christianity: An Essay on the Development of Radical Paulinist Theology in the Second Century.* Scholars Press, 1984.

Lepelley, Claude. *The Survival of the Classical World in Roman Africa: The Christianization of Cyprian's Carthage.* L'Erma di Bretschneider, 1989.

Lunn-Rockliffe, Sophie. *Ambrosiaster's Political Theology.* Oxford University Press, 2007.

Moss, Candida. *The Myth of Persecution: How Early Christians Invented a Story of Martyrdom.* HarperOne, 2013.

Novatian. *On the Trinity; Letters to Cyprian.* Translated by Herbert Moore. SPCK, 1909.

Rives, J. B. *Religion and Authority in Roman Carthage from Augustus to Constantine*. Oxford University Press, 1995.

Schoedel, William R. *Early Christian Martyrdom: A Comprehensive History*. Baker Academic, 2003.

Stevenson, J., ed. *A New Eusebius: Documents Illustrating the History of the Church to AD 337*. SPCK, 1987.

Tertullian. *Apology and De Spectaculis*. Translated by T. R. Glover. Loeb Classical Library. Harvard University Press, 1931.

— Chapter 7 —

The Rise of the Imperial Church

Despite the brutality of Emperor Diocletian's persecution, the Christian community persevered. Following Diocletian's reign, the Roman Empire underwent a series of legal and social reforms that shaped the position of Christians within society. Emperor Constantine (306–37) instituted laws that encouraged citizens to care for widows, orphans, and other vulnerable members of society, including many Christians. To fight inflation, he introduced a new currency that encouraged economic growth and expansion. Importantly, Constantine moved the capital of the empire from Rome to Byzantium, which was renamed Constantinople. Economic expansion benefitted the church, as Constantine went on a building spree, constructing church buildings around the empire. Christianity experienced remarkable growth throughout the Roman Empire and emerged as a dominant cultural and political force.

Constantine's Early Reign and Military Campaigns

Emperor Constantine reigned from 306 to 337. He is remembered for legalizing Christianity in the Roman Empire. However, Constantine's ascent to power was fraught with political intrigue and military conflict. His early reign before his conversion was one of ambitious military campaigns, political maneuvering, and personal motivations. After the death of his father, Emperor Constantius Chlorus, in 306, Constantine was proclaimed emperor by his troops in Britain, where he had been serving as a military commander. His claim to the imperial throne was initially contested by rival claimants, including Maxentius and Licinius, leading to a series of civil wars known as the Tetrarchic Wars. Constantine's defeat of Maxentius at the Battle of the Milvian Bridge in 312 paved the way for Constantine's sole rule over the western half of the empire. Constantine also waged successful campaigns against the Franks, Alamanni, and Sarmatians, securing the empire's frontiers and enhancing his military reputation.

Constantine's military successes fueled his political ambitions to reunify and stabilize the Roman Empire under his sole rule. He sought to restore the empire's political stability and economic prosperity, which had suffered from years of internal strife and external threats. Constantine's efforts to centralize power and reform the administrative apparatus of the empire reflected his desire to assert his authority and establish a strong, centralized government. Throughout his early reign, Constantine pursued a policy of religious tolerance and accommodation, granting privileges to pagans and Christians to maintain social cohesion and political stability.

Religious Landscape of the Empire

The fourth-century Roman Empire was a diverse religious landscape characterized by a multitude of beliefs, practices, and cults. Before Constantine's conversion to Christianity, paganism, mystery cults, and Christianity coexisted alongside each other, contributing to the religious pluralism of the era. The Roman pantheon consisted of numerous gods and goddesses, each associated with specific aspects of life, nature, and human affairs. The worship of Jupiter, Juno, Mars, Venus, and other deities was integral to Roman religious life, with temples, sacrifices, and festivals dedicated to their honor.

Mystery cults were secretive religious organizations that offered initiation rites and promised spiritual enlightenment or salvation to their followers. These cults, such as the Eleusinian Mysteries, the Cult of Isis, and the Cult of Mithras, attracted devotees from various social classes and backgrounds. Mystery cults emphasized personal salvation, moral purification, and the attainment of esoteric knowledge through rituals, sacraments, and communal gatherings.

Each religious tradition had a diversity of beliefs, practices, and interpretations. Paganism encompassed various cults, rites, and rituals, reflecting regional variations and local customs. Mystery cults offered different paths to spiritual fulfillment, drawing on syncretic elements from diverse cultural and religious traditions. Christianity, too, exhibited diversity, with theological disputes, doctrinal controversies, and sectarian divisions shaping the development of Christian communities and beliefs.

As the Roman Empire's official religion, the imperial cult fostered political loyalty and social cohesion. Romans often deified their emperors after their deaths, and cults dedicated to worshipping the emperor and the Roman state were widespread throughout the empire. Participation in the imperial cult was often mandatory for citizens and subjects, serving as a form of civic religion and ideological control.

The Battle of the Milvian Bridge (312)

The Battle of the Milvian Bridge took place on October 28, 312, between the forces of Constantine and Maxentius, two claimants to the title of Roman emperor. The Roman Empire was politically fragmented at the time, with multiple contenders vying for control. Constantine, ruling the western provinces, sought to consolidate his power and assert his claim to the imperial throne. According to tradition, Constantine experienced a vision on the eve of the battle that shaped his subsequent actions. As he prepared for the confrontation with Maxentius, Constantine reportedly saw a sign in the sky of the Chi-Rho—the first two letters of the name "Christ"—accompanied by *In hoc signo vinces* ("In this sign, you will conquer"). Interpreting this vision as a divine sign, Constantine vowed to convert to Christianity if he emerged victorious in battle.

The reported vision of Constantine at the Battle of the Milvian Bridge has been the subject of diverse interpretations and scholarly debate. Some historians view Constantine's conversion as a sincere religious experience, suggesting that his vision played a decisive role in shaping his religious convictions and subsequent policies toward Christianity. Others, however, question the authenticity of Constantine's conversion, arguing that it may have been motivated by political expediency. His identification with Christians promoted unity among his diverse subjects, legitimized his rule through a supposed divine sanction, and consolidated his authority over all religions in the empire. Viewed in this light, Constantine's conversion served primarily as a calculated political maneuver rather than a sincere expression of faith. Constantine's embrace of Christianity signaled a shift in the religious landscape of the Roman Empire, paving the way for the eventual Christianization of the empire and the rise of Christianity as a dominant force in Western civilization.

The Edict of Milan (313)

The Edict of Milan, issued in 313 by Emperor Constantine and his co-emperor Licinius, granted legal recognition and protection to Christianity, effectively ending the persecution of Christians and allowing them to worship freely without fear of reprisal. Additionally, the edict extended religious tolerance to all faiths, not just Christianity, ensuring that individuals were free to practice their chosen religion without interference from the state.

> We, Constantinus and Licinius the Emperors, having met in concord at Milan . . . therefore give both to Christians and to all others free facility to follow the religion which each may desire.
>
> ---
>
> The Edict of Milan

Several factors contributed to the issuance of the Edict of Milan. Constantine's conversion to Christianity was pivotal, as his newfound faith led him to adopt favorable policies for the Christian church. Constantine likely saw the legalization of Christianity as a means of fostering unity and stability within the empire and securing the support of the Christian community. Additionally, the edict reflected a broader trend toward religious tolerance and pluralism in the Roman Empire, as rulers sought to accommodate the diverse religious beliefs of their subjects.

The Edict of Milan had immediate and far-reaching consequences for Christianity and the Roman Empire. From a religious perspective, the edict granted Christians the freedom to openly practice their faith and participate in public life without fear of persecution. The edict also facilitated the growth and spread of Christianity, as it removed legal barriers and obstacles that had previously hindered the expansion of the Christian church.

Politically, the Edict of Milan helped to consolidate Constantine's power and authority as emperor. By aligning himself with Christianity and granting religious tolerance, Constantine sought to strengthen his legitimacy as a ruler and foster unity among his diverse subjects. The edict also contributed to the stabilization of the empire, as it helped to mitigate religious tensions and conflicts that had previously plagued Roman society.

As we shall see below, the Edict of Milan left a mixed legacy for both Christianity and the Roman Empire. It marked the beginning of a new era of religious tolerance and freedom, setting a precedent for future rulers to respect the rights of individuals to practice their chosen religion. The edict also paved the way for the eventual Christianization of the Roman Empire, as Christianity gradually became the dominant religion of the empire in the centuries that followed. Christians enjoyed many benefits from this freedom of worship but also faced challenges associated with this new freedom.

Constantine's Significance for Christianity

Constantine's conversion to Christianity in the early fourth century marked a dramatic shift in the relationship between the Roman Empire and Christianity. Born into a pagan family, Constantine encountered various religious traditions and beliefs during his upbringing. There is complexity surrounding his conversion because his actions and policies suggest a blend of genuine religious conviction and pragmatic statecraft. The pivotal moment of his conversion is, of course, the Battle of the Milvian Bridge in 312, where he reportedly had a vision of the first two letters of "Christ" in Greek: the Chi-Rho. He also believed he received a promise from God that he would achieve victory. Following his triumph, Constantine began to favor Christianity, issuing the Edict of Milan in 313, which legalized Christian worship and restored confiscated church properties. However, his conversion did not immediately result in the complete Christianization of his rule. Constantine continued to engage in practices rooted in Roman pagan traditions, such as retaining the title of Pontifex Maximus, and some of his coinage still bore images of pagan deities.

Constantine's involvement in ecclesiastical affairs, such as his role in convening the Council of Nicaea in 325, demonstrates the entanglement of theological and political interests in his reign. His efforts to unify the empire under a single faith may reflect both personal belief and a strategic vision for imperial cohesion. Constantine's baptism on his deathbed in 337 also complicates interpretations of his conversion, raising questions about his motives and the extent of his religious commitment throughout his life.

Following Constantine's rise to sole emperor, the church began to see immediate benefits. He became a prominent patron of the church, funding the construction of church buildings, supporting clergy, and convening the First Council of Nicaea in 325 to address theological disputes and establish doctrinal orthodoxy. He also abolished pagan sacrifices and adopted Christian symbols and iconography in imperial regalia. While he did not impose Christianity as the sole religion of the empire, Constantine's support and favoritism toward Christianity contributed to its rapid growth and spread throughout the empire. His conversion accelerated the process of Christianization, leading to the eventual establishment of Christianity as the empire's state religion under Theodosius I in 380. Constantine's patronage helped to institutionalize Christianity and integrate it into the fabric of Roman society, paving the way for the eventual Christianization of the empire.

Motivations for Supporting the Church

Constantine's motivations for supporting the Christian church were likely multifaceted and complex. From a political standpoint, his patronage of Christianity strengthened his legitimacy as emperor and fostered unity among his diverse subjects. By aligning himself with Christianity, Constantine sought to garner the support of the Christian community, which had grown significantly in numbers and influence throughout the empire. Constantine's patronage extended far beyond theology and ecclesiastical affairs, encompassing a broad spectrum of cultural, social, and political domains. Additionally, Constantine's personal experiences and convictions influenced his actions, as did his genuine belief in the moral and ethical teachings of Christianity.

From the grandeur of monumental architecture to the intricacies of bureaucratic administration, the influence of imperial patronage permeated every facet of Roman life. By exploring its multifaceted implications for the empire, its institutions, and the individuals who inhabited its diverse landscape, we gain insight into the dynamics of power and authority in the ancient world. The enduring legacy of imperial patronage shaped not only the religion, politics, and culture of the Roman Empire under Constantine's rule but the contours of human history as well.

Building Churches and Funding Institutions

Emperor Constantine's patronage of Christianity was manifest in his public support for the faith and his extensive efforts to promote the church. One of Constantine's most visible manifestations of support for Christianity was the construction of church buildings, such as St. Peter's Basilica in Rome. These churches served as centers of religious activity, hosting congregations for prayer, liturgical ceremonies, and communal gatherings. Constantine's sponsorship of construction symbolized the official recognition and elevation of Christianity within the empire, providing Christians with dedicated spaces for worship and fellowship.

In addition to promoting the physical infrastructure of the church, Constantine also provided financial support for clergy, including bishops, priests, and other church officials. He exempted clergy from certain taxes and civic obligations, granting them privileges and exemptions as a form of recognition for their religious service. This financial support enabled clergy to devote themselves entirely to their pastoral duties, ensuring the continued growth and stability of the Christian church under Constantine's patronage.

Constantine granted various privileges and exemptions to the Christian church, further solidifying its status as a favored institution within the empire. These privileges included owning property and engaging in legal disputes before ecclesiastical courts. Churches could also receive gifts of inheritance from wealthy benefactors. Constantine's granting of privileges to the church conferred a degree of autonomy and authority upon Christian institutions, enabling them to operate more effectively and independently within the framework of Roman society.

Constantine constructed church buildings and offered financial support for church leaders. On a symbolic level, these actions demonstrated Constantine's commitment to Christianity and his desire to integrate the Christian church into the fabric of Roman society. The basilicas he constructed became enduring symbols of Christian faith and identity. On a practical level, these actions provided the church with the resources and institutional framework necessary for its continued growth and development. His financial support for clergy facilitated the expansion of the church's influence and infrastructure.

Convening Councils and Shaping Orthodoxy

Emperor Constantine convened a church council in AD 325 in the city of Nicaea, a city in present-day Turkey. This was the first council designed for church leaders throughout the empire rather than for leaders in a local region. For this reason, the Council of Nicaea (325) is considered the first ecumenical council. Nicaea is the greatest example of Constantine's influence on Christian doctrine and theology. In the early fourth century, Christianity was beset by theological disputes and doctrinal controversies, particularly regarding the nature of the Trinity and the relationship between the Father and the Son, as discussed in chapter 3. These disputes threatened to divide the church. Nicaea was Constantine's effort to address these theological controversies, resolve the doctrinal disputes, and restore unity to the church. The full impact of the Council of Nicaea will be explored in the following chapter, but Constantine's involvement in this council bear mentioning here.

Constantine played a central role in convening the Council of Nicaea and presiding over its proceedings. As the Roman emperor, he provided logistical support for the council and ensured its safe conduct. While Constantine did not participate directly in the theological debates, his presence and patronage lent legitimacy to the council's decisions and helped secure the acceptance of its decrees throughout the empire.

The Council of Nicaea focused on resolving the controversy surrounding Arianism, a theological position denying Christ's full divinity. After extensive debate and deliberation, the council affirmed the divinity of Christ and condemned Arianism as heretical. The council also formulated the Nicene Creed, a statement of faith that articulated the orthodox Christian belief in the Trinity and the equality of the Father, Son, and Holy Spirit.

The Council of Nicaea was a high point in the development of Christian doctrine. By affirming the divinity of Christ and articulating the orthodox understanding of the Trinity, the council laid the foundation for subsequent theological developments and doctrinal formulations within the Christian church. The Nicene Creed, in particular, became a foundational statement of faith for Christians throughout the centuries, serving as a touchstone of orthodoxy and a rallying cry against heresy. Constantine's legacy as a theological arbiter and patron of the church remains indelibly intertwined with the history of Christianity itself.

New Roles and Structures

In the period following Constantine, the Christian church saw the emergence of the episcopate as a central institution of ecclesiastical authority. The bishop was of great importance in the church and the empire. As Christianity became a recognized religion of the empire, then eventually its official religion, the ecclesiastical authorities in the imperial church assumed more significant roles and responsibilities in society and the church.

In the early centuries of Christianity, bishops or pastors were primarily responsible for overseeing individual congregations or communities, exercising pastoral and administrative authority over their respective churches. However, with the growing size and complexity of the church, the role of bishops began to expand. Essentially, while initially the terms "bishop" and "pastor" were virtually synonymous in the church, the growth of Christianity required an evolving structure in which the bishop came to be an office of pastor to the pastors. Bishops began to oversee a network of churches rather than one congregation.

One of the most notable changes was the bishops' increased involvement in civic and political affairs. Constantine and subsequent emperors relied on bishops not only as spiritual leaders but also as administrators and mediators. Bishops were often called upon to arbitrate disputes, represent Christian communities in legal matters, and even advise imperial officials. For example, Constantine frequently consulted bishops on theological issues and relied on their leadership to maintain unity within the empire, particularly during doctrinal controversies, such as the Arian conflict. Bishops like Hosius of Cordoba (256–359) and Athanasius of Alexandria (296–373) played pivotal roles in shaping imperial religious policy.

The bishop's role as a defender of orthodoxy also expanded during this period, particularly through participation in ecumenical councils. Bishops increasingly acted as representatives of doctrinal authority in collaboration with imperial power. Their decisions at councils carried both ecclesiastical and political weight, reflecting the new partnership between church and state.

The bishops' relationship with local communities also changed. With Constantine's support for the construction of churches and the provision of imperial funding, bishops became stewards of significant wealth and property. This economic power allowed them to expand charitable activities, such as caring for the poor, building hospitals, and supporting widows and orphans. However, it also introduced new challenges, as wealth and influence occasionally led to corruption or competition for bishoprics.

Additionally, bishops' liturgical and pastoral roles became more prominent in the public sphere. Constantine's promotion of Christianity as the favored religion of the empire elevated bishops as public figures, whose sermons and rituals were attended by larger and more diverse audiences. Their ability to shape public morality and policy increased as their pastoral guidance extended beyond the Christian community to broader society.

Bishops began to organize themselves into regional associations of churches to facilitate the governance and administration of the church. A bishop would oversee an association of churches, called a diocese. These associations, much like presbyteries or Baptist associations, operated under the leadership of a single overseer. That bishop exercised spiritual and administrative authority over a specific geographic area. Typically, churches within a particular civil administrative unit would be in the same diocese or association, reflecting the close relationship between church and state in the Roman Empire.

As the church grew and expanded, certain dioceses emerged as centers of ecclesiastical authority known as metropolitan "sees." Metropolitan bishops and archbishops exercised supervisory authority over neighboring dioceses. Additionally, patriarchal sees, such as Rome, Constantinople, Alexandria, Antioch, and Jerusalem, emerged as major centers of Christian influence, with patriarchs wielding considerable authority over their respective regions. These five ancient churches were tied to the apostles themselves. As such, their prominence was already recognized among Christians. As early as the second century, Irenaeus had suggested giving deference to the church at Rome because of its affiliation with the apostles Peter and Paul. But in the imperial church, these five regional churches were given official standing to oversee those churches in their respective regions in a hierarchical ecclesiastical relationship. This ecclesiastical structure provided a framework for the organization and administration of the church, with mixed results. While hierarchy might provide stability, that stability may come at the cost of maintaining the Great Tradition. As we will see in later chapters, authoritarian structures do not guarantee fidelity to the biblical gospel.

Shifting Attitudes Toward Paganism

The ascendancy of Christianity in the Roman Empire precipitated a gradual decline in pagan practices and beliefs. As the imperial court and elite classes converted to Christianity, traditional pagan rituals, festivals, and cults began to wane in popularity. Shrines and temples dedicated to pagan gods fell into disrepair, and public observance of pagan rites declined as Christian influence spread throughout society. Additionally, the proliferation of Christian churches and the promotion of Christian values by state institutions contributed to the erosion of pagan religious practices.

Emperors such as Constantine and his successors issued edicts and decrees favoring Christianity, granting privileges to the church, and restricting the activities of pagan religious institutions. Imperial legislation and policies under emperors such as Theodosius promoted Christian hegemony and suppressed pagan practices. As mentioned before, the Edict of Milan granted religious tolerance to Christians and paved the way for the legalization of Christianity. But subsequent decrees, such as the banning of pagan sacrifices and the closure of pagan temples, further marginalized pagan religion and bolstered the dominance of Christianity.

As Christianity gained political and social ascendancy, Christian attitudes toward pagan practices became increasingly intolerant. Christian writers and theologians condemned paganism as idolatry and urged believers to reject pagan rituals and beliefs. The growing influence of Christian leaders, such as bishops and clergy, contributed to the spread of anti-pagan sentiment and the demonization of pagan deities. In some cases, Christian zealots engaged in acts of vandalism and violence against pagan temples and statues, reflecting a growing intolerance toward competing religious traditions.

Traditional pagan practices, which had been integral to Roman identity for centuries, were gradually supplanted by Christian norms and values. The erasure of pagan religious symbols and institutions reshaped the cultural landscape of the empire, paving the way for the emergence of a Christian-dominated society. However, the suppression of paganism also led to the loss of cultural heritage and traditions, contributing to a sense of cultural homogenization and religious intolerance. While the decline of paganism facilitated the spread of Christian values and institutions, it also contributed to social tensions and cultural conflicts within Roman society. Longstanding pagan temples were converted to Christian churches. The civil religion of the empire, which had been instrumental in helping Romans retain their cultural values, was being replaced by a new religion that the emperors hoped would lead the empire to even greater social and cultural flourishing. The triumph of Christianity over paganism reinforced the belief in the truth and universality of the Christian faith, leading to a sense of confidence and self-assurance among believers. The church's newfound status as the empire's dominant religious and cultural force gave rise to a sense of collective identity and purpose, as Christians saw themselves as members of a chosen and favored community.

Constantinian Legacy and Theodosius

Constantine's patronage of the church provided material support and privileges to the Christian clergy and institutions. He commissioned the construction of churches, convened ecumenical councils, and exerted influence over theological disputes, thereby intertwining the interests of the church with those of the state. However, the consolidation of Christian influence in the Roman Empire was not fully realized until the reign of Emperor Theodosius. In 380, Theodosius issued the Edict of Thessalonica, officially declaring Nicene Christianity as the state religion and proscribing other forms of worship. This edict signaled a decisive shift toward religious uniformity and asserting orthodox Christianity's dominance.

Emperor Theodosius I (379–395), also known as Theodosius the Great, reigned from AD 379 to 395 and played a significant role in solidifying Christianity's place as the dominant religion within the Roman Empire. His reign marked a critical period in the consolidation of Christianity and the suppression of competing religious traditions. With the Edict of Thessalonica in 380, Theodosius sought to unify his empire under a single religious framework, viewing Christianity as a means to foster social cohesion and moral integrity.

The theological underpinnings of Theodosius's anti-pagan stance were deeply rooted in Christian doctrine. Influenced by prominent church figures such as Ambrose of Milan and

Gregory of Nazianzus, Theodosius viewed paganism as incompatible with Christian monotheism and a threat to the moral fabric of society. The dominance of Christianity led to the replacement of pagan beliefs and practices with Christian ones in the empire.

> It is our will that all the peoples who are ruled by the administration of Our Clemency shall practice that religion which the divine Peter the Apostle transmitted to the Romans.
>
> ---
>
> Emperors Gratian, Valentinian, and Theodosius Augustuses, "An Edict to the People of the City of Constantinople" 380

Significant theological matters buttressed Theodosius's rejection of paganism and its lingering influence within the empire. Theodosius and other Christian leaders argued that paganism was fundamentally incompatible with the monotheistic tenets of Christianity. While Christianity proclaimed the belief in one God, paganism embraced polytheism, worshiping multiple gods and goddesses. Theodosius viewed paganism as a deviation from the true faith in the one God of Christianity. Central to Theodosius's theological stance was the condemnation of idolatry. In Christian theology, the worship of idols or images was a grave sin, as it diverted reverence from the one true God and broke the second commandment, against making graven images. Theodosius and his supporters regarded pagan rituals involving statues and temples as idol worship requiring eradication.

Theodosius believed that paganism fostered immoral practices and spiritual corruption. For example, Theodosius viewed pagan rituals, especially sacrifices, as not only idolatrous but also barbaric and morally degrading. Pagan sacrificial practices often involved the slaughter of animals and, in some cases, accusations of human sacrifice—practices that Theodosius and other Christians found abhorrent. By outlawing these rituals in 391, Theodosius sought to eliminate what he regarded as inhumane and spiritually corrupt practices that he believed desensitized participants to the sanctity of life.

Theodosius condemned certain pagan festivals, such as those associated with the cult of Dionysus (Bacchus), which were known for their indulgence in drunkenness, revelry, and licentiousness. These festivals often included processions, ecstatic dancing, and behavior that Christians like Theodosius viewed as promoting debauchery and undermining moral discipline. The Christian moral framework, which emphasized temperance and self-control, stood in sharp contrast to the perceived excesses of such pagan celebrations.

Although not inherently religious, gladiatorial games were closely tied to pagan cultural practices and were often held in honor of traditional gods or during pagan festivals. Theodosius, like many Christians, viewed these games as morally repugnant due to their glorification of violence and human suffering. The spectacle of combat to the death was seen as fostering cruelty and desensitizing the population to the value of human life. While Theodosius did not abolish gladiatorial games outright, his efforts to Christianize Roman society contributed to their eventual decline.

Theodosius associated paganism with practices of divination, astrology, and magic, which he viewed as not only superstitious but also morally and spiritually dangerous. These practices were often linked to attempts to manipulate the divine or gain power over others, contradicting Christian teachings of reliance on God's providence. Theodosius's laws forbade divination and condemned those who practiced or consulted such arts, often imposing severe penalties.

Certain pagan cults, particularly those of fertility deities such as Aphrodite or Cybele, were criticized by Christians for allegedly incorporating sexual practices, including temple prostitution, into their rituals. While modern scholarship questions the extent of such practices, Theodosius and other Christian leaders believed these cults promoted sexual immorality and used this as justification for their suppression. The emphasis on chastity and marital fidelity in Christian ethics stood in opposition to the perceived permissiveness of some pagan rites.

Pagan theatrical performances, often held in honor of the gods, were another source of moral concern for Theodosius. These performances, which included bawdy comedies and satirical depictions of religious or societal figures, were criticized for their crude humor, explicit content, and potential to incite immoral behavior. Christian leaders frequently condemned the theater as a venue for moral corruption, and Theodosius's suppression of pagan festivals often extended to restricting such events.

Pagan festivals, such as the Saturnalia, were often associated with excessive drinking, feasting, and temporary relaxation of social norms, including the reversal of roles between slaves and masters. While these celebrations were an important part of Roman cultural life, Theodosius and other Christians perceived them as fostering disorder and indulgence. By replacing such festivals with Christian observances, Theodosius sought to instill a sense of moral discipline aligned with Christian values.

Political considerations also drove Theodosius's turn against paganism. Theodosius consolidated his authority by aligning himself with the Christian clergy and promoting

Christianity as the state religion, bolstering his legitimacy as a ruler. The suppression of paganism served as a means of asserting control over religious institutions and undermining potential sources of opposition within the empire.

Theodosius framed the suppression of pagan religion as a defense of orthodox Christian doctrine against heresy. Theodosius and his supporters interpreted the triumph of Christianity over paganism as evidence of divine favor and providence. They believed that God had chosen Christianity as the true faith and that the suppression of paganism was part of God's plan for the salvation of humanity. Theodosius saw himself as an instrument of God's will, tasked with upholding the truth of Christianity and protecting his subjects from the dangers of paganism. Overall, Theodosius justified the suppression of paganism in theological terms, framing it as a necessary measure to uphold Christian orthodoxy, promote moral integrity, and secure divine favor for the Roman Empire.

Theodosius I also convened the Second Ecumenical Council of Constantinople in 381, reaffirming the Nicene Creed and condemning Arianism and Apollinarianism, thus solidifying orthodox Christological doctrine. By aligning himself with the Nicene party, Theodosius sought to unify the empire under a single creed and suppress theological dissent. Throughout his reign, Theodosius cultivated close ties with prominent church leaders, including bishops and ecclesiastical authorities. He consulted with influential figures, such as Ambrose of Milan and Gregory of Nazianzus, on matters of religious policy and relied on their support in implementing agenda. Theodosius's collaboration with the church facilitated the integration of ecclesiastical authority into imperial governance and reinforced the symbiotic relationship between church and state.

Emperor Theodosius II, who ruled the Eastern Roman Empire from 408 to 450, embarked on codifying Roman law to consolidate and systematize the diverse legal enactments and rulings accumulated over centuries of Roman history. The Theodosian Code was a compilation of the Roman laws enacted by Christian emperors from Constantine until Theodosius. The code aimed to provide a comprehensive and authoritative compilation of imperial legislation to facilitate the administration of justice and promote legal consistency throughout the empire. It incorporated new legislation enacted during his reign and repealed outdated laws, reflecting Theodosius's efforts to adapt Roman legal norms to contemporary circumstances. One of the distinctive features of the Theodosian Code was its integration of Christian principles and doctrines into Roman law. The code included provisions reflecting Christianity's growing influence within the empire, such as laws regulating religious practices, enforcing orthodoxy, and punishing heresy and paganism. Theodosius's own contributions to Roman law include tax exemption for churches, the recognition of Easter week as an official holiday when the courts were to be closed, and the outlawing of homosexuality in the empire. Theodosius's commitment to promoting Nicene Christianity is evident in the legal provisions of the code, which sought to uphold the authority of the church and suppress dissenting religious views. The Theodosian Code addressed various social issues, including marriage, inheritance, slavery, and taxation. It codified legal norms governing familial relations, property ownership, and contractual obligations, providing a framework for regulating interpersonal conduct and maintaining social order within the empire. The Theodosian Code was the primary source of Roman law in the Eastern Roman Empire (Byzantine Empire) and considerably influenced subsequent legal developments in medieval Europe. It provided a foundational text for Byzantine legal scholars and was a reference for legal practitioners and judges in adjudicating disputes and administering justice.

By incorporating Christian precepts into Roman law, the Theodosian Code contributed to the further Christianization of Roman society and the establishment of Christianity as the dominant religious force within the empire, reinforcing the close relationship between the imperial government and the church and promoting a vision of society guided by Christian ethics and morality. The empire had become "Christian." The church would continue to struggle with the complexities of this new relationship for centuries.

The efforts of Constantine, Theodosius I, and Theodosius II to promote Christianity and suppress paganism blurred the boundaries between ecclesiastical and imperial authority. Christianity became increasingly intertwined with the structures of imperial power, with emperors wielding ever-increasing influence over religious affairs and the church assuming a prominent role in shaping imperial ideology and governance. While the alliance between church and state brought about benefits for Christianity, it also engendered challenges and tensions. The close association with imperial power raised questions about the independence and integrity of the church as ecclesiastical leaders grappled with the complexities of navigating their relationship with the state while upholding the principles of Christian faith and morality. Navigating the complexity of church-state relations was difficult in years following the legalization of Christianity. It became even more difficult as Christian emperors involved themselves even more deeply in ecclesiastical affairs. On occasion, the complexity led to conflict, as in the conflict between Emperor Theodosius I and Ambrose of Milan.

Ambrose of Milan (340–397) was one of the most influential churchmen of the late Roman Empire. He was born into a prominent Roman family and rose to prominence as the bishop of Milan in the late fourth century. Ambrose's leadership and influence extended beyond the ecclesiastical sphere, as he played a pivotal role in shaping imperial policy and defending the interests of the church. His conflict with Theodosius I came to a head in 390 when a massacre occurred in Thessalonica in response to a riot instigated by residents. Theodosius, in a fit of rage, ordered the indiscriminate slaughter of thousands of innocent civilians as retribution for the death of a Roman official. The severity of Theodosius's response shocked the Christian community and provoked widespread condemnation. Ambrose, acting on his conscience and guided by Christian principles, confronted Theodosius over his actions in Thessalonica. In a dramatic display of ecclesiastical authority, Ambrose excommunicated Theodosius and refused to allow him to partake in the Eucharist until he had performed penance for his crimes. This unprecedented act of defiance underscored Ambrose's commitment to upholding moral standards and holding rulers accountable to divine law.

> You have a zeal for faith, I own it. You have the fear of God, I confess it; but you have vehemence of temper, which if soothed may readily be changed into a compassion, but if inflamed becomes so violent that you can scarcely restrain it.
>
> ———
>
> Ambrose of Milan, "Letter LI" to Emperor Theodosius

The confrontation between Ambrose and Theodosius eventually led to a resolution, as Theodosius submitted to the authority of the church and agreed to undergo public penance for his sins. This gesture of contrition, orchestrated by Ambrose, reaffirmed the supremacy of ecclesiastical authority over secular power and demonstrated the moral influence wielded by church leaders in the late Roman Empire.

The Theodosian Crisis left a lasting legacy on the relationship between church and state in the Roman Empire. It highlighted the potential for conflict between ecclesiastical and imperial authority and underscored the pivotal role of influential bishops like Ambrose in shaping political discourse and moral governance. The resolution of the crisis reaffirmed the principle of the church's autonomy and its ability to hold rulers accountable to divine law.

Differences Between the Eastern and Western Empires

Following the relocation of the Roman capital to Byzantium (renamed Constantinople), the empire was effectively divided in two. The Western empire was centered in Rome while the

Eastern empire was centered in Constantinople. While Roman law and institutions governed both the Eastern and Western Roman Empires, there were notable differences in the relationship between church and state in each region. These differences stemmed from various factors, including historical context, theological disputes, and the influence of critical figures. The Eastern Roman Empire, particularly under the Byzantine Emperor Justinian I, adhered to caesaropapism, where the emperor held considerable authority over religious matters. Emperors often involved themselves directly in ecclesiastical affairs, appointing bishops, convening councils, and enforcing theological orthodoxy. The Eastern church recognized the authority of the ecumenical patriarch of Constantinople. The patriarch wielded influence over religious affairs and worked closely with the emperor to maintain doctrinal unity within the church. In the Western church, Christians recognized the primacy of the bishop of Rome. The Eastern Roman Empire hosted several ecumenical councils, such as the Council of Nicaea (325) and the Council of Chalcedon (451), which played pivotal roles in shaping Christian doctrine and resolving theological disputes. These councils were often convened by imperial decree and attended by bishops across the empire. Emperors in the Eastern Roman Empire provided extensive financial and political support to the church, funding the construction of churches and monasteries and granting privileges to the clergy. This patronage reinforced the close relationship between church and state and facilitated the spread of Christianity throughout the empire.

Unlike the Eastern Roman Empire, the Western Roman Empire saw the emergence of papal primacy, with the bishop of Rome (the pope) asserting his authority over the church in the west. The pope claimed supremacy over all other bishops and exercised considerable influence over ecclesiastical affairs. The predominant form of Christianity in the Western Roman Empire was Latin Christianity, which developed distinct theological traditions and liturgical practices from its eastern counterpart. The bishop of Rome played a central role in shaping Western Christian identity and doctrine. With the eventual decline of the Western empire, the church assumed greater responsibility for providing social services, administering justice, and maintaining order.

Much of the reason for the decline of the Western empire was the focus on the east. Constantine moved the capital of the empire from Rome to Constantinople in 324. Constantine chose Byzantium for its strategic advantages. Situated at the crossroads of Europe and Asia, the city controlled key trade routes and had natural defenses, being surrounded by water on three sides. Its location allowed for better oversight of the increasingly important eastern provinces and provided a stronghold against external threats, particularly from Germanic tribes in the west and Persian forces in the east. Additionally, Constantine sought to establish a city that symbolized a new Christian era, distinct from Rome's pagan associations. Constantinople quickly grew in prominence, becoming a center of political, economic, and religious power, and it remained the capital of the Eastern Roman Empire (Byzantine Empire) for over a millennium.

This eastward focus, while strengthening the Eastern Roman Empire, left the western provinces more vulnerable to external threats and internal fragmentation. The pivotal Battle of Adrianople in 378 CE, where the Gothic forces decisively defeated Roman armies and killed Emperor Valens, underscored the growing inability of the empire to manage migratory pressures from Germanic tribes. By AD 395, the death of Emperor Theodosius I led to the formal division of the empire into eastern and western halves ruled by his sons Arcadius and Honorius, respectively. While the Eastern empire flourished, the Western empire descended into increasing turmoil.

The fifth century marked the irreversible decline of the Western Roman Empire, with a series of catastrophic events that demonstrated its growing fragility. In 406, a coalition of Vandals, Suebi, and Alans crossed the frozen Rhine River, initiating widespread devastation in Gaul. The sack of Rome in 410 by the Visigoths under Alaric I was a symbolic blow to the empire's prestige, signaling its inability to defend even its most iconic city. Meanwhile, in 429, the Vandals, led by King Genseric, crossed into North Africa, seizing one of the empire's richest provinces and cutting off crucial grain supplies to Rome. Efforts to defend the empire, such as the victory over Attila the Hun at the Battle of the Catalaunian Plains in 451, were increasingly dependent on alliances with Germanic tribes, underscoring the erosion of Roman military autonomy. The situation further deteriorated with the second sack of Rome in 455 by the Vandals, which compounded the empire's economic and psychological decline.

The ultimate collapse of the Western Roman Empire occurred in 476, when the last emperor, Romulus Augustulus, was deposed by the Germanic chieftain Odoacer. Odoacer declared himself king of Italy, effectively ending the western imperial line and marking the transition to a post-Roman world. In the decades following the fall, the western Roman territories fragmented into Germanic successor kingdoms, such as the Ostrogothic Kingdom in Italy, established by Theodoric the Great after he defeated Odoacer in 493. While the Eastern Roman Empire under Justinian I briefly reconquered parts of the former western territories, including Italy and North Africa, during the mid-sixth century, these gains were short-lived and further strained Byzantine resources.

The decline of the Western Roman Empire was not the result of a single event, but a gradual process shaped by internal weaknesses—such as political instability, economic difficulties, and military inefficiencies—and external pressures, including invasions by Germanic tribes and Huns. Key milestones, like the sack of Rome, the loss of vital provinces, and the deposition of Romulus Augustulus, serve as symbolic markers of the empire's demise. The transition from Roman rule to Germanic dominance laid the foundation for the medieval European world, highlighting the enduring legacy of the Roman Empire even in its fragmentation and decline.

Conclusion

The growth of Christianity in the fourth century can be attributed to a confluence of religious, political, and social factors that transformed it from a persecuted sect into a dominant force within the Roman Empire. Constantine's conversion was merely one of many contributing factors, but it was an important one. This endorsement by the emperor not only empowered the Christian community but also made conversion politically and socially advantageous. Additionally, Constantine's involvement in ecclesiastical matters, exemplified by his convening of the Council of Nicaea in 325, helped to unify Christian doctrine and strengthen the institutional cohesion of the church. This theological and organizational stability further solidified its appeal. The Council of Constantinople (the Second Ecumenical Council) in 381, called by Emperor Theodosius, further solidified the role of the church in the empire.

Christianity's message of salvation resonated across social strata, attracting the poor, women, and slaves, while imperial support encouraged members of the Roman elite to embrace the faith. Christianity had always been evangelistic, and Christians had operated with a missionary impulse ever since Pentecost in Acts 2, where the Spirit of God came on the disciples of Jesus and compelled them to make disciples of all nations from Jerusalem to Judea to Samaria to the ends of earth. That impulse was alive and well in the fourth century, just as it had been during the persecutions of the second and third centuries.

Public demonstrations of the emperor's Christian commitment, such as the use of the Chi-Rho symbol on public buildings and the construction of prominent Christian churches, integrated the religion into the public sphere and enhanced its accessibility. Although Constantine did not outlaw paganism outright, he implemented measures that disadvantaged traditional Roman religions, gradually shifting the sociopolitical landscape in favor of Christianity. Theodosius followed Constantine and did, in fact, outlaw paganism. These interconnected factors—imperial patronage, theological unity, social inclusivity, public visibility, and strategic centralization—collectively facilitated the rapid growth of Christianity during Constantine's reign. In the next chapter, we will turn our attention to this final contribution from these Christian emperors by looking at the Council of Nicaea and its aftermath.

Recommended Reading

Barnes, Timothy D. *Constantine and Eusebius*. Harvard University Press, 1981.

Curran, John. *Pagan City and Christian Capital: Rome in the Fourth Century*. Oxford University Press, 2000.

Drake, H. A. *Constantine and the Bishops: The Politics of Intolerance*. Johns Hopkins University Press, 2000.

Eusebius of Caesarea. *Life of Constantine*. Translated by Averil Cameron and Stuart Hall. Clarendon, 1999.

Harries, Jill. *Imperial Rome AD 284 to 363: The New Empire*. Edinburgh University Press, 2012.

Heather, Peter. *The Restoration of Rome: Barbarian Popes and Imperial Pretenders*. Oxford University Press, 2014.

Johnson, Luke Timothy. *The Creed: What Christians Believe and Why It Matters*. Darton, Longman and Todd, 2003.

Kelly, J. N. D. *Golden Mouth: The Story of John Chrysostom, Ascetic, Preacher, Bishop*. Cornell University Press, 1995.

Lenski, Noel. *The Cambridge Companion to the Age of Constantine*. Cambridge University Press, 2006.

Lieu, Samuel N. C., and Dominic Montserrat. *Constantine: History, Historiography and Legend*. Routledge, 1998.

MacCulloch, Diarmaid. *Christianity: The First Three Thousand Years*. Viking, 2010.

Markus, Robert A. *Christianity and the Secular*. University of Notre Dame Press, 2006.

Millar, Fergus. *A Greek Roman Empire: Power and Belief Under Theodosius II, 408–450*. University of California Press, 2006.

Odahl, Charles Matson. *Constantine and the Christian Empire*. 2nd ed. Routledge, 2010.

Rousseau, Philip. *The Early Christian Centuries*. Longman, 2002.

Smith, Rowland. *Julian's Gods: Religion and Philosophy in the Thought and Action of Julian the Apostate*. Routledge, 1995.

Treadgold, Warren. *A History of the Byzantine State and Society*. Stanford University Press, 1997.

Van Dam, Raymond. *The Roman Revolution of Constantine*. Cambridge University Press, 2007.

Weaver, Rebecca Harden. *Divine Grace and Human Agency: A Study of the Semi-Pelagian Controversy*. Mercer University Press, 1996.

Williams, Stephen, and Gerard Friell. *Theodosius: The Empire at Bay*. Yale University Press, 1994.

— Chapter 8 —

The Council of Nicaea and Its Theological Legacy

Nicene Christianity refers to the theological and doctrinal framework established by the First Council of Nicaea in 325. Emperor Constantine convened the Council of Nicaea to address the Arian controversy, a theological dispute concerning the nature of Christ that was threatening to destabilize the empire. The council brought bishops from across the Christian world to resolve the issue and establish doctrinal orthodoxy. The resulting Nicene Creed affirmed the divinity of Christ and articulated critical aspects of Christian belief. It affirms the belief in one God, the Father Almighty, and in one Lord Jesus Christ, the Son of God, who is of the same substance (*homoousios*) as the Father.

The Creed also affirms the belief in the Holy Spirit, the church, baptism, and the resurrection of the dead. Nicene Christianity represented a defense of orthodoxy against the teachings of Arius, who argued that the Son of God was a created being and not coeternal or consubstantial with the Father. The Nicene Creed affirmed the traditional belief in the full deity of Christ, ensuring that the church remained faithful to apostolic teaching and rejecting any deviation from orthodox doctrine. The Council of Nicaea set a precedent for future ecumenical councils and established the principle of conciliar authority in matters of doctrine and theology. When identifying proper doctrine practice, churches had always operated by a type of consensus, with church leaders gathering local councils of synods to resolve disputes. These local councils operated similarly to presbyteries or Baptist associations in which pastors and theologians address theological and ecclesiastical questions. The councils, comprised of representatives from the churches in that region, operated with some authority in relation to the questions being answered. The Council of Nicaea proposed to speak for and to the entire Christian church. Its universal nature meant that churches would look to ecumenical councils to make pronouncements that affected all Christians.

The Arian Controversy

The immediate cause of the Council of Nicaea was the Arian controversy. Arius (256–336), a pastor from Alexandria in the early fourth century, denied orthodox Christian doctrine with his teachings, leading to one of the most consequential theological controversies in church history. This section delves into Arius's teachings, their popularity, and the resulting divisions within the church. Arius taught that the Son of God, though preexistent and divine, was a created being and, therefore, not coeternal or consubstantial with the Father. According to Arius, there was a time when the Son did not exist. His teaching rejected the Christian understanding of Christ's full divinity and eternal existence.

Arius's theology concerning Christ and his relationship to God the Father is articulated in his *Thalia* and other writings. Arius argued that the Son of God was not coeternal or coequal with the Father but was instead a created being, distinct from and subordinate to God. He famously maintained that "there was a time when He [the Son] was not," emphasizing that the Son, while preeminent among creatures, had a beginning and was not of the same essence (*homoousios*) as the Father. This position, rooted in a desire to preserve the absolute transcendence and unity of God, stood in opposition to the received orthodox understanding of the Trinity.

Arius's theological stance drew upon scriptural passages that seemed to suggest Christ's inferiority to the Father, such as John 14:28 ("The Father is greater than I"), and reflected broader debates about how to reconcile monotheism with the divinity of Christ. However, his views were criticized for undermining the full divinity of Christ, which, his opponents argued, jeopardized the doctrine of salvation, as only a fully divine Christ could bridge the gap between God and humanity.

Arius's teachings, though inconsistent with the Great Tradition, gained traction due to their simplicity and accessibility to the common people. His ideas spread rapidly throughout the eastern provinces of the Roman Empire, finding support among clergy, laity, and even some bishops. Arius's emphasis on the supremacy of God the Father and the subordination of the Son appealed to those who sought a more rational and monotheistic interpretation of Christianity. Arius's teachings sparked intense debate and controversy within the church, leading to deep divisions and schisms.

Attempts at Resolution

Before convening the Council of Nicaea, several regional synods and councils attempted to address the theological controversy surrounding Arius's teachings on Christ's divinity, including a synod in Alexandria in 318 called by Bishop Alexander. Despite earnest efforts to resolve the Arian controversy, the regional synods and councils failed to achieve consensus on the nature of Christ's divinity. Differences in theological interpretation, ecclesiastical politics, and personal rivalries hindered attempts at reconciliation and led to further division within the church. The persistence of theological disagreements underscored the need for a broader gathering that could address the issue on a universal scale. As the theological controversy surrounding Arius's teachings continued to escalate, there was a growing recognition among church leaders of the need for a more comprehensive and authoritative assembly. The church's challenges transcended regional boundaries and required a unified response from the entire Christian community. The failure of earlier synods to resolve the Arian controversy highlighted the imperative for a broader ecumenical council that could represent the entire church and provide a definitive resolution to the doctrinal dispute.

Emperor Constantine recognized the situation's urgency and desired to restore unity within the church. He issued a formal summons to Nicaea. This ecumenical council brought together bishops from across the Roman Empire and beyond to address the Arian controversy and establish doctrinal orthodoxy. The Council of Nicaea marked a decisive moment in church history, providing a forum for resolving theological disputes and affirming essential Christian beliefs.

Political considerations certainly influenced Constantine's decision to convene the Council of Nicaea. The Arian controversy, which divided the church and threatened to undermine the authority of the imperial government, posed a challenge to Constantine's efforts to maintain stability and order within the empire. Constantine aimed to assert his authority as emperor and promote social cohesion among his subjects by intervening in theological disputes and seeking to reconcile opposing factions. By aligning himself with the Nicene party and endorsing the Nicene Creed, Constantine sought to establish himself as the protector and patron of orthodox Christianity, enhancing his legitimacy as ruler and reinforcing the symbiotic relationship between church and state.

As a recent convert to Christianity, Constantine likely had personal beliefs and spiritual convictions that informed his decision to convene the Council of Nicaea. Constantine's conversion experience and his perceived role as a defender of the Christian faith may have motivated him to take decisive action to address the theological controversies plaguing the church. His vision of a unified and orthodox Christianity aligned with his understanding of the faith and his desire to promote religious harmony within the empire.

The Council of Nicaea met in the city of Nicaea (modern-day Iznik, Turkey), in the province of Bithynia in Asia Minor and brought together a diverse group of bishops across the Roman Empire to address the theological controversy surrounding Arius's teachings. Constantine chose Nicaea due to its central geographic position within the Roman Empire and its accessibility to bishops traveling from various regions. The city's strategic location facilitated the assembly of a large and diverse group of participants for the council.

Image 8.1. *The Council of Nicaea*

As discussed in the previous chapter, Emperor Constantine played the central role in organizing the Council of Nicaea, providing logistical support, and overseeing the proceedings. Constantine formally summoned bishops throughout the empire, inviting them to attend the council and participate in the deliberations. Constantine presided over the council and sought to ensure order and decorum during the proceedings.

Through Constantine's effort, the Council of Nicaea attracted diverse bishops representing different regions, theological traditions, and ecclesiastical backgrounds. Bishops from the eastern and western provinces of the Roman Empire, as well as from regions beyond the empire's borders, were in attendance. Along with Constantine, the council included several other prominent figures. Hosius of Cordoba was a prominent bishop and a trusted advisor to Constantine. He played a crucial role in presiding over the council and ensuring the unity of its deliberations. Eusebius of Caesarea played an important role as well. While initially sympathetic to Arian views, he ultimately sided with the Nicene party and signed the Nicene Creed. Alexander, the bishop of Alexandria, was a staunch opponent of Arianism and a leading advocate for the Nicene position. His theological arguments against Arius were influential in shaping the council's deliberations. Although not yet a bishop at the time of the council, Athanasius of Alexandria (296–373) attended as a deacon representing Alexander of Alexandria (250–328). He later became a crucial figure in defending Nicene orthodoxy against Arianism. Eusebius of Nicomedia (275–341) was a prominent bishop and an influential supporter of Arius. His advocacy for Arianism and opposition to the Nicene Creed contributed to the theological tensions at the council.

The Eternal Son of God the Father

The council produced the Nicene Creed, employing the use of the term *homoousios* to define the relationship between the Father and Jesus. The term *homoousios* is of Greek origin, derived from *homo* (meaning "same") and *ousia* (meaning "essence" or "substance"). Translated, it signifies "of the same substance" or "consubstantial." In the context of the Nicene Creed, *homoousios* affirms the eternal relationship between God the Father and God the Son, emphasizing their shared divine nature and coequality.

The Nicene Council concluded that *homoousios* was the best way to describe biblical truth. It affirmed the unity of the Father, Son, and Holy Spirit in one divine substance while preserving their distinct persons. This concept of consubstantiality became foundational for Nicene orthodoxy and subsequent Christological formulations.

However, the term *homoousios* also sparked controversy and debate in the aftermath of the Council of Nicaea. Some theologians, including the followers of Arius, objected to its use, arguing that it was susceptible to misinterpretation and implied a form of modalism or Sabellianism, which collapsed the distinctions between the persons of the Trinity.

Despite these objections, *homoousios* endured as a hallmark of Nicene orthodoxy and a touchstone of Christian faith. It became a litmus test for doctrinal orthodoxy and served as a rallying cry for those who sought to uphold the full divinity of Christ against various theological challenges.

Scripture and the Council of Nicaea

The Great Tradition is scriptural. For Christians, theological formulation occurred through engagement with the Bible from the perspective of the gospel of Jesus guided by the rule of faith. Scripture was central to the arguments of both the orthodox, which upheld the full divinity of Christ, and the Arian faction, which contended that Christ was a created being distinct from the Father. The council revealed the profound importance of exegesis in articulating and defending Christian doctrine.

The orthodox bishops, led by figures such as Alexander of Alexandria and his deacon Athanasius, grounded their argument for the consubstantiality (*homoousios*) of the Father and the Son in the overarching narrative of salvation history as revealed in Scripture. They emphasized passages like John 1:1–3 ("In the beginning was the Word, and the Word was with God, and the Word was God. He was in the beginning with God. All things were made through him, and without him was not anything made that was made" [RSV]), which they interpreted as a clear declaration of the eternal existence and divine nature of the Word (Logos). For the Nicenes, such passages affirmed that Christ, as the Word, was not a creature but the eternal and divine agent of creation itself.

Other key texts included John 10:30 ("I and the Father are one") and Phil 2:6–11, which speaks of Christ as being "in the form of God" and yet humbling himself in obedience. These verses were interpreted not only as affirmations of Christ's divine nature but also as explanations of the unity and equality within the Trinity. The Nicenes also pointed to Jesus's titles, such as "Son of God," as evidence of a unique and eternal relationship with the Father, emphasizing that "Sonship" in this context indicated an intrinsic sharing of the Father's essence rather than a temporal origin.

The Nicene approach to Scripture was holistic and theological, seeking to interpret individual passages in light of the entire biblical witness and the church's liturgical and doctrinal traditions. Their interpretation was driven by the conviction that the full divinity of Christ was essential for the coherence of Christian worship and the efficacy of salvation. For example, they argued that only if Christ were fully God could his atoning work on the cross be sufficient to redeem humanity and restore communion with the divine.

The Arian faction, led by Arius and supported by Eusebius of Nicomedia, also appealed to Scripture but focused on passages that seemed to emphasize Christ's subordination to the Father or his role as a created being. A favorite text of the Arians was Prov 8:22–25, which they interpreted as a prophecy of Christ as the personified Wisdom of God: "The Lord created me at the beginning of his work, the first of his acts of old" (RSV). For Arians, this passage suggested that the Son had a beginning and was therefore not coeternal with the Father. Similarly, they cited Col 1:15 ("He is the image of the invisible God, the first-born over all creation") and John 14:28 ("The Father is greater than I") as evidence that the Son was subordinate to the Father and occupied a middle ground between the divine and created realms.

Arians adopted a more literal and atomistic approach to Scripture, focusing on isolated texts to support their theological conclusions. Their method often involved taking individual verses at face value without situating them within the broader context of salvation history or the unity of the biblical canon. This approach allowed them to build a case for the created status of the Son but left them vulnerable to criticism for failing to address the theological implications of the incarnation and the church's worship practices.

The divergent interpretations of Scripture at Nicaea highlighted the necessity of hermeneutical frameworks in theological debates. While both factions claimed to base their arguments on Scripture, their differing approaches revealed that the text alone could not resolve the controversy. The Nicenes appealed to the apostolic tradition and the church's liturgical practices as interpretive guides, arguing that their understanding of Scripture aligned with the faith handed down from the apostles and reflected in the worship of Christ as God. The Arians, in contrast, relied on a more speculative and philosophical interpretation, detached from this tradition.

The adoption of the term *homoousios* ("of the same essence") in the Nicene Creed exemplified this reliance on tradition and theological reasoning. Although *homoousios* is not a scriptural term, the Nicenes used it to articulate the relationship between the Father and the

Son in a way that upheld the biblical witness and safeguarded the coherence of Christian worship and doctrine. This decision demonstrated the council's recognition that Scripture, while foundational, required the guidance of theological reflection and ecclesiastical consensus to address complex doctrinal issues.

The Council of Nicaea ultimately affirmed the Nicene interpretation of Scripture, declaring that the Son is "true God from true God, begotten, not made, of one essence [*homoousios*] with the Father." This formulation rejected Arianism as incompatible with the apostolic faith and the unity of the Godhead. The council's decisions also reinforced the principle that scriptural interpretation must be grounded in the tradition and teaching authority of the church. By addressing the limitations of isolated proof texting, Nicaea set a precedent for the use of Scripture in doctrinal debates, emphasizing the need for a theological framework that reflects the fullness of the biblical narrative and the lived experience of the Christian community.

The Council of Nicaea remains a pivotal example of how Scripture was employed and contested in the articulation of Christian doctrine. The contrasting approaches of the Nicene and Arian factions illustrate the interpretive challenges posed by theological disputes and the critical role of tradition, reason, and ecclesiastical authority in preserving the unity and integrity of the faith. Through its decisions, Nicaea established a lasting foundation for trinitarian theology and set a standard for the church's engagement with Scripture in the pursuit of doctrinal clarity.

The Arian controversy was not the only controversy addressed by the Nicene Council. From at least the early second century, churches had differed regarding when to celebrate Easter, the most important day on the church calendar. The quartodeciman controversy pitted those churches who celebrated Easter on the day of the Jewish Passover (the fourteenth day of the month of Nisan) regardless of what day of the week it was against those who celebrated Easter on the Sunday following Passover.[1] The practice appears to have been limited to the churches in Asia Minor. Irenaeus tells us that Polycarp was a quartodeciman, claiming to have received the practice from the apostle John. Polycarp, representing the churches in Asia Minor, appealed to the church at Rome to adopt the practice. The bishop of Rome refused this request, but also did not condemn Polycarp and the other churches who celebrated Easter differently. This posture changed in 189 when the bishop of Rome at the time, Victor, excommunicated the quartodecimans.

---

[1] Eusebius, *Ecclesiastical History* 5.23

The condemnation from Pope Victor did not end the practice of celebrating Easter on the day of Passover. At the time of Nicaea, churches in Syria, centered at Antioch, were still using the Jewish calendar to date Easter, while the churches in Alexandria and Rome were celebrating Easter only on a Sunday. Both the bishops and the emperor preferred a standard way of determining the date of Easter each year to ensure uniformity among Christians. Complicating matters was that multiple calendars were used in different parts of the empire. A better process was required to bring a sense of unity to the church's liturgy.

The council determined that the resurrection of Jesus should be celebrated on a Sunday, as that was the day of the week on which Jesus was raised from the dead. But which Sunday? The bishops agreed to date Easter as the Sunday following the first full moon after the spring equinox. Locating the Passover in relation to the spring equinox, rather than to any particular calendar, allowed Christians to more easily conform to a common practice.

The council also addressed matters of clerical discipline and governance within the church. It issued canons regulating the behavior of clergy, such as the ordination of bishops and clergy, the prohibition of usury by clergy, and the treatment of lapsed clergy. These canons sought to establish standards of conduct and discipline within the church and ensure the integrity of its leadership. The council set forth guidelines for the ordination of bishops and clergy. It emphasized the importance of proper procedures and qualifications for ordination, seeking to maintain the integrity and authority of the clergy. The council also issued canons prohibiting clergy from the practice of usury, charging exorbitant interest rates on loans. This decision aimed to uphold ethical standards among the clergy and prevent financial exploitation of the church. The council also came up with a system of treating clergy who had lapsed or fallen into sin. It established procedures for restoring lapsed clergy to their positions, outlining steps for repentance, reconciliation, and reinstatement within the church. The council affirmed the authority of bishops and synods to discipline clergy who violated ecclesiastical norms or engaged in misconduct.

Specifically, the council addressed the question of the Meletian Schism. The Meletian Schism had arisen due to the actions of Meletius of Lycopolis (dates unknown) during the Diocletian persecution (303–313), when he accused several bishops, including Peter of Alexandria, of leniency toward Christians who had lapsed under persecution. Meletius unilaterally consecrated bishops in territories under the jurisdiction of other bishops, leading to a parallel ecclesiastical structure and significant tensions within the Egyptian church.

Canon 8 specifically addressed the Meletian schismatics and outlined terms for their reconciliation. It permitted Meletian clergy to remain in their positions but stipulated that they must recognize the authority of the canonical bishops appointed by the church. Meletian bishops and priests could retain their rank, provided they refrained from further consecrations and accepted the unity of the church. Additionally, Meletian clergy were required to present themselves to the bishop of Alexandria and be formally restored to communion. This approach aimed to balance mercy and discipline, allowing for reconciliation while upholding ecclesiastical order.

The Council of Nicaea's provisions for the Meletians demonstrated a commitment to healing divisions within the church while maintaining the authority of the Alexandrian see. By integrating Meletian clergy and laypeople under clear conditions, the council sought to end the parallel hierarchy and restore unity in Egypt. However, the schism persisted in some form even after Nicaea, as not all Meletians accepted the council's terms, and tensions continued to flare during the episcopate of Athanasius of Alexandria, a staunch opponent of both Arianism and the Meletian faction.

Formulation and Adoption of the Nicene Creed

Central to the deliberations at the Council of Nicaea was the nature of Christ. The bishops grappled with whether Christ was genuinely divine or a created being. The bishops also elucidated Christ's relationship to God the Father. By proclaiming Christ as "begotten, not made, of the same Being with the Father," the creed affirmed that Christ was coeternal with the Father.

Furthermore, the Council of Nicaea underscored Christ's significance for salvation. By affirming his full divinity, the council affirmed the efficacy of Christ's atoning sacrifice for the redemption of humanity. Christ, as the eternal Son of God, became the mediator between God and humanity, reconciling fallen humanity with the divine through his sacrificial death and resurrection. The Nicene Creed's proclamation of Christ's salvific role emphasized his central place in Christian soteriology and underscored the necessity of faith in him for salvation.

The Nicene Creed affirms the core beliefs of the Christian faith, particularly regarding the nature of God and the person of Christ. It declares belief in one God, the Father Almighty, creator of heaven and earth, and in one Lord Jesus Christ, the only-begotten Son of God, begotten of the Father before all ages, Light of Light, true God of true God, begotten, not made, consubstantial with the Father. The creed also affirms belief in the Holy Spirit, the Lord, the giver of life, who proceeds from the Father and the Son, and in one holy, catholic, and apostolic church. It concludes with a statement of belief in the resurrection of the dead and the life of the age to come.

Following the Council of Nicaea, Christians recognized the Nicene faith as a proper and correct summary and restatement of the gospel of Jesus Christ according to the Scriptures. While not inspired or authoritative Scripture, the Nicene Creed accurately summarizes and conveys Scripture's message. Later councils would look back to Nicaea as foundational to understanding and expressing the apostolic faith.

Opposition to Nicaea

> I believe in one Lord Jesus Christ, the only Son of God, begotten from the Father before all ages, God from God, Light from Light, true God from true God, begotten, not made; of the same essence as the Father. Through him all things were made.
>
> The Nicene Creed

While some opponents of the Nicene Creed fully embraced Arianism, others adopted a more moderate stance known as homoiousians. The homoiousians emerged in the post-Nicene period as a theological faction that sought a middle ground between the Nicene affirmation of the Son's consubstantiality (*homoousios*, "of the same essence") with the Father and the outright subordinationism of the Arians. The term *homoiousios*, meaning "of a similar essence," encapsulated their central theological claim: The Son is not identical in essence to the Father but is still of a similar divine nature. This subtle distinction reflected their attempt to preserve both the distinct personhood of the Father and the Son and the unity of God, avoiding what they perceived as the extremes of Sabellianism (which conflated the persons of the Trinity) and Arianism (which denied the Son's true divinity).

The homoiousians were led by figures such as Basil of Ancyra and were particularly active in the 350s and 360s during the reign of Constantius II, who sought to mediate theological disputes within the empire. They rejected the Nicene term *homoousios*, arguing that it was unbiblical and prone to misinterpretation as implying a total identity of the Father and the Son, which they feared could undermine the distinctiveness of the divine persons. However, they also opposed the radical Arian position that the Son was a mere creature, asserting instead that the Son's essence was sufficiently similar to the Father's to affirm his divinity and role in creation and salvation.

The homoiousian theology contributed to the broader debates over Trinitarian doctrine by highlighting the challenges of articulating the relationship between the Father and the Son within the framework of monotheism. Although their position was ultimately subsumed into the pro-Nicene consensus, particularly through the theological synthesis achieved by the Cappadocian Fathers, the homoiousians played a critical role in shaping the language and contours of the Nicene debate. Their emphasis on the distinctness yet closeness of the Father and the Son underscored the necessity of careful theological precision, paving the way for the eventual acceptance of the full trinitarian orthodoxy articulated at the Council of Constantinople in 381.

After the Council of Nicaea, Arius himself faced a complex fate. Despite being exiled by Emperor Constantine for refusing to renounce his teachings, Arius found sympathy and support among specific influential figures, including Eusebius of Nicomedia and other Arian bishops. He continued to propagate his theological views and gather followers, contributing to the persistence of Arianism despite its condemnation at Nicaea. The fate of Arius's supporters varied in the years following the Council of Nicaea. While some Arian bishops faced persecution and exile, others retained influence within the church and imperial circles.

Several prominent Arian bishops faced exile during the contentious theological and political struggles of the fourth century, as imperial favor alternated between Nicene and Arian factions. Among these bishops, Eusebius of Nicomedia, Aetius of Antioch, and Ursacius of Singidunum stand out as significant figures who suffered exile due to their adherence to or promotion of Arianism.

Eusebius of Nicomedia (died 341) was one of the most influential Arian bishops of his time. A close ally of Arius, Eusebius was exiled following the First Council of Nicaea in 325 due to his opposition to the Nicene Creed and his defense of Arian theology. However, his exile was short-lived, as he regained imperial favor and eventually became a key figure in the court of Emperor Constantine. Eusebius used his position to promote Arianism and orchestrated the exile of Athanasius of Alexandria, a staunch defender of Nicene orthodoxy. His eventual return to power exemplifies the volatility of imperial politics and its impact on ecclesiastical disputes.

Aetius of Antioch (313–67), a theologian and bishop associated with the radical branch of Arianism, known as anomoeanism, also faced exile. Aetius espoused the belief that the Son was *unlike* (*anomoios*) the Father in essence, taking a more extreme stance than earlier

Arians. His theological rigor and unyielding positions led to his exile during the reign of Emperor Constantius II, who sought to mediate between Arian and Nicene factions. Although Aetius's influence waned following his exile, his teachings continued to shape the more radical elements of the Arian movement.

Ursacius of Singidunum (335–70), a bishop from the Danube region, aligned himself with the Arian cause and played a prominent role in the councils that sought to undermine Nicene orthodoxy, including those at Sirmium. However, like many of his contemporaries, Ursacius faced exile when political tides shifted, particularly during the reign of pro-Nicene emperors, such as Constans (337–50) and Jovian (363–64). His repeated attempts to navigate the shifting theological landscape, including moments of retraction and reinstatement, illustrate the complexities of episcopal life during the era of the Arian controversy.

These exiles highlight the intertwining of theology and imperial politics in the fourth century, as bishops often found themselves at the mercy of shifting doctrinal allegiances within the court. The experiences of these Arian bishops underscore the broader ecclesiastical and doctrinal upheaval that characterized the post-Nicene period and the enduring tensions between orthodoxy and heresy in the early church.

Opposition to the Nicene Creed was not confined to theological circles but also to political spheres. While initially supportive of the Nicene cause, Emperor Constantine later wavered in his allegiance and sought political expediency over theological unity, sometimes favoring Arian sympathizers and even reinstating some exiled bishops. Constantine's vacillation and attempts at compromise exacerbated the theological tensions of the Nicene controversy and contributed to the persistence of doctrinal divisions within the church.

Despite initial setbacks and periods of persecution, Arianism continued to exert influence within the Roman Empire and the imperial church for several decades after the Council of Nicaea. Successive emperors, including Constantius II and Valens, openly supported Arian factions and sought to suppress Nicene orthodoxy, leading to further theological controversies and ecclesiastical divisions. It was not until the latter part of the fourth century, with the reign of Emperor Theodosius I and the Council of Constantinople in 381, that Arianism was definitively marginalized and Nicene orthodoxy established as the dominant creed within the Roman Empire. The aftermath of the Council of Nicaea witnessed the ongoing persistence of Arianism within the Roman Empire and the imperial church. Despite the condemnation of Arius and his teachings at Nicaea, Arianism remained a potent theological and political force in the empire.

Athanasius and the Defense of Nicene Orthodoxy

As already discussed, Athanasius of Alexandria emerged as a leading proponent of Nicene orthodoxy in the aftermath of the Council of Nicaea. As a deacon and later bishop of Alexandria, he vigorously opposed Arianism. Athanasius faced fierce opposition from Arian bishops and political authorities who sought to suppress Nicene orthodoxy. He endured multiple exiles and periods of persecution throughout his life due to his unwavering stance against Arianism. Despite his personal hardships, Athanasius defended the orthodox faith.

Athanasius was born around 298 in Alexandria, Egypt, and received a classical education in Greek literature and philosophy. He drank deeply from the teachings of his mentor, Bishop Alexander of Alexandria, who was a staunch opponent of Arianism. Athanasius defended the Nicene Creed's assertion of Christ's consubstantiality with the Father (*homoousios*), arguing that any compromise on this doctrine would undermine the very foundations of the Christian faith. Athanasius faced severe persecution and exile for his unwavering defense of Nicene orthodoxy. He was deposed and exiled multiple times by Arian-leaning emperors and ecclesiastical authorities who sought to suppress his influence and silence his theological dissent. Despite these challenges, Athanasius advocated for Nicene doctrine and rallied support from fellow bishops and theologians.

Perhaps his most famous work was *On the Incarnation*, which, along with its predecessor *Contra Gentes*, was not written against Arianism but does articulate Christ's divine incarnation and redemptive work to reconcile humanity to God. Written around 318, likely before the Arian controversy fully erupted but certainly in the light of Alexander's conflict with Arius, the work serves as both a theological treatise and an apologetic defense of Christian belief. Athanasius begins by explaining the purpose of the incarnation: to restore humanity's corrupted nature and to reconcile creation with God. He argues that humanity, having fallen into sin and death through disobedience, required divine intervention. The Word of God, the eternal Logos, became flesh to overcome sin and death, offering himself as a redemptive sacrifice and restoring

> For the Word, realizing that in no other way would the corruption of human beings be undone except, simply, by dying, yet being immortal and the Son of the Father, the Word was not able to die, for this reason he takes to himself a body capable of death
>
> ———
>
> Athanasius, *On the Incarnation*

the divine image in humanity. For Athanasius, the incarnation is not merely an act of divine condescension but an essential and inevitable consequence of God's love and justice, demonstrating his commitment to the renewal of creation.

Athanasius also uses *On the Incarnation* to refute objections from both pagans and Jews. He critiques pagan polytheism and idolatry, asserting the superiority of Christian monotheism and the transformative power of Christ's redemptive work. By emphasizing the futility of pagan worship and the irrationality of ascribing divinity to created objects, he underscores the unique and unparalleled nature of the incarnation. Athanasius also addresses Jewish critiques by appealing to the fulfillment of Old Testament prophecies in Christ, arguing that the incarnation was anticipated in the Scriptures and is integral to God's salvific plan.

The work's apologetic tone reflects Athanasius's broader purpose: to present Christianity as the true philosophy that fulfills both human reason and divine revelation. His rejection of paganism is not only theological but also cultural, as he portrays the incarnation as the event that overturns the moral and spiritual degradation of the Greco-Roman world. In doing so, *On the Incarnation* affirms the cosmic scope of Christ's work, presenting the Word made flesh as the answer to humanity's deepest needs and the foundation of the Christian faith.

Exile and Persecution of Athanasius

The exile and persecution of Athanasius took place amidst the broader political landscape of the Roman Empire, characterized by shifting alliances, imperial ambitions, and religious rivalries. Emperor Constantine's death in 337 ushered in a period of instability as his successors vied for control and sought to impose their theological agendas on the church. Arian sympathizers within the imperial court and ecclesiastical hierarchy wielded considerable influence, using their positions to suppress Nicene orthodoxy and persecute its proponents. The theological dispute between Nicene orthodoxy and Arianism lay at the heart of Athanasius's exile. As bishop of Alexandria, Athanasius's outspoken defense of Nicene doctrine made him a target for Arian-leaning emperors and bishops who sought to silence his dissent and promote their theological agenda.

Athanasius endured multiple periods of persecution and exile throughout his episcopate. He was first deposed and exiled in 335 by Emperor Constantine's son, Constantine II, who was sympathetic to Arianism. Tumultuous events followed Athanasius's exile, including his return to Alexandria amidst political turmoil, subsequent exiles under Emperor Constantius II, and further periods of banishment under Julian the Apostate and Valens.

Athanasius of Alexandria was revered for his defense of Nicene orthodoxy amidst theological controversies of the fourth century.

Continued Controversy and the Need for a Second Ecumenical Council

Earlier we saw that continued theological controversies led to the Second Ecumenical Council, this time in Constantinople in the year 381. Because of the continued Arian heresy, along with the rise of other heresies we will see, there was a need for further theological explication and doctrinal precision. This task was most ably executed by the Cappadocian Fathers—Basil of Caesarea, Gregory of Nyssa, and Gregory of Nazianzus—who helped shape and refine the language of Nicene orthodoxy by making essential distinctions between the persons of the Godhead.

Arianism was not the only heresy Christians faced following Nicaea. There was also the matter of the heresy of Apollinarius of Laodicea, an anti-Arian theologian who promoted the idea that Jesus was devoid of a human soul or mind. Apollinarius (c. 310–c. 390) was born in Laodicea, Syria (modern-day Latakia, Syria), receiving his early education in Alexandria, Egypt, where he studied under notable Christian theologians, such as Athanasius. Ultimately, he became bishop of Laodicea in the year 253.

Apollinarius wrote theological texts, most of which are unavailable today. His most famous work, however, was *Against the Greeks*, a polemical work in which he disputed pagan philosophical doctrines and defended Christian orthodoxy. Apollinarius also presented theological treatises and commentaries on various biblical texts, though these works are mostly lost and exist only in large part. Although Apollinarius was a prominent opponent of Arianism, his Christological missteps meant many of his allies against the Arian heresy would later become his theological opponents regarding the person and work of Christ.

According to the teachings of Apollinarius, in the incarnation, the divine Logos (Word) assumed a human body but not a human soul or mind. Instead, the divine Logos replaced the human rational soul in Christ, resulting in a composite nature comprising divinity and humanity. Apollinarius sought to unify the human and divine sides of Christ's nature in this way. By denying Christ a human soul, Apollinarius believed he could preserve the unity and integrity of Christ's person, avoiding a separation of Jesus into two persons, one divine and one human.

If Arianism denies the true divinity of Jesus, Apollinarianism denies the true humanity of Jesus. The primary opponents of Apollinarius include prominent pro-Nicene theologians and bishops. Athanasius of Alexandria argued that Apollinarianism denied the incarnation of the Son of God by destroying the humanity of Christ. Gregory of Nazianzus argued that Apollinarius undermined the saving work of Jesus by limiting the human nature. His famous dictum, "What is not assumed is not healed," was meant to convey this problem with Apollinarian Christology.

By contrast, Gregory held that Christ took on complete humanity in the incarnation. According to Gregory, for Christ to heal and save humanity, he had to take on the fullness of humanity: body, soul/mind, and spirit. If Christ failed to take on any aspect of humanity, that aspect would remain untouched—and unhealed.

The significance of Gregory's statement lies in its affirmation of the totality and completeness of Christ's salvific work. In assuming humanity in its totality, Christ redeems every aspect of human existence, reconstituting human nature back to how it was supposed to have been and reconciling it with God. More theologically, it reflects the unity of Christ's divine and human natures and, in turn, the theological significance of the incarnation for human salvation.

Emperor Theodosius I, who was a supporter of Nicene doctrine, called the council to meet in Constantinople in 381. The council comprised about 150 bishops, mostly from the Eastern Roman Empire, but with a few representatives from the Western church. The primary purpose of the Council of Constantinople was to address the ongoing theological controversies that persisted after the Council of Nicaea. The Arian controversy was still causing strife in the church. Now Apollinarianism needed to be addressed. And there were also debates over the nature of the Holy Spirit and a complete trinitarian formula, which led to the necessity of theological clarification and doctrinal consensus.

> Thus do I stand, and thus may I stand, and those I love as well, on these issues, able to worship the Father as God, the Son as God, the Holy Spirit as God—"three distinctions in personality, one Godhead undivided in glory, honor, substance, and sovereignty."
>
> ———
>
> Gregory of Nazianzus,
> *Five Theological Orations*

One of the leading figures at the council was Gregory of Nazianzus, the bishop of Constantinople. His theological writings, especially *The Five Theological Orations*, formed the backbone of a proper understanding of the Trinity and the constellation of relationships between the divine persons. As the bishop of Constantinople and a preeminent theologian of his day, Gregory was among the bishops who most organized and presided over the council of 381.

Although the council condemned Apollinarianism, the primary theological dispute at the Council of Constantinople would be the nature of the Holy Spirit. The Nicene Creed had addressed the divinity of the Son, yet it had not explicitly spoken to the divinity of the Holy Spirit. Those who denied the full divinity of the Holy Spirit were known as Pneumatomachians, or "Spirit fighters," and Macedonians because they followed the teachings of Macedonius. Proponents of this heresy argued that the Holy Spirit was not God but rather a created being. Having been created by the Father, the Spirit was subordinate to the Father and Son, being more of an instrument by which God worked rather than a divine person in the Trinity. These "enemies of the Holy Spirit" relegated the Spirit to creaturely status because they could not find biblical evidence of the Spirit's role in creation. Athanasius of Alexandria wrote against the Pneumatomachians in his *Letters to Serapion*.

The Council of Constantinople rejected Pneumatomachian teachings and affirmed the orthodox understanding that the Holy Spirit is fully divine. Building upon the Nicene Creed's affirmation of the divinity of the Son, the council expanded the creed to include a confession of faith in the Holy Spirit as "the Lord, the Giver of Life, who proceeds from the Father." This formula articulated the Spirit's eternal procession from the Father, affirming his coequality and coeternity with the Father and the Son in the Trinity.

The council condemned Pneumatomachianism and affirmed the divinity of the Holy Spirit, thus preserving and promoting the church's confession of the triune God. Nicaea ensured that the church's unity and the integrity of trinitarian doctrine would remain intact so that the church's confession of faith would remain faithful to the apostolic tradition. The recognition of the Holy Spirit as a divine person who is coequal and coeternal with the Father and the Son confirmed the Spirit's role in the economy of salvation and affirmed the central importance of trinitarian worship and devotion to the Christian life. By hailing the Nicene Creed as the standard of orthodoxy, the council ensured that Christian theology was formulated on the bedrock of the church's foundational theology and established the parameters for subsequent theological reflection. The council's pronouncements also generated the historical process of the formulation of Nicene Christianity, which conferred finality upon the definition of the Christian faith as maintained in the Nicene Creed, and it converted Constantinople into one of the five patriarchates in the Christian church.

So, while it is important to note that the bishops at Constantinople were offering supplementary affirmations to the creedal formulations of Nicaea, it is also critical to recognize that these authors understood themselves to be doing so in continuity with the original Nicene formulations, which is why their creed was accepted. The Nicene faith underscored the full divinity of Jesus Christ. Arius held that Christ was a created being and, therefore, not equal to the Father. Against Arius, Nicaea confessed Jesus Christ to be "of one essence [*homoousios*) with the Father." Additionally, while the Nicene Creed professed belief in the Spirit, it had not fleshed out a fully orbed trinitarian theology by spelling out the nature and role of the Spirit within the triune Godhead.

Conclusion

The First and Second Ecumenical Councils established Christianity's trinitarian vocabulary and grammar in the Nicene-Constantinopolitan Creed. Against the heresies of Arius, Apollinarius, and the Pneumatomachians, these councils established boundaries of orthodoxy that reflected the church's long-held faith, derived from the Scriptures of the Old and New Testaments, handed down in the rule of faith, and practiced in the church's life of prayer and worship. The Great Tradition includes both the Nicene Creed and the theological development in the centuries leading up to it. In the next chapter, we will see other doctrinal deviations from the biblical faith and observe the role which the Nicene faith played in articulating orthodox Christian theology.

Recommended Reading

Anatolios, Khaled. *Retrieving Nicaea: The Development and Meaning of Trinitarian Doctrine*. Baker Academic, 2011.

Ayres, Lewis. *Nicaea and Its Legacy: An Approach to Fourth-Century Trinitarian Theology*. Oxford University Press, 2004.

Barnes, Timothy D. *Athanasius and Constantius: Theology and Politics in the Constantinian Empire*. Harvard University Press, 1993.

Beeley, Christopher A. *The Unity of Christ: Continuity and Conflict in Patristic Tradition*. Yale University Press, 2012.

Eusebius of Caesarea. *The History of the Church*. Translated by G. A. Williamson. Penguin Classics, 1989.

Gwynn, David M., ed. *Athanasius of Alexandria: Bishop, Theologian, Ascetic, Father*. Brepols, 2012.

Hanson, R. P. C. *The Search for the Christian Doctrine of God: The Arian Controversy 318–81*. T&T Clark, 1988.

Kannengiesser, Charles. *A Handbook on Early Christianity*. Fortress, 2004.

Kelly, J. N. D. *Early Christian Doctrines*. 5th ed. HarperOne, 1978.

Lyman, J. Rebecca. *Arius: Heresy and Tradition*. Routledge, 1993.

McGuckin, John Anthony. *St. Gregory of Nazianzus: An Intellectual Biography*. St. Vladimir's Seminary Press, 2001.

Parsons, Michael H. *Athanasius*. Routledge, 1995.

Pelikan, Jaroslav. *The Christian Tradition: A History of the Development of Doctrine*. Vol. 1, *The Emergence of the Catholic Tradition (100–600)*. University of Chicago Press, 1971.

Rubenstein, Richard E. *When Jesus Became God: The Struggle to Define Christianity During the Last Days of Rome*. Harcourt, 1999.

Rusch, William G., ed. *The Trinitarian Controversy*. Fortress, 1980.

Seitz, Christopher R. *Athanasius and the Holy Spirit: The Development of His Early Pneumatology*. Yale University Press, 1988.

Torrance, Thomas F. *The Trinitarian Faith: The Evangelical Theology of the Ancient Catholic Church*. T&T Clark, 1995.

Weinandy, Thomas G. *Athanasius: A Theological Introduction*. Ashgate, 2007.

Wickham, Lionel. *The Second Council of Constantinople 553: The Three Chapters and the Failed Quest for Unity in Christendom*. Liverpool University Press, 2017.

Williams, Rowan. *Arius: Heresy and Tradition*. Rev. ed. Eerdmans, 2001.

Young, Frances M. *From Nicaea to Chalcedon: A Guide to the Literature and Its Background*. 2nd ed. Baker Academic, 2010.

—— Chapter 9 ——

Ongoing Doctrinal Development in the Church

Following the First and Second Ecumenical Councils, the church continued to pursue faithfulness to the apostolic faith, which Christians believed had been clearly articulated in the Nicene-Constantinopolitan Creed. Those councils had condemned the heresies of Arianism and Apollinarianism. In the fifth century, ongoing theological controversies over Christology and soteriology persisted. The church responded to these challenges with two additional ecumenical councils in the fifth century. In 431, the Council of Ephesus dealt with the Nestorian controversy, over whether there were two persons in Christ or only one. In 451, the Council of Chalcedon clarified the proper understanding of the union of the two natures in Christ against both Nestorian and Eutychian Christological formulations. The Definition of Chalcedon established the hypostatic union as orthodox Christology but did not settle the issue for all churches. Groups that rejected Chalcedon, known as monophysites or miaphysites, denied the two natures of Jesus Christ.

Cyril of Alexandria and the Nestorian Controversy

Nestorius (c. AD 386–450), whose theological legacy would shape one of the most significant controversies in early Christian history, was deeply influenced by his education and formation within the Antiochene tradition. Born in Germanicia (modern-day Turkey), Nestorius received his theological training in Antioch, one of the foremost intellectual and spiritual centers of the early church. The Antiochene school of theology, to which Nestorius belonged, emphasized a literal and historical approach to scriptural interpretation, a stark contrast to the more allegorical method favored by the Alexandrian school. This tradition was deeply concerned with preserving the distinctiveness of Christ's divine and human natures, reflecting a broader commitment to safeguarding both the transcendence of God and the full reality of Christ's humanity. Within this Christological tradition, however, there was a tendency to separate the natures rather than to distinguish them. We find this in Diodore of Tarsus's doctrine of two sons.

Diodore (330–90) emphasized the distinction between the divine and human natures in Christ. While Diodore did not explicitly use the term "two sons," his writings suggested a view of Christ that risked being interpreted as separating the divine Logos from the human Jesus in a manner akin to two distinct persons. For Diodore, the divine Logos, the preexistent Word of God, and the human being, Jesus of Nazareth, were united in Christ, but this union was primarily moral and functional rather than ontological. He was deeply committed to safeguarding the full humanity of Christ, emphasizing that Jesus possessed a complete human soul, will, and body. This focus was a response to heresies like Apollinarianism, which denied the completeness of Christ's humanity. At the same time, Diodore underscored the transcendence and immutability of the divine Logos, asserting that God could not be subject to human suffering or limitation. This concern led him to draw sharp distinctions between the divine and human aspects of Christ's life and work.

In Diodore's Christology, the human Jesus is the subject of suffering, growth, and death, while the divine Logos remains impassible and unchanging. Although Diodore affirmed the unity of Christ, his language sometimes suggested a partnership between the Logos and the human Jesus, leading critics to perceive a duality akin to "two sons"—the divine Son of God and the human son of Mary. This interpretation became a point of contention in later Christological debates, with opponents arguing that such a framework jeopardized the unity of Christ's person and risked separating the Savior into two distinct subjects.

Diodore's "two sons" Christology was a precursor to the teachings of his student, Theodore of Mopsuestia (350–428), and the broader Antiochene tradition. While it sought to defend the integrity of both Christ's divinity and humanity, its perceived inadequacies in articulating their union fueled the controversies that culminated in the Nestorian schism. Critics from the Alexandrian school, including Cyril of Alexandria, condemned this approach, advocating instead for the doctrine of the *hypostatic union*, which affirmed the unity of Christ's person as a single subject embodying both divine and human natures.

Nestorius's education was profoundly shaped by Theodore, a towering figure in the Antiochene tradition, whose Christological framework left an enduring mark on his pupil. Theodore insisted on the full humanity of Christ, arguing that the divine Logos and the human Jesus were united in a moral or volitional union rather than a blending of essences. This emphasis on the distinct roles and attributes of Christ's two natures became a hallmark of Nestorius's own theology. For the Antiochenes, this distinction was critical to affirming both the completeness of Christ's human experience and the immutability of the divine Logos. By highlighting the full humanity of Christ, the Antiochene theologians sought to underscore the authenticity of his suffering, death, and redemptive work for humanity. Nestorius's formation extended beyond theological study to include monastic discipline and pastoral practice, both of which shaped his approach to ecclesiastical leadership. His years as a monk instilled in him a commitment to ascetic rigor and doctrinal purity, qualities that would define his tenure as patriarch of Constantinople beginning in 428.

He entered the clergy and eventually became a monk and presbyter in the monastery of Euprepius in Antioch. Eventually, in the year 428, he was appointed to the prestigious position of the patriarch of Constantinople, which was the leading bishop in the Eastern church.

During his tenure, Nestorius instigated a theological dispute regarding the nature of Christ. He insisted there was a strict separation between Christ's divine and human natures. His teachings incited considerable controversy and opposition within the Christian community, leading to several church councils to address the dispute. The controversial teachings were condemned as heresy in 431 by the Council of Ephesus. Consequently, Nestorius was removed from his position and exiled from Constantinople to a monastery in Egypt.

After his exile, Nestorius lived a life of relative obscurity, though he still defended his theological views and wrote treatises on various theological topics. He died sometime after 451, though the exact date and circumstances of his death are unknown. Despite being labeled as a heretic by the church, the teachings of Nestorius continued to influence subsequent theological developments, particularly in the Eastern Christian tradition.

Nestorian Christology

The Antiochene tradition of Diodore and Theodore shaped Nestorius's Christology. For example, his objection to the term *Theotokos* ("God-bearer") for the Virgin Mary was rooted in a concern to avoid confusion between Christ's human and divine natures. He preferred *Christotokos* ("Christ-bearer"), believing it better preserved the integrity of each nature within the person of Christ. While Nestorius's theological perspective was consistent with the Antiochene emphasis on maintaining the distinctiveness of Christ's natures, it clashed with the Alexandrian school, which prioritized the unity of Christ's person as expressed in the *hypostatic union*.

As we have noted, the Antiochene proclivity to distinguish the natures in Christ often led to separating them from one another. This was certainly the case with Nestorius, where he conceived of Christ as the juxtaposition (he used the Greek word *synapheia*) of two persons, not one person with two natures.

Consequently, Nestorius's theological background engendered a theoretical impulse to preserve the integrity of Christ's human nature and his reluctance to ascribe divine attributes or actions to Jesus's human nature. Despite the absolute distinction Nestorius drew between Christ's divine and human natures, he posited that the two natures were functionally united in a single person, Jesus Christ. The divine Logos, Nestorius maintained, operated through Jesus's human nature, which he assumed at the incarnation and which thus enabled him to perform miracles, to teach with divine authority, and to accomplish his saving work.

While Nestorius did not overtly teach that Jesus Christ was made up of two persons, his emphasis on Christ's dual natures (divine and human) gave rise to fears about the unity of Christ's person. Nestorianism's Christological proposal suggested that Christ was composed of two distinct persons—one divine person (the Logos) and one human person (Jesus of Nazareth). By denying a single subject to whom all actions, sayings, and experiences of Jesus would be attributed, namely, the eternal Son, Nestorius divided the subject into two.

One of the pivotal controversies in Nestorius's Christology revolved around his repudiation of the term *Theotokos* ("bearer of God") used for Mary, the mother of Jesus, in favor of *Christotokos* ("bearer of Christ"). Christians had used the title *Theotokos* for Mary to emphasize the reality of the true incarnation of God in Christ. Because Jesus is God and Mary is the one who gave birth to him, then she should be called the bearer of God. Christians did not use this term to imply that Mary was the origin of the Godhead, but to insist that the child born to Mary was indeed God. Nestorius rejected the term and this reasoning because he insisted that God was impassable, or not able to suffer human experiences, and therefore could not himself be born of a woman.

Third Ecumenical Council at Ephesus (431)

The primary opponent of Nestorian Christology at the Council of Ephesus was Cyril of Alexandria.

Cyril of Alexandria (c. 376–444) was a central figure in early Christian theology and the patriarch of Alexandria during one of the most turbulent periods in the church's history. His theological legacy is most prominently associated with his defense of the doctrine of the hypostatic union—the inseparable union of Christ's divine and human natures in one person (hypostasis). This doctrine became a cornerstone of orthodox Christology, shaped largely by Cyril's writings and his role in the Council of Ephesus in 431. Cyril's theological disputes with Nestorius, patriarch of Constantinople, revealed the depth of his commitment to preserving the unity of Christ's person as essential for the efficacy of salvation.

Central to Cyril's Christology is his *Third Letter to Nestorius*, which contains the twelve anathemas, a series of theological statements designed to refute Nestorius's teachings. These anathemas articulate Cyril's understanding of the hypostatic union with remarkable clarity. The first anathema affirms that the Virgin Mary must be called *Theotokos* because she gave birth not merely to a human being but to the incarnate Word of God. This term safeguards the belief that the divine Logos and the human nature of Christ are united from the moment of conception, ensuring that Mary bore the one person of Christ. The second and third anathemas further reject any separation or division between Christ's divine and human natures, emphasizing that the divine Logos did not merely dwell in a human being as in a temple, but rather fully assumed human nature into his own person.

The hypostatic union, as articulated by Cyril, rejects any notion of two persons within Christ. The term "hypostatic" comes from the Greek word *hypostasis*, which means "person." Cyril taught that the two natures of Christ were united to the one person of the Son or Logos of God. He insisted on the unity of Christ's divine and human natures in one undivided person. This unity means that all actions and experiences of Christ—whether divine, such as performing miracles, or human, such as suffering and dying—are attributable to the one person of the Logos. The fifth anathema, for instance, directly addresses this by condemning the suggestion that the actions or experiences of Christ could be divided between the divine and human natures as though they were separate subjects. For Cyril, the divine Logos suffered in the flesh, not as a passive observer, but as God incarnate. This profound unity ensures that Christ's redemptive work is efficacious because it is both divine in authority and fully human in solidarity with humanity.

The council ultimately condemned Nestorius's teachings as heretical and affirmed the orthodox position in Christology, affirming the title *Theotokos* to honor Mary the mother of Jesus. Honoring her with this title reinforced the complete divinity of Jesus Christ. The council deposed Nestorius as patriarch of Constantinople and anathematized his teachings. The council's decision established the orthodox understanding of Christ's personhood and Mary's role in salvation. The so-called Nestorian controversy became the single most important issue of Christology in the early centuries, and Cyril's writing against Nestorius became the foundation of the council's theology.

Cyril's significant theological works include *On the Unity of Christ* and *That Christ Is One*. These texts offer insights into Cyril's doctrine of the hypostatic union. They address the theological debates of Cyril's time, particularly his opposition to Nestorianism, which proposed a problematic separation between Christ's divine and human natures. Central to both works is Cyril's insistence on the unity of Christ as one person (hypostasis) in whom divinity and humanity are inseparably joined. In *On the Unity of Christ*, Cyril asserts that Christ is "one, and not two, even though He is understood as having united two natures in Himself."[1] This statement encapsulates his core argument: While the divine and human natures remain distinct, they coexist without confusion, change, division, or separation, forming a single, unified person. Cyril further clarifies that the Word (Logos) did not merely dwell in a human being but fully assumed humanity into himself, stating, "The Word, being God, was made man, and not merely appeared as man."[2] This theological claim rejects any notion that Christ's humanity was an illusion or that his divinity was diminished in the incarnation.

In *That Christ Is One*, Cyril builds on these principles by emphasizing the indivisibility of Christ's person. This is particularly important regarding worship, for example. Cyril strongly opposes any suggestion that Christ's humanity and divinity could be worshiped separately as though the divine nature and the human nature are actually two persons. The indivisibility of the natures into two persons underscores Cyril's position that all actions and experiences of Christ—whether human or divine—belong to one person, the Logos. He further affirms the life-giving nature of Christ's flesh, asserting that it derives its salvific power from its union with the divine Word. Cyril believed that the hypostatic union

---

[1] Cyril of Alexandria, *On the Unity of Christ*, trans. John Anthony McGuckin (St. Vladimir's Seminary Press, 1995), 77.

[2] Cyril of Alexandria, *On the Unity of Christ*, 77.

is central to the efficacy of salvation, ensuring that Christ's human suffering and death are redemptive precisely because they belong to the divine person of the Logos.

Throughout these works, Cyril emphasizes the balance between unity and distinction in Christ's natures. He acknowledges that the natures are distinct, but emphasizes the importance of maintaining their perfect union. The two natures both belong to the one Person of the Eternal Son. Jesus Christ is the union of these natures. Cyril safeguards against the dualistic tendencies of Nestorianism and the monophysite confusion that would later arise. Cyril's incarnational theology highlights the transformative nature of the Word's assumption of humanity, making Christ the perfect mediator who bridges the divine and human.

He also penned commentaries on nearly every book in the Bible. His commentaries represent a significant contribution to the exegetical tradition of the early church, reflecting his theological depth and pastoral concern. His works, including commentaries on the Gospels of Luke and John, the Pentateuch, and the Minor Prophets, reveal a Christocentric hermeneutic deeply rooted in the Alexandrian tradition. Cyril approached Scripture as a unified revelation of Christ, interpreting both the Old and New Testaments through the lens of the incarnation and the salvific work of Jesus. For Cyril, the typological and allegorical meanings of Scripture often pointed toward the mystery of Christ, while he also valued the literal sense as foundational for theological reflection.

In his *Commentary on the Gospel of John*, Cyril emphasizes the divinity of Christ as revealed through the text. Reflecting on John 1:14, he argues that the incarnation involved the Eternal Son of God taking on humanity while not abandoning his divine nature. The reason for the incarnation is just as important: the Son became flesh in order to redeem the flesh. This statement encapsulates his theological approach to Scripture, wherein the events and teachings of Christ are understood as the fulfillment of God's salvific plan.

Cyril's commentaries on the Old Testament are no less significant, as he interprets the Hebrew Scriptures as bearing witness to Christ. In his commentary on Isaiah, he reflects on Isa 7:14, the prophecy of the virgin birth, declaring, "The sign of Emmanuel reveals the mystery of God dwelling with humanity. Through this child, the light of salvation dawns for the nations."[3] Here, Cyril's typological method connects the prophetic text to the incarnation, underscoring the unity of Scripture's message.

---

[3] Cyril of Alexandria, *Commentary on Isaiah*, vol. I, chaps. 1–14, trans. Robert Charles Hill (Holy Cross Orthodox Press, 2008), 115.

Cyril's hermeneutic is deeply theological, seeking to uncover the spiritual realities embedded in the text while maintaining fidelity to its literal and historical sense. He integrates Christology, soteriology, and trinitarian theology into his exegetical work, always aiming to illuminate the role of Christ as the fulfillment of God's promises. His commentaries reflect a pastoral concern to guide the faithful in understanding Scripture as a living revelation, central to the life of the church. Cyril's exegetical legacy exemplifies a method that unites rigorous theological inquiry with a deep devotion to the mystery of Christ revealed in Scripture.

The Council of Chalcedon (451)

Nestorius's insistence on separating Christ's natures led to his condemnation at the Council of Ephesus in 431, where Cyril successfully defended the unity of Christ's person. However, the rivalry between Alexandria and Constantinople, as well as tensions with other theological traditions, ensured that the Christological disputes were far from settled.

After Cyril's death in 444, his successor, Dioscorus of Alexandria, adopted a more aggressive stance, seeking to assert Alexandrian dominance over theological matters. Dioscorus allied himself with Eutyches, an archimandrite in Constantinople, who advocated for monophysitism—the belief that after the incarnation, Christ had only one nature, as his humanity was absorbed into his divinity. This doctrine directly opposed the Antiochene tradition, which stressed the distinction between Christ's two natures. When Flavian, patriarch of Constantinople, condemned Eutyches at a synod in 448, Dioscorus convened the Second Council of Ephesus in 449 to counter this decision. Known as the "Robber Synod" due to its irregular procedures and use of violence, this gathering reinstated Eutyches, condemned Flavian, and deposed bishops who opposed the Alexandrian position. Flavian's death shortly after his deposition, likely from injuries sustained during the council, further inflamed tensions, turning him into a martyr figure for opponents of monophysitism.

The theological chaos of the "Robber Synod" coincided with significant political changes in the Eastern Roman Empire. Emperor Theodosius II, who had supported the decisions of the 449 council, died unexpectedly in 450. His sister Pulcheria (399–453), a staunch defender of Nicene orthodoxy and an opponent of Dioscorus's faction, ascended to power alongside her husband, the new emperor Marcian (450–57). Pulcheria and Marcian were determined to restore ecclesiastical unity and orthodoxy, and they called for a new ecumenical council to resolve the Christological controversies. Pulcheria's influence ensured that this council would favor the Roman church's position and counter the Alexandrian dominance exemplified by Dioscorus.

A critical element at the Council of Chalcedon was the *Tome of Leo*, a letter written by Pope Leo I to Flavian of Constantinople in 449. The *Tome* articulated a clear and balanced Christological framework, affirming that Christ possessed two natures—divine and human—united in one person (hypostasis) without confusion, change, division, or separation. The *Tome* emphasized that Christ's human experiences, such as suffering and death, were real and that they occurred in the context of his fully divine person. By affirming both the integrity of Christ's humanity and the unity of his person, Leo addressed the extremes of Nestorianism, which overemphasized the distinction of natures, and Eutychian monophysitism, which conflated them.

The Definition of Chalcedon

Rather than an expansion of the Nicene Creed, the bishops instead offered a definition in which they affirmed Nicaea while also clarifying the Christian understanding of Christ. The Definition of Chalcedon affirmed the orthodox understanding of the two natures of Christ, declaring with Nicaea that Christ is "true God and true man." It further clarified that this means Christ possesses two distinct natures—divine and human—united in one person. This union of natures is qualified by the "four Chalcedonian adverbs." The two natures are united "without confusion, without change, without division, and without separation." This description of the union of natures in the one person of Christ upheld the hypostatic union, affirming that Christ's divine and human natures coexist perfectly within his personhood. By affirming the hypostatic union, the definition provided a doctrinal framework that reconciled the apparent paradox of Christ's dual nature. It safeguarded orthodox Christology against the heresies of Nestorianism and monophysitism. Nestorianism divided the two natures in Christ so that the divine actions of Christ and the human actions of Christ are separated from one another. By denying the hypostatic union, the Nestorians rejected the assumption of the human nature by the eternal Son of God for salvation. Monophysitism denied the hypostatic union by fusing the two natures into just one nature. This fusion of the natures obliterated the distinction necessary for both the divine nature and the human nature to remain intact. An analogy of monophysite theology is mixing a gallon of white paint with a gallon of black paint. The resultant mixture is neither black nor white, but gray. A mixture is a third thing formed from two constituent elements, but not actually either of them. In orthodox Christology, the two natures of Jesus remain intact. Jesus is fully God and fully human. For monophysitism, Jesus is neither God nor human, but a new, in-between kind of being. The definition also rejected Apollinarianism. As we have seen, Apollinarius taught that the human nature of Jesus was diminished, lacking a human soul or mind. Orthodox theology held that the human nature needed to be complete because of Gregory of Nazianzus's famous statement, "What is not assumed is not redeemed." Any diminishing of the human nature would produce a Christ who is less than fully human, imperiling the salvation of humanity.

The response to the Definition of Chalcedon varied among different segments of the Christian population and regions of the empire. Overall, the response was mixed, with some embracing the definition as a triumph of orthodoxy and others rejecting it, leading to subsequent theological and ecclesiastical divisions. There was widespread disagreement with the definition in many churches, stemming from its attempt to balance competing theological traditions, a compromise that left significant groups dissatisfied. The council's Christological formula declared that Christ exists in two natures—divine and human—united in one person (hypostasis) "without confusion, change, division, or separation." With these "Chalcedonian Adverbs," the theologians at the council sought to address the extremes of Nestorianism and monophysitism, it was perceived differently by various factions. For adherents of the Alexandrian theological tradition, which emphasized the unity of Christ's person, the Chalcedonian Definition appeared to lean too heavily toward Antiochene Christology, which stressed the distinction between Christ's natures. Many in this camp feared that the language of "two natures" compromised the unity of Christ that Cyril of Alexandria had defended, particularly his use of the phrase *mia physis* (one nature) to describe the incarnate Word. These concerns were exacerbated by the deposition of Dioscorus, the patriarch of Alexandria and a prominent defender of Cyril's theology, which many saw as an attack on Alexandrian influence within the church.

This dissatisfaction was particularly pronounced in Egypt, Syria, and Armenia, where opposition to Chalcedon led to the formation of what would later be known as the Oriental Orthodox Churches. These communities adhered to a Christological position often termed "miaphysitism," a nuanced theological stance affirming that Christ has one united nature (*mia physis*) that is both fully divine and fully human. Miaphysitism sought to uphold the unity of Christ's person while rejecting both the Nestorian separation of natures and the monophysite absorption of humanity into divinity. For these churches, the Chalcedonian emphasis on "two natures" was seen as a betrayal of Cyril's legacy and a potential concession to Nestorianism. The Oriental Orthodox Churches, including the Coptic Church in Egypt, the Syriac Orthodox Church, and the Armenian Apostolic Church, rejected Chalcedon's definition outright and developed distinct ecclesiastical structures that separated them from the Chalcedonian church.

The schism was not purely theological but also deeply influenced by cultural, political, and regional dynamics. The Alexandrian patriarchate, which had long been a center of theological authority, saw Chalcedon as an imperial imposition that diminished its influence in favor of Constantinople and Rome. The council's recognition of Constantinople as the second ranking see, following Rome, added to the sense of marginalization among Alexandrian clergy and their allies. Moreover, the council's decisions were enforced by imperial authority under Emperor Marcian and Empress Pulcheria, creating resistance in regions like Egypt and Syria, where local Christian traditions often viewed Constantinople's policies with suspicion. These tensions were exacerbated by the deposition of Dioscorus, which many in the Alexandrian tradition interpreted as an affront to their theological heritage and autonomy.

The Oriental Orthodox Churches emerged as vibrant Christian communities that retained their distinct Christological positions while maintaining their liturgical and cultural traditions. The Coptic Church in Egypt, for example, became a symbol of resistance to Byzantine influence, intertwining its religious identity with national and cultural pride. Similarly, the Armenian Apostolic Church and the Syriac Orthodox Church maintained their theological independence, preserving their interpretations of Cyril's teachings and rejecting the Chalcedonian Definition as incompatible with their Christological convictions. Despite their separation from the Chalcedonian church, the Oriental Orthodox Churches continued to thrive, playing significant roles in the spiritual and cultural life of their respective regions.

In addition to the theological and regional dimensions, pastoral concerns also contributed to the widespread disagreement about Chalcedon. The council's definition, while precise and intellectually rigorous, was difficult for many lay Christians and clergy to understand. The nuanced distinction between "without confusion" (rejecting monophysitism) and "without division" (rejecting Nestorianism) was not easily communicated, leading to misunderstandings and resistance among those who perceived the definition as overly philosophical or as diluting the mystery of Christ's unity. For many, the Chalcedonian language of "two natures" seemed incompatible with the more accessible and traditional expressions of faith rooted in Cyril's Christology.

The disagreements over Chalcedon ultimately led to one of the most enduring schisms in Christian history, as the Oriental Orthodox Churches formally separated from the Chalcedonian tradition. This division was not merely a theological matter but also reflected the political and cultural diversity of the Christian world. While Chalcedon sought to establish a unified doctrinal foundation for the church, its decisions highlighted the challenges of reconciling deeply entrenched theological, regional, and political differences, shaping the landscape of Christianity for centuries to come.

Severus of Antioch

Severus of Antioch (c. 465–538), also known as Severus the Great, assumed a position of prominence and leadership as a monophysite in the Eastern church. He was an erudite theologian and monk, ordained patriarch of Antioch in 512, who went on to shape the theology of his times. Severus was ardent in his opposition to the Chalcedonian Definition and a vociferous defender of monophysitism. Against the Chalcedonian doctrine of two natures in one person, Severus held that Christ's two natures were united into one nature. His numerous theological writings, including letters, treatises, and commentaries, form an articulate statement of monophysite theology, which found a popular audience among the dissident communities.

During the monophysite controversy of the sixth century, Severus encountered opposition from Chalcedonian authorities, which included the Byzantine emperors and various bishops who upheld the Chalcedonian Definition and regarded monophysitism as a heretical departure from orthodox Christology. They sought to contain and suppress its spread by imperial edicts, conciliar decisions, and theological debates and confrontations. In addition, his own church had until recently been the stronghold of Chalcedonian orthodoxy. The Antiochene clergy and their bishops were divided into two camps: those who affirmed Chalcedon and those who rejected it. Severus tenaciously propounded monophysitism, however much it shaped the theological discourse of his time.

One of Severus's central affirmations is an adherance to Cyril's formulation of the *mia physis* (one nature) of the incarnate Word, emphasizing that the two natures—divine and human—are united in a single, indivisible Person. Severus further clarifies this unity in his *Letter to Sergius*, where he argues that the natures of Christ are not confused or mingled together, but remain in an unbroken union. His defense of the integrity of Christ's natures within their unity reflects Severus's theological precision and his commitment to the miaphysite tradition.

Severus also rejected what he viewed as the dyophysite implications of Chalcedon, arguing that its language of "two natures" risked dividing Christ into two separate subjects. Any division of the two natures is Nestoriansim. For Severus, any suggestion of post-union duality was tantamount to heresy, as it undermined the soteriological significance of the incarnation, where the divine and human are united for the redemption of humanity.

Sergius the Monophysite (years unknown) was a monophysite monk who corresponded with Severus of Antioch between 512 and 518. Their exchanges were part of the unfolding response to and defense of monophysite doctrine amidst theological controversies and ecclesiastical struggles in the Eastern church. The letters between Sergius and Severus reflect the continued theological tensions and ecclesiastical divisions in the wake of the Council of Chalcedon (451). The monophysite controversy, focused as it was on the nature of Christ's person, was still very much alive in the theological discussions of the Eastern church, particularly in areas where Alexandrian Christology held sway. Forwarding monophysite beliefs from what was most likely Egypt or Syria, Sergius sought to draw the leading figure of the monophysite camp, Severus of Antioch, into an ecclesiastical and theological dialogue.

In their letters, Sergius and Severus work through several themes, including the nature of Christ's incarnation, the relation of his divine and human natures, and monophysite doctrine's soteriological and redemptive implications. Sergius's correspondence was likely an attempt to gain a precise understanding of where Severus stood on many monophysite tenets, while Severus's letters elucidated and defended the teachings of that camp against their Chalcedonian opponents.

In response to the ongoing controversy, the Byzantine emperors sought to restore church unity. These imperial interventions, motivated by both political concerns and a desire for religious uniformity, included calling ecumenical councils, issuing edicts, and using coercive methods to enforce theological orthodoxy and suppress non-Chalcedonian dissent. While the emperors strove to promote Chalcedonian orthodoxy and eliminate monophysite dissent from imperial territories, these actions often exacerbated church tensions and deepened the divide. Monophysite sects, persecuted as heretics, resisted imperial intrusion and even thrived in other regions where they could practice without imperial coercion.

Filioque Controversy and the Western Addition to the Nicene Creed

The monophysite controversy was not the only struggle faced during this time period. The Filioque controversy is a theological dispute regarding the addition of the phrase "and the Son," or *Filioque*, in the Nicene Creed. The original Nicene Creed, adopted at the First Council of Nicaea in 325, had the third article as "I believe in the Holy Spirit, the Lord and Giver of Life, who proceeds from the Father."

During the early Middle Ages, in regions of Western Europe where Latin was the standard, the Western church—the Roman Catholic Church—began to insert the phrase *Filioque* into the Nicene Creed, seemingly as an attempt to clarify their understanding of the Spirit's procession from the Father and Son. The phrase first appeared in Spain and Gaul in the sixth century. The church in the Byzantine Empire, which used Greek, adhered strictly to the original wording of the Nicene Creed without the phrase "and from the Son"—that is, without *Filioque*. The *Filioque* altered their understanding of the inner-trinitarian relationship of the Holy Spirit to Father and Son, implying that the Holy Spirit proceeds from both the Father and the Son, not from only the Father. This controversy questioned the understanding of the nature of the Holy Trinity, the relationship between the divine persons, and the authority to change the wording of an ecumenical creed.

The controversy would remain a sore spot between these two churches for centuries as the wound grew more extensive in the growing estrangement between the churches. Efforts at reconciliation and talks would continue throughout the centuries without any final resolutions. The Great Schism of 1054, which will be covered in chapter 18, refers to when the Eastern church and the Roman Catholic Church formally divided. There are several cultural and theological reasons for the split. Among them was the addition of *Filioque*.

The Churches in the West and the East

The relationship between church and state in the Eastern and Western Roman Empires was complex and evolving for political, cultural, and faith-based reasons. Church and state were tightly intertwined, with the ruling authorities wielding power over matters of faith and the church influencing political happenings. In the fourth century, the great Constantinian churches in Rome and Constantinople were designed with special doors so the emperor could avoid the common throng and have more immediate access to his praying bishops. In both ancient churches, the city's bishop came to have a religious and a partially political role in government, with realist authority over the surrounding countryside. This relational hierarchy in the ancient church reflected the organizational structure of the government. Likewise, this hierarchical organization mirrored the administrative structure of the imperial government, facilitating cooperation and coordination between church and state.

In the Eastern Roman Empire (also called the Byzantine Empire), the bishops had considerable independence and power; the emperor often sought their approval and counsel. The patriarchs of Constantinople were important imperial figures. The church assumed reign once the Western Roman Empire dissolved, and internal strife or war had rendered more or less of it leaderless. The bishop of Rome, also called the pope in the Western church, increasingly claimed "primacy" over all other bishops and spiritual authority over the entire Christian world, culminating in the claims of ultimate authority over churches by Gregory the Great from 596 onward. Another difference was that different sets of laws often governed the church and state in the Greek-speaking Roman world, the former enjoying considerable legal autonomy. In the Latin-speaking Roman world, particularly in the reign of Emperor Justinian, Roman law was often recodified and sought to encompass at least ecclesiastical law.

Figures such as Emperor Constantine the Great, Emperor Justinian I, and Patriarch Photius of Constantinople all played important roles in shaping the church-state relationship in the Byzantine Empire. Emperor Justinian I (c. 482–565), often referred to as Justinian the Great, ruled as Byzantine Emperor from 527 to 565. Justinian funded the construction of the Hagia Sophia, one of the most outstanding architectural achievements of the Byzantine Empire and a symbol of Orthodox Christianity. Byzantine architecture reflected the empire's fusion of Eastern and Western influences, with churches serving as architectural expressions of theology and worship. The Hagia Sophia in Constantinople exemplifies Byzantine architectural innovation. Its vast dome, intricate mosaics, and soaring interior spaces symbolize the heavenly Jerusalem and the majesty of God's presence. Byzantine churches were designed to facilitate liturgical worship, with centralized plans, elaborate domes, and apses facing eastward toward the rising sun, symbolizing the resurrection of Christ and the promise of eternal life. Justinian also played a role in the Three Chapters Controversy, in which he sought to reconcile theological differences between Eastern and Western Christians.

The Three Chapters Controversy

The Three Chapters Controversy was a theological and political dispute in the sixth century arising from efforts to reconcile Chalcedonian and non-Chalcedonian Christians. Following the Council of Chalcedon, churches that refused to accept the Definition of Chalcedon but rejected Nestorianism separated from the Chalcedonian churches. An effort was made to reconcile these churches to one another by condemning the works of three theologians associated with Nestorianism: the writings of Theodore of Mopsuestia, which were foundational to Nestorian thought; the writings of Theodoret of Cyrrhus, particularly his critiques of Cyril of Alexandria and the Council of Ephesus (431); and a letter by Ibas of Edessa defending Theodore and criticizing Cyril. The controversy was rooted in the aftermath of the Council of Chalcedon (451), which defined Christ as having two natures—divine and human—united in one person. While many upheld this doctrine, non-Chalcedonian Christians rejected it, viewing it as overly sympathetic to Nestorianism.

In 544, the Byzantine emperor Justinian I sought to address these divisions by issuing an edict condemning the Three Chapters, hoping to appease non-Chalcedonian Christians and strengthen imperial unity. However, this move sparked widespread opposition, particularly among Chalcedonian Christians, who saw it as undermining the authority of Chalcedon. The Second Council of Constantinople (553) was convened to resolve the issue, formally condemning the Three Chapters while reaffirming Chalcedonian orthodoxy. Although the council aimed to bridge the theological divide, it exacerbated tensions between the Eastern and Western churches. Pope Vigilius initially resisted the condemnation but eventually capitulated under imperial pressure, leading to widespread dissatisfaction among Western bishops. In regions such as northern Italy and North Africa, resistance persisted for decades, resulting in a prolonged schism known as the Schism of the Three Chapters.

This controversy underscored the challenges of maintaining doctrinal unity in the face of theological disputes and political pressures. While the condemnation was largely accepted in the Byzantine East, it deepened divisions with the West and highlighted the complex relationship between imperial authority and ecclesiastical independence.

Conclusion

Theological controversy did not end with the Councils of Nicaea and Constantinople. The Christological controversies of the fifth and sixth centuries further refined doctrinal development but also caused division within the churches of the Eastern and Western empires and between the empires themselves. Further theological and ecclesiastical division would come.

Recommended Reading

Allen, Pauline. *Cyril of Alexandria*. Routledge, 2000.

Beeley, Christopher A. *The Unity of Christ: Continuity and Conflict in Patristic Tradition*. Yale University Press, 2012.

Burgess, R. W., ed. *The Chronicle of Hydatius and the Consularia Constantinopolitana*. Oxford University Press, 1993.

Chadwick, Henry. *The Church in Ancient Society: From Galilee to Gregory the Great*. Oxford University Press, 2001.

Davis, Leo Donald. *The First Seven Ecumenical Councils (325–787): Their History and Theology*. Liturgical Press, 1990.

Fairbairn, Donald. *Grace and Christology in the Early Church*. Oxford University Press, 2003.

Frend, W. H. C. *The Rise of Christianity*. Fortress, 1984.

Grillmeier, Aloys. *Christ in Christian Tradition*. Vol. 1, *From the Apostolic Age to Chalcedon (451)*. Translated by John Bowden. 2nd ed. John Knox Press, 1975.

Gwynn, David M. *The Eusebians: The Polemic of Athanasius of Alexandria and the Construction of the 'Arian Controversy.'* Oxford University Press, 2007.

Kelly, J. N. D. *Early Christian Doctrines*. 5th ed. HarperOne, 1978.

Loon, Hans van. *The Dyophysite Christology of Cyril of Alexandria*. Brill, 2009.

McGuckin, John Anthony. *Saint Cyril of Alexandria and the Christological Controversy: Its History, Theology, and Texts*. St. Vladimir's Seminary Press, 2004.

McKinion, Steven A. *Words, Imagery, and the Mystery of Christ: A Reconstruction of Cyril of Alexandria's Christology*. Supplements to Vigiliae Christianae 55. Brill, 2000.

Pelikan, Jaroslav. *The Christian Tradition: A History of the Development of Doctrine*. Vol. 1, *The Emergence of the Catholic Tradition (100–600)*. University of Chicago Press, 1971.

Russell, Norman. *Theophilus of Alexandria*. Routledge, 2007.

Sellers, R. V. *The Council of Chalcedon: A Historical and Doctrinal Survey*. SPCK, 1953.

Weinandy, Thomas G. *The Theology of St. Cyril of Alexandria: A Critical Appreciation*. T&T Clark, 2003.

Wessel, Susan. *Cyril of Alexandria and the Nestorian Controversy: The Making of a Saint and of a Heretic*. Oxford University Press, 2004.

Wilken, Robert Louis. *The Spirit of Early Christian Thought: Seeking the Face of God.* Yale University Press, 2003.

Young, Frances M. *From Nicaea to Chalcedon: A Guide to the Literature and Its Background.* 2nd ed. Baker Academic, 2010.

Zachhuber, Johannes. *Human Nature in Gregory of Nyssa: Philosophical Background and Theological Significance.* Brill, 2000.

—— Chapter 10 ——

Ancient Christianity in Practice

As we have seen, the relationship between the church and the Roman Empire became increasingly intertwined in the fourth century. Emperors such as Constantine and his successors sought to use Christianity as a unifying force within the empire, leading to the imperial government's adoption of Christian symbols and practices. However, this alliance also raised questions about the proper role of the church concerning secular power and the potential for corruption within the church hierarchy. Christianity emerged from persecution to become the dominant religion of the Roman Empire. During times of marginalization and persecution in the first three centuries, Christians had framed their practice of the faith in contrast to the world, which rejected the truth of Christianity. Christians suffered during those centuries and could consider themselves citizens of a higher, heavenly kingdom under the rule and reign of Jesus Christ their Lord. With Christianity's acceptance in the empire and the subsequent benevolence of Roman emperors, that framing no longer fit. Christians were not a marginalized and persecuted people who suffered at the hand of their enemies while awaiting the return of Jesus and escape from the world. Christians now had a place in the world, funded and supported by the emperor no less. They needed a way of understanding the history of the church that made sense of this new context for living their faith. Eusebius of Caesarea, whose importance has already been noted previously, provided that interpretation for them.

Eusebius was born around 260 in Caesarea Maritima, a city in Roman Palestine (modern-day Israel). Eusebius became a Christian at a young age and studied with Pamphilus, a Christian presbyter and martyr renowned for his piety, learning, and devotion to the Christian faith. Origen of Alexandria also played a prominent role in his Christian journey.

Eusebius actively participated in the life of the Christian community in Caesarea, teaching the Bible and writing theological texts, such as his *Apology for Origen* and *Preparation for the Gospel*. His dedication to the Christian cause and his leadership qualities did not go unnoticed by his contemporaries. Eusebius gradually rose to prominence within the church hierarchy, serving in various capacities and gaining the trust and support of his fellow clergy and the broader Christian community. His theological knowledge, administrative skills, and commitment to the Christian faith marked him as a suitable candidate for higher ecclesiastical office, and following the death or resignation of his predecessor, Eusebius was elected as bishop of Caesarea by the local clergy and congregation. His close association with influential figures in the Christian community and his support among the broader populace also aided his election. Eusebius was ordained as bishop of Caesarea around 313, succeeding Agapius. As bishop, he played a crucial role in the administration of the church in Palestine, was involved in ecclesiastical affairs and theological controversies, and promoted Christian education.

Upon assuming the episcopal office, Eusebius continued to serve the Christian community in Caesarea with diligence and devotion. As bishop, he played a prominent role in the administration of the church, the promotion of Christian education, and the defense of Nicene orthodoxy against theological heresies.

Eusebius is best known for his extensive historical writings, which played a crucial role in preserving the early history of Christianity. His most famous work is *Ecclesiastical History* (*Church History*), a comprehensive account of the development of Christianity from its origins to the early fourth century. In this work, Eusebius chronicles the spread of Christianity, the persecutions faced by Christians (which were discussed more extensively in chapter 2), the lives of prominent Christian figures, and the theological controversies of his time. The *Ecclesiastical History* consists of ten books and covers the period from the time of Jesus Christ and the apostles to the reign of Emperor Constantine the Great. Eusebius chronicles the persecutions faced by Christians under various Roman emperors, including Nero, Domitian, Decius, and Diocletian. The work includes biographical sketches of prominent Christian figures, such as martyrs, bishops, and theologians, including Ignatius of Antioch, Polycarp of Smyrna, Origen, and Constantine the Great. Eusebius also discusses theological controversies of his time, such as the Arian controversy and the Council of Nicaea. The final books of *Ecclesiastical History* focus on the reign of Constantine and the establishment of Christianity as the Roman Empire's official religion.

> What I propose to describe are the successions of the holy apostles, and the times which have passed from that of our Savior to our own; what was done during them which affected the situation of the church.
>
> Eusebius of Caesarea, *Ecclesiastical History*

The *Ecclesiastical History* is one of the earliest and most comprehensive accounts of the early Christian church, providing valuable insights into its origins, development, and struggles. Eusebius preserved numerous documents, letters, and excerpts from earlier Christian writers that might otherwise have been lost, and his work serves as a primary source for many aspects of early Christianity. Eusebius wrote with a clear apologetic intent, aiming to defend and promote Christianity against its critics by showcasing its growth, endurance, and triumphs amidst persecution. The *Ecclesiastical History* influenced subsequent Christian historiography and theology by shaping later accounts of church history and contributing to developing Christian identity and memory. *Ecclesiastical History* served as both a foundational text and a methodological model for later historians. Written in the early fourth century, Eusebius's work was the first comprehensive effort to document the history of Christianity, tracing its development from its apostolic beginnings to his own time. He emphasized themes such as apostolic succession, the lives and martyrdoms of Christians, theological controversies, and the church's evolving relationship with the Roman Empire. This framework deeply shaped later historians, particularly those in the Byzantine tradition, who used Eusebius's work as both a source and a structural template. Authors like Socrates of Constantinople, Sozomen, and Theodoret of Cyrrhus adopted his approach, organizing their narratives around the succession of bishops and major theological events while incorporating new material relevant to their own contexts.

Eusebius's detailed accounts of Christian martyrdoms, drawn from earlier sources and his personal observations, became a model for later martyrologies and hagiographies, influencing how subsequent generations conceptualized the church's trials under persecution. His categorization of heresies and his portrayal of orthodoxy as historically continuous provided a lens through which later ecclesiastical historians framed theological disputes. Methodologically, Eusebius pioneered the integration of diverse sources, including letters, imperial edicts, and earlier histories, into a cohesive narrative. This approach set a precedent for how church history would be written, particularly in the use of documentary evidence to support theological arguments. Additionally, Eusebius blended sacred and secular history, contextualizing Christian developments within the broader Roman imperial framework and portraying Constantine as a divinely chosen ruler who ushered in a new era for the church. This integration profoundly influenced Byzantine historiography, which often presented the Christian empire as a continuation of divine providence.

Eusebius's apologetic agenda also resonated with later historians. His portrayal of Christianity as the culmination of divine providence and the true heir to classical civilization legitimized the faith in the eyes of both Christian and non-Christian audiences. His successors, such as Socrates, Sozomen, and Theodoret, extended his narrative into the post-Nicene era while maintaining his thematic and structural foundations. In the Latin-speaking West, Rufinus of Aquileia translated and adapted Eusebius's work, ensuring its transmission and influence in medieval historiography. Rufinus's adaptations later inspired figures such as Bede, whose *Ecclesiastical History of the English People* reflected Eusebius's emphasis on divine guidance in history.

Along with his historical writing, Eusebius participated in several important church councils, including the First Council of Nicaea in 325, where he played a prominent role as a defender of Nicene orthodoxy against Arianism. He was instrumental in drafting the Nicene Creed, which affirmed the divinity of Christ and condemned Arianism as heretical. Eusebius was one of the most prominent bishops from the East and held the prestigious position of bishop of Caesarea, a major city in the Roman province of Palestine. As a respected theologian and historian, both Eastern and Western bishops esteemed Eusebius for his scholarly contributions and deep understanding of Christian doctrine. Emperor Constantine appointed him one of the council's official delegates. During the council sessions, Eusebius actively participated in theological debates and discussions, advocating for a balanced position that affirmed the divinity of Christ while seeking to avoid extreme language or formulations. Eusebius's diplomatic skills and moderate stance helped facilitate dialogue between opposing factions and contributed to the crafting of the Nicene Creed. While Eusebius ultimately signed the Nicene Creed, he initially expressed some reservations about the term *homoousios* due to its philosophical implications, though he later accepted it as an orthodox formulation.

The Cappadocian Fathers

Of the many fourth-century theologians, the Cappadocians stand out as significant and influential. The Cappadocian Fathers, which is the collective name given to Basil of Caesarea, Gregory of Nazianzus, and Gregory of Nyssa, were instrumental in articulating and defending orthodox Christian doctrine, particularly regarding the Trinity and the divinity of Christ and the Holy Spirit. Their theological writings laid the foundation for much of Eastern Christian theology and contributed to the formation of the Nicene-Constantinopolitan Creed, which is still recited in liturgical worship today.

Basil of Caesarea, also known as Basil the Great, was born around 330 in Caesarea Mazaca, Cappadocia (modern-day Kayseri, Turkey). He hailed from a wealthy and influential family, and his parents, Basil the Elder and Emmelia, were devout Christians. Basil received an exceptional education in Athens, where he studied alongside fellow Cappadocian Gregory of Nazianzus. Upon returning to Caesarea, Basil embraced asceticism and dedicated himself to a life of piety and service. He became a monk and later founded a monastic community in Pontus, where he authored his monastic rule. Despite his initial reluctance, Basil was ordained as a priest by his friend Gregory of Nazianzus and later became bishop of Caesarea in 370.

Basil's ascetic ideals and monastic rule shaped the foundation of communal monastic life in Eastern Christianity. His *Rule of Saint Basil* provided guidelines for monastic communities, emphasizing communal living, prayer, and ascetic discipline. Basil also played a crucial role in defending orthodox Christian doctrine, particularly against Arianism. His theological writings, including *On the Holy Spirit*, contributed to the formulation of trinitarian theology and helped solidify the divinity of the Holy Spirit. Basil's compassion for the poor and marginalized led him to establish charitable institutions known as "Basiliads," which provided food, shelter, and medical care to those in need. Basil played a pivotal role in developing the Byzantine liturgy, influencing the structure and content of Eastern Christian worship.

> What makes us Christians? "Our faith," everyone would answer. How are we saved? Obviously through the regenerating grace of baptism. How else could we be? We are confirmed in our understanding that salvation comes through Father, Son, and Holy Spirit.
>
> ---
>
> Basil of Caesarea, *On the Holy Spirit*

Basil defended Nicene Christianity against the ongoing threat of Arianism, with his primary opponent in this controversy being

Eustathius of Sebaste. Eustathius (c. 300–377) was a semi-Arian, who denied that the Son of God was a created being but taught that he was subordinate to the Father. He opposed the Nicene Creed but also opposed the Arians. This theological conflict primarily revolved around doctrinal differences regarding the nature of the Trinity and the person of Christ. Basil adhered to Nicene orthodoxy, affirming the consubstantiality of the Son with the Father and the full divinity of the Holy Spirit. In contrast, Eustathius's theology exhibited shades of subordinationism, suggesting a hierarchical relationship within the Godhead. This theological variance caused tension between the two bishops, as Basil defended the Nicene doctrine against deviation.

The dispute also extended to Christology, particularly concerning the nature of Christ's divinity and humanity. Basil emphasized the orthodox understanding of Christ's hypostatic union—his being fully God and fully man—rejecting any notion of Christ's divinity being diminished or subordinate to the Father. Eustathius's Christological stance may have leaned toward positions considered heterodox or inadequate by Basil, further exacerbating their theological differences.

The theological conflict between Basil and Eustathius also had implications for ecclesiastical authority. As Bishop of Caesarea and a prominent figure in the Eastern church, Basil sought to uphold Nicene orthodoxy and maintain doctrinal purity within the church. Eustathius's theological deviations likely challenged Basil's efforts to safeguard the faith and promote doctrinal unity. The disagreement between Basil and Eustathius led to Eustathius's eventual deposition from his episcopal office.

Gregory of Nazianzus (329–390)

Gregory of Nazianzus (329–390), also known as Gregory the Theologian, was born in Nazianzus, Cappadocia (modern-day Turkey). He came from a devout Christian family and received an excellent education in rhetoric and philosophy. Gregory studied in Athens, where he became close friends with Basil of Caesarea and Julian the Apostate. Later, he pursued a life of asceticism and contemplation, eventually entering the priesthood. Along with Basil of Caesarea and Gregory of Nyssa, Gregory of Nazianzus is known as one of the Cappadocian Fathers. He played a crucial role in defending orthodox trinitarian doctrine against Arianism and contributed to formulating the Nicene Creed. Gregory's theological writings earned him the title "the Theologian." He composed numerous poems and hymns, including his famous *Carmina*, which express his theological and spiritual reflections in poetic form. Gregory's letters provide valuable insights into his pastoral concerns, theological discussions, and interactions with Basil of Caesarea.

Gregory reluctantly became bishop of Constantinople in 379, a position he did not seek or desire. His appointment was part of an attempt to reconcile the divided Christian community in the city, which had become deeply fractured by theological disputes. However, Gregory faced opposition from various factions within the church, mainly supporters of the Arian and Eunomian doctrines.

Gregory soon found himself involved in several theological controversies, especially concerning the doctrine of the Trinity and Christology. He faced conflicts with Arianism, Eunomianism, and Apollinarianism, writing and preaching against these heresies while also articulating the Nicene faith clearly for his congregation. Gregory encountered opposition from various quarters due to his Nicene orthodoxy and outspoken defense of trinitarian doctrine. His theological adversaries included Arian bishops and proponents of other heterodox views, such as Eunomius of Cyzicus and Apollinarius. Gregory also faced opposition from ecclesiastical and political authorities who sought to assert control over the church's affairs.

The conflict between Gregory of Nazianzus and Eunomius stemmed from their theological differences regarding the nature of God. Eunomius was a leading proponent of the Eunomian sect, which held to Arian views that diverged significantly from orthodox Nicene Christianity. Eunomius was a disciple of Aetius, who was a crucial figure in the Arian controversy, and his teachings centered on the belief that the Son (Christ) was created by God the Father and thus of a fundamentally different nature or substance from the Father. This stance contradicted the Nicene Creed, which affirmed the consubstantiality (*homoousios*) of the Son with the Father.

Gregory's five *Theological Orations* are not only theological, but are also pastoral and spiritual works, aimed at nurturing the faith and devotion of his audience. Gregory was acutely aware that theology is not merely an intellectual exercise; it is an act of worship and a means of drawing closer to God. His orations were delivered in the context of worship and intended to guide his listeners into a deeper understanding of divine mysteries that would transform their lives. For Gregory, theology served as a bridge between the mind and the heart, designed to inspire reverence, awe, and love for the triune God.

A central aspect of Gregory's pastoral approach is his emphasis on the limits of human understanding and the necessity of humility in the face of divine mystery. In the *Second*

Theological Oration, he cautions against speculative theology, stating, "Not every man is able to philosophize about God; not every man is able to speak well of Him. The subject is not so cheap and low as to be grasped by the majority."[1] This statement reflects Gregory's concern that theology, when approached arrogantly or carelessly, can lead to error and harm rather than edification. For Gregory, a proper engagement with theology begins with a posture of humility, recognizing that God's essence is ultimately beyond human comprehension. This humility is not a barrier to faith but a pathway to awe and worship. He urges his listeners to pursue a life of holiness, arguing that only a purified heart and mind can engage in the contemplation of divine truths.

Gregory's theology is also profoundly spiritual, aiming to lead believers into an intimate relationship with the triune God. He contends that theology is not an abstract discipline but a transformative experience, where the believer is drawn into deeper communion with God. Gregory insists that theological reflection must always lead to greater love for God and neighbor, integrating intellectual understanding with the practical outworking of faith in daily life.

The pastoral dimension of Gregory's orations is perhaps most evident in his reflections on the incarnation. In the *Fifth Theological Oration*, he articulates the redemptive purpose of Christ's assumption of human nature, emphasizing Christ's full assumption of humanity to underscore his pastoral concern for the salvation and healing of the believer. By highlighting that Christ's work restores the entirety of human nature, Gregory assures his audience of the comprehensiveness of God's saving grace. He encourages believers to find solace and hope in the incarnation, which demonstrates God's profound love and solidarity with humanity.

Moreover, Gregory's orations are saturated with a sense of wonder and devotion, inviting his listeners to share in his worshipful contemplation of God. In the *Third Theological Oration*, he declares, "I cannot begin to think of the One without being illumined by the splendor of the Three; nor can I discern the Three without being carried back to the One."[2] This poetic expression captures Gregory's awe before the mystery of the Trinity, which he presents not merely as a theological concept but as the heart of Christian worship. His

---

[1] Gregory of Nazianzus, *Oration 27.3*, in *On God and Christ: The Five Theological Orations and Two Letters to Cledonius*, trans. Frederick Williams and Lionel Wickham, *Popular Patristics Series* 23 (St. Vladimir's Seminary Press, 2002), 27.

[2] Gregory of Nazianzus, *Oration 40.41*, in *On God and Christ*, 132.

words encourage believers to marvel at the beauty and unity of the Godhead, inspiring both intellectual reflection and heartfelt adoration.

Ultimately, Gregory's *Theological Orations* serve a dual purpose: to defend orthodoxy and to lead his audience into a deeper experience of God. His insistence on the necessity of holiness, humility, and worship as prerequisites for theological inquiry demonstrates his pastoral care for the spiritual well-being of his listeners. By combining rigorous theological argumentation with an emphasis on the transformative power of divine truth, Gregory offers a vision of theology that is not only intellectually compelling but also spiritually enriching, drawing believers closer to the mystery and majesty of God.

The Great Tradition is both theological and liturgical, involving the worship of God in mind and in soul.

Gregory of Nyssa (c. 335–395)

Gregory of Nyssa was born around 335 in Neocaesarea, Cappadocia (modern-day Turkey), into a devout Christian family. Gregory's older brother was Basil of Caesarea, and his sister, Macrina the Younger, was a prominent ascetic and theologian. Like his brother, Gregory received an excellent education, studying rhetoric, philosophy, and theology. Despite initially intending to pursue a career in law, Gregory's life took a different turn after experiencing a spiritual awakening. He was ordained a presbyter around 362 and became bishop of Nyssa in 372, a position he held until he died in 395. Gregory of Nazianzus and Basil greatly influenced Gregory's theology, and alongside them, he played a crucial role in defending orthodoxy against various heresies, particularly Arianism and Eunomianism.

Gregory of Nyssa's work *There Are Not Three Gods* is a text that addresses the doctrine of the Trinity, particularly in response to the charge of tritheism leveled against Christians by their opponents. In this writing, Gregory argues for the unity of the Godhead while affirming the distinctiveness of the three persons: the Father, the Son, and the Holy Spirit. Gregory begins by acknowledging the challenge of articulating the mystery of the Trinity in human language. He emphasizes the importance of preserving unity and diversity within the Godhead, avoiding the extremes of modalism (which collapses the distinctions between the persons) and tritheism (which asserts three separate gods). Central to Gregory's argument is the concept of perichoresis, or mutual indwelling, within the Trinity. He contends that the three persons of the Trinity share a single divine essence and are inseparably united in their actions and operations. Despite their distinct roles in salvation history, they are ontologically inseparable and eternally coexist in perfect harmony. Gregory employs various analogies to illustrate the relationship between the Father, Son, and Holy Spirit, such as the sun, light, and heat. While distinct, they are inseparable and share the same nature. He also draws on the example of human nature, where the unity of essence does not negate the diversity of persons.

Gregory's other works include his *Great Catechism*, an extensive work intended to instruct new Christians as they prepared for their baptism. It is an introduction to the fundamentals of Christian doctrine. He also wrote *On the Soul and the Resurrection*, which explores the nature of the human soul and its destiny after death. *The Life of Moses*, which presents Moses as a model of the spiritual journey and contemplative ascent toward union with God, serves as an instructional text on living the Christian life. Gregory draws spiritual lessons from the events of Moses's life, interpreting them as symbols of the soul's progression toward divine illumination. Another theological treatise, *On the Making of Man*, explores the creation and nature of humanity as described in the book of Genesis. He reflects on the significance of humanity's creation in the image and likeness of God, as well as the purpose and destiny of human existence.

Gregory's work *The Life of Macrina* presents his sister Macrina (330–79) as a model of Christian virtue and philosophical wisdom. Written after her death in 379, the work serves both as a hagiographical tribute and a theological reflection, highlighting Macrina's asceticism, her intellectual influence, and her profound spiritual insight. Gregory presents her as a "teacher of philosophy," whose life exemplifies the integration of faith, reason, and virtue. Through a series of dialogues and descriptions, he captures her wisdom and holiness, providing readers with a rich account of early Christian spirituality.

One of the most poignant moments in the text occurs during Macrina's final hours, where Gregory recounts her prayer: "You have released us, O Lord, from the fear of death. You have made the end of this life the beginning of true life. For a little while, You give rest to our bodies in sleep and awaken them again at the last trumpet."[3] This prayer reflects her deep faith in the resurrection and her serene acceptance of death as a passage to eternal life. Gregory portrays Macrina's unwavering trust in God's promises as a source of inspiration for those who face suffering and mortality.

---

[3] Gregory of Nyssa, *The Life of Saint Macrina*, trans. W. K. Lowther Clarke, in *Nicene and Post-Nicene Fathers*, second series, vol. 5, ed. Philip Schaff and Henry Wace (Hendrickson, 1994), 189.

Macrina's theological insight is particularly evident in her dialogue with Gregory in his work, *On the Soul and Resurrection*. She explains, "The soul, being invisible, does not perish with the body but continues in a condition appropriate to its nature."[4] This statement highlights her understanding of the soul's immortality, grounded in Christian doctrine and Platonic philosophy. Through their discussion, Gregory portrays Macrina as a spiritual guide, whose grasp of complex theological truths is both profound and practical, aimed at nurturing faith and hope in the divine.

Macrina's wisdom extends to her views on suffering and providence. Reflecting on the hardships she endured, including the loss of family members, she states, "Every affliction teaches us something and is a guide to the knowledge of God."[5] Her perspective reveals a deep trust in divine providence, viewing suffering not as a punishment but as a means of spiritual growth and closer union with God. Gregory portrays her as a figure of resilience and spiritual strength, whose perspective on suffering resonates with Christian teachings on the redemptive nature of trials.

In *On the Soul and the Resurrection*, Gregory of Nyssa offers not only a tribute to his sister's extraordinary character but also a theological and philosophical dialogue that continues to inspire. Macrina's profound faith, intellectual rigor, and ascetic discipline are presented as a model for Christian living, embodying the ideals of the early church. Her words and example, as recorded by Gregory, provide a rich source of spiritual insight and a testimony to the enduring power of a life devoted to God.

John Chrysostom (347–407)

John Chrysostom (c. 349–407), often called the "Golden Mouth" for his extraordinary eloquence, was one of the most influential figures in early Christianity. Born in Antioch to a wealthy family, his father, a high-ranking military officer, died when John was still an infant. Raised by his devout Christian mother, Anthusa, John received an exceptional education under the renowned pagan rhetorician Libanius. Libanius reportedly lamented on his deathbed that John would have been his successor had he not become a Christian. This

[4] Gregory of Nyssa, *On the Soul and the Resurrection*, trans. Catharine P. Roth (St. Vladimir's Seminary Press, 1993), 61.

[5] Gregory of Nyssa, *On the Soul and the Resurrection*, 61.

classical training in rhetoric and philosophy would later distinguish John as one of the greatest preachers in Christian history, blending persuasive speech with deep theological insight.

In his early years, Chrysostom considered a legal career but abandoned it to pursue a life of asceticism and theological study. Drawn to the monastic ideals of simplicity and devotion, he spent four years as a monk in Antioch and later lived as a hermit in the mountains for two years, practicing extreme asceticism. This rigorous lifestyle permanently damaged his health, forcing him to return to the city. Recognizing his potential, the church ordained him a deacon in 381 and a priest in 386. As a priest in Antioch, Chrysostom became renowned for his sermons, delivered in the city's cathedral. His *Homilies on the Statues* in 387 marked a defining moment in his ministry. These homilies were preached during a time of great unrest, when the citizens of Antioch had rioted, destroying imperial statues, and feared retribution from Emperor Theodosius I. Chrysostom's eloquence and pastoral care calmed the terrified population, and his pleas to the emperor helped secure a pardon.

Chrysostom's reputation reached its zenith in 397 when he was appointed archbishop of Constantinople, one of the most influential sees in the Christian world. His tenure in Constantinople was marked by bold reforms and courageous preaching. He sought to root out corruption among the clergy, condemned the opulence of the aristocracy, and redirected church wealth toward charitable institutions, including hospitals, orphanages, and homes for the poor. His sermons, both inspiring and scathing, often targeted the abuses of wealth and power. "For far greater is it to feed Christ when he is hungry than to raise the dead by the name of Jesus: for in the former case you do good to Christ, in the latter He does good to you,"[6] he declared, emphasizing the centrality of charity in Christian life. His uncompromising moral stance earned him widespread admiration among the poor but created powerful enemies, particularly within the imperial court.

One of Chrysostom's most infamous conflicts was with Empress Eudoxia, whom he criticized for her lavish lifestyle and interference in ecclesiastical matters. In one sermon, he drew a veiled but unmistakable parallel between Eudoxia and Herodias, the wife of Herod, who demanded the execution of John the Baptist: "Again Herodias rages; again she dances; again she desires to see the head of John on a platter."[7] These remarks deeply offended

---

[6] John Chrysostom, *Homilies on Second Corinthians*, Homily 16, in *Nicene and Post-Nicene Fathers*, first series, vol. 12, ed. Philip Schaff (Hendrickson, 1994), 310.

[7] John Chrysostom, quoted in Socrates Scholasticus, *Ecclesiastical History*, Book VI, chapter 18, in *Nicene and Post-Nicene Fathers*, second series, vol. 2, ed. Philip Schaff and Henry Wace (Hendrickson, 1994), 150.

the empress, leading to his deposition at the Synod of the Oak in 403, orchestrated by his rivals, including Theophilus of Alexandria. Although public outrage and support from the populace briefly restored him to his position, a silver statue of Eudoxia erected near the cathedral triggered further tensions. When Chrysostom denounced the statue and its celebratory ceremonies as pagan-like idolatry, the conflict culminated in his permanent exile in 404.

Chrysostom's writings and sermons remain among the most important in Christian history. His *Treatise on the Priesthood* offers profound reflections on the spiritual and practical responsibilities of clergy, warning, "The priestly office is indeed discharged on earth, but it ranks among heavenly ordinances."[8] His *Homilies on the Gospel of Matthew* and *Homilies on the Epistles of Paul* combine meticulous scriptural exegesis with practical moral applications, addressing issues of wealth, humility, and social justice. His *Paschal Homily*, delivered during Easter, captures his rhetorical brilliance and theological insight: "Christ is risen, and the demons are cast down! Christ is risen, and the angels rejoice! Christ is risen, and life reigns!"[9]

Germanic Influence

The migration and invasions of Germanic tribes, such as the Visigoths, Vandals, and Ostrogoths, further destabilized the Western Roman Empire. These invasions resulted in widespread destruction, displacement of populations, and the decline of urban centers, including Rome itself. As Christianity spread among the Germanic peoples and the Roman Empire increasingly interacted with Germanic tribes, the Christian church began to adopt and adapt certain Germanic traditions. These adaptations facilitated the integration of these tribes into the Christian faith while allowing the church to maintain its influence in newly Christianized regions.

Christianity incorporated elements of Germanic burial traditions as it spread among these peoples. Germanic tribes often buried their dead with grave goods, reflecting their cultural beliefs about the afterlife. While early Christianity discouraged such practices, compromises were made in newly Christianized areas. Some burials of Christian converts

[8] John Chrysostom, *On the Priesthood*, 3.4, in *Nicene and Post-Nicene Fathers*, first series, vol. 9, ed. Philip Schaff (Hendrickson, 1994), 47.

[9] John Chrysostom, *Paschal Homily*, in St. John Chrysostom: *Homilies*, trans. Frederic Farrar, in *Nicene and Post-Nicene Fathers*, first series, vol. 9, ed. Philip Schaff (Hendrickson, 1994), 422.

included items like weapons or jewelry, blending Germanic customs with Christian beliefs about resurrection and eternal life. Over time, burial practices evolved, with Christian symbols, such as crosses, replacing traditional pagan motifs.

As Germanic tribes converted to Christianity, their legal traditions were often codified with Christian influences. Missionaries and bishops played a role in shaping Germanic law codes to reflect Christian values. For example, the Visigothic Code (also known as the Lex Visigothorum) and the laws of the Burgundians incorporated Christian moral teachings while retaining elements of Germanic customary law, such as trial by *ordeal* or *wergild* (compensatory payments for injury or death).

The church accommodated Germanic social structures and clan-based organization within its ecclesiastical framework. For example, the conversion of entire tribes or clans often involved the baptism of leaders first, who then influenced their followers to convert, reflecting the Germanic emphasis on tribal loyalty and leadership. Churches also incorporated Germanic cultural motifs into art and architecture, blending traditional Germanic designs with Christian symbols in illuminated manuscripts, carvings, and decorative objects.

The Germanic warrior ethos, which prized loyalty, courage, and honor, was reframed within a Christian context. The church adapted this ethos to promote the idea of Christ as a victorious warrior over sin and death. Saints and martyrs were often portrayed as spiritual warriors, and the concept of holy war or spiritual combat became an important theme in Christian teachings directed at Germanic audiences.

Christian feast days often coincided with or replaced Germanic seasonal festivals. For example, the Easter celebration, though thoroughly Christian, began to incorporate Germanic traditions in those areas. The use of eggs and rabbits reflected cultural themes of fertility and rebirth.

As Germanic leaders converted to Christianity, they often sponsored missionaries and monastic communities, blending Germanic patronage systems with Christian evangelism. Leaders like Clovis of the Franks and Theodoric the Ostrogoth supported Christian institutions while retaining elements of Germanic governance and cultural identity.

Germanic architectural and artistic styles influenced the design and decoration of Christian churches and religious artifacts. Roman Christians incorporated elements of Germanic art, such as intricate metalwork, animal motifs, and geometric patterns, into church furnishings, illuminated manuscripts, and religious iconography. The interplay between Germanic and Roman artistic traditions led to unique regional Christian art and architecture styles across post-Roman Europe.

By integrating Germanic customs into Christian practices, the church not only softened resistance to the new faith but also preserved elements of Germanic cultural identity within a Christian framework, shaping the religious and cultural landscape of early medieval Europe.

Jerome (347–420)

Jerome, also known as Hieronymus, was a prominent Christian scholar, theologian, and translator who lived during the fourth and fifth centuries. He was born around 347 in Stridon, a town located on the border between Dalmatia and Pannonia (modern-day Croatia). His family was likely of Roman descent and modest means. He received an excellent education in grammar, rhetoric, and classical literature, studying in Rome under some of the finest teachers of his time. His education exposed him to classical authors and philosophical ideas, laying the foundation for his later scholarly pursuits. Despite his Christian upbringing, Jerome initially embraced a secular lifestyle in his youth. However, he experienced a spiritual conversion during his early adulthood, leading him to renounce his former ways and devote himself to the ascetic life. He joined a community of ascetics in Aquileia and later traveled to the desert of Chalcis in Syria, where he pursued a life of prayer, fasting, and study.

Jerome produced the Latin Vulgate in the late fourth century in response to the need for a standardized Latin version of the Bible in the Western Christian church. Before Jerome's work, various Latin translations of biblical texts existed, but they were often inconsistent and inaccurate. Pope Damasus I commissioned Jerome to produce a revised Latin translation of the Bible that would adhere closely to the original Hebrew and Greek texts. Jerome embarked on translating the Bible into Latin, working primarily from the Hebrew Old Testament and the Greek New Testament. He labored meticulously, consulting with Jewish scholars and studying Hebrew and Greek manuscripts to ensure the accuracy of his translation. Jerome's language expertise and deep knowledge of biblical texts and scholarship enabled him to translate the sources faithfully.

The Latin Vulgate quickly became the authoritative version of the Bible in the Latin-speaking West, supplanting earlier Latin versions. The Vulgate provided Western Christianity with a standardized and uniform text of the Bible, ensuring consistency and accuracy in biblical study and interpretation. The Vulgate became the primary Bible for liturgical purposes. Its use in worship further solidified its authority and influence within the church.

Jerome had a complex and evolving relationship with the theological legacy of Origen of Alexandria, a highly influential figure whose teachings sparked controversy within the Christian community. Early in his career, Jerome held Origen in high esteem and admired his scholarship and intellectual achievements. He appreciated Origen's rigorous approach to biblical interpretation and his extensive knowledge of Greek philosophy and literature. Jerome's initial exposure to Origen's works left a positive impression, and he viewed him as a valuable resource for understanding the complexities of Scripture. However, Jerome's opinion of Origen began to sour as he delved deeper into his writings and encountered theological concepts that he found objectionable.

One of the primary points of contention was Origen's allegorical method of interpretation, which Jerome criticized as overly speculative and prone to doctrinal error. Specifically, he argued that Origen's allegorical interpretations often departed from the plain, literal meaning of the text and introduced speculative interpretations that could lead to confusion and heresy. Jerome also took issue with certain theological doctrines espoused by Origen, particularly his teachings on the preexistence of souls and the eventual salvation of all beings, including demons. Origen's belief in the preexistence of souls, wherein he taught that souls existed before birth and were subject to a process of purification and progression, was incompatible with orthodox Christian doctrine, and Jerome accused Origen of introducing foreign philosophical concepts into Christian theology. Origen's teachings on universal salvation, which posited that all rational beings, including demons, would ultimately be reconciled to God and restored to their original state, were opposed by Jerome. Jerome argued that Origen's doctrine of universal salvation undermined the seriousness of sin and the necessity of redemption through Christ. Origen's trinitarian theology, particularly his subordinationist view of the Son to the Father, was another point of contention for Jerome. While Origen affirmed the divinity of Christ, he also emphasized the hierarchical relationship between the Father and the Son, which Jerome believed compromised the equality and coeternality of the divine persons.

As Jerome's theological views solidified and became more closely aligned with orthodox Christian doctrine, he increasingly distanced himself from Origen's teachings and actively opposed the spread of Origenism within the church. Jerome viewed Origenism as a dangerous heresy that threatened the integrity of Christian faith and doctrine, and he sought to refute Origen's ideas through his writings and polemical works. Jerome articulated his criticisms of Origen and his followers in various theological treatises and letters, where he vigorously attacked Origenist doctrines and defended orthodox Christian beliefs. In particular, Jerome's *Against Rufinus* and *Apologia to Pammachius* are notable works in which he refutes Origenist teachings and defends the authority of Scripture and the traditional teachings of the church.

Rufinus of Aquileia (345–411) was a contemporary of Jerome and an admirer of Origen, and he sought to defend Origen's theological legacy against criticism, particularly from figures like Jerome, who had reservations about Origen's teachings. Rufinus affirmed Origen's contributions to Christian theology and sought to portray Origen in a favorable light, emphasizing his intellectual brilliance and spiritual depth. Rufinus defended Origen's allegorical method of interpreting Scripture, arguing that it was a legitimate and spiritually enriching approach to understanding the deeper meaning of biblical texts. He believed that Origen's allegorical interpretations helped uncover hidden truths and spiritual insights that were not apparent in the text's literal sense. Rufinus also sought to demonstrate that Origen's theological teachings were fundamentally orthodox and in harmony with the teachings of the early church fathers. He argued against accusations of heresy leveled against Origen, insisting that Origen's writings were consistent with the core tenets of the Christian faith, including the belief in the Trinity, the divinity of Christ, and the authority of Scripture.

Rufinus defended Origen's controversial doctrine of universal salvation, arguing that Origen's views on the ultimate reconciliation of all rational beings with God were compatible with Christian theology's overarching themes of divine mercy and redemption. He asserted that Origen's teaching on universal salvation fits within the broader context of God's salvific plan for humanity. Rufinus also defended Origen's character and integrity against accusations of heresy and immorality. He portrayed Origen as a devout and pious Christian who dedicated his life to the pursuit of truth and the service of God, rejecting allegations of moral wrongdoing or theological deviance. Overall, Rufinus's defense of Origen was motivated by a desire to vindicate Origen's reputation as a theologian and to preserve his legacy for future generations. While Rufinus acknowledged that Origen's teachings were not without controversy, he believed that Origen's contributions to Christian theology deserved recognition and appreciation.

Rufinus had a significant theological conflict with his friend Jerome over the theology of Origen of Alexandria. Jerome and Rufinus first met in Rome, where they formed a close friendship and shared a common interest in biblical studies and monasticism.

Together, they translated and interpreted theological texts, collaborating on projects, such as translating Origen's works into Latin. However, their friendship soured due to theological disagreements and personal animosities. The catalyst for the conflict between Jerome and Rufinus was their differing attitudes toward Origen, whose teachings had been condemned by some church authorities. Jerome, influenced by his mentor Didymus the Blind (313–98), emphasized the importance of literal interpretation of the Bible. On the other hand, Rufinus was more sympathetic to Origen's allegorical approach and inclined toward speculative theology. While Jerome became increasingly critical of Origen's doctrines, Rufinus defended Origen's theological legacy and sought to promote his ideas within the Christian community. Despite their bitter conflict, Jerome and Rufinus both contributed to the development of Christian scholarship and theology. Jerome's translation of the Bible into Latin (the Vulgate) remains one of his most enduring legacies, while Rufinus's translations of Origen's works introduced his ideas to Western audiences.

Ambrose of Milan

Ambrose was among the most influential figures in the early Christian church, particularly in the Latin West. Born around 340 into a Christian family of Roman nobility, Ambrose received an excellent education in rhetoric and law, which would later shape his theological writings and pastoral leadership.

After practicing law in Rome, Ambrose entered the political arena and eventually became the governor of the province of Aemilia-Liguria, with his seat in Milan. It was during this time that Ambrose's life took a significant turn. In 374, the bishopric of Milan became vacant, and a fierce conflict arose between Arian and Nicene Christians over the selection of a new bishop. Ambrose, although not yet baptized and not a clergyman, intervened to restore peace and order. Ambrose's eloquence and charisma impressed both the Arians and Nicenes. To everyone's surprise, he was acclaimed as the new bishop of Milan by popular acclamation despite his lack of formal theological training or ordination. After undergoing a course in theology and receiving baptism, Ambrose was ordained a priest and consecrated as bishop in December 374.

As bishop of Milan, Ambrose quickly distinguished himself as a fearless defender of orthodox Christianity against Arianism and other heresies. He also became known for his ascetic lifestyle, personal piety, and passionate preaching. Ambrose's theological writings, such as *On the Christian Faith* and *The Holy Spirit*, reflect his commitment to Nicene orthodoxy and his defense of the divinity of Christ and the Trinity.

In *On the Christian Faith*, Ambrose provides a systematic exposition of the Christian faith, focusing on the essentials of Christianity. He begins by affirming the foundational belief in the Trinity as necessary for saving faith.

Ambrose articulates a robust doctrine of salvation centered on the redemptive work of Christ, the transformative power of divine grace, and the necessity of faith. Ambrose emphasizes the incarnation as the pivotal event in God's plan for human salvation, affirming that Christ's dual nature—fully divine and fully human—was essential for the restoration of humanity. Drawing on Phil 2:7–8, he highlights Christ's humility: "He emptied Himself, taking the form of a servant, being made in the likeness of men, and being found in fashion as a man, He humbled Himself, becoming obedient even unto death, yea, the death of the cross."[10] Ambrose interprets this as evidence of Christ's solidarity with humanity, which enables his sacrificial death to redeem the fallen human condition.

A key element of Ambrose's soteriology is the concept of substitutionary atonement. Christ, as both God and man, bridges the gap between sinful humanity and the divine. Ambrose states, "He took upon Himself what was ours, that He might impart to us what was His" (*De Fide* 2.8.65), emphasizing that through Christ's death and resurrection, believers are made participants in divine life. This idea is grounded in 2 Cor 5:21, where Paul writes, "He made the one who did not know sin to be sin for us, so that in him we might become the righteousness of God." Ambrose underscores that Christ's suffering and death were not only acts of obedience but also acts of substitution, through which he bore the punishment for human sin and restored the possibility of eternal communion with God.

Ambrose also stresses the role of grace in salvation, emphasizing its transformative and initiating power. Echoing Eph 2:8—"For you are saved by grace through faith, and this is not from yourselves; it is God's gift"—Ambrose asserts that salvation is entirely the work of divine grace, not human merit. He writes, "No one can redeem himself by his own works; redemption is through the blood of Christ" (*De Fide* 3.11.80). For Ambrose, grace not only initiates salvation but also sustains the believer, enabling growth in holiness and perseverance in faith.

---

[10] Ambrose of Milan, *Exposition of the Christian Faith*, 3.81, in *Nicene and Post-Nicene Fathers*, second series, vol. 10, ed. Philip Schaff and Henry Wace (Hendrickson, 1994), 264.

Faith, in Ambrose's theology, is the means by which individuals appropriate the benefits of Christ's redemptive work. Ambrose ties faith to baptism, the sacrament through which believers are united with Christ and cleansed of sin. Drawing on Rom 6:3–4, he describes baptism as a participation in Christ's death and resurrection: "For all who are baptized in Christ Jesus are baptized into His death . . . so that, as Christ was raised from the dead, we too might walk in newness of life." Ambrose views faith and baptism as inseparable, with the latter serving as the visible expression of the believer's entry into the saving grace of Christ.

In *On the Christian Faith*, Ambrose integrates exegesis of Scripture and theological formation with a deeply pastoral concern for the spiritual growth of his audience. His doctrine of salvation emphasizes the incarnation, the necessity of grace, and the centrality of faith, presenting a cohesive vision of how humanity is redeemed and transformed through Christ. By rooting his theology in the biblical narrative and the church's life, Ambrose provides a framework for understanding salvation that continues to resonate in Christian thought.

Furthermore, Ambrose stressed the ongoing process of sanctification in the believer's life. Salvation is not merely a past event, but an ongoing transformation brought about by the Holy Spirit in the believer's life. Repentance and confession of sins are essential to the Christian life. Ambrose's pastoral approach to penance reflects his concern for the spiritual well-being of believers and his belief in the transformative power of God's grace to restore and renew the repentant sinner.

Ambrose found himself in the middle of a political controversy when Emperor Theodosius I ordered the massacre of civilians in Thessalonica in retaliation for rioting against the government. Ambrose condemned the massacre in no uncertain terms and demanded that the emperor perform public penance for his actions. The emperor complied with Ambrose's demand, demonstrating the bishop's considerable influence over secular affairs.

Ambrose's lasting legacy extends beyond his theological writings and ecclesiastical leadership. He introduced hymn singing into the Western church and composed several hymns, including the famous *Te Deum*. Ambrose also played a crucial role in the conversion of Augustine of Hippo, whom he baptized in 387. Ambrose died on April 4, 397, leaving a legacy of theological insight, moral courage, and pastoral leadership.

Expansion and Growth of the Church

The church engaged in significant missionary endeavors and evangelization efforts that contributed to the expansion and growth of Christianity during the fourth and fifth centuries. In particular, the conversion of Emperor Constantine to Christianity in the early part of the fourth century marked a turning point, as it led to the legalization and subsequent promotion of Christianity throughout the Roman Empire. Missionaries and evangelists traveled far and wide, preaching the gospel and establishing Christian communities in regions previously untouched by the message of Christ. Christians in the empire took Jesus's commission to "make disciples of all nations" seriously. The efforts of figures such as Athanasius, Ambrose, Augustine of Hippo, and John Chrysostom were instrumental in spreading Christianity to urban centers, rural areas, and even to the remote corners of the Roman Empire. Through their preaching, teaching, and example, these missionaries and evangelists brought countless souls into the fold of the church, contributing to its growth and expansion.

By the end of the fourth century, Christianity had grown considerably, with a sizable portion of the population of the empire identifying as Christians. While precise figures are difficult to ascertain, estimates suggest that Christians may have constituted as much as 15 percent of the total population by this time, with higher concentrations in urban areas and regions where missionary activity was particularly successful. The Christian community encompassed people from all walks of life, including enslaved people, freedmen, merchants, artisans, soldiers, and members of the imperial household. Christianity appealed to individuals from diverse social, economic, and cultural backgrounds, offering hope, salvation, and redemption that resonated with people's spiritual and existential needs.

Recommended Reading

Behr, John. *The Nicene Faith: Formation of Christian Theology*. Vol. 2. St. Vladimir's Seminary Press, 2004.

Brown, Peter. *The Body and Society: Men, Women, and Sexual Renunciation in Early Christianity*. Columbia University Press, 1988.

Brown, Peter. *Through the Eye of a Needle: Wealth, the Fall of Rome, and the Making of Christianity in the West, 350–550 AD*. Princeton University Press, 2012.

Cameron, Alan. *The Last Pagans of Rome*. Oxford University Press, 2011.

Daley, Brian E. *Gregory of Nazianzus*. Routledge, 2006.

Elm, Susanna. *'Virgins of God': The Making of Asceticism in Late Antiquity*. Oxford University Press, 1994.

Gwynn, David M. *The Eusebians: The Polemic of Athanasius of Alexandria and the Construction of the 'Arian Controversy.'* Oxford University Press, 2007.

Hill, Robert C. *St. John Chrysostom: Homilies on Genesis 1–17*. Catholic University of America Press, 1998.

Humphries, Mark. *Communities of the Blessed: Social Environment and Religious Change in Northern Italy, AD 200–400*. Oxford University Press, 1999.

Kelly, J. N. D. *Jerome: His Life, Writings, and Controversies*. Duckworth, 1975.

McLynn, Neil B. *Ambrose of Milan: Church and Court in a Christian Capital*. University of California Press, 1994.

Meredith, Anthony. *Gregory of Nyssa*. Routledge, 1999.

Murphy, Francesca A. *The Comedy of Revelation: Paradise Lost and Regained in Gregory of Nyssa's Exegesis*. Oxford University Press, 2008.

Rousseau, Philip. *Basil of Caesarea*. University of California Press, 1994.

Russell, Norman. *The Doctrine of Deification in the Greek Patristic Tradition*. Oxford University Press, 2004.

Schaff, Philip, and Henry Wace, eds. *Nicene and Post-Nicene Fathers*. Second series. 14 vols. Christian Literature Company, 1890–1900.

—— Chapter 11 ——

Augustine and His Legacy

Thou movest us to delight in praising Thee; for Thou hast formed us for Thyself, and our hearts are restless till they find rest in Thee.

—Augustine, *Confessions*[1]

While our approach in this volume is slow to dedicate too much attention to single figures, events, or works, Augustine of Hippo is a necessary exception. His life serves as a watershed moment in the history of Christian thought and development, especially in the West. As such, and in keeping with our approach in this volume, we will consider Augustine's legacy in light of the Great Tradition. Augustine's work as author, bishop, and public spokesman for the church advanced apostolic authority, trinitarian doctrine, proper Christian living, and deep reflection on the church's liturgical practice. In this chapter we will briefly survey who Augustine was, his legacy through the four aspects of the Great Tradition, and what he teaches the church of today.

Aurelius Augustinus was born November 13, 354, in the little-known town of Thagaste (modern-day Souk Ahras), approximately sixty miles south of Hippo (modern-day Annaba),

---

[1] Augustine, *Confessions* 1.1, in Philip Schaff, ed., *Nicene and Post-Nicene Fathers*, first series (repr., Hendrickson, 2012), 1:45.

where he would be ordained a priest and then bishop in the mid-390s. Not much is known about Augustine's hometown, but his biographer, Possidius, described Augustine's parents as belonging to a middle/upper-middle class of people in the town.[2] Thagaste specifically, and North Africa in general, no doubt had a certain draw for Augustine as, despite his travels and regional fame during his lifetime, he returned home often in his early years and ultimately careered only sixty miles from where he grew up.

North Africa was one of the epicenters of Christianity from as early as the late second century, though Carthage was no Rome and Hippo was no Carthage. Ultimately, the Muslim invasion of the late seventh century would overtake North Africa, leaving little trace today of its once buzzing and contagious Christian energy.[3] Even while Augustine lay reciting the Psalms on his deathbed in August of 430, the Arian Vandals were laying siege to the city.

Augustine was raised in a half-Christian home. His mother, Monica, was a committed Catholic (Nicene) Christian, and she recited Scripture to her son and prayed for him from his infancy. Augustine speaks of this in book 3 of his *Confessions*, where he writes, "For by your mercy, Lord, from the time when my mother fed me at the breast my infant heart had been suckled dutifully on his name, the name of your Son, my Saviour."[4]

His father, Patricius, was not a Christian during Augustine's upbringing, though he did convert late in life before his death. Nonetheless, Augustine does not speak of him often, having far more affection and respect for his mother. Patricius is remembered as a hard man, likely abusive and unfaithful to Monica during Augustine's youth, though he cared for his family and saw to it that their needs were met.

Augustine's parents recognized his unique intellectual and rhetorical abilities early, so they sacrificed to provide him with the best education available. Augustine was thus trained in the liberal arts, where he studied the "art of eloquence" and read the great poets, philosophers, and politicians of the past, including Homer, Plato, Aristotle, Virgil, Cicero, and more.[5]

---

[2] Cf. "Thagaste" in Allan D. Fitzgerald, ed., *Augustine Through the Ages: An Encyclopedia* (Eerdmans, 1999), 824.

[3] J. Patout Burns and Robin Jensen, *Christianity in Roman Africa: The Development of Its Practices and Beliefs* (Eerdmans, 2014), 84–86.

[4] *Confessions* 3.4, trans. R. S. Pine-Coffin (Penguin, 1961), 59.

[5] *Confessions* 3.4. See *City of God*, book 8, where Augustine quickly surveys much of this great literature, ultimately arguing that none are closer to the Christians than the Platonists, by which he means the Neoplatonists.

By age nineteen he was teaching rhetoric in his hometown of Thagaste and cultivating a reputation as a skilled orator. Around this time, he read Cicero's work *Hortensius*. This work, now lost to history, was an exhortation to philosophy—the love of wisdom. Augustine recounts this in his *Confessions*:

> It altered my outlook on life. It changed my prayers to you, O Lord, and provided me with new hopes and aspirations. All my empty dreams suddenly lost their charm and my heart began to throb with a bewildering passion for the wisdom of eternal truth. . . .
>
> My God, how I burned with longing to have wings to carry me back to you, away from all earthly things, although I had no idea what you would do with me! For *yours is the wisdom*. In Greek the word "philosophy" means "love of wisdom," and it was with this love that the *Hortensius* inflamed me. . . .
>
> But, O Light of my heart, you know that at that time, although Paul's words were not known to me, the only thing that pleased me in Cicero's book was his advice not simply to admire one or another of the schools of philosophy, but to love wisdom itself, whatever it might be, and to search for it, pursue it, hold it, and embrace it firmly. These were the words which excited me and set me burning with fire, and the only checks to this blaze of enthusiasm was that they made no mention of the name of Christ.[6]

This selection from *Confessions* reveals Augustine's passion for God, his abiding pursuit of eternal wisdom, and his remarkable ability with words. Few before or after Augustine rival his gift of eloquence both with the tongue and pen.

After reading *Hortensius*, Augustine turned briefly to the Bible in search of wisdom, but he found the Scriptures unsophisticated and hard to understand. So he joined the Manichees, a gnostic religious sect who associated themselves with Jesus and wisdom, but did not associate with the Nicene faith. For the next ten years Augustine would remain a "hearer" in the Manichean religion, meaning he participated on the fringes but was not recognized as a leader. During this decade he took a mistress, had a son, Adeodatus (meaning "gift of God"), taught rhetoric in Thagaste, and eventually was appointed as the official orator in Milan in 384. Just before his appointment in Milan, however, Augustine met with Faustus of Milevis, the leader of the Manichees. Augustine approached this meeting with a great deal of anticipation that

[6] *Confessions* 3.4, 59.

Faustus would answer the many philosophical, theological, and moral questions that haunted him. He came away from this meeting woefully disappointed and disillusioned.

Augustine's move to Milan was a step up the social ladder, but personally it was a low point. His disappointment with Manichaeism pushed him toward the school of skepticism as he relocated to Milan. Yet, as Augustine remembered these events, he recognized God's sovereign hand at work, for soon after arriving in Milan he heard the preaching of Ambrose, bishop of Milan. Ambrose was revered for his preaching, a true attraction for a teacher of rhetoric. Further, Ambrose was trained in the Alexandrian school of interpretation known for its allegorical approach to Scripture, something unknown to Augustine up to this point. This was timely as Augustine was once again open to the veracity of the Christian faith despite his turning away from the Scriptures years earlier. Ambrose also introduced Augustine to the *libri Platonicorum*, the books of the Platonists, which offered a philosophical (especially metaphysical) scaffolding that caused Augustine to rethink his view of God and all of reality.

By August of 386, the combination of Augustine's past, Ambrose's preaching and influence, and the weight of Scripture collided toward a moment of repentance and conversion. Augustine recounts this in *Confessions*, book 8. The story takes place in a backyard garden with his friend Alypius:

> In this way I wrangled with myself, in my own heart, about my own self. And all the while Alypius stayed at my side, silently awaiting the outcome of this agitation that was new in me.
>
> I probed the hidden depths of my soul and wrung its pitiful secrets from it, and when I mustered them all before the eyes of my heart, a great storm broke within me, bringing with it a great deluge of tears. I stood up and left Alypius so that I might weep and cry to my heart's content, for it occurred to me that tears were best shed in solitude. . . . Somehow I flung myself down beneath a fig tree and gave way to the tears which now streamed from my eyes, the sacrifice that is acceptable you. . . .
>
> I was asking myself these questions, weeping all the while with the most bitter sorrow in my heart, when all at once I heard the sing-song voice of a child in a nearby house. Whether it was the voice of a boy or a girl I cannot say, but again and again it repeated the refrain "Take it and read, take it and read." . . . I stemmed my flood of tears and stood up, telling myself that this could only be a divine command to open my book of Scripture and read the first passage on which my eyes should fall. . . .

> So I hurried back to the place where Alypius was sitting, for when I stood up to move away I had put down the book containing Paul's Epistles. I seized it and opened it, and in silence I read the first passage on which my eyes fell: *Not in revelling and drunkenness, not in lust and wantonness, not in quarrels and rivalries. Rather, arm yourselves with the Lord Jesus Christ; spend no more thought on nature and nature's appetites* [Rom. 13:13, 14]. I had no wish to read more and no need to do so. For in an instant, as I came to the end of the sentence, it was as though the light of confidence flooded into my heart and all the darkness of doubt was dispelled.[7]

In August of 386, the thirty-one-year-old Augustine was thus converted to the true Wisdom of God, Jesus Christ. The following Easter, he was baptized in Milan by Ambrose. However, Augustine's conversion did not mean that his life would be without hardship. In the summer of that same year, his mother, Monica, died. Within two years, his son, Adeodatus, and a dear friend, Nebridius, died as well.

After his conversion, Augustine quickly disentangled himself from the profession of teaching rhetoric, seeking instead the monastic and intellectual life. But, in 391, amidst a recruiting trip for his monastic community, the church in Hippo insisted that Augustine be ordained to the priesthood and dedicate his life to the service of the church. Interpreting this as God's will, Augustine obliged. In 395 or 396, he succeeded Valerius as bishop of Hippo, and thus began what we may call Augustine's mature work and ministry. Between 396 and his death in August of 430, Augustine wrote his *Confessions*, *City of God*, *On the Trinity*, *On Christian Doctrine*, *Enchiridion*, *Retractions* and dozens more works, including polemics against the Donatists and Pelagians, plus hundreds of letters and sermons.

Augustine and the Authority of Scripture

While there are many areas of debate in Augustine's thought among scholars, there is little debate about Augustine's view on the authority of Scripture. Augustine held Scripture in the highest regard and left to the church some of the most sophisticated and insightful exegesis in all of Christian literature.

Three points deserve mention regarding Augustine's view of the Bible. First, Augustine held a very high view of Scripture, with a strong emphasis on authorial intent. Similar to

[7] *Confessions* 3.11–12, trans. Pine-Coffin, 177–78.

the contemporary, especially North American, language of inerrancy, Augustine emphasizes Scripture's accuracy in its form, order, and meaning. Interpretations may err, but the words of Scripture are right and true as given by God. Moreover, the interpreter is responsible for pursuing the original intent of the biblical author to keep the interpretation and teaching of Scripture tethered to its apostolic authority and power of the Spirit.[8]

Second, Augustine's approach to the interpretation of Scripture defies categorization. He does not fit into the Antiochene or Alexandrian schools, oversimplified though these classifications may be. Augustine's *On Christian Doctrine* (*De doctrina christiana*) is his textbook on interpretation and preaching, which he summarizes as "wisdom and eloquence." Wisdom, ultimately and most directly understood by Augustine as the incarnate Christ, is both what is required for proper interpretation of Scripture and what we seek in Scripture. Eloquence is the skill of communicating this wisdom in a form that befits the divine message.

Third, among the many notable insights in Augustine's *On Christian Doctrine*, one of the most important is Augustine's insistence that any interpretation of Scripture must undergird the double love of God and neighbor. Any interpretation that fails to do so is an invalid interpretation. He writes, "So if it seems to you that you have understood the divine scriptures or any part of them, in such a way that by this understanding you do not build up this twin love of God and neighbor, then you have not yet understood them."[9]

While the Scriptures flow easily from Augustine's tongue and pen, the portions of Scripture most dear to him include Genesis, the Psalms (which he refers to as the *totus Christus*—the whole Christ), the Sermon on the Mount in Matthew 5–7, Paul's letters, and the Johannine literature. His reliance on these books is associated with the various polemical and theological occasions that motivated his writing.

De Trinitate

Around the year 400, as he completed his *Confessions*, Augustine took up the task of writing a dedicated volume on the Trinity entitled *De Trinitate* (*On the Trinity*). The immensity

---

[8] For more on Augustine's view of Scripture, see Pamela Bright, *Augustine and the Bible* (University of Notre Dame Press, 1999); Peter Sanlon, *Augustine's Theology of Preaching* (Fortress, 2014); and John D. Woodbridge, *Biblical Authority: A Critique of the Rogers/Mckim Proposal* (Zondervan, 1982).

[9] Augustine, *Teaching Christianity* [*De doctrina christiana*], ed. John E. Rotelle (New City Press, 1996), 1.36, 40 (p. 124).

of the task, coupled with pastoral demands, meant that Augustine took the better part of twenty years to complete the work. An incomplete version of the book was stolen by the Donatists in the mid-410s and published without Augustine's permission, pressuring Augustine to finish the work and publish the complete version c. 422–26.

On the Trinity holds a unique place in Augustine's corpus, as it is arguably his only "gratuitous" work, as Rowan Williams suggests. Across fifteen books, Augustine considers God's mission of sending the Son and the Spirit; the essential equality of the Father, Son, and Spirit; divine simplicity; and the eternal generation of the Son. Moreover, Augustine's interest in divine Wisdom features strongly in the work as he argues against the Arians in favor of the Son's equality with the Father and as he distinguishes between wisdom and knowledge (*sapientia* and *scientia*).

Perhaps most significantly, *On the Trinity* demonstrates Augustine's mature "faith seeking understanding" method, coupled with a pro-Nicene conviction. He begins the work boldly, "The reader of these reflections of mine on the Trinity should bear in mind that my pen is on the watch against the sophistries of those who scorn the starting-point of faith, and allow themselves to be deceived through an unseasonable and misguided love of reason."[10]

Augustine wrote *On the Trinity* as though he has the Bible in one hand and the Nicene Creed in the other, leaving no opportunity for Arian arguments, while also creatively exploring the relationship between God and man, man's fallenness and marred *imago*, and the way back to God and the *imago* in Christ, the power and wisdom of God.

> The Trinity is the one, only, and true God, and that one rightly says, believes, and understands that the Father, the Son, and the Holy Spirit are of one and the same substance or essence.
>
> ———
>
> Augustine,
> *On the Trinity*

Confessions and *City of God*

It is no overstatement to suggest that Augustine's *Confessions* is both a masterpiece of Christian spirituality and a work of literary novelty, as it combines prayer with autobiography.

[10] *The Trinity (De Trinitate)*, ed. John E. Rotelle (New City Press, 1991), 1.1 (p. 65).

Likely written in the late 390s, Augustine recounts his life story from birth to baptism and the death of his mother in the form of prayer. Through the lens of God's sovereignty, Augustine reads back into his life how God was at work even before his conversion. He speaks of being "suckled dutifully" on the name of Christ by Monica while she nursed him as an infant.[11] He tells how he and friends stole pears for no reason other than out of the desire to sin. He shares stories of love and promiscuity, of friendship and loss, of confusion and disappointment, of curiosity and hope, all life experiences that God used to draw Augustine to himself. And in book 8, as seen above, Augustine recounts in vivid detail his emotional conversion to Christ in a friend's Italian garden.

Confessions is truly a book for all Christians, a first-person account of God at work in one's life even before conversion. In this timeless work, Augustine models prayer, sincerity, confession, transparency, and faith in ways rarely seen before or since.

Arguably, however, Augustine's best-known work, due to its impact both inside and outside the church, is *City of God*. It was written in response to a letter sent to Augustine by his friend Marcellinus, who asked how to respond to the accusation that Rome's fall was due to the Christians angering the Roman gods. Augustine's answer was the twenty-two-book (what we today refer to as a chapter) tome whose influence has been arguably unmatched in the West by any other literature excepting the Bible.

In the first half of this allegorical "tale of two cities," Augustine essentially tells the Roman story of the world, its view of the gods, the origin of all things, the virtues and vices of the various philosophical schools, and more, while systematically dismantling the coherence of their worldview. In book 11, Augustine pivots to tell the Christian story of the world, which has a particular beginning in the Creator God, a particular end (*telos*) in the new heavens and earth, and a pilgrimage in between.

Augustine uses the imagery of Ps 87:3 to compare the City of God with the City of Man. He parallels these cities both to show the superiority of the City of God as the eternal city for which people are made, but also to argue for how we should live in between the time of Christ's first and second coming. This gives rise to discussions of politics and civil propriety, history and providence, war and its relation to justice, and the call to wisdom and virtue for individuals and societies, as well as an amillenial view of eschatology (the view that the thousand year reign of Christ is not a literal thousand years but a symbolic description for the age of the church), among many other important themes.

---

[11] Augustine, *Confessions* 3.4, trans. Pine-Coffin (p. 59).

One would try in vain to quantify the impact of *City of God* across the globe, especially in the West. As has been suggested, Augustine imagined the kingdom of God in the early fifth century, and the church sought to materialize Augustine's imagination in the centuries that followed.[12]

Against Donatism and Pelagianism

The Donatist dispute at the beginning of the fifth century (c. 400–411) put pressure on Augustine the pastor to clarify his views on baptism and the church, especially on the relationship between the person administering the sacrament and the effect of the sacrament itself. The Donatists, named after Donatus of Carthage (died c. 355), emerged in the early fourth century when some refused to acknowledge the baptism of someone who defected (*traditor*, or someone who "handed over" the Scriptures) under the Diocletian persecution (c. 303–11). Taking this view further, Donatists also refused to acknowledge the baptism of one who was baptized by a priest or bishop who defected under persecution, arguing that ordination or baptism by a *traditor* contaminated the sacrament and all who participated therein.

In North Africa, the Donatists became the majority church by the 360s, though pressure began to build in the 390s with resistance from both Augustine of Hippo and Aurelius of Carthage. For Augustine, the Donatist controversy was primarily a pastoral one that cut to the heart of the church's unity. While Donatist and Catholic churches were "indistinguishable in worship and creed" in North Africa during Augustine's time,[13] the lack of ecclesial and theological unity was unacceptable to Augustine, and the division had lasted long enough.

As William Harmless proposes, "Augustine's anti-Donatist writings gravitate around two main issues: the theology of the church and the theology of baptism."[14] J. Patout Burns and Robin M. Jensen offer the following four points as a helpful summary of Augustine's position:

---

[12] Cf. Christopher Dawson, *Medieval Essays* (Catholic University of America Press, 1954) especially the opening essay, "The Study of Christian Culture," 5–14.

[13] William Harmless, SJ, *Augustine in His Own Words* (Catholic University of America Press, 2010), 234.

[14] Harmless, *Augustine in His Own Words*, 235.

1. Christ himself gave baptism through the minister as his agent, so that the properly performed ritual was always effective. This became known as *ex opera operato*, meaning, "It is worked by the work."
2. The church was the necessary mediator of the sanctifying effect of the sacrament because the Holy Spirit conferred upon it the power to forgive sins.
3. Although the ritual of baptism was always effective in conferring forgiveness and grace, only those who repented of sin and believed in Christ actually retained these baptismal gifts.
4. The enduring efficacy of baptism could restore an originally insincere recipient who later converted and repented.[15]

Augustine thus differed from Cyprian on the validity of baptism "outside the church," but he maintained Cyprian's insistence on the church's unity. In the end, his solution sought to promote the church's unity while undermining Donatist separatism, honoring the legacy of Cyprian, and clarifying the nature of the sacrament.

Augustine's dispute with Pelagius also contributed to his liturgical legacy, as well as to his theological and moral legacy. Pelagius (c. 354–418) served as a British monk and spiritual director in the late fourth and early fifth centuries. Having visited Rome in the 380s, and seeing the relaxed morals of Christian leaders, Pelagius sought to promote a rigorous moral and ascetic commitment to Christ. After reading Augustine's *Confessions*, Pelagius was struck by Augustine's prayer in 10.29, which reads, "Give what you command, and then command whatever you will."[16] Pelagius rejected this perspective, insisting instead for a more libertarian free-will approach.

This resulted in what we know as the Pelagian controversy, which was settled rather quickly at the Council of Carthage in 418. Pelagius's view of the human will, which suggested people could merit salvation without divine grace, proved too simplistic and found little biblical support. Augustine, on the other hand, promoted a robust view of human depravity, a high view of God's sovereignty, and the necessity of divine intervention for salvation without the assistance of the human will. Moreover, he argued for a *prevenient grace* that made possible the confession of Christ for those who truly believed. Additionally,

---

[15] J. Patout Burns Jr. and Robin Jensen, *Christianity in Roman Africa: The Development of Its Practices and Beliefs* (Eerdmans, 2014), 215–16.

[16] Augustine, *The Confessions*, trans. Maria Boulding, ed. John E. Rotelle, vol. 1.1 of *The Works of Saint Augustine: A Translation for the 21st Century* (New City Press, 1997), 264.

Augustine's view found strong biblical support, especially in Paul's writings, thus overwhelming Pelagius's weaker position.

While Pelagius was swiftly defeated by Augustine, his followers were not so quickly dismissed. In the ensuing decades, the semi-Pelagians developed Pelagius's reasoning toward a defense of libertarian free will with greater depth and biblical support. However, Pelagianism and various forms of semi-Pelagianism were eventually condemned at the Council of Orange in 529. The council articulated twenty-five canons, which accomplished the following:

1. Reaffirmed original sin
2. Denied any opportunity for a truly libertarian (free) view of the will
3. Denied any synergistic (as opposed to monergistic) view of justification or unaided merit toward God—meaning that justification is solely (mono) the work of God
4. Reaffirmed Augustine's view that grace must precede any movement toward God

This debate continued through the Middle Ages at various times, but it was especially reignited in the Reformation as Luther and the Magisterial Reformers sought to inject a higher view of God's sovereignty into the discussion of human salvation. This divided Augustine's legacy in the Reformation, making him ostensibly the soteriological hero of the Reformers and the ecclesiological hero of the Catholics.

So What for the Church Today?

Augustine remains a pivotal figure to the present day across the various Christian traditions and thus deserves a concluding reflection for the contemporary church. While still foundational for much Roman Catholic teaching, Augustine is much more palatable to Protestants than a figure like Thomas Aquinas, whose legacy is more directly bound up with the form of Catholicism that divides Catholics and Protestants today. Even conservative Protestants seek to retrieve Augustinian thought for its rigorous biblical engagement, depth of spirituality, and a certain theological familiarity—especially regarding soteriology. After all, it is said that John Calvin quoted Augustine more than any other source except the Bible.

We must note, however, that the Eastern church does not share the depth of appreciation for Augustine as is found in the West. Augustine was known by reputation in the East, but his works remained largely unknown there until the thirteen century, when his *De Trinitate* was translated into Greek.[17] His beginning with the divine essence of God has been met with criticism by Eastern theologians, who place a stronger accent on the threeness of God following the Cappadocian Fathers. Further, the East generally rejects Augustine's doctrines of sin and grace in response to Pelagius.[18] The soteriological differences between East and West are more than simple matters of nuance concerning free will versus sovereignty. Instead, the East approaches the doctrine of salvation from a different framework altogether, one that struggles to recognize or appreciate an Augustinian approach. For these reasons and more, the Eastern church has, at best, held Augustine's legacy at arm's length, and at worst decried his work altogether.[19]

Nonetheless, Augustine remains an exemplar for modern Christians as one whose heart was on fire for Christ and as one who tirelessly promoted and defended the faith. At times this defense concerned internal church matters, protecting the flock of God against false doctrine. At other times it concerned civil matters regarding how Christians live between the advents. Augustine challenges Christians of every tradition to a deeper and more vigorous love for God and neighbor as we pilgrimage together toward the City of God.

Recommended Reading

Augustine. *City of God.* Translated by Henry Bettenson. Penguin Classics, 2004.

Augustine. *Confessions.* In *Nicene and Post-Nicene Fathers*, Series 1. Edited by Philip Schaff, vol. 1. Hendrickson, 1886/2012.

Augustine. *Confessions.* Translated by R. S. Pine-Coffin. Penguin, 1961.

---

[17] George E. Demacopoulos and Aristotle Papanikolaou, "Augustine and the Orthodox: 'The West' in the East," in *Orthodox Readings of Augustine*, ed. Aristotle Papanikolaou and George E. Demacopoulos (St. Vladimir's Seminary Press, 2008), 11.

[18] Cf. Demacopoulos and Papanikolaou, "Augustine and the Orthodox," 21–24.

[19] "[Augustine] has always been regarded with some reserve in the East. In our own days, especially among Western converts to Orthodoxy, there have arisen two opposite and extreme views of him. One view, influenced by Roman Catholic opinions, sees rather more importance in him as a Father of the Church than the Orthodox Church has given him in the past; while the other view has tended to underestimate his Orthodox importance, some even going so far as to call him a 'heretic.' Both of these are Western views, not rooted in Orthodox tradition. The Orthodox view of him, on the other hand, held consistently down the centuries by the Holy Fathers of the East and (in the early centuries) of the West as well, goes to neither extreme, but is a balanced appraisal of him with due credit given both to his unquestioned greatness and to his faults." Seraphim Rose, *The Place of Blessed Augustine in the Orthodox Church* (Saint Herman of Alaska Brotherhood, 2007), 30.

Augustine. *Teaching Christianity* [*De doctrina christiana*]. Edited by John E. Rotelle. New City Press, 1996.

Augustine. *The Trinity (De Trinitate)*. Edited by John E. Rotelle. New City Press, 1991/2015.

Burns, Patout, and Robin Jensen. *Christianity in Roman Africa: The Development of Its Practices and Beliefs*. Eerdmans, 2014.

Demacopoulos, George E., and Aristotle Papanikolaou. "Augustine and the Orthodox: 'The West' in the East." In *Orthodox Readings of Augustine*, edited by George E. Demacopoulos and Aristotle Papanikolaou. St. Vladimir's Seminary Press, 2008.

Fitzgerald, Allan D. *Augustine Through the Ages: An Encyclopedia*. Eerdmans, 1999.

Harmless, William. *Augustine in His Own Words*. Catholic University Press of America, 2010.

Martin, Thomas F. *Our Restless Heart: The Augustinian Tradition*. Orbis, 2003.

Rose, Seraphim. *The Place of Blessed Augustine in the Orthodox Church*. Saint Herman of Alaska Brotherhood, 2007.

—— Chapter 12 ——

Antony, Benedict, and Early Monasticism

The monastic tradition played a critical role in the development and expansion of Christianity, especially in the West. While many Protestant Christians may be less familiar with monastic and ascetic practices, these figures and their institutions still occupy an important place in the historical imaginations of Catholics, Orthodox, and Protestants alike. One can hardly recall the medieval stories of King Arthur, the *Canterbury Tales*, or the legendary Robin Hood apart from the church and the monastic organizations alongside it. And it's fair to say that the monastic and ascetic traditions from early and medieval Christianity remain respected by Christians everywhere, even if they are little known and even less understood.

When considering Protestant—even evangelical—spirituality and devotional practices, there's a certain seriousness and depth found in ancient ascetic practices that is lacking in the comparatively short history of Protestantism. This chapter surveys the beginnings of the Christian ascetic and monastic traditions roughly until the time of Gregory I (d. 604), leaving the rest of the medieval monastic story for a later chapter. The bulk of attention here will be given to Antony and the tradition of the desert fathers, Benedict of Nursia and his important *Rule*, Patrick of Ireland and his impact on Christian mission, and the relationship of the monastic movement to the Great Tradition. Others, such as Basil, Simeon the Stylite, John Cassian, Augustine, and Jerome, will receive brief consideration along the way.

Emergence of Ascetic Movements

Ascetic practices do not originate with Christianity. Rather, early Christians repurposed in a distinctly Christian manner strict communal exercises that first developed in Greek philosophical communities, turning toward material minimalism and prayer. The Christian versions of these communities first appeared in Egypt in the late third and early fourth centuries and flourished in the Middle Ages across the church of the East and West, and, while not as popular as they once were, they persist to the present day.

At least three motivations gave rise to early ascetic movements. First was the sporadic persecution of the middle to late third century, along with economic hardship that left much of the Roman Empire in disarray, pushing some to the desert for isolation and prayer.[1] Second was the enjoyment of worldly privilege and relaxation of moral standards that followed the legalization of Christianity in the West in the early fourth century. Diarmaid MacCulloch writes, "It was hardly surprising that the sudden sequence of great power and great disappointment for the imperial church in the West inspired Western Christians to imitate the monastic life of the Eastern church."[2] The cultural whiplash felt by church leaders going from the intense Diocletian persecution of c. 303–311 to the politically privileged position of the emperor's personal invitation to the Council of Nicaea in 325 was doubtless destabilizing for Christians. Especially as people poured into the churches following Constantine's conversion, those who had suffered for Christ for generations felt a need to hold the world's acceptance and privilege at arm's length. And while theological debates persisted in the following decades, the Edict of Thessalonica on February 27, 380—what would have been Emperor Constantine's one hundredth birthday—declared Christianity the official religion of the Roman Empire. As decreed by Emperor Theodosius, "We desire that all peoples who are governed by the moderation of Our Clemency shall practice that religion which was handed down by the divine

---

[1] Mark Noll, *Turning Points: Decisive Moments in the History of Christianity*, 2nd ed. (Baker Academic, 2000), 88.

[2] Diarmaid MacCulloch, *Christianity: First Three Thousand Years* (Penguin, 2011), 312.

Apostle Peter to the Romans."[3] Soon thereafter, Theodosius actively opposed pagan worship in the empire and closed pagan temples in 391.

With political opposition now aimed at pagans, Arians, and Manichaeans, Christians enjoyed a measure of freedom and privilege previously unknown to them. Even early in the fourth century, after Christianity was legalized but not yet the law of the land, Emperor Constantine's mother, Saint Helena, became the "face of Christianity" as part of her son's Christianization campaign, making visible through architecture, art, and cultural symbol the invisible faith of the church.[4] This cultural flourishing of Christian privilege and symbolism led many to ask anew what it meant to be "in the world but not of the world" (John 17:14–17). One prominent answer to that question was monasticism.

A third motivation is what Mark Noll calls "inner motivations." These are less reactionary to external and political developments and more concerned with personal commitments to Scripture and prayer. It was important for early monastics to remove themselves from worldly distractions to adhere to a single-mindedness and unceasing posture of prayer toward God. Noll urges, "The life of prayer, in turn, would transform them into a charitable and hospitable people."[5] Moreover, Noll insists that "immersion in Scripture remained a permanent characteristic" of monastic communities, even during times of Christian history when attention to Scripture seemed more obligatory than sincere.[6]

Antony and Eastern Monasticism

The two prominent forms of early monasticism from Egypt are represented by Antony (251–356) and Pachomius (292–346). Antony represented the hermitic (individualized and isolated) monastic life while Pachomius modeled an early cenobitic (communal) style. While Pachomius's communal approach became the dominant monastic approach, we will attend more closely to Antony's life below due to the breadth of his influence, not least because of Athanasius's biography, *Vita Antonii* (*Life of Antony*). Antony's life as told by Athanasius and corroborated by many contemporaries inspired the imagination of future

[3] Bruce Frier, ed., *The Codex of Justinian: A New Annotated Translation, with Parallel Latin and Greek Text Based on a Translation by Justice Fred H. Blume* (Cambridge University Press, 2016), 14–15.

[4] Lynn H. Cohick and Amy Brown Hughes, *Christian Women in the Patristic World: Their Influence, Authority, and Legacy in the Second Through Fifth Centuries* (Baker Academic, 2017), 116.

[5] Noll, *Turning Points*, 90.

[6] Noll, 90.

monastics, for his sincerity and strict discipline were applicable at both the individual and communal levels.

> For simply to remember Antony is a great profit and assistance for me also. I know that in even hearing, along with marveling at the man, you will want also to emulate his purpose, for Antony's way of life provides monks with a sufficient picture for ascetic practice.
>
> ———
>
> Athanasius, *The Life of Antony*

Antony, known as "the Great One," was born in Egypt into a wealthy family in c. 251 to devout Christian parents who raised him in a distinctly Christian manner. Athanasius informs us that while Antony was never in need as a child, he also was not spoiled; "he didn't pester his parents for food of various and luxurious kinds, nor did he seek the pleasures associated with food, but with merely the things he found before him he was satisfied."[7]

Athanasius goes on to describe that soon after the death of his parents, Antony was divinely inspired by the call of Christ: "Go, sell your belongings and give to the poor, and you will have treasure in heaven. Then come, follow me" (Matt 19:21). He sold all he had, entrusted his sister's well-being and care to the virgins of a local convent, and then set out for a life of discipline and isolation. As he sought this isolation within the confines of society, Antony experienced intense attacks from the devil, tempting him with memories, material things, and sexual desires. Ultimately, these temptations led him to the tombs of the desert, away from the village, where he would spend the next twenty years in isolation.

After a time, people sought Antony to emulate his asceticism. Those who went to him were amazed at his good health, both physical and spiritual. "The state of his soul was one of purity. . . . He maintained utter equilibrium, like one guided by reason and steadfast in that which accords with nature."[8] He performed miracles of healing and exorcisms, comforted the grieving, and restored relationships. Moreover, he modeled godliness, shepherding, and a devoted life to Christ. Antony was also a beloved teacher. The collection of sayings from the desert fathers known as the *Apophthegmata* includes some forty wise sayings and anecdotes from Antony. While he viewed the ascetic life through a warrior's lens, ever on guard against the attacks of the devil, he simultaneously demonstrated a calmness and sober-mindedness

---

[7] Athanasius of Alexandria, *Athanasius: The Life of Antony and the Letter to Marcellinus*, ed. Richard J. Payne, trans. Robert C. Gregg, Classics of Western Spirituality (Paulist Press, 1980), 31.

[8] Athanasius of Alexandria, *Athanasius*, 42.

exemplary for Christians of all times, places, and vocations. Antony described this spiritual warfare in apocalyptic visions:

> But changes of form for evil are easy for the devil, so in the night they made such a din that the whole of that place seemed to be shaken by an earthquake, and the demons as if breaking the four walls of the dwelling seemed to enter through them, coming in the likeness of beasts and creeping things. And the place was on a sudden filled with the forms of lions, bears, leopards, bulls, serpents, asps, scorpions, and wolves, and each of them was moving according to his nature. . . . Nor was the Lord then forgetful of Antony's wrestling, but was at hand to help him. So looking up he saw the roof as it were opened, and a ray of light descending to him. The demons suddenly vanished, the pain of his body straightway ceased, and the building was again whole.[9]

Antony's asceticism inspired the likes of Simeon the Stylite (c. 390–459) of northern Syria and John Cassian in southern France. As early monasticism grew in popularity, drawing sizeable crowds who visited the monks to learn from them and observe their way of life, Simeon grew weary of the crowds and erected a pillar approximately twenty meters high, upon which he lived for some twenty years until his death. Food and drink were hoisted up by a basket, and despite his desire for solitude, pilgrims traveled from far distances to see and hear from Simeon. He is remembered both for his disciplined commitment to the ascetic life and for his promotion of Nicene and Chalcedonian teaching about Jesus and the Holy Trinity.

John Cassian (c. 360–435) was the first to introduce Eastern forms of monasticism to the West. After some time in the monastery at Bethlehem, Cassian and his friend Germanus moved to Egypt to learn the more extreme ways of holiness from the desert monks, then from Egypt to Constantinople, where Cassian was discipled by John Chrysostom. Eventually, Cassian landed in Marseille, on the southern coast of France, where he founded two monasteries—one for men and the other for women—introducing Eastern ways to Western monastics.[10]

---

[9] Athanasius, *The Life of Antony*, in *Nicene and Post-Nicene Fathers*, ed. Philip Schaff and Henry Wace, second series, vol. 4 (Hendrickson, 2012), 198–99.

[10] Cassian's works *The Institutes* and *The Conferences* were also quite influential in shaping both the inner and outer monastic life. Cassian is not without controversy, however, especially for his views on free will in reaction to Augustine's teaching, earning him a reputation as an early proponent of semi-Pelagianism. Cassian was also respected, however, for his opposition to Nestorius's teaching and his support of the term *Theotokos*.

Basil of Caesarea (330–79) further advanced the Eastern monastic tradition through his legacy, establishing a rule (a daily order of life that typically includes spiritual practices, work routines, and habits for both communities and individuals) that persists as the basis for the rule followed in the Eastern church today. This approach is more cenobitic in nature and less friendly toward the extreme asceticism of the early desert monks.

Despite the influence of Basil's rule for Eastern monastics, Saint Antony's legacy looms largest among the early monks of the East. And while the Western tradition charted its own course, Antony's legacy and inspiration carried over to the West, influencing Augustine, Benedict, and many more. Antony represents the earliest of the ascetic Christian tradition, establishing an inspiring precedent for personal holiness, commitment to orthodoxy, and dedication to Christ. As one historian recently argued, Saint Antony was considered a "super star" of the faith in the fourth century.[11]

Benedict's Rule and Legacy

Saint Augustine speaks of Antony's inspiring reputation in his conversion story in *Confessions*, book 8, and soon after his conversion in 386, Augustine began recruiting for a monastic community. One of the earliest monastic rules in antiquity is attributed to Augustine, though it is unlikely that he was the author.

Saint Jerome was also attracted to monasticism at least in part as a means of fleeing sexual temptation. By 389 he was director of a newly founded monastery in Bethlehem, where he would remain until his death, establishing his own legacy of biblical scholarship and translation. But the monasticism that became best known in the West originated a century after Augustine and Jerome. It was the hard-working, fiercely communal, spiritually accountable, level-headed monasticism of Benedict of Nursia (c. 480–c.583).

By Benedict's time there were four types of recognized monasticism. First were the Anchorites (or Hermits) who chose to live in isolation. Second were the Sarabites, whom Benedict called the most wicked for they had proven some measure of discipline and looked like monks in appearance, but they acted like pagans in their self-gratification and appeasement of appetites. Third were the Gyrovagues, who wandered from community to community and were despised for their lack of accountability and commitment. In his *Rule*,

[11] Stefana Dan Laing, "The Life of St. Antony," lecture presented at the Sixth Annual Evangelical Voices in the Academy, Wake Forest, NC, October 28, 2021.

Benedict identifies the fourth group, the Cenobites, who live in communities or convents and were subject to an abbot, as his own preferred approach. Early in his journey Benedict tried the solitary ascetic life, and while he respected it, he felt that he most needed the discipline of community.

Stories abound about Benedict's strictness and deep commitment to the disciplined life. Gregory the Great tells of the early days of Benedict's leadership, when the monks hated him and sought to poison him. When Benedict learned of their attempt, he called them together, forgave them, and admitted that he may not be a suitable abbot for them.[12] And yet, some years later he wrote the *Rule* that would serve as the blueprint for western monasticism for centuries.

> "We have therefore to establish a school of the Lord's service, in the institution of which we hope we are going to establish nothing harsh, nothing burdensome."

Benedict's aim was a rule for Cenobites and a school for training in virtue, for such is "the most formidable to the powers of hell."[13] In 529 he founded the monastery at Montecassino some eighty-five miles southeast of Rome, where he would live until his death in 547.[14] Following his death the monastery was destroyed, and it seemed that the Benedictine tradition and way of life had been lost until around 594, when Gregory the Great praised Benedict and his *Rule*, renewing interest in Benedictine monasticism.[15]

Benedict was particularly committed to the principle of an occupied mind, for as he famously declared, "[I]dleness is the enemy of the soul." Thus, *ora et labora*—prayer and work—became the mantra of Benedict's monastic community, for manual labor was not merely necessary for

> Having our loins, therefore, girded with faith and the performance of good works, let us walk in his paths by the guidance of the gospel, that we may deserve to see him who hath called us to his kingdom.
>
> ———
>
> Benedict of Nursia,
> *The Rule of St. Benedict*

---

[12] Mark Galli and Ted Olsen, introduction to *131 Christians Everyone Should Know* (B&H, 2000), 199. Also, Bruce Shelley, *Church History in Plain Language*, 4th ed., updated by R. L. Hatchett (Thomas Nelson, 2013), 129.

[13] Benedict, *The Holy Rule of St. Benedict* (Thomas Richardson and Son, 1865), chapter 1.

[14] "A Brief History of the Benedictine Order," OSB.org, https://www.osb.org/our-roots/a-brief-history-of-the-benedictine-order/.

[15] "Brief History of the Benedictine Order."

survival, but was intrinsically good for the body and soul. The Benedictines commitment to work contrasted that of the Roman mindset, which scorned manual labor as the business of slaves and the lower class. Benedictines, however, found dignity in labor as seen in the ancient Jewish tradition reflected in the positive view of work from Genesis 1 and 2 to Proverbs 31 and beyond.[16]

Benedict's *Rule* is his most enduring legacy. This brief seventy-two-chapter (more like short sections of instruction) manual covers all the bases of monastic living, from the "Instruments of Good Works," "Obedience," "Silence," and "Humility" (chapters 4–7) to the quantity and frequency the Psalms and the alleluia are to be sung (9–17). Benedict was not only attentive to personal devotion and liturgical practices in his *Rule*, but he was also attuned to the challenges of communal living. Thus, he offered instruction for excommunication and how to treat those who had been excommunicated (24, 26, 27) and for those who had been repeatedly corrected but had not amended their ways (28). He also gave instruction on the care of sick brethren (36), the amount of food and drink given to each (39–40), and how the brothers are to treat one another (69–71).

Patrick and the Monastic Missions Movement

Another important thread in the monastic legacy is the missional impulse, which was especially modeled by Patrick of Ireland. Patrick was raised in a wealthy, Romanized British family until he was taken into slavery by Irish raiders at age sixteen. He remained in Ireland for the next six years, where he suffered severely from cold and hunger. His faith was his great solace during these years. At age twenty-two, Patrick escaped, returning to Britain, where he was eventually reunited with his family. He tells in his *Confession* that after returning to Britain, he had a dream calling him to return to Ireland and "walk among us once more."[17]

Compelled by Christ's commission in Matt 28:19 to make disciples of all nations, Patrick returned to the land where he was taken and suffered greatly as a boy. There he

---

[16] Klaus D. Shulz, Robert G. Clouse, and Marianka S. Fousek, *The Church from Age to Age: A History* (Concordia, 2011), 180.

[17] St. Patrick, *The Works of St. Patrick; St. Secundinus; Hymn on St. Patrick*, ed. Johannes Quasten and Joseph C. Plumpe, trans. Ludwig Bieler, vol. 17 of *Ancient Christian Writers* (Paulist Press, 1953), 28.

would spend the rest of his life preaching the gospel, baptizing converts, founding monasteries, and establishing dioceses.[18]

While Patrick's ministry was met with constant threat of possible martyrdom and resistance by officials both local and abroad, Patrick persisted in preaching and teaching, and in honoring local officials. His conciliar-while-confident missional approach remains an example for modern-day missionaries.

> For this we can give to God in return after having been chastened by Him, to exalt and praise His wonders before every nation that is anywhere under the heaven.
>
> ---
>
> Saint Patrick,
> *Confession*

Macrina the Younger

Macrina, sister to Gregory of Nyssa and Basil of Caesarea, is another important figure within the ascetic tradition. She was one of many who had all the talent and privilege necessary to enjoy a life of worldly success yet was willing to forsake it all and influence others to do the same. Much credit is given to the three Cappadocian Fathers, Basil of Caesarea, Gregory of Nyssa, and Gregory of Nazianzus, for their role in galvanizing the church to affirm Nicene orthodoxy in the years between Nicaea and Constantinople. Less known is the fourth "great Cappadocian," Macrina, whose example of godliness inspired a whole community of believers, and who had a pivotal role in the conversion of Basil and Gregory of Nyssa.[19]

Everything we know about Macrina comes from Gregory of Nyssa's pen in the form of two works, *The Life of Saint Macrina* and *On the Soul and Resurrection.* In the first work, Gregory describes a woman whose marvelous beauty was only surpassed by her radiant godliness.[20] She was an example of devotion even to her own mother, and it was Macrina that set Basil on his course of service to the church:

---

[18] An article previously available at the International Mission Board website, the world's largest Christian missions-sending agency, recounts Patrick's legacy: "After just a few decades, more than a thousand Irish would profess faith, by Patrick's own reports. But his influence didn't end with his converts. The zeal and scope of his mission served as a model for his newly-planted Celtic churches. Their desire for and devotion to global gospel advance would lead to the evangelization of the British Isles, Gaul, and Central Europe in the centuries that followed." Robert Wells, "The Legacy of St. Patrick," International Missionary Board, March 17, 2017, https://www.imb.org/2017/03/17/the-legacy-of-st-patrick/.

[19] Justo González, *Early Christian Literature* (Westminster John Knox), 217.

[20] St. Gregory of Nyssa, *The Life of Saint Macrina*, trans. Kevin Corrigan (Wipf & Stock, 2005), 24.

> The great Basil . . . came back from the school where he had been trained for a long time in the discipline of rhetoric. Although when [Macrina] took him in hand he was monstrously conceited about his skill in rhetoric, contemptuous of every high reputation and exalted beyond the leading lights of the province by his self-importance, so swiftly did she win him to the ideal of philosophy that he renounced worldly appearance, showed contempt for the admiration of rhetorical ability and went over of his own accord to this active life of manual labour, preparing for himself by means of his complete poverty a way of life which would tend without impediment toward virtue.[21]

Not only does Gregory's writing portray a godly woman, but also a woman of deep intellectual capacity. His admiration for his sister is both tender and moving. Two of his works take place mainly at her deathbed: in *The Life of Saint Macrina* as a way to show how strong her effect was on the community gathered around her and in *On the Soul and the Resurrection* as the setting for the titular dialogue. Gregory, bishop of Nyssa, calls Macrina "the Teacher" throughout the dialogue, as she is the primary speaker.[22] He puts himself in the position of the puzzled student asking difficult questions, and his older sister gives answers that reveal a keen philosophical mind that nonetheless is deeply devoted to Christ. Macrina serves as a compelling example that the theological depth that the saints of old possessed was never separated from a very real devotion to Christ.

This devotion to Christ deeply influenced Macrina, and she dedicated herself to a life of piety and asceticism from an early age. She embraced a monastic lifestyle, living in seclusion and practicing rigorous self-discipline, prayer, and contemplation. Macrina's commitment to asceticism and her unwavering and inspiring devotion to God yielded a fitting reputation for wisdom, holiness, and compassion. However, Macrina's influence extended beyond her immediate family and monastic community. She also shaped the theological landscape of her time through her engagement in theological discussions with her brothers, Basil of Caesarea and Gregory of Nyssa, contributing to the development of orthodox Christian doctrine and offering insightful reflections on theological controversies of the era.

---

[21] St. Gregory of Nyssa, *Life of Saint Macrina*, 26.

[22] St. Gregory of Nyssa, *On The Soul and the Resurrection*, trans. Catharine P. Roth (St. Vladimir's Seminary Press, 1993), 27.

Early Monasticism and the Great Tradition

Much can and should be said about the legacy of the early monastics. Especially during a time when the light of the martyrs and early Christians was dimming due to cultural compromise, when the popularity and even convenience of Christianity were increasing, and following political devastation with the fall of Rome, these early monastics were quiet "cities on a hill" that shined bright for Christ by discipline, prayer, and denial of material luxuries. As Richard Tarnas observed,

> Despite an awareness of their specially graced spiritual status, intellectually conscious Christians of the early Middle Ages knew themselves to be living in the dim aftermath of a golden age of culture and learning. But in the church's monasteries, a few kept alive the classical spark. In that politically and socially unsettled era, it was the Christian cloister that provided a protected enclosure within which higher pursuits could be safely sustained and developed.[23]

This is not to suggest that the ascetic life is beyond critique. The extreme separatist approach to culture such as that of Antony or Simeon found critique even within monasticism as contrary to the life of Christ, the apostles, and the call of ordinary Christians. As addressed by Benedict, the isolated life such as that modeled by Antony and Simeon the Stylite neglects responsibility to the community of faith. Benedict noted in his *Rule* that this monastic approach lacks fellowship and the accountability of the brethren. For these reasons and more, we cannot recommend a lifelong monastic commitment such as that of Antony or the Benedictines. This does not mean, however, that seasons of extended prayer, solitude, and self-denial are unimportant for followers of Christ. In fact, we affirm that there is much to learn from their way of life and commitment to Christ. In loose connection with our threads of the Great Tradition, we consider the following four lessons from the early monastics.

1. Morality and Spirituality

From Antony's retreat from worldly trappings to Jerome's flight from sexual temptation, monasticism has sought to pursue holiness and depth of spirituality above all. At every

[23] Richard Tarnas, *The Passion of the Western Mind* (Ballantine, 1991), 189.

turn, the early monastics strove to resist the devil and pursue the righteousness of Christ through intense discipline and dedication to scripture and prayer. They teach us not merely to read Scripture, but to see ourselves in the text through practices such as *lectio divina*, an active spiritual reading of Scripture that begins with *lectio* (reading), then *meditatio* (meditation), followed by *oratio* (prayer), ending with *contemplatio* (contemplation). Such a reflective devotional practice is deeply formative for Christians and honors God's Word as the uniquely living text that it is.

One critique of early monasticism is the prioritization of soul over body that undermines a proper biblical theology of the body. Like the Platonists before them, the prominent view of early monastics was that the body weighed down the soul and neglecting the body served to purge the soul unto purity. Yet, despite such an over-emphasis of soul over body, these spiritual forebearers left the church a remarkable legacy of prayer and militance against temptation and sin.

On the moral front, while monastics preferred to avoid worldly matters, it was not uncommon for them to oppose the authorities over matters of injustice. As Antony ministered to those who suffered under the Diocletian persecution of the early fourth century, so respected was he by the officials that he was left alone to minister to others even when he volunteered himself as a martyr. Decades later, near the end of his life of 105 years, Antony publicly defended Athanasius's pro-Nicene agenda in Egypt.

2. Doctrine

In his later years and amidst the ongoing battles with Arian factions following the Council of Nicaea, Antony publicly defended Athanasius's pro-Nicene agenda. While Antony is best remembered for his godliness and not as a theologian, Antony cared deeply about holding on to orthodoxy and threw his influence behind Athanasius to affirm the voice of the church at Nicaea. Basil of Caesarea, a father of Eastern cenobitic monasticism, clarified the church's understanding of the Holy Spirit. Jerome in the West produced the Vulgate, a new Latin version of the Bible translated from the Greek and Hebrew texts; wrote commentaries on much of Scripture; and made important contributions to the history of interpretation.

Of course, monastics did not guarantee orthodox theology. Pelagius, one of the most famous heretics in history, was a British monk who promoted a works-based righteousness now known as Pelagianism (see previous chapter). This aberrant theological position did not emerge from mere theological theorizing but represented Pelagius's reaction to the relaxed morals of Christians, especially Christian clergy, in the late fourth century. Interestingly, Augustine of Hippo, better known for his ministry as bishop but who inspired the earliest monastic rule in the West and lived in a cenobitic context, refuted Pelagius's teachings, promoting instead a thoroughgoing Pauline view of grace through faith. Moreover, Augustine too advanced the pro-Nicene agenda, especially in his work *On the Trinity*, and remained a looming influence in the Christological debates that ensued in the mid-fifth century.

3. Liturgy of Life

The communal dedication to eating, drinking, sleeping, praying, working, and reading for the rest of one's life, such as that found in the Benedictine communities, may sound to modern Christians like a complete forsaking of freedom. But our monastic forefathers would argue otherwise, insisting that committing to the ascetic life *is* freedom: freedom from the many trivial daily decisions that distract us from God.

Submitting oneself to a rule frees one from the when's and what's of daily decision-making about food, clothing, and other trivialities, and pre-commits each moment of the day to all that is necessary for life and godliness. It is a liturgy for all of life. While the separatist cultural approach is not commendable, we do well to learn from the early monastics and are careful to apply what we can to contemporary Christian living.

4. Legacy of Labor

In connection with the emphasis on holy living as an essential thread of the Great Tradition, *ora et labora* remains the mantra of the Benedictine tradition as the rhythm of prayer and work serves as a distinctive of this remarkable community. Benedict begins chapter 48 of his *Rule* with the following:

> As idleness is the enemy of the soul, the brethren are to be employed alternately in *manual labour and pious reading*. Hence, we think it well to regulate the time to be allotted to both these daily exercises, in the following manner. From the Feast of Easter till the 14th of September, exclusively, the brethren going forth in the morning shall be employed at whatever is to be done, from the 1st till about the 4th

hour; from the 4th until near the 6th hour, they will apply themselves to *pious reading*. Having dined after Sext, they will retire to the Dormitory to take some repose, observing in the mean time a profound *silence*.[24]

The Benedictines believed work to be an intrinsic good for both personal wholeness and communal flourishing. But, in highlighting the legacy of prayer and work, we must not miss the emphasis on study. We have already seen the scholarly legacy of Jerome and Benedict; in the decades that followed, the monasteries carried on this legacy by leading the way in theological education and development. This cannot be separated from the earnest commitment to "pious reading" of the monastic communities.

While both inspiring and instructive, the lives of these remarkable men and women must not be received uncritically. Nevertheless, the influence of early monasticism on the following centuries cannot be overstated, and contemporary Christians of all traditions do well to remember these spiritual forebearers with fondness and gratitude, while wisely appropriating their example of holy living into contemporary life.

Recommended Reading

Athanasius of Alexandria. *The Life of Antony and the Letter to Marcellinus*. Edited by Richard J. Payne. Translated by Robert C. Gregg. Paulist Press, 1980.

Behr, John, ed. *Give Me a Word: The Alphabetical Sayings of the Desert Fathers*. Translated by John Wortley. Popular Patristics Series 52. St Vladimir's Seminary Press, 2014.

Cohick, Lynn H., and Amy Brown Hughes. *Christian Women in the Patristic World: Their Influence, Authority, and Legacy in the Second Through Fifth Centuries*. Baker Academic, 2017.

Dan Laing, Stefana. "The Life of St. Antony." Lecture presented at the Sixth Annual Evangelical Voices in the Academy, Wake Forest, NC, October 28, 2021.

Frier, Bruce. *The Codex of Justinian: A New Annotated Translation, with Parallel Latin and Greek Text Based on a Translation by Justice Fred H. Blume*. Cambridge University Press, 2016.

Galli, Mark, and Ted Olsen. *131 Christians Everyone Should Know*. B&H, 2000.

González, Justo. *Early Christian Literature*. Westminster John Knox, 2019.

[24] Saint Benedict, *Holy Rule of Saint Benedict*, 90–91, emphasis added.

Noll, Mark. *Turning Points*. 2nd ed. Baker Academic, 2000.

Shelley, Bruce. *Church History in Plain Language*. Zondervan Academic, 2021.

Shulz, Klaus D., Robert G. Clouse, and Marianka S. Fousek. *The Church from Age to Age: A History*. Concordia, 2011.

St. Benedict Abbot of Monte Cassino. *The Holy Rule of Saint Benedict*. Thomas Richardson and Son, 1865.

St. Gregory of Nyssa. *On the Soul and the Resurrection*. Translated by Catharine P. Roth. St. Vladimir's Seminary Press, 1993.

St. Gregory of Nyssa. *The Life of Saint Macrina*. Translated by Kevin Corrigan. Wipf & Stock, 2005.

St. Patrick. *The Works of St. Patrick; St. Secundinus; Hymn on St. Patrick*. Edited by Johannes Quasten and Joseph C. Plumpe. Translated by Ludwig Bieler. Vol. 17 of *Ancient Christian Writers*. Paulist Press, 1953.

Tarnas, Richard. *The Passion of the Western Mind*. Ballantine, 1991.

—— Chapter 13 ——

Gregory the Great and the Rise of the Papacy

Gregory the Great rose to prominence as one of the most influential figures in the history of the papacy during a dramatic period of cultural and political upheaval in the Western Roman Empire. Gregory's role as bishop of Rome would mark the beginning of a new era for the church and the papacy, as he sought to assert the authority of the church in both spiritual and temporal matters and to promote the Christian faith in the face of political and social challenges.

Gregory the Great

Gregory the Great, born into a prominent Roman family in 540, enjoyed the privileges and opportunities afforded by his noble birth. His father, Gordianus, served as a senator and held high-ranking governmental positions. Gregory grew up in a wealthy family, where he was educated and exposed to late antique Rome's cultural and intellectual life. He received a thorough education, common among the nobility, in secular and religious subjects, studying grammar, rhetoric, law, and literature. Following in his family's footsteps, Gregory embarked on a career in civil service, serving in various administrative roles within the Roman government. His talent and dedication soon caught the attention of Emperor

Justinian I, who appointed him prefect of Rome—an esteemed position responsible for overseeing the city's governance and administration. As prefect, Gregory demonstrated competence and integrity, earning a reputation for fairness and compassion in his dealings with the people of Rome.

Despite his success in secular life, Gregory deeply longed for a more contemplative and ascetic existence. Inspired by the foundational guide for monastic life in the Western church, the *Rule of St. Benedict* by Benedict of Nursia (480–547), and the example of his mother, who had devoted herself to a life of prayer and charity, Gregory decided to renounce his worldly ambitions and embrace the monastic life. Gregory's career trajectory soon transitioned from the corridors of power in Rome to the solitude of the monastic cell. In 574, Gregory resigned from his position as prefect and withdrew to the seclusion of a monastery on his family's estate in Rome. There he dedicated himself to prayer, meditation, and asceticism, seeking spiritual enlightenment and union with God. His decision to embrace monasticism reflected a deep commitment to holiness and spiritual perfection. This pivotal moment in Gregory's life would set the stage for his later achievements as a monk, theologian, and, eventually, as one of the most influential popes in the history of the Western church.

Gregory's time in the monastery proved transformative, deepening his faith and shaping his spiritual outlook. He embraced the rigors of monastic discipline with zeal, fasting, praying, and practicing self-denial with fervor. His ascetic lifestyle and devotion to prayer earned him admiration and respect among his fellow monks, who recognized him as a model of piety and holiness. In the monastery, Gregory also immersed himself in the study of Scripture, theology, and the writings of the church fathers, honing his intellectual faculties and theological insights. His erudition and theological acumen would later distinguish him as one of his time's greatest theologians and thinkers.

Gregory Becomes Bishop of Rome

In 590, Pope Pelagius II passed away during a devastating plague that ravaged Rome and its surrounding territories, leaving the church in need of a new leader. At this time, Rome faced numerous challenges, including political instability, social unrest, and the looming threat of invasion by barbarian tribes. The church struggled with internal divisions and doctrinal controversies, adding to the uncertainty and turmoil. During these tumultuous circumstances, Gregory, who had distinguished himself as a monk, scholar, and administrator, emerged as a consensus candidate for the papacy. His reputation for piety, wisdom, and administrative competence made him a natural choice to lead the church through this crisis.

Despite his qualifications and the overwhelming support of his fellow clergy, Gregory viewed the prospect of assuming the highest office in the church with a deep sense of apprehension and humility. He saw himself as unworthy of such a lofty responsibility, preferring instead the quietude and anonymity of monastic life to the burdensome duties and worldly entanglements that came with the papacy. Nevertheless, in obedience to God's will and his peers' unanimous affirmation, Gregory reluctantly accepted the solemn charge of leading the church as bishop of Rome. His reluctance, far from being a sign of weakness or inadequacy, demonstrated humility and reverence for the sacred office he occupied.

Gregory became pope at a critical juncture in the history of the church and the Roman Empire. The Western Roman Empire had collapsed. The church faced internal challenges, including theological controversies, doctrinal disputes, and the spread of heresies. The devastating plague that had claimed the life of Pope Pelagius II continued to wreak havoc, further exacerbating the suffering and despair of the people. The city of Rome faced famine, disease, and social unrest, exacerbating the already dire conditions facing the population.

Despite the challenges and uncertainties facing the church and the Roman Empire, Gregory's papal authority was quickly accepted and confirmed by both clergy and laity alike. His reputation for piety, humility, and leadership qualities inspired confidence and endeared him to those in the church, who looked to him for guidance and support during these troubled times. Gregory's diplomatic skills and political acumen enabled him to navigate the complex dynamics of Roman and Byzantine politics, securing the support and cooperation of key political figures and institutions. Maurice, emperor of the Eastern Roman Empire, supported his ascension to the position of Bishop of Rome and recognized him as the legitimate pope. With the support of both the people and the imperial authorities, Gregory's papacy paved the way for an enduring legacy in the history of the Western church.

Gregory's Role as Bishop of Rome

In the following years, Gregory enjoyed a series of remarkable achievements, including his efforts to reform the church, promote Christian unity, and provide for the welfare of the people of Rome. Despite his formidable challenges, Gregory's leadership and pastoral care would shape the course of the church for centuries to come. Upon becoming pope, Gregory wasted no time setting forth his initial priorities for reform and administration. Chief among these was his unwavering commitment to purifying the church of corruption and restoring its moral integrity. Gregory recognized that clergy misconduct and the lax enforcement of ecclesiastical discipline undermined the church's credibility and moral authority. To address these pressing concerns, Gregory embarked on a rigorous program of reform aimed at rooting out simony, nepotism, and other abuses within the clergy.

Simony refers to the buying or selling of ecclesiastical offices, sacraments, or spiritual benefits, a practice named after Simon Magus, who, according to Acts 8:18–24, attempted to buy the power of the Holy Spirit from the apostles. In Gregory's time, simony was a widespread problem, particularly in the appointment of bishops and clergy. Wealthy individuals or influential families would use financial or political leverage to secure ecclesiastical positions, often placing unqualified or unspiritual individuals in roles of significant authority.

Gregory strongly condemned simony as a grave sin and a threat to the spiritual integrity of the church. He emphasized that ecclesiastical offices were not commodities to be traded but sacred responsibilities entrusted to those called by God. He sought to ensure that clerical appointments were based on merit, spirituality, and adherence to church doctrine rather than wealth or influence. Gregory's reform efforts included stricter oversight of episcopal appointments and the enforcement of canonical laws prohibiting simony.

Nepotism refers to the practice of favoring relatives, particularly in the granting of ecclesiastical positions. In Gregory's era, it was common for bishops, abbots, and other church leaders to appoint family members to influential roles, regardless of their qualifications. This practice often led to abuses of power, weakened the moral authority of the church, and fostered divisions within ecclesiastical communities.

Gregory took a firm stance against nepotism, advocating for a church leadership that prioritized spiritual qualifications over familial ties. He recognized that nepotism not only compromised the integrity of the church but also hindered its mission by placing unworthy individuals in positions of authority. In his *Pastoral Rule*, Gregory laid out the qualities required of clergy, emphasizing humility, piety, and a genuine commitment to pastoral care, which nepotistic appointments often disregarded.

Gregory the Great's reforms targeted both simony and nepotism as part of a broader effort to purify the church and restore its credibility. He implemented measures to ensure the accountability of bishops and clergy, including the establishment of stricter criteria for appointments and the promotion of monastic leaders, whom he saw as exemplars of discipline and virtue. Gregory's own commitment to reform was evident in his rejection of luxury and his emphasis on pastoral care, which set an example for the church hierarchy.

By addressing these practices, Gregory sought to strengthen the spiritual authority of the church and its leaders, ensuring that ecclesiastical offices were held by individuals who were genuinely devoted to serving God and the Christian community. His reforms had a lasting impact, influencing subsequent efforts to combat corruption and promote clerical discipline throughout the medieval church.

Gregory the Great's commitment to pastoral care was a cornerstone of his papacy, and it manifested in tangible ways through the establishment and support of numerous charitable institutions, including hospitals, orphanages, and homeless shelters. Gregory understood that the church had a duty not only to address the spiritual needs of the faithful but also to provide for their physical well-being, particularly the poor and vulnerable. His initiatives were deeply rooted in his theology, which viewed acts of mercy and care for the marginalized as essential expressions of Christian love and pastoral responsibility.

Gregory's tenure as pope coincided with a period of social and economic turmoil, marked by the collapse of Roman infrastructure, frequent invasions, famine, and disease. In response, Gregory mobilized the resources of the church to meet the pressing needs of the people. He directed the vast wealth of the Roman church, particularly its landholdings, toward charitable activities. The income from these estates was used to establish and maintain hospitals to care for the sick, including both clergy and laity, regardless of their ability to pay. These hospitals provided not only medical care but also spiritual support, reflecting Gregory's holistic approach to human well-being.

Orphanages were another key focus of Gregory's charitable efforts. Recognizing the plight of children left destitute by war, famine, or disease, he directed the church to provide shelter, education, and sustenance for orphans. These institutions were often attached to monasteries, which Gregory saw as ideal settings for instilling Christian values and providing structured care. Similarly, Gregory championed the establishment of homeless shelters, where the destitute could find food, lodging, and protection. In these shelters, the church sought not only to alleviate immediate suffering but also to restore dignity and hope to the lives of the poor.

Gregory's personal involvement in these efforts set an example for clergy and laypeople alike. He personally distributed alms and ensured that resources were allocated efficiently to meet the needs of the community. His letters frequently mention his concern for the poor and his efforts to mitigate the suffering of those affected by famine and pestilence. In one famous instance, he organized the church's grain supplies to feed Rome's starving population during a particularly harsh period of scarcity.

Through these initiatives, Gregory institutionalized the church's role as a provider of social services, a legacy that endured throughout the medieval period. By establishing hospitals, orphanages, and shelters, Gregory not only addressed the immediate needs of his time but also laid the groundwork for the church's broader mission of charity and social justice. His commitment to pastoral care exemplified the integration of spiritual leadership with practical compassion, embodying the ideal of the church as a refuge for all in need.

As the bishop of Rome and de facto ruler of Rome during political instability, he assumed the responsibilities of secular governance with prudence and diplomacy. He negotiated with barbarian invaders, administered justice, and provided for the welfare of the populace, earning him the title of "Servant of the Servants of God." One of Gregory's enduring legacies is his literary contributions, most notably his extensive correspondence and theological writings, which encompass various topics, including pastoral care, moral instruction, liturgy, and spirituality.

Gregory Reforms the Church

Upon assuming the papacy, Pope Gregory the Great inherited a church in dire need of administrative reform. One of his priorities was reorganizing the management of papal estates and finances, which had become disorganized and inefficient due to years of neglect and mismanagement. Gregory implemented strict financial oversight and accountability measures, appointing competent administrators to oversee the administration of church properties and ensuring that revenues benefited the poor and supported charitable works. Furthermore, Gregory took steps to expand the church's economic resources through prudent investments and strategic acquisitions of land and properties. By consolidating and expanding the church's financial base, Gregory sought to ensure its long-term stability and viability, enabling the church to fulfill its mission of serving the spiritual and material needs of believers.

Central to Gregory's administrative reforms was his efforts to overhaul the management of papal finances. Recognizing the critical importance of financial solvency to the effective functioning of the church, Gregory implemented a series of measures designed to streamline revenue collection, eliminate wasteful expenditures, and ensure fiscal accountability. He instituted regular audits of ecclesiastical finances, appointed competent stewards to oversee the administration of church properties, and enforced strict standards of financial transparency and integrity among the clergy—a radical departure from the lax fiscal practices that had plagued the church in previous eras.

In addition to reforming the church's financial administration, Gregory also sought to centralize ecclesiastical authority under the papacy. Recognizing the need for robust and centralized leadership to address the church's challenges, Gregory asserted the primacy of the Roman church in matters of doctrine, discipline, and governance. He convened synods and councils to address doctrinal controversies and disciplinary issues, asserting the authority of the papacy to adjudicate disputes and enforce ecclesiastical norms.

Central to Gregory's vision of effective governance was the establishment of a professional bureaucracy staffed by competent and dedicated officials. Gregory recruited talented individuals from diverse backgrounds to serve in critical administrative roles, irrespective of their social status or ecclesiastical rank, who were skilled administrators to manage the complex affairs of the church. Under Gregory's leadership, the papal administration evolved into a well-organized and efficient bureaucracy with clear lines of authority, standardized procedures, and specialized departments overseeing various aspects of church affairs. Gregory's emphasis on meritocracy and competence led him to fill administrative positions based on merit rather than nepotism or favoritism, fostering a culture of professionalism and integrity within the papal office. He established schools and seminaries to educate future church leaders and bureaucrats, equipping them with the skills and knowledge necessary to navigate the complexities of ecclesiastical administration.

Gregory's creation of a professional bureaucracy was a departure from the ad hoc and decentralized administrative structures that characterized the early medieval church. An implication of this reorganization was a greater centralization of power. Drawing inspiration from the administrative models of the Roman Empire, Gregory established a cadre of skilled bureaucrats and administrators—known as the papal curia—to assist him in the day-to-day governance of the church. These bureaucrats, drawn from the ranks of the clergy and the laity alike, were charged with a wide range of responsibilities, including the management of papal correspondence, the supervision of ecclesiastical appointments, and the execution of papal directives—a model of bureaucratic efficiency that would become a hallmark of the papal administration in the centuries that followed.

Papal diplomats played a crucial role in Gregory's efforts to extend papal authority and influence beyond the borders of Rome. Acting as envoys of the papacy, they represented the interests of the church in diplomatic negotiations and international relations, advocating for the rights and privileges of the church and promoting Christian unity and cooperation.

In particular, the pope's representatives were entrusted with resolving disputes and conflicts between rival factions within the church, mediating between warring bishops, and reconciling schismatic communities. They also played a crucial role in promoting papal policies and initiatives, disseminating papal decrees and pronouncements, and ensuring compliance with ecclesiastical norms and regulations. Papal diplomats were dispatched to foreign courts and kingdoms to negotiate treaties, alliances, and agreements on behalf of the papacy.

An example of this diplomatic strategy in action mediating church disputes is the Schism of the Three Chapters in northern Italy. This schism arose after the condemnation of the "Three Chapters" at the Second Council of Constantinople (553), which many Western bishops viewed as undermining the authority of the earlier Council of Chalcedon (451).

When Gregory became pope, the schism persisted in northern Italian regions, such as Milan and Aquileia, where bishops and clergy refused to accept the council's rulings. Gregory sought to restore unity in the church by balancing firmness with diplomacy. He dispatched papal ambassadors to engage in negotiations with the schismatic bishops, seeking to reconcile their opposition while maintaining the orthodoxy of Chalcedonian doctrine.

Through his representatives, Gregory emphasized the pastoral responsibility of the bishops to preserve church unity and avoid prolonged division. His diplomatic efforts, conducted both directly and through his representatives, eventually contributed to the gradual reconciliation of the schismatic churches with Rome. This success not only healed a significant rift in the Western church but also reinforced the authority of the papacy as a mediator in ecclesiastical disputes, highlighting Gregory's skillful use of legates as instruments of papal diplomacy, fostering unity and resolving theological conflicts while respecting local concerns.

A Legacy of Holiness and Evangelization

Pope Gregory the Great's commitment to monasticism and missionary work is a testament to his fervent devotion to the spread of the gospel and the spiritual welfare of humanity. Throughout his pontificate, Gregory dedicated himself to the monastic life, founded numerous monasteries, and dispatched missionaries to evangelize pagan populations. Gregory's commitment to monasticism was evident from an early age. Despite his noble birth and promising career in civil administration, Gregory felt called to renounce the trappings of worldly success in favor of a life devoted to prayer, contemplation, and asceticism. He established a monastery on his family estate in Rome, where he lived a life of rigorous self-discipline and communal worship—a testament to his unwavering commitment to the monastic ideal. Gregory's advocacy for monasticism extended beyond the confines of his monastery. Recognizing the spiritual benefits of monastic life and its potential to revitalize the church in an age of moral decline, Gregory founded numerous monasteries throughout the Western Roman Empire, providing havens of piety, learning, and charitable works for monks and nuns alike. These monasteries served as centers of spiritual renewal and cultural preservation, preserving the rich legacy of Christian tradition and transmitting it to future generations.

Gregory devoted himself to the contemplative life and asceticism. Having forsaken a promising career in civil administration to embrace the monastic vocation, Gregory understood firsthand the spiritual benefits of renunciation and withdrawal from the world's distractions. Throughout his pontificate, Gregory sought to cultivate a culture of monasticism within the church, encouraging clergy and laity to embrace lives of prayer, austerity, and self-denial to draw closer to God and attain spiritual perfection. His founding of monasteries as centers of spiritual and intellectual life was central to Gregory's promotion of monasticism. Recognizing the need for havens of prayer and scholarship amidst the chaos and upheaval of the early Middle Ages, Gregory established a network of monastic communities throughout the Western Roman Empire and beyond—providing refuge for the weary pilgrim, solace for the troubled soul, and a beacon of hope in a world wracked by uncertainty and despair. These monasteries, guided by the *Rule of St. Benedict* and inspired by the ideals of poverty, chastity, and obedience, served as bastions of stability and sanctity in an age of turmoil and transition.

In addition to his efforts to promote monasticism, Gregory was a tireless champion of missionary outreach and evangelization. Recognizing the imperative to spread the gospel to every corner of the earth, Gregory dispatched missionaries to the farthest reaches of the known world—bringing the light of Christ to pagan peoples and establishing the church in lands untouched by the gospel message. One of Gregory's missionary endeavors was to the Lombards, a Germanic tribe that had invaded Italy in the late sixth century. Despite the political tensions between the Lombards and the Roman Empire, Gregory saw an opportunity for evangelization and reconciliation. The Lombard court during Gregory the Great's papacy was located in Pavia, the capital of the Lombard Kingdom in northern Italy. Pavia, known as Ticinum in Roman times, became the center of Lombard political and administrative power after the Lombards established their kingdom in Italy in AD 568.

Gregory dispatched representatives, including bishops and other church representatives, to Pavia to negotiate peace treaties and promote diplomatic relations. These representatives also worked to mitigate conflicts between the Lombards and the Roman population while fostering the spread of Christianity among the Lombard rulers and their subjects. The Lombards presented both a military and religious challenge. Many Lombards followed Arian Christianity, which was considered heretical by the Roman church, while others adhered to traditional pagan beliefs. Gregory sought to convert them to Nicene Christianity, aiming to reduce religious divisions and integrate them into the broader Christian world.

Gregory's strategy included negotiating directly with Lombard rulers, particularly Queen Theodelinda, a Bavarian princess and devout Catholic. Theodelinda's influence proved pivotal in the success of Gregory's mission among the Lombards. She supported the establishment of Nicene Christianity in Lombard territories, and her son, Adaloald, was baptized in the Catholic faith, marking a significant step toward the conversion of the Lombard leadership. Gregory also sent letters and gifts, such as a jeweled cross and theological writings, to strengthen ties with Theodelinda and promote orthodox Christianity.

However, Gregory's mission faced significant challenges. The Lombards were politically fragmented, with different dukes holding varying degrees of influence and adhering to diverse religious practices. While Theodelinda's court embraced Catholicism, other Lombard leaders and regions retained Arian or pagan practices, slowing the broader acceptance of Nicene Christianity. Additionally, the military threat posed by the Lombards to Rome and surrounding regions created ongoing tensions that hindered purely spiritual efforts.

Augustine of Canterbury and the Gregorian Mission

One of Gregory's most enduring legacies in missionary expansion is the conversion of England to Christianity. In 596, Gregory dispatched a mission led by a Benedictine monk, Augustine of Canterbury, and around forty other monks to evangelize the Anglo-Saxon kingdoms of England. They established a monastery at Canterbury as a mission center. Augustine (died c. 604) became the first archbishop of Canterbury and is often called the "Apostle to the English" because of his evangelism of Anglo-Saxon England.

The mission, known as the Gregorian Mission, was a resounding success, leading to the conversion of King Ethelbert of Kent and the establishment of Christianity as the dominant religion in England. Under Augustine's leadership, the Gregorian Mission achieved remarkable success, baptizing thousands of converts and establishing a network of churches, monasteries, and schools throughout England, spreading the gospel and laying the foundation for the Christianization of the Anglo-Saxon kingdoms. Augustine's mission also fostered cultural exchange and collaboration between the Roman and Anglo-Saxon churches, contributing to a unified Christian identity in England. Augustine's missionary efforts laid the groundwork for the Christianization of England and the emergence of the English church as a bastion of faith and culture in the medieval world.

Gregory's missions to the Lombards, barbarian tribes, and England led to the spread of Christianity throughout the continent, transforming Europe from a patchwork of pagan tribes into a Christian civilization. His missionary zeal and commitment to evangelization paved the way for converting countless people and establishing a Christian witness across the continent.

Gregory's missionary endeavors contributed to Western civilization's spread and European culture's Christianization. Through establishing churches, monasteries, and schools, Gregory fostered the development of a Christian society characterized by piety, learning, and cultural flourishing. By sending missionaries throughout Europe, Gregory contributed to the expansion of Christianity, but he also contributed to the expansion of Roman influence on the continent and beyond. By establishing Christian communities and ecclesiastical structures in newly converted territories, Gregory strengthened the ties between the Roman church and secular rulers, creating a symbiotic relationship between church and the state in their regions. This close relationship would only become greater in the Holy Roman Empire, which we will examine later.

Gregory the Great: Defender of Rome

Pope Gregory was defender and protector of the Roman people. When he became the bishop of Rome, Gregory could not have imagined the part he would soon play in protecting the people within his city and church. One of Gregory's most notable contributions as the defender of Rome was his adept management of food distribution during periods of scarcity and famine. Recognizing the acute suffering experienced by the city's inhabitants during times of food shortages, Gregory organized relief efforts to provide sustenance to the hungry and alleviate their plight. Through the establishment of granaries, the distribution of alms, and the mobilization of resources from ecclesiastical estates, Gregory ensured that the basic needs of the Roman populace were met, thereby earning the enduring gratitude and admiration of the city's residents.

As bishop of Rome and spiritual leader of the Western church, Gregory assumed a central role in defending the city of Rome against external threats, including barbarian invasions and incursions by hostile forces. He organized the city's defense, fortified its walls, mobilized troops, and coordinated relief efforts to protect the population from harm. Gregory's leadership during times of crisis earned him the admiration and gratitude of the Roman people, who looked to him for guidance and protection in the face of adversity.

Gregory recognized the importance of maintaining diplomatic relations with the Lombards to ensure the safety and security of Rome and its surrounding territories. He negotiated with the Lombard kings, seeking to secure peace treaties and agreements that would protect the interests of the church and the Roman people. Through diplomatic overtures and negotiations, Gregory managed to secure temporary peace agreements with the Lombard kings, averting outright conflict and preserving the integrity of the papal territories.

Similarly, Gregory engaged in diplomatic initiatives with the Byzantine Empire, the successor state to the Eastern Roman Empire. As we will see, Gregory had some significant disagreements with the Byzantine church, but he maintained a generally amicable relationship with the Byzantine emperors, collaborating on matters of mutual concern. For example, Gregory referred to Emperor Maurice as his "lord" (*dominus*) and expressed loyalty to the emperor in his correspondence. In one letter, Gregory described himself as "the faithful servant of your Piety," signaling his recognition of the emperor's overarching authority. This deference was part of Gregory's strategy to maintain a cooperative relationship while advancing the church's interests.

During Gregory's papacy, Italy faced ongoing threats from the Lombards, who were encroaching on Byzantine territories. Although Gregory was frustrated by the Byzantine military's inability to decisively deal with the Lombards, he worked to coordinate defense efforts with the Byzantine administration, particularly the exarch in Ravenna, who acted as the emperor's representative. Gregory often used his resources to organize local defenses and negotiate truces with the Lombards, effectively supplementing Byzantine efforts and stabilizing the region. Despite occasional tension over these issues, Gregory consistently sought to align his actions with Byzantine policies.

While Gregory sought to maintain good relations with the Byzantine Empire, he also found himself embroiled in disputes with the Byzantine patriarchate, typically over matters related to ecclesiastical authority. Notable conflicts arose between the Roman and Byzantine churches, reflecting growing tensions over authority, jurisdiction, and theological differences. One of the most prominent disputes concerned the title "ecumenical patriarch," used by the patriarch of Constantinople, John IV (John the Faster). Gregory viewed the title as an overreach and a claim to universal authority over the church, which he believed diminished the primacy of the bishop of Rome. Gregory argued that such a title was incompatible with the humility expected of church leaders and instead emphasized his own title, "servus servorum Dei" (servant of the servants of God), to underscore his vision of leadership as service rather than domination. This conflict symbolized broader tensions regarding the balance of power between Rome and Constantinople.

The ongoing Schism of the Three Chapters also created friction. This controversy, which we examine in chapter 9, had left many Western bishops, particularly in northern Italy, in opposition to Byzantine-imposed decisions. These bishops felt the condemnations undermined the authority of the earlier Council of Chalcedon (451). Gregory worked to reconcile these bishops with the broader church while maintaining unity, but his efforts often conflicted with the more uncompromising stance of Byzantine authorities. This situation highlighted Gregory's delicate balancing act as he sought to preserve Western autonomy without severing ties with Constantinople.

Administrative and jurisdictional disputes further strained relations. Gregory often clashed with Byzantine officials over the governance of churches in regions under imperial control, such as southern Italy, Sicily, and the Balkans. While Gregory sought to assert Roman authority in these areas, the Byzantine emperor and the patriarch of Constantinople maintained their influence, leading to ongoing administrative tensions. Liturgical differences, such as variations in the timing of feasts and fasting practices, added to the strain, with Gregory defending the autonomy of Roman traditions against Byzantine customs.

Another area of divergence was monasticism. Gregory's strong promotion of the *Rule of St. Benedict* as the ideal for Western monasticism and church reform sometimes conflicted with Byzantine monastic traditions, which emphasized different spiritual practices, including hesychasm (inner stillness). These disputes over authority, liturgy, and monastic ideals reflected the growing divergence between the Eastern and Western churches. While Gregory worked to maintain unity, his firm defense of Roman primacy and traditions foreshadowed the deeper divisions that would later lead to the East-West schism.

Despite these tensions, Gregory defended papal authority and the integrity of the Roman church as primary among all bishops. He asserted the primacy of the papacy in matters of doctrine and discipline, rejecting attempts by the Byzantine patriarchate to dictate ecclesiastical policy and undermine papal prerogatives. Gregory's resolute defense of papal authority, coupled with his commitment to church unity and orthodoxy, played a crucial role in shaping the course of theological debates and ecclesiastical governance in the early medieval period. This conflict reflected broader tensions between the Eastern and Western churches and foreshadowed future disputes over papal authority and the nature of the relationship between the churches.

Gregory's leadership during times of crisis extended beyond mere military defense to encompass spiritual protection and pastoral care. He comforted the people of Rome in times of distress, offering prayers and spiritual guidance to sustain their faith and courage.

Gregory: Theologian and Author

Along with being a capable ruler and diplomat, Gregory the Great was also a prolific author. One of his most influential works is his *Pastoral Rule*, a treatise on pastoral ministry and spiritual leadership. This influential text serves as a guidebook for clergy, offering practical advice and spiritual wisdom on the duties and responsibilities of pastoral ministry. Written around 590, shortly after Gregory became pope, the work served as both a manual for bishops and an examination of the spiritual and practical aspects of church leadership. Its enduring relevance lies in several key features.

First, *Pastoral Rule* emphasizes the moral and spiritual formation of the pastor as foundational to effective leadership. Gregory insists that clergy must embody the virtues they preach, living lives marked by humility, holiness, and compassion. He stresses that a pastor's moral integrity and personal sanctity are indispensable for guiding others, as spiritual authority is rooted in the authenticity of one's example.

Second, Gregory offers practical advice for addressing the diverse needs of a congregation. He recognizes that pastoral care must be tailored to individuals, taking into account their spiritual maturity, life circumstances, and struggles. Gregory advises pastors to use discernment in their teaching and discipline, adapting their approach to nurture and strengthen the faith of their flock. His nuanced understanding of human nature makes the *Pastoral Rule* particularly insightful for leaders navigating the complexities of ministry.

Third, the *Pastoral Rule* underscores the dual role of the pastor as both a shepherd and a servant. Gregory draws on the image of Christ as the Good Shepherd, calling pastors to lead with gentleness while safeguarding their congregation from spiritual dangers. He balances this with a reminder that pastors must also serve their people, prioritizing their welfare over personal ambition or comfort.

Gregory offers practical advice on the art of preaching, urging clergy to speak with clarity, conviction, and compassion and to tailor their message to the needs and capacities of their audience. He emphasizes the importance of biblical literacy and theological acumen as foundational for effective pastoral leadership. He insists that pastors must be deeply rooted in Scripture, not only to gain intellectual knowledge but to allow its teachings to transform their own lives. Gregory views Scripture as the ultimate guide for life and ministry, containing divine wisdom applicable to all aspects of human existence. He also emphasizes the need for pastors to interpret and present Scripture in ways that resonate with their congregation, adapting their teaching to the spiritual maturity, background, and circumstances of their listeners. This adaptability requires a profound understanding of biblical principles and theological frameworks, enabling pastors to address the diverse needs of their communities meaningfully.

Gregory further highlights the role of theological knowledge in defending the faith against heresy and correcting misunderstandings within the church. He stresses the importance of doctrinal precision and the ability to discern truth from error, particularly in an era rife with theological disputes. For Gregory, Scripture is not only a source of teaching but also a tool for pastoral care, providing moral and spiritual insights to comfort, correct, and inspire. At the same time, he urges pastors to approach their study with humility, recognizing that the depths of Scripture cannot be fully mastered. This commitment to lifelong learning ensures that their engagement with Scripture is not an intellectual exercise alone but a spiritual discipline that deepens their relationship with God. By emphasizing the centrality of biblical literacy and theological acumen, Gregory reflects his conviction that a pastor's preparation directly impacts their ability to lead and nurture their congregation faithfully.

In addition to his insights on leadership and preaching, Gregory encourages clergy to cultivate a spirit of pastoral solicitude, attending to their flock's physical, emotional, and spiritual needs with compassion and empathy. He underscores the importance of regular visitation, counseling, sacramental ministry, and the administration of discipline and correction when necessary—all to nurture the spiritual growth and maturity of Christians.

Finally, Gregory acknowledges the burdens of pastoral ministry, offering guidance on how to maintain spiritual vitality amidst the challenges of leadership. He emphasizes the importance of prayer, self-examination, and reliance on God's grace as essential practices for sustaining a life of service.

Gregory's *Dialogues* is a collection of biographies and hagiographies of saints, martyrs, and miracles, recounting the lives of saints and documenting miraculous events attributed to their intercession, written around 593. The work covers various topics, including the lives of saints, the power of prayer and miracles, the nature of sin and redemption, and the reality of spiritual warfare. These dialogues, which include accounts of Gregory's encounters with the supernatural, serve as both edifying narratives and theological treatises on the nature of divine providence and the workings of grace in the lives of believers. Through vivid storytelling and theological reflection, Gregory's *Dialogues* offers insights into the spiritual struggles and triumphs of the early church, seeking to inspire faith and devotion in his readers while also providing moral and spiritual instruction for the Christian life. Gregory composed this work to inspire faith, moral virtue, and devotion among Christians during a time of widespread societal upheaval, including invasions, plagues, and the decline of the Roman world.

The *Dialogues* is structured as a series of conversations between Gregory and his deacon, Peter, which allows Gregory to address theological and spiritual questions in a narrative format. The text focuses particularly on the lives of holy men and women in Italy, showcasing their sanctity, miraculous deeds, and steadfast faith in the face of challenges. Gregory intended the *Dialogues* to demonstrate the active presence of God in the world, reinforcing the belief that divine grace and intervention were accessible to all who sought holiness. The *Dialogues* also contains accounts of miracles and visions, including healings, exorcisms, and revelations of the afterlife, which Gregory used to underscore the reality of divine providence and the hope of salvation. While the text reflects popular piety and elements of folklore, it also serves as a theological treatise, exploring themes such as the intercession of saints, the nature of the soul, and the moral lessons drawn from the lives of the righteous. By blending narrative storytelling with theological insight, Gregory's *Dialogues* became a helpful tool for teaching and evangelization, preserving the memory of early saints and inspiring Christians to pursue holiness in their own lives.

Throughout his theological writings and commentaries, Gregory champions allegorical methods and moral interpretations as essential tools for unlocking the hidden depths of Scripture and discerning its spiritual significance for Christians. Gregory revered the sacred texts, convinced that they contain spiritual truths that transcend mere literalism. Gregory recognizes the multilayered nature of Scripture—that is, the conviction that sacred texts contain not only historical narratives and doctrinal teachings but also allegorical symbols, moral lessons, and spiritual insights that speak to the deepest longings and aspirations of the human soul. In his commentaries on the Bible, Gregory employs allegorical methods to uncover the spiritual meanings hidden beneath the surface of the biblical texts, drawing connections between Old Testament figures, events, and rituals and their fulfillment in the person and work of Christ.

Gregory emphasizes the moral dimension of Scripture, viewing the sacred texts as a repository of timeless wisdom and ethical guidance for the Christian life. He encourages believers to discern the moral lessons and spiritual truths embedded within the biblical narratives, drawing inspiration from the exemplary lives of the saints and the teachings of the church fathers to illuminate the path of virtue and holiness. In Gregory's view, the purpose of biblical interpretation is not merely to acquire intellectual knowledge or doctrinal certainty but to cultivate love for God and neighbor and to be transformed in mind and heart by the Word of God.

For example, in his *Morals on the Book of Job*, Gregory offers a moral and spiritual interpretation of the trials and sufferings of the biblical patriarch Job, drawing parallels between Job's experiences and the struggles of the Christian soul in its journey toward God. The work is a theological commentary that blends biblical exegesis, moral instruction, and allegorical interpretation. Written during Gregory's time in Constantinople (AD 578–86), this work offers profound insights into the nature of human suffering, virtue, and the pursuit of divine wisdom. One of the central themes Gregory explores is the role of patience in the Christian life, using Job's unwavering endurance in the face of suffering as a model for all believers. For Gregory, Job exemplifies the ideal Christian virtue of patience, which he describes as "the root and guardian of all the virtues."[1] Through Job's steadfastness, Gregory teaches that suffering, though difficult, can serve as a means of spiritual growth and purification when approached with faith and perseverance.

Gregory also offers a detailed allegorical interpretation of Job's three friends, who, rather than comforting Job, accuse him of sin. Gregory suggests that these friends represent false teachers or misguided counselors who rely on human logic rather than divine wisdom. Their failure to recognize Job's righteousness serves as a warning against trusting in worldly reasoning when confronting spiritual matters. Similarly, Job's physical affliction through the boils is understood by Gregory as an allegory for the spiritual wounds caused by sin. He interprets the boils as a visible manifestation of inner sin, asserting that, just as Job's suffering was visible to others, so too are the consequences of sin evident to the Christian community. This interpretation highlights the need for repentance and the grace of God to heal spiritual wounds.

---

[1] Gregory the Great, *Forty Gospel Homilies, Homily 35.7*, David Hurst, OSB, in Fathers of the Church, vol. 123 (Catholic University of America Press, 1990), 287.

Gregory's interpretation of Job's wife further contributes to his moral teachings. Job's wife, who urges him to curse God and die, is seen by Gregory as a symbol of temptation. Her suggestion represents the internal voices that seek to draw believers away from their faith during times of trial. Gregory contrasts Job's faithful response to his wife's despairing counsel with the Christian call to resist temptation and remain loyal to God, even in the most challenging circumstances.

Gregory also views Job's trials as representative of the universal Christian experience. Job's story, in Gregory's reading, is not simply an individual account but an allegory for the entire church, which must endure suffering and persecution in the world. In this context, Job's story prefigures Christ's own passion, with Job's endurance symbolizing the Christian's ultimate triumph over sin and death through Christ's resurrection.

Overall, Gregory's *Moralia in Job* presents a comprehensive moral and theological framework that uses the story of Job to instruct Christians in how to understand suffering, embrace patience, and resist temptation. By offering both literal and allegorical readings of Scripture, Gregory's work remains a significant contribution to Christian thought, illustrating how biblical narratives can serve as models for moral living and spiritual development.

Gregory the Great's *Homilies on the Gospels* is a collection of sermons that offers a rich blend of biblical exegesis, moral teaching, and theological reflection. Through his homilies, Gregory seeks to interpret the Gospel texts in ways that speak to the spiritual and practical needs of the Christian community. One example of Gregory's exegesis can be found in his interpretation of the parable of the good Samaritan (Luke 10:25–37). Gregory sees the good Samaritan as a symbol of Christ, who, through his compassion, heals the wounds of humanity caused by sin. In this allegorical reading, Gregory identifies the robbers as the forces of evil; the priest and the Levite as the Old Testament law, which could not offer salvation; and the Samaritan as a representation of Christ, who, through his incarnation, came to tend to the wounded humanity. Gregory's interpretation emphasizes the need for Christians to follow Christ's example by showing mercy and compassion to others, particularly those who are suffering or marginalized.

In another homily, Gregory offers an insightful exegesis of the Sermon on the Mount (Matthew 5–7), focusing specifically on the Beatitudes. Gregory interprets the Beatitudes not just as ethical teachings but as a blueprint for the spiritual ascent of the soul. For Gregory, each beatitude corresponds to a particular stage of spiritual purification and growth. For example, in his interpretation of "Blessed are the poor in spirit, for theirs is the kingdom of heaven" (Matt 5:3), Gregory explains that spiritual poverty is the first step toward holiness, as it requires humility and the recognition of one's need for God. He argues that poverty of spirit enables the soul to be filled with divine grace, making it receptive to God's kingdom.

Gregory's exegesis often integrates both literal and allegorical interpretations. In his homily on the miracle of the loaves and fishes (John 6:1–14), Gregory offers a typological reading, where the loaves represent the teachings of Christ and the fish symbolize the apostles. Gregory interprets the miracle as an allegory for the nourishment of the soul, with Christ as the provider of spiritual sustenance. He further connects this to the Eucharist, suggesting that the multiplication of the loaves foreshadows the abundance of grace available to Christians through the sacrament of Communion. In this way, Gregory's exegesis not only explains the Gospel events but also ties them to the lived experience of the church, making the teachings of Scripture relevant to the practice of faith.

Overall, Gregory's *Homilies on the Gospels* exemplifies his ability to blend literal, moral, and allegorical readings of Scripture. His exegesis is deeply rooted in the belief that the Gospel is not only a historical account of Jesus's life but also a living text, rich with spiritual and moral insights that guide the Christian toward salvation. Through his homilies, Gregory invites his audience to understand Scripture as both a source of theological knowledge and a guide for virtuous living.

Conclusion

Gregory's theological insights and pastoral wisdom informed the teachings of subsequent theologians and spiritual leaders, including Thomas Aquinas, Bernard of Clairvaux, and Francis of Assisi. Gregory's liturgical reforms and promotion of Gregorian chant laid the foundation for the development of the Western liturgical tradition, influencing the Roman church's worship practices.

Gregory's theological writings, including the *Pastoral Rule* and the *Dialogues*, offered practical guidance for clergy and spiritual leaders, emphasizing the importance of humility, compassion, and spiritual discipline in the Christian life. He emphasized the mercy and providence of God, reflected on the nature of sin and redemption, and devoted himself to the saints and miracles, inspiring generations of Christians to deepen their faith and seek holiness in their lives. His efforts to standardize liturgical practices and promote sacred music enriched the church's worship experience and helped cultivate a sense of unity and continuity in the Christian liturgical tradition.

The establishment of centralized authority represented a decisive break with the early Middle Ages' fragmented and decentralized ecclesiastical structures. Recognizing the need for robust and centralized leadership to confront the church's myriad challenges, Gregory asserted the primacy of the papal office as the ultimate arbiter of ecclesiastical authority and discipline. Through a combination of diplomatic finesse and judicious exercise of papal prerogatives, Gregory sought to assert papal supremacy over the various patriarchates, bishoprics, and monastic orders that composed the sprawling ecclesiastical landscape of medieval Christendom—establishing the foundation of the papacy as the preeminent authority in the Western church with unparalleled influence on the political, social, and religious landscape of Europe. Gregory's ecclesiastical reforms strengthened the papacy, particularly in the Western church. The Roman church of the Middle Ages came to reflect Gregory's emphasis on the authority of the bishop of Rome.

Recommended Reading

Brown, Peter. *The Rise of Western Christendom: Triumph and Diversity, A.D. 200–1000*. 10th anniversary rev. ed. Wiley-Blackwell, 2013.

Collins, Roger. *Keepers of the Keys of Heaven: A History of the Papacy*. Basic Books, 2009.

Demacopoulos, George E. *Gregory the Great: Ascetic, Pastor, and First Man of Rome*. University of Notre Dame Press, 2015.

Duffy, Eamon. *Saints and Sinners: A History of the Popes*. 4th ed. Yale University Press, 2014.

Heather, Peter. *Rome Resurgent: War and Empire in the Age of Justinian*. Oxford University Press, 2018.

Herrin, Judith. *The Formation of Christendom*. Princeton University Press, 1987.

Leyser, Conrad. *Authority and Asceticism from Augustine to Gregory the Great*. Oxford University Press, 2000.

Llewellyn, Peter. *Rome in the Dark Ages*. Faber and Faber, 1970.

Mann, Horace K. *The Lives of the Popes in the Early Middle Ages*. Vol. 1, *The Popes Under the Lombard Rule*. Kegan Paul, 1902.

Markus, Robert A. *The End of Ancient Christianity*. Cambridge University Press, 1990.

Markus, Robert A. *The Gregorian Mission to Kent: Anglo-Saxon Christianity and the Church in the West*. Routledge, 1990.

Markus, Robert A. *Gregory the Great and His World*. Cambridge University Press, 1997.

Mayr-Harting, Henry. *The Coming of Christianity to Anglo-Saxon England*. 3rd ed. Penn State University Press, 1991.

McNeill, John T. *The Celtic Churches: A History A.D. 200 to 1200*. University of Chicago Press, 1974.

Moorhead, John. *Gregory the Great*. Routledge, 2005.

Noble, Thomas F. X. *The Republic of St. Peter: The Birth of the Papal State, 680–825*. University of Pennsylvania Press, 1984.

Richards, Jeffrey. *Consul of God: The Life and Times of Gregory the Great*. Routledge, 1980.

Richards, Jeffrey. *The Popes and the Papacy in the Early Middle Ages, 476–752*. Routledge, 1979.

Smith, Julia M. H. *Europe After Rome: A New Cultural History, 500–1000*. Oxford University Press, 2005.

Straw, Carole Ellen. *Gregory the Great: Perfection in Imperfection*. University of California Press, 1988.

—— Chapter 14 ——

Sixth and Seventh Ecumenical Councils

In the previous chapter, we traced the development of the papacy in the church of the Western Roman Empire. In this chapter, we will focus on controversies in the Eastern Roman Empire that resulted in the Sixth and Seventh Ecumenical Councils. As noted previously, the Eastern Roman Empire is often called the Byzantine Empire to highlight its capital of Constantinople, which had previously been called Byzantium. Citizens of the Eastern Roman Empire would have considered themselves Romans. But, to keep the two empires distinct, we will refer to the Eastern empire as the Byzantine Empire.

The Byzantine Empire was a complex state of political and religious interrelationships in the period leading up to the Sixth and Seventh Ecumenical Councils. Byzantine emperors exercised influence over theological debates and ecclesiastical affairs, often aligning themselves with particular theological factions to advance their agendas. The relationship between the imperial court and the church hierarchy was often tense, as both vied for power and authority. Moreover, the Byzantine Empire faced external threats from neighboring powers, such as the Persians, the Slavs, the Arabs, and the Normans. The empire also faced internal challenges, such as social unrest and economic instability.

It is within this politically unstable environment that the church continued its important work of maintaining and passing along the Great Tradition. Christian leaders still had to care for the souls of men and women, evangelize non-Christians, and help Christians live out their faith. Ongoing theological conflicts required additional theological formation.

Christological Debate Beyond Chalcedon: Monothelitism

One controversy that emerged in this period was the monothelite controversy, a theological dispute centered on the nature of Christ's will. The monothelite doctrine was initially proposed as a political and religious compromise by Byzantine emperors, such as Heraclius (r. 610–41). The aim was to reconcile the Chalcedonian majority with the miaphysite (non-Chalcedonian) Christians, who rejected the Council of Chalcedon and were particularly strong in regions like Egypt, Syria, and Armenia. These regions were vital to the empire but had become increasingly estranged due to theological and cultural differences. By promoting monothelitism, the emperors hoped to bridge these divisions and maintain political cohesion within the empire, especially as it faced external threats, such as the rise of Islam.

Monothelitism, derived from Greek roots meaning "one will," was the doctrine that Christ possessed only one will, a divine will, rather than two wills, one divine and one human, as confirmed by the Council of Chalcedon, as previously discussed. The monothelite controversy emerged in the aftermath of the Council of Chalcedon, which had affirmed that Christ had two natures, divine and human. This doctrine is called dyophysite Christology, from the Greek term meaning "nature," *physis*.

Despite the Definition of Chalcedon's language, questions remained regarding the unity of Christ's person and how his divine and human natures related to each other. Monoenergism, the doctrine that Christ had one divine energy, had previously been proposed as a compromise between opposing theological factions. Monothelitism built upon this idea, asserting that Christ also possessed only one divine will, which acted harmoniously with his divine nature. Monothelitism taught that while Christ had two distinct natures (divine and human), he operated with only one divine will. Proponents of monothelitism argued that this doctrine preserved the unity of Christ's personhood and avoided the perceived pitfalls of Nestorianism (emphasizing a separation between Christ's divine and human activities).

Maximus the Confessor (b. 580) was a prominent opponent of monothelitism, advocating for the orthodox position that Christ possessed both divine and human wills. Maximus the Confessor used several Scripture passages to argue for the existence of both a divine and human will in Christ, which was central to his defense of *dyothelitism*. One of the primary passages he cited was Luke 22:42, in which Jesus prays in the garden of Gethsemane, saying, "Not my will, but yours, be done." Maximus emphasized that this statement clearly distinguishes between Christ's divine will and his human will, as Christ voluntarily submits his human will to the will of the Father. Similarly, John 5:30—"I seek not to please myself but him who sent me" (NIV)—was used to demonstrate that Christ's human will was active and capable of seeking the Father's will, further reinforcing the concept of two distinct wills in Christ.

Maximus also turned to Matt 26:39, another passage from the garden of Gethsemane, where Jesus expresses His anguish and desire for the cup of suffering to pass, yet submits to the Father's will. This, for Maximus, was another clear sign that Christ had both a human will, which could desire something different, and a divine will, which was always in perfect alignment with the Father. In Heb 5:7–8, Maximus found further evidence of Christ's dual wills, as the passage describes Jesus offering prayers with fervent cries and tears, learning obedience through his suffering. This active submission highlights that Christ's human will was involved in his obedience and passion.

Maximus also referenced 2 Cor 5:21, which says that Christ "had no sin" (NIV) but became sin for humanity, implying that he fully assumed human nature, including a human will. Similarly, Phil 2:7–8, which speaks of Christ "taking the very nature of a servant" (NIV) and becoming obedient unto death, was used to argue that Christ's obedience required a human will capable of choosing submission, which could not be achieved if he had only one divine will. Lastly, Rom 8:3–4, which describes Christ as being sent "in the likeness of sinful flesh" to fulfill the law, was cited to underscore that for Christ to truly overcome sin and fulfill his mission, he must have fully participated in human nature, including a human will.

Maximus opposed monothelitism and argued that Christ's human nature was complete and integral, possessing all the faculties and attributes of humanity, including a human will. According to Maximus, to deny Christ a human will would compromise the integrity of his human nature and the fullness of the incarnation. Maximus actively engaged in theological debate and wrote extensively against monothelitism, particularly in his work *Disputation with Pyrrhus*, in which he refuted the monothelite arguments of Pyrrhus, the patriarch of Constantinople. He also corresponded with Pope Martin I, who shared his opposition to monothelitism. The monothelite controversy led to several ecclesiastical councils and debates over the seventh century, including the Lateran Synod of 649 and the Third Council of Constantinople (the Sixth Ecumenical Council) in 680–81, that at times came to differing conclusions. Maximus's stance against monothelitism led to his trial and condemnation at the Lateran Synod in 649 under the orders of the Byzantine emperor Constans II.

Maximus and his followers were subjected to persecution by the Byzantine Empire, which sought to suppress their views and enforce the monothelite doctrine. In 653, Maximus was arrested by imperial forces, along with his companions, including Anastasios, a bishop, and Theodore, a monk. Maximus was initially exiled to the region of Garda, and later to Bizya (modern-day Bulgaria), a remote area far from the centers of ecclesiastical influence. This exile, while harsh, did not silence him, and Maximus continued to defend his theological position.

The punishment escalated further when Maximus was summoned to Constantinople, where he was subjected to torture to force him to recant his beliefs. He had his right hand was cut off and his tongue cut out as a symbolic act of silencing his writing and preaching, which were central to his theological advocacy. He was also subjected to other physical torment, but he remained steadfast in his convictions. Maximus was ultimately condemned as a heretic by the Byzantine authorities, and in 655, he was sent into further exile to Cherson, on the Crimean Peninsula.

Maximus died in exile around 662, having endured years of suffering and punishment for his defense of the doctrine that Christ possessed two wills. His steadfastness in upholding the orthodox understanding of Christ's nature eventually led to his posthumous vindication. In 680–81, the Third Council of Constantinople officially condemned monothelitism as a heresy and reaffirmed the dyothelite position, recognizing Maximus as a champion of the true Christian doctrine.

The monothelite controversy exacerbated cultural and regional tensions within the Byzantine Empire. While it was intended to reconcile Chalcedonian and monophysite Christians, it instead alienated both groups. Monophysites rejected monothelitism as a superficial concession that failed to address their theological concerns, while many Chalcedonians viewed it as a deviation from established orthodoxy. This theological polarization mirrored and reinforced existing cultural and political divides between the Greek-speaking, Chalcedonian-dominated imperial core and the Semitic- and Coptic-speaking populations of the eastern provinces, many of whom leaned toward monophysitism.

The controversy also influenced relations between the Byzantine Empire and the Latin West. While the papacy initially sought to navigate a middle ground, figures like Pope Martin I and Maximus the Confessor vehemently opposed monothelitism. Pope Martin I's imprisonment and Maximus's exile and mutilation by imperial authorities underscored the cultural and theological rift between East and West. The eventual rejection of monothelitism reinforced the papacy's role as a defender of orthodoxy but also highlighted growing tensions between the Eastern and Western churches.

Sixth Ecumenical Council: Constantinople III (680–81)

The Sixth Ecumenical Council, also known as the Third Council of Constantinople, was convened in 680–81 by Emperor Constantine IV (668–85) to address the monothelite controversy. The controversy had been fueled by Emperor Heraclius and Patriarch Sergius I of Constantinople, who sought to reconcile the Chalcedonian definition of Christ's two natures with a more simplified doctrine of one will. This theological compromise, however, was met with resistance from many in the church, particularly from the West and key theologians, such as Maximus the Confessor, who argued that monothelitism undermined Christ's full humanity and divinity.

The council was attended by approximately 170 bishops, primarily from the Eastern church, though representatives from the West, including Pope Agatho, were also influential. The participants were united in their opposition to monothelitism and in their desire to reaffirm the orthodox Christological position established by the Council of Chalcedon (451), which defined Christ as one person in two distinct natures, divine and human. The main proceedings of the council focused on the theological debate surrounding Christ's will. The council condemned monothelitism as a heresy, asserting that Christ, as both fully human and fully divine, must possess two distinct wills, corresponding to his two natures. This doctrinal stance was necessary to preserve the integrity of Christ's humanity, allowing him to fully experience human suffering and temptation.

The bishops also made a series of theological clarifications regarding the relationship between Christ's divine and human wills. The council emphasized that these two wills must be distinct but never in conflict. The divine will, as part of Christ's divinity, is always in perfect alignment with the Father's will, while the human will, reflecting Christ's true humanity, is capable of freely choosing and acting in accordance with divine will. However, in Christ, the human will is always subject to and harmonized with the divine will, ensuring that both natures are fully expressed without contradiction.

In addition to condemning monothelitism, the council also issued a posthumous condemnation of Pope Honorius I, who had been accused of supporting monothelitism in his correspondence with Patriarch Sergius I. Although Honorius did not explicitly advocate for monothelitism, his failure to oppose the heresy was seen as a grave error, leading to his excommunication. The council's proceedings also reaffirmed the Chalcedonian Definition of 451, emphasizing that Christ's two wills must be distinct but never in conflict, as both wills were perfectly aligned in the person of Christ.

However, perhaps most surprising was the council's decision to condemn Patriarch Sergius I of Constantinople for his role in promoting the monothelite doctrine. Sergius had argued that Christ had only one will, which was divine, and the council's condemnation of his teachings reflected the church's determination to eliminate the influence of monothelitism. The council's condemnation of Sergius and his ideas was part of a broader effort to affirm orthodox Christology.

The acts of the council also underscored the authority of the papacy in matters of faith and doctrine. Pope Agatho of Rome, who played a crucial role in shaping the theological direction of the council, sent a letter to the emperor and the council's participants, which was read aloud at the gathering. His letter explicitly rejected monothelitism and supported the position of dyothelitism, reinforcing the pope's authority to define doctrine within the universal church. The council's final decrees were also confirmed by Pope Leo II after Agatho's death, further solidifying the papal support for the decisions made at the council.

While the Third Council of Constantinople settled the monothelite controversy, another decree, which affirmed the use and veneration of icons in Christian worship, would lead to further controversy. This decision would continue to be debated as those who rejected the use of icons, known as iconoclasts, continued to argue against the use of images in Christian worship. This controversy would persist into the eighth century and lead to the calling of another ecumenical council.

Background to the Iconoclastic Controversy

In the early centuries of Christianity, attitudes toward images and iconography varied among different Christian communities. While some early Christians embraced the use of religious images as aids to devotion and sources of spiritual inspiration, others were more cautious of the potential for idolatry and superstition. The catacombs of Rome, for example, contain numerous examples of early Christian art depicting biblical scenes, martyrs, and symbols of faith, suggesting a positive attitude toward images among some early Christians.

However, the use of images also sparked controversy within the early church, particularly among those influenced by Jewish and Greco-Roman traditions that cautioned against idolatry and the worship of graven images. For instance, the early Christian theologian Origen expressed reservations about using images in worship, warning against the temptation to attribute divine qualities to material objects.

Despite these concerns, the use of images gradually became more widespread in Christian worship, particularly following the legalization of Christianity by Emperor Constantine in the fourth century. Icons, or sacred images, came to play a central role in Christian devotional practices, serving as visual aids to prayer, meditation, and contemplation of the divine mysteries. This issue was addressed at the Sixth Ecumenical Council convened in 680–81 in Constantinople, which reaffirmed the use of icons in Christian worship.

Iconoclasm's Resurgence and the Controversy Deepens

Despite the affirmation of the use of icons, at the Sixth Ecumenical Council, the Eastern Roman Empire witnessed the growth of iconoclasm during the reign of Emperor Leo III (717–41). This movement gained traction among certain factions within the church, including clergy, theologians, and even emperors, leading to widespread controversy and division. In this context, the rise of iconoclasm represented both a theological dispute and a reflection of broader social, political, and religious dynamics within the Byzantine Empire.

John of Damascus (676–749), a theologian and monk, emerged as a leading defender of icons during the iconoclastic controversy. His key writings, including the *Three Treatises on the Divine Images*, provided a robust theological defense of the veneration of icons and affirmed their legitimacy in Christian worship. John grounded his defense of icons in the theological concept of the incarnation of Christ. He argued that just as Christ became incarnate in human form, the material form of icons could also express divine truth. According to the Damascene, icons were not objects of worship but were vehicles for encountering the divine presence and fostering spiritual devotion. John provided a theological framework defending the use of icons against iconoclastic attacks. His arguments resonated with many orthodox Christians, who saw in icons a tangible expression of their faith and a means of encountering the divine mystery.

> It is obvious that when you contemplate God becoming man, then you may depict Him clothed in human form. When the invisible One becomes visible to flesh, you may then draw his likeness.
>
> ---
>
> John of Damascus,
> *On the Divine Images*

In 726, Emperor Leo III issued his Edict of Iconoclasm, banning the veneration of religious images, citing concerns about idolatry and the need to purify Christian worship. This edict marked the beginning of a systematic campaign against icons, which included the destruction of religious images, the persecution of iconophiles, and the imposition of harsh penalties on those who defied imperial decrees.

The theological rationale for iconoclasm stemmed from concerns about the potential for idolatry and superstition in the veneration of icons. Some iconoclasts argued that religious images detracted from the worship of the one true God and were contrary to the biblical commandments against graven images. Politically, iconoclasm served as a means for imperial authorities to assert their authority over the church and to consolidate power within the Byzantine Empire. By aligning themselves with the iconoclastic cause, emperors sought to promote unity and stability within the empire and suppress dissenting voices within the church. The Edict of Iconoclasm precipitated theological and political turmoil within the Byzantine Empire, leading to divisions within the church and widespread opposition among Christians. The iconoclastic controversy deepened as theological debates intensified and tensions between iconoclasts and iconophiles escalated.

The reigns of Leo III's successors, Leo IV and Constantine V, witnessed a second period of iconoclasm in the Byzantine Empire, marked by further persecution of icon venerators and debates around biblical interpretations. Emperors Leo IV and Constantine V continued their predecessor's iconoclastic policies, seeking to suppress the veneration of icons and to enforce imperial authority over the church. During this period, theological debates around iconoclasm intensified, with iconophiles marshaling biblical, patristic, and theological arguments in defense of icon veneration. Constantine V convened a series of iconoclastic councils to codify and enforce iconoclastic doctrine. These councils issued decrees condemning the veneration of icons as idolatrous and heretical, and they sought to eradicate the use of icons from Byzantine religious life. The iconoclastic controversy divided the church and led to periods of persecution and theological suppression.

The tumultuous period leading up to the Seventh Ecumenical Council saw iconoclasm gaining traction among certain factions within the church, leading to iconoclastic persecutions and the destruction of religious art and artifacts. However, the defenders of icon veneration, led by key figures such as John of Damascus, Theodore the Studite, and Empress Irene of Constantinople, vigorously opposed iconoclasm, asserting the theological legitimacy and spiritual significance of icons in Christian worship. The ensuing conflict between iconoclasts and iconophiles—those who upheld the veneration of icons—threatened to divide the church and undermine its unity.

Seventh Ecumenical Council: Nicaea II (787)

The Seventh Ecumenical Council, also known as the Second Council of Nicaea, was convened in 787 by Emperor Constantine VI and his mother, Empress Irene, in Nicaea. The emperor called the council in response to the ongoing controversy surrounding the use and veneration of icons in Christian worship and the continued threat posed by iconoclasm—the rejection of religious images and their veneration. Empress Irene, who ruled as regent for her son Constantine VI, sought to reconcile the opposing factions and restore unity to the church by convening the Seventh Ecumenical Council.

The *iconodule* movement, led by key figures such as John of Damascus and Theodore the Studite, vigorously defended the use and veneration of icons in Christian worship. The word "iconodule" means "one who venerates icons." The iconodules' defense of icons was grounded in orthodox Christology, affirming the reality of Christ's humanity and the transformative power of divine grace. They rejected the iconoclastic assertion that icons constituted idolatry, emphasizing instead the spiritual significance of icons as aids to prayer and meditation. The council's deliberations centered on the theological significance of icons and the distinction between their veneration and worship. It claimed that icons were not objects of worship but aids to devotion, serving as tangible expressions of the divine mystery and conduits of spiritual grace. Iconodules argued that icons served as visible reminders of the incarnation of Christ and the communion of saints, facilitating the worshipper's encounter with the divine and fostering spiritual growth and devotion. The key distinction is that veneration of icons is directed toward the person or event depicted in the icon, acknowledging their holiness and helping the believer connect with God, whereas worship is directed exclusively to God, as the ultimate object of adoration and devotion. This theological framework was central during the iconoclastic controversy, where iconoclasts (those who opposed the use of icons) accused iconodules (those who supported icon veneration) of veering into idolatry by venerating images. The iconodules claimed that iconoclasm at least implied a Docetic Christology. As we saw in chapter 3, Docetism was the view that the humanity of Christ was not genuine humanity but only appeared so. Any Christology that does not take seriously the full humanity of Jesus is Docetic, at least in tendency. Because the iconoclasts denied the use of physical representations of divine realties in word, refusing to show icons veneration, the iconodules accused them of not taking seriously the humanity of Christ. This Christological question is the fundamental question in the controversy. Fundamentally, the controversy is about Christology, not liturgy.

Patriarch Tarasius of Constantinople played a central role in the proceedings of the Seventh Ecumenical Council at Nicaea II. As the patriarch of the church in the Eastern empire, Tarasius presided over the council and provided theological guidance and leadership to defend the orthodox position on using icons. He worked closely with Empress Irene and the imperial authorities to ensure the success of the council and the restoration of icons following the teachings of the church. Tarasius's diplomatic skills were instrumental in securing the condemnation of iconoclasm.

Theodore the Studite (759–826), an influential monk and theologian, played a crucial role in defending icon veneration and advocating for the restoration of icons in Christian worship. His writings and theological insights provided a foundation for the council's pronouncements on the theological significance of icons. Pope Adrian I of Rome sent legates to the Seventh Ecumenical Council to express his support for the restoration of icon veneration and to reaffirm the Roman church's commitment to orthodoxy. His participation in the council underscored the unity of the Eastern and Western churches in affirming the theological legitimacy of icons.

The council adopted a definition of faith that articulated the theological rationale for using icons and condemned the iconoclastic position as contrary to the teachings of the church. Furthermore, the council issued a series of canons reaffirming the use and veneration of icons in churches, monasteries, and private homes and prescribing penalties for those who sought to destroy or deface religious images. The decisions of the Seventh Ecumenical Council marked the definitive triumph of orthodoxy over iconoclasm and ensured the enduring place of icons in orthodox Christian worship and spirituality.

The council articulated a robust defense of icon veneration, affirming the orthodox belief that icons were legitimate aids to devotion and expressions of Christian faith. The council clarified the distinction between worship (reserved for God alone) and veneration (appropriate for icons as representations of Christ and the saints), emphasizing that the veneration of icons did not constitute idolatry. The council's pronouncements affirmed the theological significance of icons as tangible expressions of the divine presence and as a means of fostering spiritual devotion. It condemned iconoclasm as heresy and reaffirmed the church's commitment to restoring icon veneration in Christian worship.

Aftermath of the Seventh Ecumenical Council

Nicaea II's affirmation of icons as vehicles of divine grace and channels of spiritual communion resonated with Christians worldwide, leading to the widespread adoption of iconographic practices in churches and religious communities across the Christian East and West. Following the Seventh Ecumenical Council, the Byzantine emperors, under the guidance of the church hierarchy, implemented iconodule policies to promote the use and veneration of icons in Christian worship. The decision of the council repealed iconoclastic decrees and took measures to restore and preserve religious images destroyed or defaced during the iconoclastic persecutions. Iconodule bishops and clergy were appointed to oversee the enforcement of iconophile policies and to ensure the proper use and maintenance of icons in churches and monasteries.

The council's decisions also established an iconographic tradition in Byzantine art, characterized by a rich and vibrant array of religious images depicting Christ, the virgin Mary, saints, and biblical scenes. Iconographers, inspired by the theological insights of Nicaea II, sought to capture the spiritual essence and divine presence conveyed through icons, employing symbolic imagery, vibrant colors, and intricate details to convey the mysteries of the Christian faith. The legacy of the Seventh Ecumenical Council extends far beyond its immediate historical context, shaping the trajectory of Byzantine Christianity and Christian art for centuries to come. The council's affirmation of icon veneration as an integral part of orthodox spirituality established a theological foundation for the enduring significance of icons in the life of the church.

Conclusion

The Sixth and Seven Ecumenical Councils highlighted the ongoing need for attention to theological matters. Monothelitism was inconsistent with the Definition of Chalcedon and needed to be addressed. The question of whether churches could or should use icons in worship was dividing Christians from one another and likewise needed to be addressed. Theologically, both councils were ultimately concerned with the question of Christ's human nature. In the monothelite controversy, the matter was the human will of Christ. Monothelites denied the human will, contrary to Gregory of Nazianzus's famous statement "What is not assumed is not healed." In the iconoclast controversy the central question was whether the human nature of Jesus meant that God was worshipped through that which was created (i.e., his humanity). Regardless of the specific matter of the veneration of icons, the most important implication of the Seventh Ecumenical Council was the reaffirmation of the true humanity of Christ.

Recommended Reading

Allen, Pauline, and Bronwen Neil. *The Sixth Century: End or Beginning?* Australian Association for Byzantine Studies, 1996.

Booth, Phil. *Crisis of Empire: Doctrine and Dissent at the End of Late Antiquity*. University of California Press, 2014.

Brubaker, Leslie, and John Haldon. *Byzantium in the Iconoclast Era, c. 680–850: A History*. Cambridge University Press, 2011.

Cameron, Averil. *The Byzantines*. Blackwell, 2006.

Demacopoulos, George E., and Aristotle Papanikolaou, eds. *Orthodox Readings of Augustine*. St. Vladimir's Seminary Press, 2008.

Grillmeier, Aloys. *Christ in Christian Tradition*. Vol. 2, part 2, *The Church of Constantinople in the Sixth Century*. Mowbray, 1995.

Haldon, John F. *Byzantium in the Seventh Century: The Transformation of a Culture*. Cambridge University Press, 1990.

Herrin, Judith. *Byzantium: The Surprising Life of a Medieval Empire*. Princeton University Press, 2009.

John of Damascus. *On the Divine Images: Three Apologies Against Those Who Attack the Divine Images*. Translated by David Anderson. St. Vladimir's Seminary Press, 1980.

Louth, Andrew. *St. John Damascene: Tradition and Originality in Byzantine Theology*. Oxford University Press, 2002.

Mango, Cyril, and Roger Scott, eds. *The Chronicle of Theophanes Confessor: Byzantine and Near Eastern History AD 284–813*. Oxford University Press, 1997.

Meyendorff, John. *Christ in Eastern Christian Thought*. St. Vladimir's Seminary Press, 1975.

Noble, Thomas F. X. *Images, Iconoclasm, and the Carolingians*. University of Pennsylvania Press, 2009.

Ostrogorsky, George. *History of the Byzantine State*. Translated by Joan Hussey. Rev. ed. Rutgers University Press, 1969.

Pelikan, Jaroslav. *The Spirit of Eastern Christendom (600–1700)*. University of Chicago Press, 1974.

Price, Richard, and Michael Gaddis, eds. *The Acts of the Council of Chalcedon*. Liverpool University Press, 2005.

Ware, Kallistos. *The Orthodox Church*. New ed. Penguin, 1997.

Wessel, Susan. *The Iconoclast Controversy, 726–843: History, Theology, and Legacy*. Routledge, 2021.

—— Chapter 15 ——

Liturgical and Ecclesial Development in the Middle Ages

What was Christian worship like in the early to high Middle Ages? What did it sound, look, smell, taste, and feel like? Answering these questions takes us far beyond hymns and preaching styles. It includes architecture, incense, icons, prayers, and consideration of the Eucharist. It's a conversation about the church's liturgy.

Liturgy simply refers to the order of things, especially the order of a worship service, though it may also refer to one's order and routine in life. Anyone who has ever attended an older rural church where the "order of service" never changes understands the traditional nature of liturgical routines that cement themselves in corporate worship. And this was certainly true in the Middle Ages. In fact, while doctrinal clarity and vocabulary was still underway, the church sought to retain an ancient style of worship to connect to early Christianity in an effort to preserve the gospel and tradition of the apostles. And once established, the liturgical cement is difficult to alter. When it does, it is a slow and painful process.

Of course, describing with precision what worship was like for ordinary Christians during these centuries is difficult and requires some amount of guesswork. Speaking to this, Andrew Louth admits, "The basis on which we make these guesses mostly consists of extant liturgical evidence, supplemented by what can be deduced from surviving monuments and archaeological investigation, to which can be added hints and guesses from letters that have been preserved, and especially from the *Lives* of the saints."[1] This chapter thus traces key contours of liturgical practices of this period across both Eastern and Western churches, followed by special attention to the first eucharistic controversy as an important medieval theological development concerning the liturgy of the church.

Liturgy Leading up to the Middle Ages

The earliest centuries of Christian worship represent a period of liturgical development and, to some degree, innovation. Some suggest it is more accurate to refer to the worship of the early "churches" rather than of the early "church," for one's liturgical experience would have differed from region to region across various Christian communities depending on language, culture, and broader religious context.[2] And yet, there were also deep continuities across Christian communities, including regular gathering, celebrations of baptism and Eucharist, the reading and teaching of Scripture, and prayer.

By the fourth and fifth centuries, various liturgical families began to emerge across the East and the West. For the Eastern church, centered in Constantinople, the liturgical evolution is complex, but its legacy was informed by ancient Jewish practices and early texts, such as the *Apostolic Tradition* (third century); the *Apostolic Constitutions* from Antioch, particularly book 8 (fourth century); and the *Liturgy of St. James*, which was active by the fifth century in Jerusalem. Further, by the end of the fourth century, two *anaphoras* (prayers of consecration) had become central for Eastern liturgy.[3]

The Byzantine liturgy of the East followed the fourth-century Liturgy of St. Basil of Caesarea. This was likely passed down through Gregory of Nazianzus and John Chrysostom, though it may have been slightly modified by John.[4] This was the most common liturgy used in Constantinople by the ninth century and consisted of the following:

---

[1] Andrew Louth, *Greek East and Latin West: The Church AD 681–1071*, ed. Andrew Louth, vol. 3 of *The Church in History* (St. Vladimir's Seminary Press, 2007), 193.

[2] "A History of Christian Worship: Part 2 (2010)," posted Nov. 9, 2020, by Vision Video, Youtube, https://www.youtube.com/watch?v=sMQCRsAP1_I&feature=youtu.be.

[3] Robert Webber, *Twenty Centuries of Christian Worship*, vol. 2 of *The Complete Library of Christian Worship* (Star Song, 1994), 152.

[4] Webber, *Twenty Centuries*, 102.

I. The Rite of Preparation

II. The Liturgy of the Word or Synaxis
- a. The antiphons (short corporate chants recited during worship)
- b. The entrance of the clergy (ministers)
- c. The readings
- d. The dismissal of the catechumens (those preparing for baptism)

III. The Liturgy of the Faithful
- a. The prayers of the faithful
- b. The Great Entrance
- c. The kiss of peace and creed
- d. The anaphora (the central prayer for the Eucharist)
- e. The Lord's Prayer and Communion
- f. The final prayers and dismissal[5]

Liturgy is everything for the Eastern church. From the opening rite of preparation to final prayers and dismissal, the liturgy is ordered as a journey for Christians to enter the kingdom of God, climaxing at the Eucharist (Communion). John Warren Morris captures this well:

> The major theme of the Byzantine liturgy is the entrance of the faithful into the kingdom of God. The clergy and faithful also considered the liturgy a sacrifice or offering. As the principal act of worship of the church, it was a sacrifice of praise and thanksgiving. It was also the offering of bread and wine as symbols of the offering of creation to God by a grateful people. The believers of ancient Byzantium also considered the Eucharist a remembrance of the sacrifice of Christ. Finally, the faithful offered themselves to God by their participation in the liturgy.[6]

While much was the same between Eastern and Western liturgical practices of the Middle Ages, Eastern worship distinguished itself by the Greek language, leavened bread, wine unmixed with water, and the "epiclesis," the special invocation of the Holy Spirit asking

---

[5] Taken from Webber, *Twenty Centuries*, 154.

[6] John Warren Morris, "The Byzantine Liturgy," in Webber, *Twenty Centuries*, 153.

that the elements be made into the body and blood of Christ.[7] Additionally, we offer three brief observations about the distinctives of the liturgy of the East.

1. Worship with the Saints

The liturgy began with the procession of the bishop into the basilica, though in more prominent cities, such as Constantinople, bishops may have processed through the city to the church for what was known as "stational liturgies."[8] These processions included relics for the veneration of the saints, the greatest of which was the blessed virgin Mary, the *Theotokos*, Mother of God.[9] Andrew Louth notes, "In these ways, Christian worship throughout Christendom articulated a sense that the worshippers on earth were joining in their worship of God with all the saints who had lived on earth before them. As well as joining their worship with the angelic hosts, they also joined with saints who had once lived on earth, on the very earth on which they themselves were standing."[10] Eastern Christians understand joining their worship with the heavenly hosts to be in keeping with the biblical imagery of being surrounded by the cloud of witnesses (Heb 12:1) and of the angel holding the prayers of the saints as incense and offering them on the heavenly altar (Rev 5:8; 8:3–4).

2. Worship and Icons

As will be discussed further in chapter 18, icons and iconography are the clue to the thought and practice of Eastern Orthodoxy. Bruce Shelley remarks, "In Orthodoxy the idea of image is key to understanding the ways of God with man. Man is created 'in the image of God'; he carries the icon of God within himself."[11] Icons therefore serve as windows into the heavenly realm, elevating worshippers toward God, inspired by the person of Christ, the very "icon" of the invisible God (Col 1:15).

By the ninth century, the liturgy itself became an icon in words, "an action of the mystery of salvation through Christ."[12] Ornate clerical robes, lofty architectural design that

[7] James Hitchcock, *History of the Catholic Church* (Ignatius Press, 2012), 193.
[8] Louth, *Greek East and Latin West*, 196.
[9] Louth, 197.
[10] Louth, 198.
[11] Bruce L. Shelley, *Church History in Plain Language* (Zondervan Academic, 2013), 152.
[12] Morris, "Byzantine Liturgy," 153.

evoked transcendence and lifted the eyes of worshippers toward God, and incense that filled the room and stimulated the senses all became important features of Byzantine worship. The famed Hagia Sophia, erected in Constantinople (modern-day Istanbul) by emperor Justinian in 537, redefined the standard for worship spaces. At the time, it was believed to be the largest building in existence and served as the epicenter for Byzantine Christianity for nearly a thousand years.

3. Participatory Worship

Congregational participation is common for both Eastern and Western traditions in responsive readings, corporate prayers, and the reciting of creeds. But the Eastern liturgy incorporates even greater public participation, with frequent kneeling, kissing of the icons, and the kiss of peace. The kiss of peace is shared clergy to clergy, men to men, and women to women as a sign of putting aside division and promoting unity among the people of God. It is a way of carrying out the apostle Paul's frequent instruction to greet one another with a holy kiss, included in both letters to the Corinthians, in the letter to the Romans, and in the letter to the Thessalonians. After all, as the Savior was betrayed with a kiss, it is fitting that God would repurpose such an intimate action as a means of promoting unity among his people.

Distinctives of the Western Liturgy

The liturgical legacy of the West is even more complex than the East, as uniformity in worship was not achieved until after the Council of Trent in 1570, despite Emperor Charlemagne's best efforts centuries before. The missals (books containing the order and contents of Roman mass) that inform the Western liturgical legacy include the *Gothic Missal* (c. 700), the *Bobbio Missal* (c. seventh–eighty century), and the *Roman Missal* (c. fifteenth century). Additionally, prayer booklets known as sacramentaries were collected over the centuries to organize prayers for the mass, the earliest of which dates to the mid-fifth century with Pope Leo I. We must also note the role of the monasteries in the liturgical development of the Middle Ages. As James White observes, "Most liturgical changes in the Middle Ages seem to originate from the religious orders."[13] The monasteries sought to *preserve* liturgical legacy and *promote* liturgical development, both

[13] James F. White, *A Brief History of Christian Worship* (Abingdon, 1993), 78.

in theory and in practice. One example of this trend in the Western church includes the ninth century Eucharistic controversy in southern France between Radbertus and Ratramnus discussed below. But first we will look at another example in Pope Gregory I, the first monk to become pope, and the trajectory he set for liturgical developments in the West. In fact, from a bird's-eye view, the story of liturgical development in the West may be outlined as "Gregory to Gregory to Francis to the press."

Gregory the Great to Gregory the VII

Pope Gregory I, better known as Gregory the Great (540–604), is considered one of the four great Latin fathers of the church (see chapter 13). He left a remarkable legacy of leadership, unity, and care for the church. In his *Pastoral Rule*, Gregory insisted that the primary role of the pastor is the ministry of the Word in preaching. Gregory also stressed the importance of character among pastors, dedicating the final book of his *Rule* to the personal virtue and humility of pastors. Gregory's papacy, which began in 590 after Pope Pelagius II died of the plague, came at a time of incredible political and social upheaval in Europe. Much of the political prestige that popes enjoyed during the Middle Ages was due to the expansion in papal influence that Gregory caused not by political ambition, but by decisive leadership in the face of unrelenting invasions, plagues, and famines.

Regarding liturgy in the West, Gregory is a representative of that connection we have mentioned between liturgical developments and monasteries. "With Gregory monasticism for the first time ascended the papal throne."[14] And when the monk became the pope, monastic practices became papal imperatives. The liturgical commonplaces of penance, merit, purgatory, and the Holy Eucharist so characteristic of medieval Catholicism were not original to Gregory, but his papacy ensured they would become the dominant themes of it. As a result of Gregory's papacy, medieval piety became centered around the Holy Eucharist, and Roman Catholic liturgy became incomprehensible without it.

A notable distinctive of the liturgy of the West in the medieval era is the Mass as a more private experience. This contrasts with the corporate, participatory experience in the East. In the West, private prayers—once the exclusive practice of monks—reinforced a more personal or private faith. Reasons for this shift from the participatory to the private may

---

[14] Shelley, *Church History in Plain Language*, 178.

vary—from illiteracy among large portions of the congregation to the waning familiarity with the Latin language in which the Mass was performed. However, the influence of the monk Pope Gregory I is undeniable.

Almost 500 years later, the expansions and innovations which Pope Gregory I brought to the papacy had calcified into avenues for political ambitions. By the time Pope Gregory VII (1073–85) ascended to the papacy, the problem had reached a fever pitch. Using the authority that Gregory the Great brought to the papacy, the feisty Gregory VII urged both clerical and liturgical reforms in the church. Of the many issues of concern during this time, simony (buying or selling positions in the church), investiture (authority over the installation of bishops and abbots), and clerical celibacy topped the list. Gregory saw much success in his reform efforts, though this was not without much trial and political expense. Along the way, however, Gregory successfully persuaded political and religious leaders in the north to adopt the Roman Rite, further expanding the liturgy of the Western church.

Francis to the Printing Press

The legacy of Francis of Assisi (c. 1181–1226) is most often associated with his love for the natural world and his life of poverty. In his own day, however, Francis was almost singularly concerned with one thing: the Holy Eucharist. It could be said that Francis's devotion to the natural world and his reverence for poverty were means to an end—they were ways of purifying his life so that he could encounter God more fully in the bread and the wine. Augustine Thompson argues, "The locus of Francis's 'mysticism,' his belief that he could have direct contact with God, was in the Mass, not in nature or even in service to the poor."[15] His life as a radical monastic began with the restoration of crumbling chapels because that was where the Mass was held. His harshest words were reserved for those who trifled with the holy Host. And as sincere as his preaching was against worldliness and lavish living, he had no qualms with lavish displays of wealth when it involved the various elements on the altar. The unprecedented popularity of his movement ensured that his passionate devotion to the Holy Eucharist would only become further ingrained in the liturgy and piety of the Western church.

[15] Augustine Thompson, OP, *St. Francis of Assisi: A New Biography* (Cornell University Press, 2012), 61.

The First Eucharistic Controversy: Radbertus and Ratramnus

Returning to the theme of the influence of monasteries on liturgical development, in the early Middle Ages, the church freshly considered the nature and number of sacraments. By the thirteenth century, the West recognized seven sacraments, including baptism, Eucharist, confirmation, penance (confession or reconciliation), marriage, ordination (holy orders), and extreme unction (anointing of the sick). Due to its centrality throughout the history of Christ's worship, we give particular attention here to the theological development of the eucharist.

In the 840s, the grandson of Charlemagne, Emperor Charles II (also known as Charles the Bald) elicited two treatises on the Eucharist to be written by two Benedictine monks at Corbie Abbey in northern France. This was likely not intended to stir up controversy but rather to produce comprehensive treatments on this central practice of the church. Of particular concern was the presence of Christ in the Eucharist. If Christ were present in the bread and wine, exactly how was he present? Was this merely metaphorical language from Jesus in John 6 concerning "eating his flesh" and "drinking his blood"? Was it literal? Spiritual? Hyperbolic? Simply mystery?

Paschasius Radbertus (c. 785–c.860) and his colleague Ratramnus (c. 800–c. 868) were assigned the tasks of writing treatises on the subject. Both entitled their works *De Corpore et Sanguine Domini* (*On the Body and Blood of the Lord*), though they reached quite different conclusions on the question of the presence of Christ.

Radbertus, abandoned as a child, rose from nothing to become the headmaster of Corbie Abbey. Founded in the mid-seventh century under the patronage of the Merovingian dynasty, it was a center of classical learning internationally famed for its library. In his treatise, Radbertus wrote, "Though the body and blood of Christ remain in the figure of bread and wine, yet we must believe them to be simply a figure and, after consecration, they are nothing else than the body and blood of Christ. . . . [We must believe them] to be clearly the very flesh which was born of Mary, and suffered on the cross and rose from the tomb."[16]

Radbertus drew on Matt 26:26, where Christ states, "This is my body," and on the lengthy passage in John 6:22–65, where Christ identifies himself as the true bread come down from heaven. In this passage, Jesus famously insists, "Truly I tell you, unless you

[16] Henry Bettenson and Chris Maunder, eds., *Documents of the Christian Church*, 4th ed. (Oxford University Press, 2011), 162.

eat the flesh of the Son of Man and drink his blood, you do not have life in yourselves" (John 6:53). Such direct language provided Radbertus plenty of fuel for his argument, though hermeneutical clarity remained. Radbertus stressed the difference in the *real* flesh and blood of Jesus, and the *figure* of the bread and wine. He further stressed the role of faith in taking the Eucharist, without which a person eats and drinks judgment on himself.

> Though the body and blood of Christ remain in the figure of bread and wine, yet we must believe them to be simply a figure and, after consecration, they are nothing else than the body and blood of Christ.
>
> ---
>
> Paschasius Radbertus
> *On the Body and Blood of the Lord*

In response to Radbertus's position, Geoffrey Bromiley critiques,

> What [Radbertus] does not explain is why it is only by faith that visible things like body and blood can be seen. Certainly Christ's deity cannot be sensorily perceived, since it is in itself invisible, but if the truth behind the figure in the Eucharist is the Incarnational body, which lies in the sensory sphere, then why should the demand be made for faith in the change in order that it may be discerned? The analogy breaks down here.[17]

Ratramnus, a colleague and fellow scholar of Radbertus at Corbie, took a different interpretation on the body and blood of Christ. For brevity, we offer Bromiley's helpful summary of Ratramnus's view in contrast to that of Radbertus:

1. The elements of bread and wine are placed on the altar as a figure or memorial of the Lord's death.
2. The body and blood are taken by believers "when faith receives what the eye does not see but what it believes."
3. Thus it is "spiritual food spiritually feeding the soul."[18]

While Ratramnus's "spiritual presence" position was more intuitive and seems better supported by the church fathers, Radbertus's view won the day and had lasting effects. In the eleventh century, the archdeacon Berengar of Tours was condemned three times for

---

[17] Geoffrey W. Bromiley, *Historical Theology* (Eerdmans, 1978), 162.
[18] Bromiley, *Historical Theology*, 164.

advocating a view more like that of Ratramnus rather than the "physicalist" view of Radbertus. Radbertus's position eventually became known as *transubstantiation* and was codified in canon law at the Fourth Lateran Council in November of 1215. This council called by Pope Innocent III declared some seventy decrees, and the first of them was the confirmation of this view of the Eucharist. The council also required all Catholics to attend confession and receive communion at least once per year.

> Outwardly, the form of bread, is presented, its color is exhibited, its taste is perceived, but inwardly, a far different thing is signified . . . that is, Christ's Body is shown forth, which is beheld, is taken, is eaten, not by the bodily senses, but by the gaze of the believing soul.
>
> Ratramnus,
> *On the Body and Blood of the Lord*

In the following decades, Thomas Aquinas (1225–74) would further clarify the church's position using Aristotelian categories that distinguish between "essentials" and "accidents." In this scheme, faith confirms that while the "accidents" (that which is perceived by the senses) of the bread and wine do not change, the "essential" nature transforms into the real body and blood of Christ.

Transubstantiation remains the official position of the Roman Catholic Church, though only a few centuries later, the Protestant Reformers took great issue with the doctrine. In particular, Martin Luther criticized this view in his *The Babylonian Captivity of the Church*, arguing that "transubstantiation . . . must be considered as an invention of human reason, since it is based neither on Scripture nor sound reasoning."[19] The reaction of the Reformers sparked heavy debate about the nature of the Eucharist, resulting in diverse positions even among themselves.

Further Liturgical Developments During the Middle Ages

The Calendar and Feast Days

The church's liturgy extended beyond the church buildings on Sundays. It quickly enveloped all of time, covering the calendar throughout the year. In fact, these liturgical rhythms resulted in a new approach to the annual calendar all together. Christians were not satisfied with holidays that were organized around pagan calendars decided by pagan rulers.

[19] Bettenson and Maunder, eds., *Documents of the Christian Church*, 210.

They preferred a calendar that considered the life of Christ throughout the year, assisting Christians in remembering and celebrating the life and work of Christ in every season.

By the beginning of the fifth century, the Christian calendar was well established, with two cycles and four seasons. The two cycles included nativity and pascha, while the four seasons were coupled together as Advent and Christmas, Lent and Easter. The Middle Ages contributed additional feast celebrations, including All Saints Day and various Marian feasts, such as the Immaculate Conception, Trinity Sunday, and the Feast of Corpus Christi. Many other feast days for the saints were added, further complicating the daily recital of the mass.[20] Feast days and celebrations do not originate with Christians but rather harken back to Christianity's Jewish roots with annual celebrations such as Passover. Yet, in keeping with the already-renovated Christian calendar, feast days were to be reconsidered in light of Christ.

The first three festivals incorporated into the Christian calendar were Passover (Pascha or Easter), Pentecost, and Epiphany. The week-long paschal commemoration was originally held in a single day. By the end of fourth century, however, this had become a multi-day celebration in an effort to remember the final week of Christ's life. In her well-known diary, the late fourth-century nun Egeria recorded her pilgrimage to the Holy Land, providing a detailed account of the events of Holy Week, beginning with the procession from the Mount of Olives on Palm Sunday led by the bishop. She continues describing the events of each day of the week up through Easter Sunday.[21] This account illustrates how well developed the Paschal celebration had become by that time, at least in Jerusalem, from which it spread.

Music and Hymnography

Both in monasteries and in parish churches, music was central. Early in the medieval era, unison-style singing was prominent, as had been the case in the early church. In her diary, Egeria speaks of songs and hymns being sung throughout the day in Jerusalem at various appointed times. Music had a sorted reputation among early Christians, originally due to its association with Jewish and pagan culture, but also for its use in promoting false teaching, such as Arianism. Further, some early Christians, such as Augustine, though he had written

---

[20] James F. White, *A Brief History of Christian Worship* (Abingdon, 1993), 92–93. See also 62–65.

[21] M. L. McClure and C. L. Feltoe, trans., *The Pilgrimage of Etheria* (Society for Promoting Christian Knowledge, 1919), 63–85.

a work entitled *De musica* soon after his conversion admiring the orderliness and mathematical precision of music, warned against delighting in music in idolatrous ways. Hence the carefulness with which Christians of the early medieval period engaged with music, especially in worship. Even still, polyphonic-style singing (singing with multiple parts or harmonies) emerged by the end of the Middle Ages, breaking with the tradition of unison singing that was developing simultaneously. New hymns were frequently added during this time, complementing the growing number of feast day celebrations for the saints.[22]

Architecture

In keeping with the times, church architecture gradually transitioned from the simpler basilica structures to large and architecturally impressive buildings with multiple spaces dedicated to various parts of the liturgy and communal functions. In the West, the more modest Romanesque style, with thick stone walls, pillars, and archways, were common until the twelfth century (see the San Liberatore a Maiella in Abruzzo, Italy, for example). As resources and the presence of the church increased, especially in the west, the more baroque Gothic architecture emerged in high-late medieval church buildings. These Gothic features include the flying buttress truss system combined with pointed archways, ribbed vaults, rose windows, and ornate decor throughout the building as it welcomed worshippers to experience the greatness and loftiness of God (examples: Notre Dame, Basilica of Saint-Denis).

Church pews made their first appearance in the West around the thirteenth century in England. A seemingly small and necessary thing to contemporary Christians, but for a people of such tradition, adding pews into the worship spaces after some 1300 years was no small matter. James White suggests that "the seated congregation was arguably the greatest shift in Christian worship since Constantine."[23] Pews caught on quickly in the late Middle Ages, however, and were common in the West by the time of the Protestant Reformation.

Eastern churches differed from the longitudinal shaped buildings of the West. They typically included a more centralized building capped with a dome. Pews were not introduced in the East like they were in the West. Only in the past century have some Orthodox churches began to incorporate seating in their worship spaces. This topic still seems rather hotly debated among the Orthodox.

---

[22] McClure and Feltoe, *Pilgrimage of Etheria*, 101.

[23] McClure and Feltoe, *Pilgrimage of Etheria*, 102.

Liturgy and the Great Tradition

By the early sixth century, both the Apostles' and Nicene Creeds were present in Eastern and Western liturgies. Hymns, prayers, and antiphons were also handed down across the centuries to new generations of Christians in an effort to move the faith forward by reaching back, not to mere tradition, but to a familiar and faithful one, a tradition preserved in songs, prayers, confessions, baptism, the eucharist, the teaching of Scripture and the regular gathering of Christians that even the apostles would have recognized.

The church of this era was by no means perfect or pure. One could even argue that some of the church's greatest moral and theological missteps occurred from the early to high Middle Ages. And yet liturgy maintained a link to the great faith once for all delivered to the saints.

Recommended Reading

Allison, Greg. "On the Body and Blood of the Lord." In *Historical Theology*. Zondervan, 2011.

Bettenson, Henry, and Chris Maunder, eds. *Documents of the Christian Church*. 4th ed. Oxford University Press, 2011.

Bromiley, Geoffrey W. *Historical Theology*. Eerdmans, 1978.

Cyril of Alexandria. "The Third Letter of Cyril to Nestorius." In *Christology of the Later Fathers*. Edited by Edward R. Hardy. Westminster John Knox, 2006.

Hitchcock, James. *History of the Catholic Church*. Ignatius Press, 2012.

Louth, Andrew. *Greek East and Latin West: The Church 681–1071*. Vol. 3 of *The Church in History*. St. Vladimir's Seminary Press, 2007.

McClure, M. L., and C. L. Feltoe, trans. *The Pilgrimage of Etheria*. Society for Promoting Christian Knowledge, 1919.

Shelley, Bruce L. *Church History in Plain Language*. Zondervan Academic, 2013.

Thompson, Augustine, OP. *St. Francis of Assisi: A New Biography*. Cornell University Press, 2012.

Webber, Robert. *Twenty Centuries of Christian Worship*. Vol. 2 of *The Complete Library of Christian Worship*. Star Song, 1994.

White, James F. *A Brief History of Christian Worship*. Abingdon, 1993.

—— Chapter 16 ——

The Rise of Islam and the Crusades

The Middle Ages tell a story of remarkable cultural, ecclesial, political, economic, and theological development all over the globe. From brilliant architectural development and the proliferation of monastic communities to the founding of hospitals and universities, there are numerous bright spots throughout the story of the sixth century to the fifteenth.

And yet, many have dubbed this period the "Dark Ages." For some, the rise of Islam in the early seventh century signals the foil to Christian progress and the decline of the East. For others, the Crusades of the twelfth and thirteenth centuries, followed by the Black Death of the fourteenth century, cast a shadow across the entire Middle Ages.

The "Dark Ages" language is a gross mischaracterization of this roughly 1000 years of history because it fails to recognize the remarkable advancements made throughout the Middle Ages. There are *dark* parts of the story, however, such as the fall of major Christian cities to Islam as well as the role of the church in the Crusades. As such, this chapter will consider the rise and spread of Islam from approximately the seventh to the eleventh century, followed by reflections on the Crusades of the twelfth to thirteenth centuries.

Rise of Islam

Muhammad was born in 570 in the town of Mecca (in modern-day Saudi Arabia), some forty miles east of the Red Sea. He was orphaned at an early age and raised by his paternal uncle, Abu Talib. He soon took up the role of a merchant, married a well-off widow, and had multiple children. According to his account, around 610, he was visited in a cave by the angel Gabriel, who delivered to him special messages from Allah insisting that he become the prophet of the "true religion." At first, he only shared these messages with his wife and a few friends who encouraged him to write them down. Eventually he did so and these messages from Allah became the foundational text for the Islamic faith, now known as the Qur'an.

This new faith found some association with the Jewish and Christian faiths already present in the East, though there were important distinctions. Islam celebrated Jesus as a prophet, but not as the Son of God as proclaimed in Christian Scripture and confessed by the church. Islam has arguably more continuity with the Jewish faith, with its relentless monotheism. But the Jews did not recognize Muhammad as a prophet of God, nor did they accept the Qur'an as the words of the God of Abraham, Isaac, and Jacob. Thus, these faiths quickly diverged and eventually opposed one another.

Muhammad's new faith also met immediate cultural and local tribal resistance, as the Arab peoples of his region were far from monotheists during this time. They were classic polytheists who revered many gods, especially the gods of the natural elements, and thus found Muhammad's call to monotheism a threat to all social, political, and economic stability. After all, what if he was wrong and the gods were angered?

Despite gaining a sizeable following, resistance and an assassination plot led Muhammad to flee from Mecca to Medina in 622, some 200 miles north, where he established a theocratic government and continued to gain followers. Muslims mark Muhammad's move to Medina in 622 as year one on the Islamic calendar. By 630 Muhammad's army and influence was great enough that he returned home to Mecca, which quickly and rather peacefully converted to Islam. Muhammad managed to gain authority over his native tribe, the Quraysh, and claim the Kaaba, the cubic shaped building that was believed to be built by Abraham and Ishmael and was revered by the locals as a sacred space. Muhammad thus established Mecca as the epicenter of the Islamic faith and the destination for generations of Muslim pilgrimage.

According to Islamic tradition, Muhammad died June 8, 632, only two years after returning home to Mecca. Who would succeed Muhammad as leader of the Islamic faith sparked no small amount of turmoil for the young Muslim community. Some insisted that Muhammad had appointed his son-in-law, Ali, as his successor ("caliph"). Others argued that no such appointment had been made and opted for Muhammad's father-in-law Abu Bakr.

This divide is the genesis of the two Muslim parties that are still at odds today. The Shia (or Shiites) supported Ali, and the Sunnis, who made up the majority, supported Abu Bakr.

Over the next decade, Abu Bakr united Muslims and led them to conquer the majority of the Middle East, overtaking major Christian cities, including Damascus, Jerusalem, and Alexandria. As the Islam expert John Renard describes, "To the north, [Bakr's] forces ended the Byzantine domination of the Fertile Crescent, including Iraq, greater Syria, and the holy city of Jerusalem. Further to the west, Umar established garrisons in Egypt. And to the east, he made serious inroads into the realm of the Zoroastrian Sasanian dynasty of Persia."[1] Bakr's successor, Uthman, expanded Islam's boundaries even farther into Libya and deeper into Persia, and he overtook the Sasanian empire. Despite more controversy over the rightful successors of Muhammad, Islam continued to spread. By 750, Islam's presence would dominate North Africa, much of Spain and Portugal, the entire Arabian Peninsula, and most of India. By 1300, the Islamic-led Ottoman empire emerged to become one of the greatest dynasties in world history, lasting from the 1300s to 1922, when it fell during World War I. The historian Robert Louis Wilken does not exaggerate when he claims, "No event during the first thousand years of Christian history was more unexpected, calamitous, and consequential than the rise of Islam."[2]

Five Pillars of Islam

Islam begins with a simple confession of faith, the Shahada. It states, "There is no god but Allah, and Muhammad is his messenger," and it is to be recited five time each day. It is whispered into the ear of a newborn and is to be the final words heard by a Muslim at death. It is a daily testimony of devotion to the one god, Allah. The Shahada is the first of the Five Pillars of the Islamic faith.

The second pillar is salat (or salah), the observance of five prayer times throughout each day. Muslims are expected to wash before prayer, face the direction of Mecca, lift their hands

---

[1] John Renard, *101 Questions and Answers on Islam* (Paulist Press, 1998), 15.

[2] Robert L. Wilken, *The First Thousand Years* (Yale University Press, 2012), 288. This section on the rise of Islam accords with the traditional story of Islamic origins, though we recognize the work of Patricia Crone, Michael Cook, and Jay Smith, who question the traditional story. Crone and Cook's work argue that the evidence suggests Islam developed slower and much later than traditionally believed, possibly after the seventh century. Cf. Crone and Cook, *Hagarism: The Making of the Islamic World* (Cambridge University Press, 1977); Crone, *Meccan Trade and the Rise of Islam* (Princeton University Press, 1987).

beside their head and declare "Allahu Akbar" ("God is great") followed by the specific salat for the time of day. Bowing (ruku) and the prostrate position (sujud) are also expected during prayer to involve the entire body and maintain focus.

The three remaining pillars are occasional in nature and are almsgiving, fasting, and pilgrimage. While not unique to Islam, Muslims have the strongest tradition of pilgrimage of any faith in the world, and they are expected to visit Mecca at least once during their lifetime. Almsgiving promotes a certain generosity and social awareness among Muslims. Fasting is especially associated with Ramadan, the ninth month in the Muslim calendar, commemorating when Allah gave the message of the Qur'an to Muhammad.

Effects on the Church

As Islam spread across the Middle East, both Christian and Jewish communities were deeply affected by the cultural and religious shift taking place under their feet. Eventually everything changed throughout the Middle East, and by 750 half of the Christian world was under Muslim rule. Those who lived in Spain and Portugal, across North Africa, and throughout India were among the earliest to feel the effects of Islamic takeover. The Muslims had especially set their sights on Syria and Jerusalem given their connections with the Abrahamic tradition, of which they believed themselves to be the true heirs. Following the Muslim victory at the Battle of Yarmuk in August 636, the conquest of Syria was a foregone conclusion, with most cities offering little resistance. After a period of siege, Jerusalem also surrendered to the caliph Umar by 638, and before the end of the century, Islam had erected the Dome of the Rock in Jerusalem where Solomon's Temple once stood. Jerusalem, along with Mecca and Medina, was one of the holiest places on earth for the Islamic faith. As Wilken describes, Muslims were

> harbingers of a new civilization that would displace the language, transform the institutions, and remake the architecture of a region that had been dominated for centuries by the cultures of Israel, Greece, Rome, and Christianity. . . . In two hundred years many of the Christians of the region would be speaking Arabic, and territories that were once provinces of the Roman empire would be ruled from Baghdad, not Constantinople.[3]

---

[3] Wilken, *First Thousand Years*, 294.

Historians previously described these events as brutally militaristic. But more recent scholarship suggests that while military force was used occasionally, Islamic takeover was generally more peaceful and allowed Christians and Jews, as well as Buddhists, Hindus, and Zoroastrians, to continue in their faiths, though their political and economic status differed from Muslims. Requiring the Islamic religion was originally understood to go against Muhammad's teaching, and military force was to be reserved for defense. Concerning forced faith by Muslims, Diarmaid MacCulloch writes, "This is not the whole story—in fact forced conversions were not at all the rule in early Islam, even while it was extending its reach by military campaigns."[4] If not out of military force, it is difficult to say precisely why so many people converted to Islam. Various explanations include political and economic stability, attraction to a monotheism in the Arabic language, and a culturally dominant alternative to Christianity, and certainly some were compelled in a heavy-handed way.

The effect of Islam on the church in North Africa is a sadder story. It is safe to say that no former Christian epicenter from the early centuries was diminished as severely as that of North Africa. This was the birthplace of the Latin tradition represented by the likes of Tertullian and Augustine. While North Africa did not fall as early as Syria and Egypt, its fall was more complete. Following the Vandal invasion in the mid-fifth century and almost a century of the Arian kingdom they established, Byzantine rule was restored in 534 by Emperor Justinian. But, the church had been weakened by the Vandals and never regained the vibrancy it knew from the third through mid-fifth centuries. By 647 the Arabs had taken control of Sbeitla, some 170 miles southwest of Carthage, and by 698 Carthage was conquered and destroyed by Hassan ibn al-Nu'man. Various artifacts indicate that Christianity, as well as the Latin language, lingered until at least the eleventh century, but its flame was almost entirely extinguished. Wilken captures it well:

> In the centuries immediately after the Muslim conquest, Christianity remained alive in North Africa. But through a combination of social constraints, the displacement of Latin by Arabic . . . , the atrophy of ecclesiastical structures, and lack of leadership, the number of Christians dwindled, and by the twelfth century this most ancient Christian region had become wholly Muslim. Unlike the Middle East and Egypt, today there is no indigenous Christian community in North Africa that can

[4] Diarmaid MacCulloch, *Christianity: The First Three Thousand Years* (Penguin, 2009), 256.

> trace its history back to the time of Tertullian, Cyprian, Augustine, and Fulgentius of Ruspe.[5]

While the "Dark Ages" is a mischaracterization of the Middle Ages, the near extinction of Christianity in the Middle East casts at least a shadow on the medieval era of Christian history.

Cultural Developments Under Islam

MacCulloch speaks to the aesthetic dimension of the Qur'an as a great attraction to Islam. He writes,

> At the centre of Muhammad's achievement was the extraordinary poetry which enshrined his revelations. Muslim sources have often ascribed the Qur'an's power to its exceptional beauty in the Arabic language, and the Qur'an does not translate well, particularly into English. Conversion to Islam can therefore be a deeply felt aesthetic experience that rarely occurs in Christian accounts of conversion.[6]

Islam's cultural influence did not stop with the Qur'an's poetry. Rather, as religions are prone to do, it stretched into every dimension of society and culture. Under Islamic rule, the arts, sciences, literature, architecture, and education in general were all advanced, integrating their Greek ideological building blocks with Persian and Indian thought. Algebra, for example, was added as a third branch of mathematics in addition to geometry and arithmetic. Ibn-Sina (also known as Avicenna, 980–1037) wrote a medical textbook based on Galen's physiology that set a new standard in medicine and was later assigned in Western schools as a primary medical text.[7] Elsewhere, new forms of pumps and pipes were designed to improve infrastructure, and artistic expression was seen especially in architecture.

It would be hard to overstate the educational impact of Arabs during this time. Not only did the Arabic language replace Greek and Latin, but eventually the Western vocabulary was expanded as new ideas and cultural artifacts were introduced. John Riddle notes that words like "alcohol," "elixir," "zero," "almanac," and "chemistry" moved East to West from

---

[5] Wilken, *First Thousand Years*, 323.

[6] Wilken, *First Thousand Years*, 257.

[7] John M. Riddle, *A History of the Middle Ages, 300–1500* (Rowman & Littlefield, 2008), 150.

Arabic vocabulary, influencing language and learning.[8] Education became readily available for children of virtually any economic status, and schools of higher learning called *madrasas* were developed, attending to "grammar, philology, rhetoric, literature, logic, mathematics, and astronomy."[9] Despite whatever misgivings the West may have about the Islamic takeover in the East, much may be appreciated with regard to cultural development, especially in literature and education.

Both Jews and Christians also had a strong educational heritage. The rise of Islam only served to stoke the fires of learning with fresh vigor and new insights. But the religious and ethnic distinctions between these three did not allow for a synthesis of faiths and cultures. Over time, many Christians converted to Islam, though this was not necessarily encouraged. Since non-Muslims paid higher taxes, conversions to Islam reduced tax revenue. Nevertheless, many Christians adopted the ways and means of Arabic culture, including language, fashion, celebrations, and festivals.

While Islam, Judaism, and Christianity resisted a synthesis of religion, the Arabic appetite for learning led to much collaboration with studied Christians and scholars. Monasteries such as Mar Saba (southeast of Jerusalem) and Saint Catherine (in south Sinai in Egypt) emerged as intellectual centers where Greek and Latin classics, as well as the Bible and the church fathers, were translated into Arabic. Aristotle's works became particularly popular among both Muslims and Arabic-speaking Christians. Capable translators, such as Anthony David of Baghdad and Stephen of Ramla, were instrumental in these translation efforts, a movement of scholarship that lasted some 300 years, from the eighth to the eleventh century.

While Italy and Asia Minor represented the heart of Christian monasticism after Jerusalem fell to Islam, Palestinian monasteries eventually restabilized and found renewed purpose in advancing education and literature, while also engaging Muslims in apologetic dialogue concerning Christianity. Numerous Arabic-speaking Christians—including the great John of Damascus; Timothy I, who became patriarch of the Eastern church; and the lesser-known Theodore Abu Qurrah—all defended the truth of Christianity and its practices against the accusations of Islam.[10]

---

[8] Riddle, *A History of the Middle Ages, 300–1500*, 147.

[9] Riddle, *A History of the Middle Ages, 300–1500*, 147.

[10] For an excellent overview, see Robert L. Wilken's chapter "Arabic-Speaking Christians," in *First Thousand Years*, 307–15.

The Crusades

By the end of the eleventh century, the world had known some five centuries of Muslim conquest; religious tension between the Christians, Muslims, and Jews; territorial disputes; tectonic cultural shifts; a schism between the Western and Eastern churches; and significant economic discrepancies by all parties. The ground was ripe for conflict fueled by religious, political, and economic concerns.

In brief, the Crusades were a series of five to seven wars from 1096 to 1291 fought by Western Christians against Muslims, Jews, and/or Eastern Christians under the authority of the pope seeking to reclaim the Holy Land for Christian purpose and pilgrimage. The Cambridge Crusade scholar Jonathan Riley-Smith adds that the Crusades included those who "were called upon to take up the Cross" taking vows to join the military with its particular aims of war. Second, the taking up of the cross was a call that could only be issued by the pope. And third, for answering the pope's call and for their service, crusaders were guaranteed certain privileges, such as pardon for sin (indulgences) and that their "families, interests and assets would be protected in their absence."[11]

In the fifth century, Augustine taught the church a notion of *Jus ad bellum* or just war that neither celebrated nor pursued such gruesome conflict without just cause. It was a level-headed approach that was neither naïve to the inevitability of war at times nor bent in pursuit of unnecessary conflict. The criteria for just war included:

1. *Just cause*—proper reasons for declaring war, such as self-defense, protecting the innocent, assisting allies for just reasons
2. *Proportionality*—going to war is likely to cause less damage than not going to war
3. *Right intention*—the motives for going to war must align with the command to love God and neighbor
4. *Right authority*—must be authorized by a legitimate governing authority, such as that recognized in Romans 13
5. *Reasonable chance of success*—without the likelihood of success, there is little chance of restoring peace
6. *Last resort*—nonviolent options must be exhausted before pursuing warfare

[11] Jonathan Riley-Smith, *What Were the Crusades?* (Rowman & Littlefield, 1977), 12–13.

While the notion of just war was recognized by the church of the twelfth century, the notion of holy war was not. Holy war, or *jihad*, was the business of the Muslim armies as they spread across the Middle East, but this was not the way of Christ or the church. At least it hadn't been.[12]

The beginning of the end for the East was signaled by the fall of Bari in Southern Italy to the Normans and the loss at the Battle of Manzikert to the Seljuk Turks in 1071. The East was losing control of the empire, including easy access for pilgrimage to Jerusalem. Emperor Alexius Comnenus thus called out to the West for help.

At this point, Pope Urban II saw the opportunity to rally the church of the West to rescue the church of the East while reclaiming the Holy Land and reestablishing Christianity as the dominant global religion. No doubt such a demonstration of power and rescue would elevate the West and restore both peace and proper Christian authority.

In 1095 at Clermont in southeastern France, Pope Urban II appealed to the people, calling for a crusade to "rescue Jerusalem from the infidels."[13] Robert the Monk records a portion of Urban's speech as follows:

> From the confines of Jerusalem and from the city of Constantinople a grievous report has gone forth and has repeatedly been brought to our ears; namely, that a race from the kingdom of the Persians, an accursed race . . . has violently invaded the lands of those Christians and has depopulated them by pillage and fire. . . . They destroyed the altars, after having defiled them with their uncleanness. . . . This royal city [Jerusalem] is now held captive by the enemies of Christ and is subjected, by those who do not know God, to the worship of the heathen. She seeks, therefore, and desires to be liberated and ceases not to implore you to come to her aid.[14]

The crowd responded with shouts of "*Deus vult!*"—"God wills it!"—eerily reminiscent of the cry of Muhammad's army as they marched across the Middle East. Whatever stated or unstated motivations there may have been, Urban had certainly touched a nerve with the people. The blend of religion and rescue rallied the crowd toward crusade. People from

---

[12] See Thomas F. Madden, *The New Concise History of the Crusades* (Rowman & Littlefield, 2005), 1–4.

[13] John M. Riddle, *A History of the Middle Ages, 300–1500* (Rowman & Littlefield, 2008), 275.

[14] Robert the Monk, quoted in John M. Riddle, *A History of the Middle Ages, 300–1500* (Rowman & Littlefield, 2008), 276.

around Europe, especially France, heeded the call and found creative ways to finance their journey. The initial expense seemed worthwhile given the pope's promise of indulgence (forgiveness of sins), a practice made popular a few decades earlier for those who gave money toward the building and maintenance of church buildings. Those willing to go to war, or who financed someone to fight in their stead, were promised remission for temporal punishments from sin. Moreover, there was the prospect of plunder, offering hope for increased personal wealth and betterment of one's family.

First Crusade—1096–99

The first crusade took place between 1096 and 1099 with the stated goal of retaking the Holy Land, especially Jerusalem, while also protecting Eastern Christians and ensuring safe travel for pilgrimage. Jerusalem was indeed reclaimed with the help of leaders such as Peter the Hermit (c. 1050–1115), a French priest with more zeal and charisma than military training who rallied a sizeable following. Peter's army included some 20,000 peasants eager to fight for the cause under the banner of the cross. It was an amateur army of soldiers without sergeants and is known to history as "The People's Crusade." Following a series of battles along the Rhine in Germany, their passion gave way to inexperience, and they were badly defeated by the Turks at Civetot in 1096. Peter may well have been the sole survivor but continued to fight and was present for Jerusalem's capture in 1099.

In response to the defeat at Civetot, a more proper military effort was put forward, referred to as "The Princes' Crusade" and led by the likes of Raymond IV of Toulouse, the brothers Godfrey of Bouillon and Baldwin of Boulogne, Bohemond of Taranto, and other dignitaries from across France, Italy, and the Flemish region. With an army of approximately 100,000, the crusaders sieged Nicaea in June 1097, Antioch in June 1098, and Jerusalem in July 1099. The Kingdom of Jerusalem was established, led first by Godfrey, though he soon died. Upon his death, his brother Baldwin was crowned king of Jerusalem on December 25, 1100. This Latin legacy in Jerusalem survived until 1291, when Jerusalem fell again and finally to the Muslims.

Despite their success, the battles from Nicaea to Antioch to Jerusalem took a toll on the crusaders, many of whom suffered from sickness and disease as well as thirst and starvation. Moreover, eyewitness accounts of the battles are far from flattering for those who donned the cross of Christ on their breastplate. The savagery, looting, and indiscriminate killing of men, women, and children, not to mention tales of cannibalism, followed by prayers on the battlefield and the celebration of the Eucharist with hands blood-stained from battle—these are common refrains from the accounts of the battles.

Second Crusade—1145–48

In the decades following the first crusade, the Hospitallers of John of Jerusalem were established to care for sick and ailing pilgrims, the Knights Templar were founded to protect Christian pilgrims to Jerusalem, and the practice of inquisition proliferated and would continue for several centuries more. Bernard of Clairvaux founded a Cistercian monastery and heralded the next crusade in his preaching. Edessa was taken by Muslims in 1144, and the new Pope Eugenius III declared a new campaign that resonated with Pope Urban II's rhetoric from before.

As Peter the Hermit was the preacher of the First Crusade, Bernard of Clairvaux carried this mantle for the Second Crusade. Inspired by Bernard's preaching and led by King Louis VII of France and Conrad III, emperor of Germany, armies set out to regain Edessa. But internal strife and poor leadership led to swift failure, principally at Damascus in 1148. Following various failures and strategic errors, the mission to recapture Edessa was abandoned. By virtually all historical accounts, the Second Crusade was an abject failure.

> Hasten then to expiate your sins by victories over the infidels, and let the deliverance of the holy places be the reward of your repentance.
>
> ———
>
> Bernard of Clairvaux,
> "Sermon at Vezelay" March 31, 1146

Upon his return to Europe, Louis's embarrassment was mixed with fury at the Byzantine Empire, which he now regarded as the real enemy of Christ. While Louis received no papal support to return to crusade, the perception that the Byzantines were enemies took hold in the West, further dividing the it from the East.

Third Crusade—1189–92

Despite earlier division among Islamic armies and communities that were exploited by the first crusaders, by the 1160s Islam was remarkably unified from Egypt to Syria. And the unifying leader remains one of the most revered figures in Islamic political and military history, Saladin (Salah ad-Din, 1138–93). From July to October 1187, Saladin's army defeated Christians at Hattin in Galilee (July 4, 1187) and Jerusalem on October 2.

The Battle of Hattin was particularly gruesome, only adding to Saladin's already fierce reputation. Saladin's secretary described the events as follows, particularly stressing the religious distinctives and superiority of Islam over Christianity:

> Islam passed the night face to face with unbelief, monotheism at war with trinitarianism, the way of righteousness looking down upon error, faith opposing polytheism. . . . Humiliation was inflicted on the men of Sunday, who had been lions and now were reduced to the level of miserable sheep. I passed by them and saw the limbs of the fallen cast naked on the field of battle, scattered in pieces over the site of the encounter, lacerated and disjointed, with heads cracked open.[15]

After the bloodbath at Hattin, crusaders simply surrendered at Jerusalem, and Saladin accepted, celebrating the restoration of "true" worship in the Holy City. News traveled fast of Jerusalem's capture, and the response was strong, especially from the royalty, lending the Third Crusade the title of "Crusade of the Kings."

Holy Roman Emperor Frederick I Barbarossa ("Redbeard"), King Philip II of France, and Richard I ("Lionheart"), who would later become King of England, all took the cross, leading armies of more than 100,000 on a mission to retake Jerusalem from Saladin. Barbarossa drowned en route, and eventually Richard I emerged as the leader of the crusade. Richard captured Cyprus and Jaffa and aided Philip in taking Acre. However, he was unable to capture Jerusalem. All was not lost, however, as the crusade ended with an unlikely treaty between Richard and Saladin on September 2, 1192, during which Saladin gave crusaders control of some sixty miles of the Mediterranean coast from Jaffa to Acre, and Christian pilgrims were granted safe passage from Jaffa to Jerusalem.

Fourth Crusade—1198–1204

By the beginning of the thirteenth century, the treaty between Richard and Saladin was old and unsatisfying news for Pope Innocent III. He wanted Jerusalem back under Christian

---

[15] Quoted in John Dickson, *Bullies and Saints: An Honest Look at the Good and Evil of Christian History* (Zondervan, 2021), 11.

control and out from under Muslim authority. And while a sizeable number of crusaders heeded the pope's call, he struggled to get European royalty on board. What was accomplished in the Fourth Crusade was not what was planned, though it had sizeable impact on the future of Europe.

Innocent III's campaign struggled financially and thus contracted with Venice to ship soldiers to Egypt. When the crusaders were unable to cover the shipping cost, they agreed in return to pay the bill by assisting the Venetians in taking over Zara, a port city across the Adriatic Sea. After successfully taking Zara, crusaders joined forces with the Venetian ruler Enrico Dandolo and turned their attention not to Egypt or Jerusalem, but to Constantinople. Many in the West were disappointed with the commitment level from the East, and thus felt justified in taking from Constantinople what they felt was owed to them.[16] Against the pope's wishes, crusaders sacked Constantinople in April 1204 and replaced the Greek patriarch with the Venetian Thomas Morosini. John Dickson observes, "For the following half-century Constantinople was *Latin* and *Catholic*, when it had been the capital of everything Greek and Orthodox since the AD 300s."[17] The story could be told as though a "union" between East and West was established in Constantinople under Innocent III. But the union was illusory. It was an imposition by the West that aggravated old and existing tensions.

Fifth and Final Crusades—1212–91

Various crusades or related events, such as the Children's Crusade of 1212, popped up throughout the thirteenth century, leading historians to differ on the total number of crusades. After the dissolution of the Fourth Crusade in 1204, Innocent III began planning another. His 1213 encyclical *Quia maior* is arguably the strongest call to crusade by any church leader throughout the crusader era. Arguing that defeating the dangerous and heretical Cathars (meaning "pure"), an Albigensian dualistic religious heretical movement that emerged in the twelfth century, was an act of neighbor-love and with the apocalyptic association of Muhammad with the "beast" whose sign is "666," Innocent held nothing back. At the Fourth Lateran Council, in November 1215, called by Innocent III, plans were made, and crusaders were to report to Brindisi and Messina on June 1, 1217. Innocent

[16] Dickson, *Bullies and Saints*, 13.

[17] Dickson, *Bullies and Saints*, 14.

died on July 16, 1216, but his successor, Honorius III, remained committed to the campaign. Despite the prospects of success, the crusade ended in failure. In the years that followed, various men, such as Frederick II, Louis IX of France, his brother Charles of Anjou, and Prince Edward of England, would all lead efforts toward toppling Egypt or retaking Jerusalem with very little success. Crusaders battled far more than Muslims during the thirteenth century as the commitment levels among crusaders were unreliable, sickness crippled many, and financial needs were a regular distraction.

The end of the story comes in 1291 with the fall of Acre, the coastal stronghold in northern Israel. The siege on Acre began on April 6 and by May 18 the city was under Muslim control and Christians were banished from the Holy Land. With praise to Allah, Muslims celebrated the "purification" of the Franks from Syria and the coastal areas.

The Crusades and the Great Tradition

The crusades had complex consequences for interfaith relations, as they brought Christians into direct contact with Muslims, Jews, and other religious communities. While the stated goal of the Crusades was to reclaim Christian territories and defend Christendom, they often resulted in religious persecution, violence, and forced conversions of non-Christians. Jewish communities, in particular, faced persecution and pogroms during the Crusades, as Christian crusaders targeted them in their zeal to combat perceived enemies of the faith. Similarly, Muslims in the Holy Land and other regions subjected to crusading campaigns suffered displacement, destruction of property, and loss of life, leading to enduring animosities and resentments between Christian and non-Christian communities.

The crusades left a legacy of religious conflict and animosity between Christian and non-Christian communities, shaping interfaith relations in the following centuries. The memory of the Crusades, as well as the violence and persecution associated with them, continued to fuel tensions and mistrust between different religious groups. Moreover, the crusades contributed to the demonization of the "other" and the perpetuation of stereotypes and prejudices, further exacerbating divisions and hostilities between Christian and non-Christian communities.

Nevertheless, we must consider both the moral and theological dimensions of what took place. The notion of Holy War was more at home in the Islamic worldview than the Christian one, and there was precedent from the spread of Islam in this regard. This certainly fueled the rhetoric of popes and animated crusaders to take up the cross. But it was hardly justified by Scripture. After all, this is the faith of the one who preached the Sermon on the Mount, "Blessed are the merciful . . . the peacemakers . . . those who are persecuted because of righteousness, for the kingdom of heaven is theirs" (Matt 5:7–10). And this kingdom that Christ spoke of was not one to be imposed by force, at least not before his return. Yet, both the injustice of Islam and the blocking of the Holy Land reached a boiling point, providing strategic opportunity for the West to reclaim Jerusalem and "rescue" the Eastern church. It didn't take too much rhetorical flare to ignite imaginations and justify the cause for crusaders of the West for the sake of the cross and kingdom.

But it was wrongheaded. The rationale for going to war was above all emotional and political, hardly meeting the just war criteria laid out by Augustine. And by the end of the thirteenth century, Jerusalem was in full control of the budding Ottoman Empire, the Byzantine church as it had been known was effectively dissolved, and the church of the West was weak, tired, and unstable. And, while one may argue that the crusader spirit lived on into the Reformation, the fighting moved from the battlefield to the writing desk fueled by the printing press.

The authority of the church was also dealt a blow during this time. By the thirteenth century, multiple cultural movements were already underway with the rumblings of a classical renaissance, the rise of Scholasticism, and the proliferation of new universities. But the division of the papacy and its ongoing power struggles with European countries cast a dark cloud over the church in the West. The fourteenth century did not begin any prettier than the thirteenth ended. It was understandable for the world to wonder if the church could be trusted.

Recommended Reading

Dickson, John. *Bullies and Saints: An Honest Look at the Good and Evil of Christian History*. Zondervan, 2021.

Madden, Thomas F. *The New Concise History of the Crusades*. Rowman & Littlefield, 2005.

Renard, John. *101 Questions and Answers on Islam*. Paulist Press, 1998.

Riddle, John M. *A History of the Middle Ages, 300–1500*. Rowman & Littlefield, 2008.

Riley-Smith, Jonathan. *What Were the Crusades?* Rowman & Littlefield, 1977.

Wilken, Robert L. *The First Thousand Years*. Yale University Press, 2012.

—— Chapter 17 ——

Medieval Monasticism, Mysticism, and New Religious Orders

Following the publication of Benedict's *Rule* and the proliferation of monastic communities that followed, the influence of monasteries is hardly paralleled by any other social institution save the government and the church—and at certain times, the monasteries may have had greater influence than either of these. Serving as the custodians of learning and scholarship, models for morality and holy living, leaders in farming and agriculture, and preachers and pioneering missionaries, monastic communities indelibly shaped the story of medieval Christianity.

Picking up some of the threads of chapter 11, this chapter considers the ongoing impact of the monastic movement throughout the Middle Ages, including the Cluniac Reform of the tenth century, the founding of the Cistercians, and the rise of various mendicant orders. Further, we consider important theological developments that emerge during this time in direct relation to monasteries, as well as the tension that persisted between monks and clergy, monasteries and churches, throughout the Middle Ages.

Monastic Contours in the Early Middle Ages

At the time of Gregory the Great's death (604), Christianity was almost entirely an urban religion. By the death of Charlemagne in 814, however, Christianity had moved to the countryside in rural areas all over northern Europe. Much of Hungary and northward, through Poland and into Scandinavia, was evangelized. Germany, once a loose conglomeration of pagan villages and holds ruled by warlords, was thoroughly Christianized. Much of this transformation was due to the work of monks.

Monasticism originated as a lay movement. But with monasticism's tendency to build in rural locations, it was inevitable that locals would look to the monasteries, the home of the spiritual athletes, for pastoral care. Certainly, tensions existed in places where Christianity was new; yet for many in rural areas, the monks were the ones who taught them how to pray and practice their faith. Locals often attended the church of the monasteries and were encouraged to value manual labor and order all of life unto God. Over time this led to territorial conflicts of authority concerning the propriety of monks being ordained and performing sacramental duties. In addition to all this, the monastic attention to reading and scholarship made monasteries a natural home for local education moving into the twelfth century with the advent and proliferation of universities.

Before we look at some of the most important monastic orders that arose during this period, we need to consider one of the most important monks to lead this missionary movement into less urban areas of Europe.

Boniface

Boniface (c. 675–754) was an Anglo-Saxon whose name in Latin means "doer of good." He led the Saxons in the charge in missionary work among the peoples of what is now Germany. He preached the gospel to thousands among a once firmly pagan stronghold and became known as the apostle to the Germans. He was supported by both the Frankish kings and Pope Gregory II—who changed his name from Winfred to Boniface—and this support afforded him a great deal of protection as he rooted out paganism from Germanic lands. One particularly dramatic episode tells of Donar's Oak (or Thor's Oak), which was venerated by the Germanic people. Boniface took an axe to the tree, but before he made much headway in chopping it down, a great wind came and blew it down. When the gods did not strike Boniface down for his sacrilege, the people immediately converted to

Christ. Under Boniface's direction, a chapel dedicated to Peter was built from the wood of the oak tree.

Due to his success, Boniface enjoyed the favor of the pope and of the Frankish rulers. On behalf of the Franks, Boniface led the way in weakening the hold of paganism in Germanic lands, which increased their ability to expand their political hold. On behalf of the pope, Boniface exerted considerable influence in restructuring and reforming the Frankish church. Many of the dioceses and administrative arrangements that Boniface established are still in place today. Boniface served to bring Rome closer in alliance to the Frankish rulers of Gaul, present-day France. Aside from Rome itself, Gaul was the last remaining historically Christian kingdom that had not become entrenched in the battle against Islam. This meant a papal ally with a strong standing army that could be called upon in times of need.

> Moved by zeal for the task entrusted to us, as well as by the Gospel precept, "Pray ye, therefore, the Lord of the harvest that he send forth laborers into his harvest," we directed you in imitation of the Apostles ordered by the Lord: "Go forth and preach the Gospel!"
>
> ———
>
> Pope Gregory II,
> "Letter to Boniface," December 4, 724

Despite his vast political and ecclesial influence, Boniface remained a missionary until his death. He remained resolute in his desire to see converts among the Frisians and so, at nearly eighty years old, he set out with a group on a missionary journey. He baptized many of the Frisians and called for a confirmation meeting. But at the meeting in 1207, bandits ambushed the group. They killed Boniface and those with him, thinking they would find gold and silver in the luggage, which instead contained books and manuscripts of Holy Scripture. His body is entombed in the Fulda Cathedral in Germany.

Cluny

In 909, Duke William III of Aquitaine donated his favorite hunting grounds, called Cluny, for a new monastery. William chose Berno to serve as the inaugural Abbot of the new Monastery at Cluny with the purpose of returning to the spirit and discipline of Benedict's *Rule* with all its emphasis on prayer, work, devotion, and obedience. Having deeded the land to Saints Peter and Paul, William thus placed the new monastery under the oversight of

Rome. The Cluniac Reform addressed perceived deficiencies in monastic life, such as negligence of discipline, secular interference, and moral laxity. Central to the Cluniac Reform was the establishment of a network of monasteries affiliated with the mother house of Cluny, each adhering to a strict rule of life focused on liturgical prayer, manual labor, and asceticism. Imperial support, particularly from the Holy Roman Empire and local rulers, provided crucial backing for the Cluniac Reform movement, enabling it to gain traction and influence across Europe. Emperors and nobles granted lands, privileges, and exemptions to Cluniac monasteries, bolstering their economic and political power and facilitating their charitable endeavors, such as providing food, shelter, and education to needy people. Ironically, Cluny is not remembered for its reform and return to Benedictine ideals. Rather, in a short time, Cluny became incredibly wealthy due to donations of land and monetary gifts. So much so that manual labor was outsourced to hired hands as monks argued that they were purer when not dirtied by work in the fields. By the time of Cluny's eighth abbot, Peter the Venerable (1122–57), Cluny had garnered an aesthetic reputation commensurate with its wealth. Everything was ornate. Buildings, dress, liturgy—everything was what one might call "over the top" in decor and style. Cluny defended this as appropriate for devotion to God, but others felt it was too much and that Cluny, the original monastic reform movement, needed reforming.

Cistercians

The grandiose reputation of Cluny motivated others toward monastic reform. Though Cluny had been a reform movement, many felt that it hardly represented the spirit of Benedict. Thus, in 1098 the Cistercian movement, named after the French city of Citeaux ("Cistercium" in Latin), was begun by Robert of Molesme. The Cistercians emphasized manual labor, self-sufficiency, and contemplative prayer, eschewing the wealth and luxury associated with many monastic establishments of the time. Imperial support, particularly from rulers such as Henry II of England and Frederick Barbarossa of the Holy Roman Empire, played a crucial role in the expansion and consolidation of the Cistercian order. Imperial patronage provided the Cistercians with land grants, charters, and legal protections, enabling them to establish new monasteries, cultivate extensive agricultural estates, and engage in charitable works, such as the provision of alms to the poor and the care of the sick and infirm. Though Robert was its first abbot, the Cistercian movement remains unique among monastic traditions as it is not named after one inspirational or founding leader. Rather, one might say that Cistercian monasticism was a communal movement founded by its first three abbots, Robert, Alberic, and Stephen, successively.

Robert led for only a short time before being succeeded by Alberic, who insisted the monks be clothed in white rather than the traditional Benedictine black garb. This was in part because Alberic felt black was too opulent for the monastic life, but also to distinguish this new monastic movement from the Cluniacs, hence the Cistercian nickname, "White Monks." Cistercians continue to wear a white robe with a leather belt today.

Citeaux's third abbot was the Englishman Stephen Harding, who was chiefly responsible for the Cistercian *Carta caritatis*, Charter of Love, drafted in 1119. Among other things, the Charter articulated independence for each Cistercian monastery, in contrast to the over-centralized form of government that Cluny had over hundreds of Benedictine monasteries. The Cistercian houses maintained a legal relationship with a federal form of oversight and mutually supported one another's work. In a short time, four daughter houses were established in the eastern-central region of France that shared the governing responsibilities for one another. Included in these four daughter houses was the monastery at Clairvaux, made famous by its founder, Bernard.

Bernard of Clairvaux

While not the founder of the Cistercian movement, one can hardly speak of the Cistercians without speaking of Bernard (1090–1153). In fact, modern-day Cistercians refer to Bernard's time as the beginning of the "golden age" of the Cistercian movement. Born in 1090 in southern Dijon, France, to parents of Burgundy's nobility, Bernard excelled in learning as a child, and around 1113 he, along with multiple family members, including eventually his father, chose to join the new Cistercian movement in Citeaux. After three years at Citeaux, Bernard was chosen to establish a new monastery in Clairvaux, a town renamed by Bernard for its "clear view" of the landscape and that rose to become a center for spirituality and devotion to God. As Clairvaux grew, the monastery planted its first daughter house in 1118. Some 170 other monasteries attribute their beginnings to Bernard's leadership and influence during his lifetime.

Bernard served as the abbot of the monastery in Clairvaux until his death in 1153. His popularity spread quickly as people flocked to join the new work in Clairvaux and to learn alongside Bernard. His preaching and writing were particularly popular, earning him recognition as a doctor of the church by Pope Pius VII in 1830. Bernard also held a position of arbiter of Europe from 1130 until his death in 1153, placing him frequently before kings and dignitaries to discuss matters of church and state. Nevertheless, his core aim was to carry out the monastic manner of piety and sincerity in deep devotion to God.

Despite his desire to focus on the monastic life, in 1130 Bernard found himself in the middle of a papal schism following the election of two popes in the wake of Honorius II's death (1060–1130). Innocent II (1088–1143) and Anacletus II (d. 1138) both claimed the papacy. While Bernard and many nobilities, including Holy Roman

Image 17.1. *The spread of Cistercian monasticism in Europe.* Taken from *Christian History* 24, *Bernard of Clairvaux, Medieval Reformer and Mystics* (Christian History Institute, 1989).

Emperor Lothair II, supported Innocent, Anacletus retained the support of the majority of the Christian world. Bernard devoted much time and energy to Innocent's cause over the next eight years, even losing some financial support for his monastery as a result. In 1138 Anacletus died, ending the schism. Innocent II was properly recognized as pope, and living supporters of the schism were condemned by the Second Lateran Council, in 1139.

One might have hoped for Bernard's political work to be behind him, but alas it was only the beginning. After Innocent II's death in 1143, Eugenius III (Eugene), a former student of Bernard's at Clairvaux, was elected pope. Recognizing that Bernard's influence was greater than his own, when Eugene called for the Second Crusade around 1146, he turned immediately to Bernard to promote the effort. Bernard's pen, known for beautiful prose about the love of God, turned to the call for crusading. He wrote, "But now, O brave knight, now, O warlike hero, here is a battle you may fight without danger [to the soul], where it is glory to conquer and gain to die. Take the sign of the cross, and you shall gain pardon for every sin that you confess with a contrite heart."[1]

Ultimately, the Second Crusade was a failure, a disaster in fact. And, as Thomas Madden notes, "No one was more disappointed than Bernard. The crusade built on his prestige and reputation had been an unmitigated fiasco." Why? In Bernard's view, "The armies of Christendom failed because of the sins of Europe. God withheld victory from his knights to chastise them and all Christians. . . . If crusades were ever to succeed, [Bernard] argued, Europe must purify itself."[2]

Bernard's influence in the twelfth century was vast, and his legacy is variegated. While not without critique, Bernard's greatest legacy is a spiritual one. As one historian said, "from any corner of [Bernard's] thought we are led back always to the center, to the love of God."[3] His spirituality involved steps of progress toward proper fear and love of God and proper love of self. He describes this journey in various ways, as in his *On Loving God*, with a multistep process that culminates in "for now we do not love ourselves except for his sake,"[4] and in his *Sermons on the Song of Songs*, in which the process culminates with the bride asking to

---

[1] Quoted in John Dickson, *Bullies and Saints: An Honest Look at the Good and Evil of Christian History* (Zondervan, 2021), 11.

[2] Thomas F. Madden, *The New Concise History of the Crusades* (Rowman & Littlefield, 2005), 61.

[3] Dennis Martin, "The Spirituality of St. Bernard of Clairvaux," in *Christian History Magazine* 24, *Bernard of Clairvaux Medieval Reformer and Mystics* (Christian History Institute, 1989).

[4] Martin, "Spirituality of St. Bernard," 35.

kiss her bridegroom out of confidence, not out of fear. "She has kissed his feet in repentance, kissed his hand in spiritual growth as the bridegroom guides her toward maturity, and now in confidence, she kisses his mouth and joins him in the sweet embrace of love (sermons 1–8)."[5] This legacy of spirituality and early mysticism is particularly noteworthy during the time of rationalism, Aristotelian retrieval, and emerging Scholasticism. As such, we turn briefly to the medieval mystical tradition of the twelfth–fourteenth centuries.

The Mystical Movement

A mystical approach to life and doctrine threads back to the earliest Christians. While scholars differ on definitions, at its root Christian mysticism may be described as "that part of its belief and practices that concerns the preparation for, the consciousness of, and the reaction to what can be described as the immediate or direct presence of God."[6]

Mystical experiences and approaches were commonly attested by early Christians, including Antony and the desert fathers and Dionysius the Areopagite in his sixth century *On Mystical Theology*. These experiences are spoken of with some frequency over the next thousand years. However, a fresh movement of mysticism emerged in the twelfth century. The movement stretched across Europe, including influential men and women, such as Hildegard of Bingen (1098–1179), Bonaventure (c.1217–74), and Meister Eckhart (c.1260–c.1328) in Germany and France; Bridget of Sweden (c. 1303–1373), who founded the Bridgettine nuns recognized as the Order of the Most Holy Savior by Pope Urban V in 1370; Julian of Norwich in England (c.1343–c.1416); and Catherine of Siena (1347–1380) in northwest Italy. For our purposes here, we will briefly consider Julian and Catherine as two examples of medieval mysticism and will return to Bonaventure in chapter 19 as a Franciscan counterpart and contemporary of Thomas Aquinas. Julian operated with a more

---

[5] Martin, "Spirituality of St. Bernard."

[6] Bernard McGinn, *Foundations of Mysticism: Origins to the Fifth Century* (Crossroad, 1991, 2002), xvii. Alister McGrath carefully distinguishes between "mysticism" and "spirituality," arguing for the latter as the more helpful term for today. In teasing out three senses of the word "mysticism," McGrath suggests the third sense as "used to refer to specific schools of Christian spirituality, including the 'English mystics' of the fourteenth century . . . and the 'German mystics' of the latter Middle Ages." Alister McGrath, *Christian Spirituality: An Introduction* (Blackwell, 1999), 6. We approach the discussion of the medieval mystical movement in a similar vein, recognizing it as part of the larger story of Christian spirituality, though offering a distinct flavor of spirituality that emerges at a notable time in the history of the church.

secluded and private ministry, and Catherine with a more public ministry—both of which carry lasting legacies that reverberate across subsequent centuries.

Julian of Norwich (c. 1342–c. 1416)

While little is certain concerning the personal life of the English anchoress (female ascetic) Julian of Norwich, her mystical life and legacy continue to inspire Christians around the world. It has been speculated that she was married, as she writes as one who knew first-hand the tender experience of motherhood. It is also possible that she lost loved ones to the Black Plague, which she is believed to have contracted multiple times and survived. Even her name was likely not Julian. Rather, she may simply have been named after the church of Julian in Norwich, England.

According to her account, in May 1373, during a period of intense sickness, Julian experienced a series of visions of the passions of Christ. Her meditations on these visions are recorded in her *Revelations of Divine Love*. It was after this experience on her supposed deathbed that, upon her recovery, she chose to dedicate her life to isolation and meditation.

From her hut at Julian's church, Mother Julian, as she was often called, became a trusted counselor and adviser to many. The emphasis on the goodness and love of God for the world and the importance of prayer are prominent themes in Julian's writing. McGrath notes that "for Julian, prayer is a thing of great delight to God, who rejoices when we pray. We should persevere in prayer, even when that prayer seems dry and useless."[7] She writes,

> God rejoices that he is our Father, and God rejoices that he is our Mother, and God rejoices that he is our true spouse, and that our soul is his beloved wife. And Christ rejoices that he is our brother, and Jesus rejoices that he is our saviour. These are five great joys, as I understand, in which he wants us to rejoice, praising him, thanking him, loving him, endlessly blessing him, all who will be saved. . . .
>
> I contemplated the work of all the blessed Trinity, in which contemplation I saw and understood these three properties: the property of fatherhood, and the property of motherhood, and the property of lordship in one God. In our almighty Father we have our protection and our bliss, as regards our natural substance, which is ours by our creation from without beginning; and in the second person, in knowledge and

[7] McGrath, *Christian Spirituality*, 156.

> wisdom we have our perfection, as regards our sensuality, our restoration and our salvation, for he is our Mother, brother and saviour; and in our good Lord the Holy Spirit we have our reward and our gift for our living and our labour, endlessly surpassing all that we desire in his marvellous courtesy, out of his great plentiful grace. For all our life consists of three: In the first we have our being, an in the second we have our increasing, and in the third we have our fulfillment. This first is nature, the second is mercy, the third is grace.[8]

This short selection from Julian immediately alerts readers to, first, her creative courage within her robust Catholic theological framework. The number three remains important to Julian throughout her writing, and rightly so for it offers a safe and familiar framework for her readers who might otherwise have greater concern for her creativity, especially concerning the "motherhood" of God. Secondly, readers are struck by not merely her theological carefulness (though some will doubtless take serious issue), but also the depth of personal experience woven through her prose. Different than the flavor of the Scholastic school of thought dominating Julian's day, Julian employs her philosophical, theological, and biblical education in the service of spiritual growth toward God. Hers is a thoroughgoing experience elevating the whole of the human soul. Other noteworthy themes in Julian include the motherhood of God, vision of the bleeding Christ, struggles with the devil, sin and anxiety, salvation, and the comfort of Christ.

Catherine of Siena (1347–80)

Catherine was born to a lower-middle class family during the late Italian Middle Ages in the republic of Siena, on the western coast of Italy. This was a time of great turmoil in Roman Catholicism, a downslope of Catholic cultural dominance in Europe, though the church's influence still loomed large.

Catherine was the youngest of twenty-five children, though many of her siblings did not survive. After the death of her sister while Catherine was a teenager, she committed herself to lifelong virginity and joined the Dominican Order, giving her a religious association while still living at home. She quickly garnered a reputation for generosity and giving away material possessions.

---

[8] Hugh T. Kerr, ed., *Readings in Christian Thought*, 2nd ed. (Abingdon, 1990), 127–28.

At age twenty-one, Catherine experienced a mystical vision of marriage to Christ, which encouraged her toward a life of service and toward public matters, especially concerning the poor, the sick, and the uneducated. However, working among the sick contributed to her own consistently poor health. In 1377 she established a monastery for women but died only a few years later, in 1380, at the age of thirty-three.

Catherine's influence extended beyond ecclesiastical affairs, as her letter-writing influenced Pope Gregory XI to leave Avignon and return the papacy to Rome. Moreover, on a religio-political front, she further influenced Gregory XI to crusade against the Muslims and reclaim Jerusalem.

Interest in Catherine's thought and writing spiked following her death and was relatively consistent into the late seventeenth century. The most significant spike came, however, around 1850 and continues into the present with a resurgence of interest in mystical thought. Among some 400 letters and a series of "Prayers," Catherine's best-known work is her *Dialogue*, which treats the spiritual life in the form of a series of conversations between God the Father and the human soul, Catherine in this case.

> God's Son is the peaceful sea providing drink to all who have been at war and want to be reconciled with him. The sea pours out a fire that can warm any cold heart; it warms so well that all base fear is lost, and only perfect charity remains.
>
> ———
>
> Catherine of Siena,
> *Letters*

> She [the soul] therefore arises, with hatred of that imperfection and with love of perfection, and, through this charity, which is of the Holy Spirit, she participates in His will, fortifying her own to be willing to suffer pain, and, coming out of the house through My Name, she brings forth the virtues on her neighbor. Not that by coming out to bring forth the virtues, I mean that she issues out of the House of Self-Knowledge, but that, in the time of the neighbor's necessity she loses that fear of being deprived of her own consolations, and so issues forth to give birth to those virtues which she has conceived through affection of love. The souls, who have thus come forth, have reached the fourth state, that is, from the third state, which is a perfect state, in which they taste charity and give birth to it on their neighbors, they have arrived at the fourth state, which is one of perfect union with Me. The two last-mentioned states are united, that is to say, one cannot be without

> the other, for there cannot be love of Me, without love of the neighbor, nor love of the neighbor without love of Me.[9]

Like many theologians before her, Catherine emphasized the importance of the love of God in her writings. Her writings in the dialogue are written mainly as if God himself were speaking.

New Orders

Monastic reform did not begin and end with Cluny and the Cistercians. Other movements emerged as well, the strictest of which was the Carthusians, founded by Bruno of Cologne in 1084. In an effort to return to the original hermitic style of the desert fathers, Bruno and six others settled in a rocky area of Grenoble, France, seventy miles southeast of Lyon. They soon became known by locals as "Christ's poor men." The movement grew and was recognized by Pope Innocent II in 1133. By the 1170s, the Carthusians made their way to England at the invitation of King Henry II as part of his penance for the murder of Thomas Beckett. The Carthusians lived solitary lives in their own cells, only seeing one another at dedicated times to celebrate Mass, and only eating meals together on Sundays or feast days. Though respected and influential, the Carthusian way wasn't for everyone.

Peter Waldo and the Waldensians

An important precursor to the mendicant movement was the twelfth-century Peter Waldo (died c. 1218) and the Waldensians. Waldo, an Italian merchant from Lyons, learned of a monk who dedicated his life to extreme poverty and was thus inspired to do the same with the added activity of preaching. His followers became known as the Waldensians, and though Waldo had received permission to preach from Pope Alexander III in 1179, it was given with the caveat that permission must also be granted by local clergy. This proved difficult, but Waldo and friends preached anyway.

Their unofficial preaching led to persecution, and they were officially excommunicated by the church in 1183. They eventually took refuge in the Alps and were considered heretics

[9] Catherine of Siena, "A Treatise on Prayer," in *The Dialogue of Catherine of Siena* (Cosimo, 2007), 162.

and schismatics by Rome. The Waldensians joined the Protestant Reformation and came to be viewed as spiritual forerunners.

Mendicant Movements

In the wake of the Investiture Controversy of the late eleventh and early twelfth centuries concerning whether the Pope or the Emperor had the authority to appoint (or invest) authority, the stage was set for the emergence of the mendicant movement. Mendicant simply means "beggar" (Latin, *mendicare*), and members of mendicant orders were dedicated to absolute poverty and the ascetic way of life, allaying the concerns about monks owning property. Unlike traditional monastic communities, mendicants were quite public in their work, active in serving their community through teaching, prayer, preaching and evangelism, and ministry to the poor and sick. They modeled both the active and contemplative life, embodying their motto *non sibi soli vivere sed et aliis proficere*, "to live not for themselves only, but to serve others." The two dominant mendicant movements were the Franciscans and the Dominicans.

Francis and the Franciscans

By all accounts, Francis of Assisi (1181–1226) was a strange man—but one whose devotion to God demands the deepest respect. Originally named Giovanni (John) after John the Baptist, Francis was born in Assisi, about 100 miles north of Rome, in 1181. Once his father returned home from a business trip, he renamed his son Francesco in light of his own interests as a Francophile and in hopes that his son would follow in his footsteps as a man of business and not a man of God. Francis's upbringing was a privileged one, and his early aspirations were that of knighthood. In 1202 as a young man, he defended his hometown of Assisi in the battle against Perugia, during which he was captured and held prisoner for approximately a year. He also suffered greatly from sickness during this time. Following his release and after receiving a vision in which he heard God tell him, "Go and rebuild my house that is in ruins," Francis dedicated his life to God.

Francis committed himself to prayer and deep pursuit of God, experiencing other visions of Christ in prayer and practicing poverty while on pilgrimage to Rome. While there, he begged alongside the poor and ministered to a leper, who was part of a group of outcasts Francis was known to have publicly ridiculed and been repulsed by. Eventually, this new way of life put Francis at odds with his father, who locked him in the cellar for a time, then summoned him before the authorities, including the bishop of Assisi. Francis arrived dressed like the wealthy young son of a cloth merchant that he was, then proceeded to renounce all he had, removed his clothes, and went into the woods naked to live as a hermit and repair worn-down chapels. He began with the church in San Damiano, where he received his initial vision from God.

The once ringleader of rambunctious and mischievous upper-class boys in Assisi had now refused all inheritance from his father and rejected all material possessions save his cloak. While his ambitions had changed, his joyful personality and leader's spirit continued to attract others to this new way of life. By 1209 Francis had gained about a dozen disciples, so he drafted a rule for himself and his followers and sought Pope Innocent III's approval to establish a new order and preach the gospel. Surprisingly, Innocent III approved on two conditions. First, the group had to swear obedience to the papacy under Francis's headship; second, they had to receive the tonsure (shaving the top of the head) as a sign of dedication and humility.

Francis's original name for the group was *Ordo Fraturam Minorum* (Order of Brothers Minor, or Order of Little Brothers). His first *Rule* is lost to us today, but Francis drafted a second *Rule* in 1221, just after resigning as the head of the OFM. He drafted a third *Rule* in 1223, which was approved by Pope Honorius III. This rather short, twelve-chapter *Rule* touches on all manner of life, work, preaching permissions, correction of other brothers, and directives about how to relate to nuns. And it opens with the unambiguous chain of authority:

Chapter I. In the name of the Lord, the life of the lesser brother begins.

The rule and life of the lesser brothers is this: To observe the holy gospel of our Lord Jesus Christ, living in obedience without anything of our own, and in chastity. Brother Francis promises obedience and reverence to the Lord Pope Honorius and his canonically elected successors, and to the Roman church; and the rest of the brothers are obliged to obey Francis and his successors.[10]

Among the many facets of Francis's important legacy, we give particular attention to his piety, preaching, and his influence. Regarding piety, few in the history of the church have

[10] St. Francis, "The Rule of St. Francis," OFM, accessed May 9, 2025, https://ofm.org/en/the-rule.html.

been more dedicated than Francis. It is said that in 1224, amidst a lengthy retreat to La Verna, Francis received the stigmata (Greek, *stigma*), the signs of the wounds of Christ in his own flesh. Francis's stigmata are considered the first instance in the history of the church, a sign believed to be experienced only by the holiest of God's servants. Moreover, Francis's prayers continue to inspire Christians today, including this one, which is said to originate at the foot of the crucifix in the church in San Damiano.

Most High,
glorious God,
enlighten the darkness of my heart
and give me, Lord,
a correct faith,
a certain hope,
a perfect charity,
sense and knowledge,
so that I may carry out Your holy and true command.[11]

Despite the oft-quoted phrase attributed to Francis that says, "Preach at all times, and use words when necessary," the phrase does not appear in his writings. Rather, Francis is said to have preached in up to five villages per day. While Francis may appreciate the spirit of such a saying, his practice was one of both words and deeds. Francis is even remembered for preaching to the birds, as captured in the well-known painting by Giotto Di Bondone (c. 1299), exhorting them to praise their Creator. This is illustrative of his deep love for nature and shows why he is recognized as the patron saint of both animals and ecology in the Roman Catholic Church. Among his most famous prayers is Canticle of the Creatures (sometimes called the Canticle of the Sun).

Finally, Francis's influence extended to his support not only of the brothers of his community (friars) but also to the sisters. Early in the journey of this new way of life, Francis gained a follower named Clare (c. 1193–1253) and accepted her into the ranks of his order, thus establishing a nunnery known as the "Poor Clares." The sisters took up residence at the church in San Damiano, where they earned the respect of Rome and where Clare would be the first woman to write a rule to be approved by the papacy.

---

[11] Francis and Clare, *Francis and Clare: The Complete Works*, ed. Richard J. Payne, trans. Regis J. Armstrong and Ignatius C. Brady, Classics of Western Spirituality (Paulist Press, 1982), 103.

Dominicans

Unlike the Franciscans, whose origins are nonclerical, the Dominicans formed behind a leader who served as a canon in the cathedral of Osma but who also felt that significant reform was in order. Dominic (c. 1170–1221) was born in the little town of Caleruega in the Castile-Leon community of northern Spain. Like Francis, Dominic enjoyed a privileged upbringing, as his parents were members of the Spanish nobility, affording him a strong Christian upbringing, during which he was originally educated by his uncle who was a priest. He went on to study art and theology at Palencia and later joined the canons at Osma, where he eventually became prior.

Around 1203 Dominic joined his bishop, Diego, on a diplomatic mission that eventually led them to southern France to defend the Catholic faith against the Albigensian (or Cathar) heresy. Despite their false teaching, Dominic was impressed by their success, especially noticing that their leaders were ascetics. Dominic thus coupled the disciplined monastic lifestyle with that of an evangelist, teaching and preaching the faith, and he soon saw success in converting heretics. He sought support from Pope Innocent III for the founding of a new monastic order, but Innocent refused on the grounds that the church did not want too many new orders. This was short-lived, however, as Pope Honorius III confirmed the new community in December of 1216, giving them the title of "preachers." The Dominican order continues to use the abbreviate "OP" for Order of Preachers (*Ordo Praedicatorum*) to this day. In contrast to the Cistercians, who were known for wearing white, Dominicans wore a black *cappa* (cloak) and even today are often referred to as "Black Friars."

Dominic desired to return to Tolouse, but the pope held him in Rome, giving him the office of "Master of the Sacred Palace," a position that has been held by Dominicans ever since. From 1216 until his early death in 1221, Dominic had accomplished a lifetime of work. And after beginning with only a handful, by his death, Dominic's followers were numbered in the thousands.

The Dominican legacy boasts some of the greatest preachers and teachers in the church's history, including Thomas Aquinas, Albert the Great, Savonarola, and many others. Dominicans never wavered from their commitment to the doctrine of the church. Often, this bore fruit in magnificent theological works. Sometimes, this took a less intellectual path. For example, Pope Gregory IX appointed the Dominicans to carry out the work of the Inquisition, and Tomás de Torquemada (1420–98), the first grand inquisitor, was drawn from the ranks of the Dominican order.

Order of Saint Augustine

Adding to the proliferation of new orders in the thirteenth century, the Order of Saint Augustine (OSA) was founded in Italy in 1244 at the approval of Pope Innocent IV. He insisted that a group of hermits living around Tuscany, Italy, be united under a common rule and thus gave to them the *Rule of Saint Augustine*. He then insisted that the house be properly organized and led by a prior general. In 1256 the growing group that began with strong hermetic tendencies formed the Grand Union of the Order. Soon the new order moved toward a more cenobitic style of contemplation, pastoral ministry, and evangelization.

Within 100 years, the Order of Saint of Augustine had grown to 8,000 friars across multiple countries working across pastoral ministry and preaching, education and scholarship, as well as other ordinary vocations, such as carpentry and farming. Missions and education remain strong threads of OSA heritage. As stated on the official website for the Augustinians Province of Thomas of Villanova,

> During periods of great missionary effort in the church, Augustinians were counted among the religious of various Orders and Congregations who ventured into foreign lands to extend the message of the gospel and to lay the foundations for religious life. They ventured throughout Europe, as well as to North and South America, Africa, Japan, Persia, India, and China. Augustinians were among the founding fathers of the first university of the New World, and were the first evangelizers of the Philippine Islands.[12]

Order of Saint Benedict

The Benedictine approach to monasticism and Benedict's *Rule* (see chapter 11) dominated the church until the Cistercian movement in the late eleventh century. As such, much of the monastic reform we have discussed is a reaction against what had become an overly opulent and authoritative Benedictine establishment. In both the thirteenth and fourteenth centuries, there were papal attempts to restructure the Benedictines but with little success. Not until 1893 was a central organization established over the Benedictines, when Pope Leo XIII installed the Benedictine Confederation.

---

[12] "The Augustinian Order," The Augustinians, https://www.augustinian.org/order.

Developments and Legacy

Among other things, perhaps what the era of monastic reform signals most strikingly is a return to the apostolic tradition, especially in the moral sense. From the Cistercians forward, a common thread of material poverty marked these radical followers of Christ, inspired as Antony was to "go, sell your belongings and give to the poor, and you will have treasure in heaven. Then come, follow me" (Matt 19:21). Lady Poverty was their bride, as was said of Francis, for this was the way of Christ.

Additionally, it was a time of tension, though various leaders and authorities desired a common end of a pure church. The ideal for theological purity extended beyond canon law and into the private opinions and confessions of ordinary citizens. While the rise of monastic orders stimulated many to seriously consider afresh what it meant to follow Christ, it also gave rise to dissenting and heretical groups that threatened the unity of the church and thus the kingdom of God.

The Cathars, also known as the Albigenses, were one such heretical group, a dualistic religious movement that emerged in the twelfth century. They posed a significant challenge to the established Catholic Church and its doctrines. The Cathars rejected fundamental tenets of Roman Catholicism, such as the sacraments and the authority of the church hierarchy, advocating instead for asceticism, simplicity, and spiritual purity. The spread of Catharism and other heretical views raised alarm among ecclesiastical and secular authorities, prompting concerted efforts to suppress these perceived threats to religious orthodoxy and social cohesion. The Inquisition was the church's response to these heretical groups.

Originally, the responsibility of inquisition belonged to local bishops to ensure common doctrine among their subjects. But after conflict with the Cathars, the Fourth Lateran Council of 1215 joined ecclesial and civil punishment for heretics. Inquisitors employed a range of tactics, including interrogation, surveillance, and the use of informants, to identify and apprehend suspected heretics, and in 1252 Pope Innocent IV permitted torture for inquisitorial practice. Bruce Shelley explains, "Canon Law, it is true, forbade a cleric from shedding blood. He who served the altars of the One Sacrifice must not sacrifice men. He could only hound, and interrogate, and torture the prisoner. If he found the unfortunate person guilty of heresy he turned him over to civil authorities, usually for burning at the stake."[13] The use of torture and coercion to extract confessions from suspected heretics

[13] Bruce Shelley, *Church History in Plain Language* (Thomas Nelson, 2013), 221.

raised ethical concerns regarding the treatment of religious minorities and the abuse of state power in the name of orthodoxy.

Thus, the era of monastic reform was one of excitement at renewed spiritual vibrancy but was also darkened with the cloud of civil and ecclesiastical authorities ensuring things did not get too far out of their control. This tension persisted, and the spirit of renewal was further fanned into flame or reform in the centuries to come.

Recommended Reading

Bainton, Roland H. *The Medieval Church*. Nostrand, 1962.

Catherine of Siena. "A Treatise on Prayer." In *The Dialogue of Catherine of Siena*. Cosimo, 2007.

Francis and Clare. *Francis and Clare: The Complete Works*. Edited by Richard J. Payne. Translated by Regis J. Armstrong and Ignatius C. Brady. Paulist Press, 1982.

Julian of Norwich. *Revelations of Divine Love*. Translated by Barry Windeatt. Oxford World's Classics. Oxford University Press, 2015.

Kerr, Hugh T. *Readings in Christian Thought*. 2nd ed. Abingdon, 1990.

Martin, Dennis. "The Spirituality of St. Bernard of Clairvaux." *Christian History Magazine-Issue 24: Bernard of Clairvaux, Medieval Reformer and Mystics*. Christian History Institute, 1989.

McGinn, Bernard. *Foundations of Mysticism: Origins to the Fifth Century*. Crossroad 1991, 2002.

McGrath, Alister. *Christian Spirituality: An Introduction*. Blackwell, 1999.

—— Chapter 18 ——

The Holy Roman Empire

The origins of the Holy Roman Empire go back to the Carolingian Dynasty, particularly the reign of Charlemagne, who expanded the Frankish Kingdom through conquests and alliances in the late eighth and early ninth centuries. Charlemagne's military campaigns, known as the Carolingian Renaissance, not only expanded the territory of the Frankish Kingdom but also promoted intellectual and cultural renewal throughout Western Europe.

Frankish Dominance and Carolingian Legacy

Competing claims to authority and shifting identities shaped the development of Western civilization. This complexity is evident in the relationship between the Papacy and Frankish kings and the evolving concept of a "Roman" Empire in the West. From the early Middle Ages, the papacy asserted its spiritual authority over Christendom, claiming a direct line of succession from the apostle Peter and asserting primacy over the universal church. Popes participated in both ecclesiastical and secular affairs, with the power to crown kings, depose rulers, and adjudicate disputes among Christian princes. The papacy's claim to spiritual sovereignty often intersected with political considerations, as popes sought to extend their influence beyond the confines of Rome and assert their authority over the Christian West. The Frankish kings emerged as powerful rulers in Western Europe following the collapse of the Roman Empire, consolidating their dominance over former

Roman territories and establishing the foundations of medieval governance. Kings such as Charlemagne sought to revive the legacy of the Roman Empire in the West, portraying themselves as heirs to the imperial title and champions of Christian civilization. The coronation of Charlemagne as Roman emperor by Pope Leo III in 800 symbolized the fusion of Frankish kingship with Roman imperial aspirations, blurring the lines between secular and spiritual authority.

The concept of a "Roman" Empire in the West reflected shifting political realities and cultural influences. While the Roman Empire in the East continued to exist as the Byzantine Empire, the West saw the emergence of new forms of political organization and identity. The Carolingian Empire, established by Charlemagne, represented a revival of Roman imperial ideals tempered by Germanic customs and Christian values.

Charlemagne and the Carolingian Empire

Charlemagne, also known as Charles the Great, emerged as a powerful ruler in the late eighth and early ninth centuries, consolidating the Frankish kingdoms and expanding his domains through military conquests. His reign witnessed the Carolingian Renaissance, a revival of learning and culture inspired by classical antiquity and Christian theology. Charlemagne's patronage of scholars, artists, and theologians contributed to Western Europe's intellectual and spiritual renewal, laying the groundwork for a new era of Christian civilization.

In 800, Pope Leo III crowned Charlemagne as Roman emperor in a meaningful ceremony held in Rome. This event symbolized the revival of the Roman Empire in the West and the restoration of imperial authority under Charlemagne's rule. Pope Leo III sought to legitimize his reign and establish a close alliance between the church and the Frankish monarchy by bestowing the imperial title upon Charlemagne. The coronation affirmed the close relationship between Christianity and political power, reinforcing the idea of a Christian universal monarchy guided by divine providence.

The coronation of Charlemagne as Roman emperor set a precedent for future rulers in Europe, establishing the principle of imperial authority derived from papal recognition. Charlemagne practiced a unique blend of spiritual and temporal authority. He assumed responsibilities ranging from defending Christendom against external threats to promoting Christian education and welfare within his realms. The Carolingian Empire represented a synthesis of Roman, Germanic, and Christian traditions, forging a new European identity that would endure for centuries.

Charlemagne's legacy as a Christian ruler and statesman looms large in European history, shaping the political, cultural, and religious landscape of the Middle Ages. His efforts to promote Christian unity, education, and governance laid the groundwork for the Holy Roman Empire and influenced the development of feudalism, chivalry, and medieval monarchy. The Carolingian Renaissance fostered a renewed interest in learning and literature. Charlemagne's reign symbolized the fusion of Christian faith and political power, setting a standard for rulership that would resonate throughout the medieval period and beyond.

Following Charlemagne's death in 814, his empire was divided among his three grandsons in the Treaty of Verdun in 843. This division led to the fragmentation of the Carolingian Empire into three distinct regions: West Francia, Middle Francia, and East Francia.

The empire's emphasis on Christian unity and universal sovereignty contributed to developing a distinctively European identity rooted in Roman heritage and Christian faith. The relationship between the papacy and Frankish kings was evolving the concept of an empire in Gaul that reflected the glories of ancient Rome. Aspirations of an empire with a common civil religion, a common culture, and a common set of virtues guided both church and state. The relationship between secular and ecclesiastical leaders led to competing claims to authority and conflicting loyalties. Popes sought to assert their spiritual sovereignty over the Christian West, often challenging the political power of secular rulers. Frankish kings, in turn, sought to establish their legitimacy through close alignment with the papacy and the imperial title while also asserting their independence from papal interference.

The nascent Holy Roman Empire faced many challenges and threats that tested its cohesion and stability during its formative years. Among these challenges were the Viking invasions. Beginning in the late eighth century, the Viking invasions threatened the security and stability of the emerging Holy Roman Empire. Viking longships swept across the coasts of Europe, raiding towns, plundering wealth, and terrorizing local populations. These raids disrupted trade routes, undermined agricultural productivity, and destabilized political authority in the affected regions. The empire's decentralized structure made it difficult to mount a coordinated defense against the Viking incursions, leading to widespread devastation and loss of life.

Internal divisions among the nobility also challenged the cohesion of the nascent empire. Feudal lords, vying for power and influence, often pursued their agendas at the expense of imperial unity. Rivalries between noble families, conflicts over territorial boundaries, and disputes over succession rights weakened the central government's authority and hindered efforts to establish effective governance. The lack of robust central control exacerbated these internal divisions, leading to a fragmentation of power and a breakdown of law and order in many regions.

Political instability further undermined the cohesion of the Holy Roman Empire during its early years. The decentralized nature of governance, characterized by a patchwork of independent states, principalities, and ecclesiastical domains, created fertile ground for political rivalries and power struggles. Successive rulers faced challenges in asserting their authority over the various constituent parts of the empire, leading to frequent conflicts and power struggles. The absence of a centralized administrative apparatus made it challenging to coordinate policies and respond effectively to external threats, leaving the empire vulnerable to external aggression and internal discord. Overcoming these challenges required a concerted effort to forge alliances, consolidate power, and establish effective governance structures, laying the groundwork for the eventual consolidation of the empire under stronger centralized rule.

The revival of imperial authority began in East Francia with Otto I, also known as Otto the Great, who became king of the Germans in 936. He reigned from 936 to 973 and was crowned emperor of the Romans in 962, marking the beginning of the Holy Roman Empire. Otto was a member of the Ottonian or Saxon dynasty, which rose to power in East Francia following the collapse of the Carolingian Empire. Otto sought to centralize authority within the empire and assert imperial control over the German territories. He defeated rebellious nobles and expanded the empire's borders through military campaigns in Italy and Eastern Europe.

The Ottonian Dynasty, spanning from 962 to 1024, marked a period of consolidation for the Holy Roman Empire. Central to this era was the coronation of Otto I as Holy Roman emperor. This coronation reaffirmed the close relationship between the imperial throne and the papacy. By receiving the imperial crown from the pope, Otto I strengthened the legitimacy of his rule and established the precedent for future emperors to seek papal approval for their coronation. This act symbolized the fusion of spiritual and temporal authority within the empire and set the stage for closer collaboration between the imperial court and the church.

Recognizing the importance of ecclesiastical support for the stability and legitimacy of their reign, the Ottonian emperors fostered closer ties with the church. Otto I and his successors sought to strengthen the influence of the church within the empire, promoting the appointment of loyal bishops and abbots who would support imperial authority. In return, the church provided crucial support to the emperors, both politically and militarily, helping to maintain order and stability within the realm. This alliance between the imperial throne and the church laid the groundwork for the empire's expansion and consolidation in the following centuries. Under Otto I and his successors, the Holy Roman Empire expanded its territorial holdings and established its core territories in central Europe. The Ottonian emperors secured control over crucial regions, such as Saxony, Bavaria, and Lotharingia, through diplomacy, warfare, and strategic alliances, laying the foundation for the empire's territorial integrity. Establishing these core territories provided a solid base from which the emperors could project their authority and influence throughout the empire, consolidating their power and strengthening imperial governance.

The Investiture Controversy

The Investiture Controversy, spanning from 1076 to 1122, stands as one of the defining struggles for power between the church and the state in medieval Europe. At its core was the conflict between Emperor Henry IV of the Holy Roman Empire and Pope Gregory VII over the appointment of bishops and other high-ranking clergy. The Investiture Controversy emerged from centuries of tension between secular rulers and the church over the control of ecclesiastical appointments. Since the Carolingian era, rulers had asserted their authority to appoint bishops and abbots, viewing these positions as instruments of secular governance. However, the church increasingly sought to assert its independence and autonomy in spiritual matters, advocating for the freedom of ecclesiastical appointments from secular interference. From the origin of the hierarchical episcopacy, church leaders had typically been appointed, either by bishops who oversaw associations of churches (called dioceses) or the pope. Following Gregory the Great's time as pope, the papacy had become even more influential. Within the Holy Rome Empire, the emperor had attempted to exert what the pope deemed undue influence over the appointment of church leaders. The problem, of course, was that the church and state had become intertwined with one another. Often the pope wanted to influence political matters; and the emperor, ecclesiastical ones. Either way, the lines were blurred between the two spheres of authority.

Emperor Henry IV, seeking to assert his authority over the church, appointed bishops and abbots loyal to him, disregarding papal authority in ecclesiastical appointments. The Holy Roman emperor's desire to appoint bishops and abbots loyal to him was rooted in the intertwined nature of secular and ecclesiastical authority in medieval Europe. Bishops and abbots were not only spiritual leaders but also influential political figures who controlled vast estates and resources, making their loyalty essential to the emperor's governance. By appointing church leaders loyal to him, the emperor could ensure that the revenues and wealth generated from church lands supported imperial policies and objectives. This practice also allowed the emperor to consolidate his political authority, as loyal bishops and abbots often acted as advisors, administrators, and military allies. Their allegiance ensured that the church's considerable influence bolstered the emperor's rule rather than undermined it. Additionally, bishops and abbots wielded significant local power, often serving as quasi-secular rulers who administered justice, levied taxes, and governed their regions. Loyal appointees enabled the emperor to extend his influence into these areas, reinforcing his control over the empire's decentralized structure.

Furthermore, appointing loyal church leaders helped the emperor balance the power dynamic between the secular and ecclesiastical realms. As the protector of Christendom, the emperor sought to ensure that the church's policies aligned with his own interests and that the clergy remained subordinate to imperial authority. This also served as a counterbalance to papal ambitions, as loyal bishops and abbots could resist papal interventions that might challenge the emperor's sovereignty over the church within his realm. Ultimately, the practice of appointing loyal bishops and abbots reflected the emperor's need to integrate the church into the political framework of the empire, ensuring that it functioned as a supportive institution for his rule.

This disregard for papal authority challenged the longstanding tradition of papal supremacy in spiritual matters and threatened the independence of the church from secular control. Pope Gregory VII, a staunch advocate for papal primacy and reform within the church, viewed Henry's actions as a direct affront to papal authority and launched a campaign to assert the church's independence. Pope Gregory VII issued a series of papal decrees known as the Dictates of the Pope, affirming papal authority over ecclesiastical appointments and condemning secular interference in church affairs. In response, Emperor Henry IV convened a council of bishops who declared Gregory deposed from the Papacy, effectively excommunicating him from the church. However, in return, Gregory VII excommunicated Henry IV, leading to a deepening rift between the church and the empire.

The Investiture Controversy ended at the Concordat of Worms in 1122, brokered by Pope Calixtus II and Emperor Henry V, Henry IV's son. The agreement affirmed the church's authority to appoint bishops and abbots while granting secular rulers the right to invest them with the symbols of their temporal authority. This compromise helped to restore peace between the church and the empire. Still, it also marked a victory for papal authority and the principle of spiritual independence from secular control.

Frederick Barbarossa and the Hohenstaufen Dynasty (1152–1254)

The reign of Frederick Barbarossa and the subsequent rule of the Hohenstaufen Dynasty from 1152 to 1254 was a period of struggle for control within the Holy Roman Empire. These dynamics showcased the empire's complexities and the challenges faced by its rulers in maintaining unity and stability. Under Frederick Barbarossa, the territory of the Holy Roman Empire expanded as the emperor sought to consolidate and extend imperial authority over neighboring regions. Barbarossa launched military campaigns aimed to assert imperial power over the Lombard cities and assert his claim to the Kingdom of Italy. Additionally, Barbarossa sought to expand imperial influence in Germany, fostering closer ties with regional princes and nobles to strengthen his grip on the empire's core territories.

Frederick fought with the pope incessantly as the emperor sought to assert imperial authority over ecclesiastical appointments and his supremacy over the church. This conflict closely resembled the Investiture Controversy a century earlier and represented a continuing struggle for power between the emperor and the papacy over the appointment of bishops and other high-ranking clergy. Despite attempts at reconciliation, tensions between Barbarossa and the papacy persisted, leading to excommunications and interdicts that further strained relations between the empire and the church.

> On Earth, God has placed no more than two powers, and as there is in Heaven but one God, so is there here one Pope and one Emperor. Divine providence has specially appointed the Roman Empire to prevent the continuance of schism in the Church.
>
> ---
>
> Frederick Barbarossa,
> "Letter in Radewic or Rahewin" in
> *Monumneta Germaniae Historica*

The Hohenstaufen Dynasty also faced internal struggles for control within the Holy Roman Empire as rival factions vied for power and influence at the imperial court. Regional princes and nobles who sought to maintain their autonomy and privileges often resisted Barbarossa's efforts to centralize authority and assert control over the empire's constituent parts. This internal strife weakened imperial power and hindered efforts to govern effectively, contributing to periods of instability and unrest within the empire.

As we have seen, the Investiture Controversy was a protracted struggle between the papacy and the Holy Roman Empire over the appointment of bishops and other church officials, highlighting the tensions inherent in their relationship. The conflict reached its zenith in the eleventh and twelfth centuries, as successive popes and emperors vied for supremacy in spiritual and temporal matters. Ultimately, the resolution of the Investiture Controversy through the Concordat of Worms in 1122 affirmed the papacy's authority in ecclesiastical appointments while acknowledging the emperor's role in investiture with temporal symbols. Despite periodic conflicts, the papacy often sought to assert its independence from imperial influence, particularly in doctrine, canon law, and papal prerogatives. Papal claims to universal spiritual authority, exemplified by the doctrine of papal supremacy, occasionally clashed with the aspirations of the emperors to assert their dominance over the church. This tension between papal and imperial authority helped to define the boundaries of ecclesiastical and secular power within medieval Christendom.

Conflict in the Holy Roman Empire

The Holy Roman Empire was a vast and heterogeneous entity, comprising a patchwork of territories, duchies, bishoprics, and free cities, each with its laws, customs, and rulers. This decentralized structure, inherited from the Carolingian era and perpetuated by the Treaty of Verdun in 843, resulted in a weak central authority and a lack of effective governance at the imperial level. Emperors struggled to assert their control over the myriad of regional princes, bishops, and nobles, leading to a fragmentation of power and the emergence of semiautonomous territories within the empire.

This decentralization of power gave rise to the proliferation of territorial principalities as local rulers sought to consolidate their control over their domains and assert their independence from imperial authority. In the territorial principalities of the Holy Roman Empire, churches were deeply integrated into the political, social, and economic fabric of their regions, reflecting the fragmented and localized nature of power within the empire. Each principality had its own distinct relationship with the church, shaped by the political ambitions of local rulers, the influence of the imperial church system, and the broader role of the church in medieval society.

Churches in the principalities were often closely tied to the ruling prince or noble, who wielded significant influence over ecclesiastical appointments and the administration of church lands within their territory. This relationship was a result of the proprietary church system (*Eigenkirchentum*), where many churches were effectively owned by local lords who treated them as part of their estate. These lords exercised the right to appoint clergy, manage church revenues, and oversee religious institutions, ensuring that the church served their political and economic interests. This practice created a localized structure of ecclesiastical authority, often subordinating the church to the secular goals of the territorial rulers.

Architecturally, the churches within these principalities varied greatly, reflecting the wealth and prestige of their patrons. Cathedrals and larger parish churches were centers of both religious and civic life, often built or expanded as expressions of a principality's prosperity and piety. Smaller rural churches, by contrast, served the local population but were often modest in design, with limited resources. Many churches were richly decorated, funded by noble patronage, and served as symbols of territorial identity and status.

Ecclesiastically, the church in the Holy Roman Empire was part of the imperial church system, which tied the clergy to the empire's governance. Bishops and abbots were often important political figures, controlling vast estates and acting as imperial administrators. In the territorial principalities, this meant that bishops frequently aligned with the interests of the local ruler or the emperor, depending on the political context. Monasteries also played a significant role, serving as centers of learning, cultural preservation, and economic activity and often acting as landlords of large agricultural estates.

Religiously, the church was central to daily life, providing sacraments, moral guidance, and education, and its festivals shaped the rhythm of the calendar year. However, the decentralized nature of the empire meant that ecclesiastical practices could vary widely across regions, reflecting local traditions and the influence of specific rulers or bishops. Despite this diversity, the church maintained a unifying presence, connecting the fragmented principalities of the Holy Roman Empire to broader Christian traditions and the authority of the papacy, albeit often contested by local and imperial ambitions.

This perpetual struggle for power and autonomy characterized the relationship between emperors and local rulers in the Holy Roman Empire. Emperors sought to centralize authority and assert their supremacy over the empire, while local rulers jealously guarded their prerogatives and resisted imperial encroachments on their independence. This tension manifested in frequent military and diplomatic conflicts as emperors sought to impose their will on the princes and bishops, often with limited success. The limited imperial authority and decentralized governance structure of the Holy Roman Empire often led to political instability and conflict within the empire. Rivalries between the emperor and the imperial princes and among the princes frequently erupted into open warfare, civil unrest, and power struggles.

Moreover, the lack of effective governance hindered the empire's ability to respond to external threats and challenges, leaving it vulnerable to invasion, conquest, and disintegration.

In contrast to the centralized monarchies of the time, the Holy Roman Empire's fragmentation and internal conflicts were defining features of its history, shaping its political landscape and governance structure. The decentralization of power, the rise of territorial principalities, and constant struggles between emperors and local rulers contributed to perpetual instability in the empire. Centralized monarchies, such as France or England, concentrated power in the hands of the monarchs and their administration. Conversely, the empire lacked a centralized cultural or political power, and operated in a more federal fashion. This decentralized structure made it difficult for the emperor to exert centralized control over the empire, resulting in a weak imperial authority. This distinctive political arrangement set the empire apart from its contemporaries and contributed to its complex and multifaceted history.

Another distinctive feature of the Holy Roman Empire was its system of legal pluralism, whereby diverse legal systems and traditions governed different regions and territories. This legal diversity further contributed to the decentralized nature of the empire and made it challenging to establish uniform laws and regulations across the entire realm. This led to the establishment of imperial courts and bureaucracies to centralize authority and administer the empire's vast territories. These courts, such as the Aulic Council and the Imperial Chamber Court, served as judicial bodies responsible for resolving disputes and administering justice within the empire. Bureaucracies managed the day-to-day affairs of the empire, including taxation, justice administration, and law and order maintenance.

The Imperial Diet emerged as a representative assembly where the emperor could consult with the princes, bishops, and other nobles of the empire on matters of policy and governance. Initially convened by the emperor, the Imperial Diet evolved into a more formalized institution with the participation of elected representatives from the various regions of the empire. The Imperial Diet was crucial in mediating conflicts between the emperor and the princes and enacting legislation and taxation policies.

Local rulers resisted the emperor's efforts to centralize authority. Independent city-states and municipal governments emerged, exercising control over their own affairs, further bolstering local autonomy. The decentralized nature of the Holy Roman Empire made it difficult for emperors to exert centralized control over the entire realm. Imperial reforms aimed at curbing feudal power and asserting imperial authority were often met with resistance from the nobility and local elites, leading to periodic conflicts and tensions within the empire.

Golden Bull of 1356: Formalization of Electoral Procedures and Consolidation of Princely Power

The Golden Bull of 1356 formalized electoral procedures for the imperial crown and solidified the power of seven German princes. This pivotal decree, issued by Emperor Charles IV, sought to establish clear guidelines for the selection of future emperors, thereby stabilizing the imperial succession and ensuring the continued cohesion of the empire. Before the issuance of the Golden Bull, the process of electing the Holy Roman emperor was ambiguous and often contentious. Electors were chosen from among the nobility, clergy, and imperial cities, leading to frequent disputes and power struggles. Emperor Charles IV recognized the need to codify these procedures to prevent future conflicts and secure the legitimacy of the imperial title. The Golden Bull of 1356 established a standardized electoral process for choosing the Holy Roman emperor, designating seven electors granted the exclusive right to elect the emperor. These electors included the archbishops of Mainz, Trier, and Cologne; the king of Bohemia; the count palatine of the Rhine; the duke of Saxony; and the margrave of Brandenburg. By conferring this privilege upon a select group of princes, the Golden Bull sought to streamline the election process and reduce the likelihood of disputed successions. In addition to formalizing electoral procedures, the Golden Bull consolidated the German princes' power within the Holy Roman Empire. The seven electors represented some of the empire's most powerful and influential rulers. By entrusting them with the responsibility of electing the emperor, Charles IV effectively recognized and reinforced their authority, cementing their status as critical players in imperial politics.

> We have promulgated, decreed and recommended for ratification the subjoined laws for the purpose of cherishing unity among the electors, and of bringing about a unanimous election, and of closing all approach to the aforesaid detestable discord and to the various dangers which arise from it.
>
> ---
>
> Charles IV,
> *Golden Bull of 1356*

The relationship between the Holy Roman Empire and the papacy was a central dynamic in shaping the prestige and authority of the papal office. The Holy Roman Empire, as the self-proclaimed successor to the ancient Roman Empire, held considerable sway over much of Western Europe during the Middle Ages. Papal coronations of emperors, such as the crowning of Charlemagne by Pope Leo III in 800, served to legitimize both the papal and imperial claims to authority, reinforcing the symbiotic relationship between the two institutions.

Crusades and the Holy Roman Empire

Motivated by religious fervor, political ambitions, and promises of spiritual rewards, emperors and nobles eagerly joined the Crusades to defend Christendom and reclaim the Holy Land from Muslim control, as we have seen. Emperors, such as Frederick Barbarossa and Frederick II, led crusading expeditions, demonstrating their commitment to the cause of crusading and their desire to assert imperial authority in the East. These emperors sought to expand the influence of the Holy Roman Empire beyond its borders and to establish a presence in the Middle East, particularly in Jerusalem and the entire Holy Land, aligning themselves with the broader goals of the Crusades as articulated by the papacy.

Nobles and knights from the Holy Roman Empire also played crucial roles in the Crusades, raising armies, financing expeditions, and leading troops into battle. Their participation in the Crusades enhanced their status and prestige within the empire while providing opportunities for adventure, plunder, and advancement.

The involvement of Holy Roman emperors and nobility in the Crusades underscored the close relationship between the empire and the broader Christian world. Their participation in these holy wars reflected the shared commitment of the empire to the defense of Christendom and the promotion of Christian values while highlighting the emperors' and nobles' ambitious political and territorial aspirations.

Additionally, the diversion of financial and human resources to the Crusades disrupted economic activities, such as agriculture, trade, and commerce, leading to economic hardship and social upheaval in some regions. Despite the economic challenges posed by the Crusades, they also created opportunities for trade and commerce within the empire. The influx of wealth from the East, captured through conquest or acquired through trade with Muslim merchants, enriched imperial coffers and stimulated economic growth in certain regions. Crusader states and ports along the Mediterranean served as hubs for commercial activity, facilitating the exchange of goods and ideas between East and West and fostering the development of merchant networks and trading routes.

The Crusader States and the Holy Roman Empire's Influence in the East

The establishment of crusader states in the Middle East created opportunities for the Holy Roman Empire to extend its political and ecclesiastical influence in the East. These crusader states of the Kingdom of Jerusalem, the Principality of Antioch, the County of Tripoli, and the County of Edessa were established during and after the First Crusade (1096–99) and were governed by European nobles and knights for varying durations. These states served as Christian footholds in the Levant and were integral to the crusaders' efforts to maintain control over the Holy Land. The Kingdom of Jerusalem, established in 1099 following the capture of Jerusalem, was the most prominent crusader state. It reached its zenith under leaders such as Baldwin IV and Baldwin V, but its power declined after the loss of Jerusalem to Saladin in 1187. Although a diminished kingdom persisted with its capital in Acre, it eventually fell to the Mamluks in 1291, marking the end of crusader rule in the region, with European control lasting for 192 years.

The Principality of Antioch, founded in 1098, was strategically important due to its location near Byzantine and Muslim territories. It remained under European control for nearly two centuries before falling to the Mamluks under Sultan Baibars in 1268, ending 170 years of crusader rule. The County of Tripoli, the last crusader state to be established, was founded in 1102 by Raymond IV of Toulouse and served as a vital coastal stronghold for European trade and diplomacy. It endured until 1289, when it was conquered by the Mamluks, bringing an end to 187 years of European governance. The County of Edessa, established in 1098, was the first crusader state and initially one of the strongest. However, its location deep in Muslim territory made it vulnerable, and it fell to the forces of Zengi, the Atabeg of Mosul, in 1144, after just forty-six years under crusader control. The loss of Edessa was a significant blow to the crusaders, sparking the Second Crusade in an attempt to reclaim it.

Holy Roman emperors and nobility saw the crusader states as potential allies and strategic footholds in the East. They sought to assert imperial authority in these territories and establish diplomatic and commercial ties with local rulers. The motivation for joining the Crusades was not merely religious but had diplomatic and economic factors as well.

The Holy Roman Empire maintained diplomatic relations with the crusader states, forging alliances and treaties to advance mutual interests. Emperors and imperial envoys negotiated agreements with rulers of the crusader states, offering military assistance, financial support, and political recognition in exchange for territorial concessions and strategic alliances.

The crusader states served as important centers of trade and commerce, connecting the East and West through lucrative trade routes and commercial networks. Merchants from the Holy Roman Empire traded goods, such as textiles, spices, and luxury goods, with merchants in the Levant, enriching both parties and stimulating economic growth in the region. The presence of crusader states provided opportunities for merchants to establish trading colonies and engage in profitable business ventures in the East.

Rise of Free Imperial Cities and Economic Prosperity

The rise of free imperial cities contributed to economic prosperity and reshaped the political landscape of medieval Europe. These cities emerged as centers of commerce, industry, and innovation, driving economic growth and fostering a vibrant urban culture. Free imperial cities enjoyed a range of privileges and liberties granted to them by the emperor, including self-governance, exemption from feudal obligations, and the right to regulate trade and commerce within their territories. These freedoms empowered the citizens of free imperial cities to govern according to their laws and customs, enabling them to pursue economic opportunities and social advancement with greater autonomy and independence.

Free imperial cities became magnets for merchants and artisans seeking economic opportunities and social mobility. These cities thrived as commercial hubs, facilitating the exchange of goods and services domestically and internationally. The influx of skilled labor and entrepreneurial talent fueled the growth of industries, such as textiles, metalwork, banking, and shipping, contributing to the overall prosperity of the empire.

The prosperity of free imperial cities fostered cultural exchange and intellectual innovation, attracting scholars, artists, and intellectuals from across Europe. These cities became centers of learning, creativity, and artistic expression, where citizens exchanged ideas, artisans created artistic masterpieces, and cultural movements flourished. The cultural diversity of free imperial cities enriched the intellectual and artistic life of the empire, contributing to the Renaissance of the twelfth and thirteenth centuries.

The rise of free imperial cities in the Holy Roman Empire had far-reaching consequences for the church, fundamentally altering its role in urban governance, its economic influence, and its relationship with the laity. Free imperial cities were granted autonomy directly by the emperor, placing them under imperial protection and outside the jurisdiction of local princes or bishops. This newfound independence disrupted the traditional dual role of bishops, who often served as both spiritual leaders and secular rulers of cities. In many cases, bishops had controlled city governance, judicial matters, and administrative functions, making them central figures in both the spiritual and political life of urban centers. However, the establishment of free imperial cities transferred much of this authority to local councils composed of burghers and representatives of merchant and artisan guilds, thereby significantly reducing the secular power of ecclesiastical leaders within these cities. This shift often led to friction between the church and the emerging civic authorities, as bishops struggled to retain influence in areas where they had historically dominated.

Economically, the flourishing of free imperial cities as centers of trade, commerce, and craftsmanship further diminished the church's traditional control. These cities were hubs of economic activity, and their growing prosperity created a powerful merchant and artisan class that was often resistant to ecclesiastical taxes, tithes, and other financial obligations imposed by the church. Tensions frequently arose over the ownership and use of resources, particularly land, as city leaders and wealthy burghers sought to assert control over economic affairs that had previously been managed or influenced by the church. Furthermore, the economic independence of these cities reduced their reliance on ecclesiastical institutions for charitable and social services, such as hospitals and poor relief, weakening the church's traditional role as the primary provider of these essential services.

The social and religious consequences of this shift were equally profound. Free imperial cities created spaces for increased lay participation in both civic and religious life, which often resulted in a diminished role for ecclesiastical authorities. Lay councils and guilds frequently assumed responsibilities traditionally managed by the church, such as organizing public festivals, overseeing schools, and managing charitable institutions. This growing lay involvement sometimes led to conflicts with the church over jurisdiction and authority. Moreover, the relative autonomy of these cities provided fertile ground for reformist ideas during the late medieval period. Many free imperial cities became centers of intellectual and religious ferment, where new ideas challenging church authority could take root with less interference. During the early sixteenth century, this climate made free imperial cities crucial strongholds for the Protestant Reformation. Reformers such as Martin Luther and Ulrich Zwingli found support among urban elites and guilds, who were receptive to calls for reduced ecclesiastical control and greater local autonomy. The economic and social dynamics of these cities further bolstered the appeal of reformist movements, as merchants and artisans often saw Protestantism as aligned with their aspirations for independence from traditional church structures.

The rise of free imperial cities thus marked a critical shift in the balance of power between the church and secular authorities in medieval Europe. By reducing the church's influence in governance and economic affairs and fostering environments open to lay participation and reformist ideas, these cities became agents of change that significantly reshaped the religious and political landscape of the Holy Roman Empire. While they often retained their Christian identities, their autonomy eroded the dominance of the church and laid the groundwork for the broader transformations of the Reformation and beyond.

Free imperial cities served as advocates for their own interests and concerns in imperial diets and assemblies. Their economic wealth and social prestige afforded them a voice in imperial politics, allowing them to negotiate treaties, form alliances, and assert their rights and privileges against the encroachments of feudal lords and rival city-states. The political clout of free imperial cities helped balance the empire's power dynamics and promote stability and cooperation among its diverse constituents.

Conflict Between Imperial Cities and Feudal Lords

Imperial cities frequently faced conflict with neighboring feudal lords over territorial boundaries and jurisdictional rights. Feudal lords sought to expand their domains and consolidate their power and often encroached upon the territories of free imperial cities, leading to land-ownership, taxation, and legal-jurisdiction disputes. These territorial conflicts sometimes escalated into armed confrontations as both sides sought to assert their claims and defend their interests.

Economic competition between imperial cities and feudal lords was another source of conflict within the Holy Roman Empire. Feudal lords, reliant on agrarian revenues and feudal dues, often viewed the prosperity of urban centers with suspicion and sought to curtail their economic activities through restrictive trade policies, tolls, and tariffs. Imperial cities, on the other hand, sought to protect their economic interests and expand their commercial networks, leading to conflicts over trade routes, market access, and commercial regulations.

Competing visions of governance and sovereignty fueled the political rivalry between imperial cities and feudal lords. Imperial cities, governed by municipal councils and elected officials, sought to preserve their autonomy and independence from feudal authority. In contrast, feudal lords sought to assert control over urban centers and subordinate them to their feudal obligations. This rivalry often played out in imperial diets and assemblies, where both sides vied for influence and sought to advance their interests through diplomacy and alliances.

Legal disputes between imperial cities and feudal lords were common in medieval Europe, as both sides sought to enforce their rights and privileges through the legal system. Feudal lords often attempted to impose their laws and customs upon urban centers, challenging the autonomy and jurisdiction of municipal authorities. Imperial cities, in turn, appealed to the emperor and imperial courts to uphold their charters and defend their liberties against feudal encroachments.

Consequences for Christianity

The emergence and evolution of urban centers within the Holy Roman Empire had consequences for Christianity, shaping the development of the faith and its interaction with broader society in numerous ways. Urban centers were often melting pots of religious diversity, where Christians of different denominations and beliefs coexisted alongside Jews, Muslims, and adherents of other faiths. This diversity often fostered a spirit of religious tolerance and dialogue, encouraging Christians to engage with alternative perspectives and theological interpretations. Urban centers became centers of religious debate and exchange, where scholars and theologians conversed with representatives of other faith traditions, contributing to developing Christian theology and fostering interfaith understanding.

Urban centers served as bases for Christian missionary activity. Churches in populated areas dispatched missionaries to evangelize rural areas, frontier regions, and distant lands. The presence of established churches, monasteries, and religious institutions in urban centers provided a strong foundation for missionary endeavors, offering resources, support networks, and trained clergy to carry out the work of evangelization. Urban centers also served as hubs for the training and education of missionaries, equipping them with the knowledge and skills needed to spread the Christian message effectively.

Urban centers facilitated the synthesis and integration of diverse cultural and religious traditions, leading to hybrid Christian expression and belief forms. The encounter between Christianity and indigenous cultures in urban settings often led to syncretic religious practices, blending Christian theology and ritual elements with local customs and traditions. This process of cultural syncretism enriched the diversity of Christian worship and spirituality, allowing the faith to adapt and evolve in response to changing social and cultural contexts. Wealthy patrons and benefactors from urban elites provided financial support to churches, monasteries, and religious orders, enabling them to expand their influence and undertake ambitious building projects. The economic resources generated by urban centers also funded charitable activities, social welfare programs, and educational initiatives sponsored by the church, further cementing its role as a critical player in medieval society.

Role of the Church in Shaping Imperial Policy and Governance

Bishops, abbots, and theologians, provided spiritual guidance to rulers and advised them on matters of governance and justice. The church's teachings on morality, justice, and the common good often influenced imperial policy decisions, shaping laws, regulations, and social norms. The church played a central role in the administration of justice within the Holy Roman Empire, operating its legal system alongside secular courts. Bishops and canon lawyers presided over ecclesiastical courts that adjudicated disputes involving church law, morality, and sacraments. The church's legal authority extended to marriage, inheritance, and heresy, where ecclesiastical courts often held jurisdiction over secular authorities.

The church also provided social welfare and charitable assistance to the poor, sick, and marginalized members of society. Monasteries, convents, and religious orders operated hospitals, orphanages, and almshouses, offering food, shelter, and medical care to those in need. The church's commitment to charitable works and Christian charity helped alleviate poverty, alleviate suffering, and promote the dignity and well-being of all members of society.

The church served as a mediator and arbitrator in diplomatic and political disputes within the Holy Roman Empire, facilitating negotiations and peace settlements between warring factions. Popes and bishops often acted as intermediaries between rival rulers, helping to resolve and prevent armed conflict. The church's diplomatic efforts helped maintain stability and order within the empire, promoting peace and reconciliation among its diverse constituents.

Promotion of Christian Education and Monasticism

Within the Holy Roman Empire, the church played a crucial role in promoting Christian education and the development of monasticism, fostering spiritual growth, intellectual inquiry, and cultural preservation. The church was a primary patron of education and intellectual life, establishing monastic schools, cathedral schools, and universities. These institutions provided instruction in theology, philosophy, Latin, and the liberal arts, aiming to educate clergy, scholars, and the broader population. Monastic schools, in particular, served as centers of learning and cultural preservation, where monks dedicated themselves to studying scripture, theology, and classical literature. The church's commitment to education and intellectual inquiry fostered a culture of scholarship and innovation, advancing knowledge and cultivating critical thinking within medieval society.

Through its educational initiatives, the church promoted a culture of learning and intellectual inquiry within medieval society. Educational initiatives in the Holy Roman Empire, particularly during the early medieval period, were closely tied to the efforts of rulers like Charlemagne (r. 800–814) and his successors to strengthen the church, improve governance, and promote cultural renewal. These initiatives, often referred to as the Carolingian Renaissance, laid the foundation for formal education in medieval Europe by emphasizing literacy, the preservation of classical knowledge, and the training of clergy and laity alike.

Charlemagne recognized that a well-educated clergy was essential for the spiritual cohesion of the empire. In a series of reforms beginning in the late eighth century, he encouraged the establishment of schools attached to monasteries, cathedrals, and royal courts. His *Admonitio generalis* (789), a sweeping set of directives, mandated the creation of schools to educate both clergy and laypeople. This capitulary emphasized the importance of studying Scripture, classical texts, and practical skills necessary for governance.

Charlemagne invited renowned scholars, such as Alcuin of York, to his court at Aachen to oversee educational reforms. Alcuin and other scholars helped develop a standardized curriculum based on the seven liberal arts, divided into the trivium (grammar, rhetoric, logic) and quadrivium (arithmetic, geometry, music, astronomy). These disciplines formed the foundation of medieval education.

Monasteries and cathedrals became the primary centers of education in the Holy Roman Empire. Monastic schools, such as those at Fulda, Corbie, and Saint Gall, focused on training monks in theology, Latin literacy, and the copying of manuscripts. These schools preserved classical texts and biblical manuscripts, ensuring the survival of ancient knowledge.

Cathedral schools, often located in urban centers, educated future priests and bishops but also began to attract lay students, particularly those from noble families. Notable cathedral schools, such as those in Reims, Chartres, and Cologne, became hubs of intellectual activity, influencing the broader development of European education.

A key aspect of the educational initiatives in the Holy Roman Empire was the establishment of scriptoria—centers for manuscript copying and production—within monasteries.

Charlemagne and his successors prioritized the standardization of texts, particularly biblical and liturgical works. The creation of the Carolingian minuscule, a clear and legible script, facilitated the dissemination of knowledge and became the standard writing style for centuries.

Monastic communities played a crucial role in preserving and transmitting classical knowledge and literature during the early medieval period. Monks painstakingly copied and illuminated manuscripts of ancient texts, preserving works of philosophy, science, and literature that would otherwise have been lost to history.

While the primary focus of education was on clergy, there were efforts to educate laypeople, especially members of the nobility. Lay education emphasized practical skills, such as governance, military leadership, and the management of estates, alongside exposure to classical and religious texts. Charlemagne himself set an example by learning to read and encouraging his court to pursue intellectual enrichment.

Influence of Imperial Patronage on Church Architecture and Art

Imperial patronage within the Holy Roman Empire influenced the development of church architecture and art, shaping the aesthetic and symbolic expression of Christianity in medieval Europe. Imperial patronage contributed to the construction of magnificent cathedrals and monasteries throughout the empire, symbolizing imperial power, religious devotion, and cultural achievement. Emperors and imperial authorities provided financial support, land grants, and royal privileges to ecclesiastical institutions, enabling them to undertake ambitious building projects showcasing the Christian faith's grandeur and majesty. Cathedrals, such as Cologne Cathedral, Speyer Cathedral, and St. Stephen's Cathedral in Vienna, are prime examples of imperial patronage in church architecture, featuring soaring spires, intricate stone carvings, and stunning stained glass windows that testify to the wealth and power of the empire.

Imperial patronage also influenced the production of religious imagery and iconography within church art, as rulers sought to promote specific religious doctrines, political agendas, and dynastic aspirations. Emperors and imperial families commissioned lavish artworks, such as illuminated manuscripts, altarpieces, and frescoes, that glorified the Christian faith and celebrated the achievements of the empire. These artworks often depicted biblical scenes, saints, and imperial symbols, conveying messages of divine authority, political legitimacy, and spiritual piety to worshippers.

Imperial patronage was crucial in promoting sacred relics and pilgrimage sites within the Holy Roman Empire as rulers sought to enhance their realms' religious prestige and cultural significance. Emperors and imperial authorities sponsored the acquisition and translation of relics, such as the Crown of Thorns or the Holy Lance, which were believed to possess miraculous powers and attracted pilgrims from far and wide. Pilgrimage sites, such as Santiago de Compostela, Aachen, and Rome, became centers of religious devotion and cultural exchange, drawing pilgrims, merchants, and artisans to their sacred precincts and stimulating economic growth and cultural exchange.

Decline and Legacy of the Holy Roman Empire

The Holy Roman Empire, once a formidable political and religious entity in medieval Europe, experienced a gradual decline in power and influence over the centuries, leading to its eventual dissolution and transformation. Several factors contributed to this decline, shaping the empire's legacy in European history.

One of the primary factors contributing to the decline of the Holy Roman Empire was the fragmentation and disunity among its constituent territories and rulers. The empire was a complex patchwork of autonomous states, principalities, bishoprics, and free cities governed by their own laws, customs, and interests. This decentralization of power weakened the authority of the emperor and hindered efforts to centralize governance and maintain imperial cohesion.

The Holy Roman Empire faced numerous external threats and challenges from rival powers. Wars, invasions, and territorial disputes weakened the empire's borders and strained its military resources, diverting attention and resources away from internal governance and stability. Additionally, the rise of powerful nation-states in Western Europe, such as France and England, challenged the imperial authority of the Holy Roman emperor and undermined the empire's geopolitical position on the continent.

Attempts to reform and modernize the Holy Roman Empire in the late medieval and early modern periods were largely unsuccessful in addressing its underlying structural weaknesses. Efforts to centralize authority, rationalize administration, and strengthen imperial institutions were hampered by resistance from powerful princes and entrenched interests, limiting the effectiveness of imperial governance and perpetuating the empire's decline.

Originating from the ashes of the Western Roman Empire, the Holy Roman Empire emerged as a unique amalgamation of secular and religious authority, encompassing diverse territories, cultures, and political systems. Founded on the principle of a Christian universal monarchy, the empire served as a symbol of continuity with the Roman past while adapting to the shifting political and cultural landscapes of the medieval period. The Holy Roman Empire shaped medieval Europe's political, social, and religious dynamics. As a decentralized confederation of states and principalities, it provided a framework for governance and diplomacy, fostering a sense of collective identity among its diverse constituents. The empire's rulers, from Charlemagne to Frederick II, sought to maintain imperial unity while accommodating regional powers' and ecclesiastical authorities' interests and aspirations.

The intricate relationship between Christianity and political authority lay at the heart of the Holy Roman Empire. Emperors and rulers sought to legitimize their power through their association with the church, while popes and ecclesiastical leaders wielded spiritual influence to assert their authority over temporal affairs. This dynamic tension between church and state, exemplified by conflicts such as the Investiture Controversy, shaped the balance of power within the empire and influenced the development of European political theory.

Despite its aspirations for unity and universal rule, the Holy Roman Empire was fragmented. Princely states, free cities, and ecclesiastical territories enjoyed considerable autonomy, leading to a patchwork of overlapping jurisdictions and conflicting allegiances. This decentralized structure allowed for cultural diversity and regional development but hindered efforts to achieve centralized governance and imperial cohesion. The Holy Roman Empire was a bulwark of Christian civilization, defending Europe against external threats and promoting cultural exchange and integration.

Effects of the Creation of the Holy Roman Empire on Christianity

The creation of the Holy Roman Empire shaped the religious landscape of medieval Europe in various ways. First, it provided a robust patronage network for the Christian church. Emperors and imperial authorities often supported and promoted Christianity to legitimize their rule and assert control over their subjects. This political patronage bolstered the influence of the church and facilitated the spread of Christianity throughout the empire.

Second, The Holy Roman Empire played a central role in the governance of the church, with emperors exerting considerable influence over the appointment of bishops, abbots, and other ecclesiastical officials. Imperial control over ecclesiastical appointments sometimes led to conflicts between secular and religious authorities, as emperors sought to assert dominance over the church hierarchy. These tensions shaped the relationship between the imperial throne and the papacy, influencing the course of medieval religious and political history.

Third, the Holy Roman Empire served as a melting pot of cultures, languages, and traditions, facilitating the exchange and synthesis of diverse religious and cultural influences. Christianity in the empire absorbed elements of indigenous pagan beliefs, Roman traditions, and Germanic customs, developing a uniquely Germanic Christian identity. This process of cultural syncretism enriched the diversity of Christian practice and belief within the empire, contributing to the formation of distinct regional variations of Christianity.

Fourth, the Holy Roman Empire played a central role in the Christianization of Europe, as missionaries and evangelists went to convert pagan peoples within its borders. Emperors and imperial authorities supported missionary endeavors through patronage, protection, and endorsement, facilitating the spread of Christianity among the various Germanic tribes, Slavic peoples, and other ethnic groups of Europe. The Christianization of the empire led to the establishment of churches, monasteries, and ecclesiastical institutions, which served as centers of religious life and cultural transformation.

Finally, the creation of the Holy Roman Empire forged a complex relationship between the church and the state, characterized by a delicate balance of power and authority. While the church wielded spiritual and moral influence over the empire, emperors and imperial leaders asserted their secular authority over ecclesiastical matters, leading to occasional conflicts and tensions between church and state. These tensions manifested in disputes over ecclesiastical appointments, taxation, jurisdictional authority, and doctrinal issues, shaping the dynamics of church-state relations throughout the medieval period.

Recommended Reading

Blumenthal, Uta-Renate. *The Investiture Controversy: Church and Monarchy from the Ninth to the Twelfth Century*. University of Pennsylvania Press, 1988.

Cantor, Norman F. *Church, Kingship, and Lay Investiture in England, 1089–1135*. Princeton University Press, 1958.

Collins, Roger. *Charlemagne*. University of Toronto Press, 1998.

Davis, R. H. C. *A History of Medieval Europe: From Constantine to Saint Louis*. 3rd ed. Routledge, 2000.

Gillingham, John. *The Holy Roman Empire and the Ottonian Renaissance*. Longman, 2001.

Head, Thomas, ed. *Medieval Hagiography: An Anthology*. Routledge, 2000.

Leyser, Karl. *Rule and Conflict in an Early Medieval Society: Ottonian Saxony*. Edward Arnold, 1979.

Morris, Colin. *The Papal Monarchy: The Western Church from 1050 to 1250*. Oxford University Press, 1989.

Robinson, I. S. *The Papacy, 1073–1198: Continuity and Innovation*. Cambridge University Press, 1990.

Southern, R. W. *Western Society and the Church in the Middle Ages*. Penguin, 1970.

Tellenbach, Gerd. *The Church in Western Europe from the Tenth to the Early Twelfth Century*. Cambridge University Press, 1993.

Tierney, Brian. *The Crisis of Church and State, 1050–1300*. University of Toronto Press, 1988.

Ullmann, Walter. *The Growth of Papal Government in the Middle Ages: A Study in the Ideological Relation of Clerical to Lay Power*. Methuen, 1955.

Wickham, Chris. *The Inheritance of Rome: A History of Europe from 400 to 1000*. Viking, 2009.

Wolfram, Herwig. *History of the Goths*. University of California Press, 1988.

—— Chapter 19 ——

The Great Schism Between East and West

In 1054, the Roman Catholic Church and the church of the Byzantine Empire formally split over a host of theological and ecclesiastical issues. This seismic event, which ruptured the unity of Christendom, reverberated across theological, ecclesiastical, and geopolitical spheres, shaping the trajectory of European and Byzantine civilization for centuries to come.

Political, Theological, and Cultural Differences Between East and West

The Great Schism did not happen in a vacuum but in a complex world of cultural and theological differences at the root of the identity of the Western and Eastern churches. These differences contributed to the conflicts that precipitated the formal rupture between East and West. To comprehend the genesis and evolution of the Great Schism, one must first grasp the contextual backdrop of political, theological, and cultural disparities that characterized relations between the Eastern and Western empires and the churches within them.

The division of the Roman Empire in the fourth century into the Eastern Roman Empire (Byzantine Empire) and the Western Roman Empire laid the foundation for divergent political trajectories. While the Byzantine Empire, centered around Constantinople, thrived as a bastion of Greek culture and Christianity in the East, the Western Roman Empire faced the challenges of barbarian invasions, eventually leading to its collapse in the fifth century. The emergence of the Carolingian Empire in the West and the Byzantine Empire's contestation with Islamic forces in the East further underscored the geopolitical distinctiveness of the two regions. These differing political landscapes fostered unique power dynamics and imperial ambitions that would influence ecclesiastical relations between East and West.

Cultural disparities between the Greek-speaking East and the Latin-speaking West also contributed to estrangement and alienation between the two regions. The Eastern church developed its distinct liturgical traditions, theological emphases, and cultural expressions, while the Roman Catholic Church in the West evolved its unique ecclesiastical practices and cultural norms. Additionally, differences in ecclesiastical governance, such as the prominence of the papacy in the West and the conciliar model of governance in the East, further underscored the cultural divergence between the two branches of Christianity. Ecclesiastical politics and power struggles within the church precipitated the Great Schism. Rivalries between the patriarch of Constantinople and the pope of Rome and conflicts over jurisdictional authority and ecclesiastical prerogatives fueled tensions between the Eastern and Western churches. Competing claims to ecclesiastical authority and administrative control contributed to a sense of division and discord within the Christian church. As we have seen previously, differences in liturgical practices and cultural sensitivities further exacerbated the rift between East and West. These liturgical differences became flashpoints for contention and discord within the Christian community.

One of the central issues that created deep distrust between East and West was the question of ecclesiastical authority and the extent of papal primacy within the Christian church. This contentious issue revolved around the role of the bishop of Rome, or the pope, and his claims to universal jurisdiction and supremacy over all other bishops.

In the West, the bishop of Rome asserted primacy based on the belief that he was the successor of Peter, to whom Jesus had given the keys of the kingdom of heaven according to the gospel of Matthew (Matt 16:18–19). This doctrine of papal supremacy asserted that the pope held a unique and supreme authority over the entire Christian church, with the power to depose bishops, establish doctrine, and adjudicate ecclesiastical disputes.

However, in the East, the concept of papal primacy was met with skepticism and resistance. The Eastern church adhered to a more conciliar model of ecclesiastical governance, distributing authority among bishops and patriarchs, with no single bishop claiming universal jurisdiction. As the leader of the Eastern church, the patriarch of Constantinople asserted the principle of *primus inter pares* ("first among equals"), whereby he held a position of honor and respect among the other patriarchs but did not claim supremacy over them.

The divergence in ecclesiastical authority between East and West became a source of tension and contention as the bishop of Rome sought to extend his influence and authority into the Eastern church. Attempts by the popes to assert jurisdictional control over Eastern bishops and patriarchs were met with resistance, leading to a breakdown in relations between the two branches of Christianity.

Liturgical practices and religious customs deepened the divisions between the Eastern and Western churches, contributing to the Great Schism. The veneration of icons, or religious images, held a central place in Eastern Christian worship, aiding devotion and conduits for spiritual contemplation. Eastern Christianity believed that icons manifested the divine presence and facilitated communication with the heavenly realm. Using icons in liturgical settings, private devotions, and religious processions was integral to spirituality in the Eastern church. In contrast, the Western church adopted a more cautious approach to religious imagery, particularly during iconoclastic controversies in the Byzantine Empire. While the Roman church acknowledged the legitimacy of religious images, it emphasized a more restrained and symbolic use of icons in liturgical contexts, eschewing the elaborate iconography found in the churches of the East.

Linguistic differences also contributed to the divergence in liturgical practices between East and West. The Eastern church conducted its worship services primarily in Greek, the language of the Byzantine Empire, and the language of the New Testament. Greek liturgical texts, hymns, and prayers formed the backbone of Eastern Christian worship, reflecting the cultural and linguistic heritage of the Eastern Christian tradition. In contrast, the Western church gradually adopted Latin as its primary liturgical language, owing to the influence of the Roman Empire and the spread of Christianity throughout Western Europe. Latin became the language of the Roman Catholic liturgy, shaping the prayers, chants, and rituals of the Western church and reinforcing its cultural and ecclesiastical identity.

Differences in the celebration of sacraments further underscored the liturgical divergence between East and West. While both traditions recognized the seven sacraments (baptism, confirmation, Eucharist, penance, anointing of the sick, holy orders, and matrimony), their liturgical rites and theological interpretations differed. The Eastern church emphasized mystical participation in the sacraments, particularly in the Eucharist, celebrated as the "Mystical Supper" or "Divine Liturgy." The Eastern Eucharistic liturgy, characterized by elaborate rituals, solemn chants, and mystical symbolism, emphasized the real presence of Christ in the consecrated elements. In contrast, the Roman church developed distinct liturgical rites for the celebration of sacraments, with an emphasis on doctrinal precision and ritual uniformity. The Roman Rite, characterized by its liturgical texts, rubrics, and ceremonial gestures, reflected the theological priorities and ecclesiastical norms of the Western church.

Filioque Controversy and the Procession of the Holy Spirit

The Filioque controversy contributed to the Great Schism between the Eastern and Western churches by highlighting the divergent understandings of the nature of the Trinity and the relationship between the Father, Son, and Holy Spirit. The Filioque controversy revolved around the inclusion of the phrase "and the Son" (Latin: *Filioque*) in the Nicene Creed, specifically in the clause concerning the procession of the Holy Spirit. In the original Nicene Creed, as affirmed by the Ecumenical Council of Nicaea in 325 and the First Council of Constantinople in 381, the creed stated that the Holy Spirit "proceeds from the Father." However, in the West, particularly in the Frankish and later Roman churches, the phrase *Filioque* was gradually added to the Nicene Creed, asserting that the Holy Spirit proceeds from both the Father and the Son. This addition was motivated by theological and doctrinal concerns, including affirming the Son's divinity and equality with the Father. Eastern Christians strongly resisted the inclusion of *Filioque* in the Nicene Creed, viewing it as a doctrinal innovation and a departure from the ecumenical consensus established by the early church councils. Eastern theologians argued that the procession of the Holy Spirit from the Father alone was the traditional and scriptural teaching of the church and that any alteration to the creed constituted a violation of doctrinal orthodoxy.

> They say that the Spirit proceeds not only form the Father but "also from the Son." For they do not get this statement from the evangelists, nor does this blasphemous dogma derive from an ecumenical council.
>
> ---
>
> *Edict of Constantinople*, 1054

The Filioque controversy is about the Christian doctrine of the Trinity and the inner life of God. In the East, the procession of the Holy Spirit from the Father alone (often referred to as the "monarchy of the Father") emphasized the unity of the Godhead and the distinct roles of the divine persons. In the West, including the Filioque in the Nicene Creed reflected a desire to affirm the Son's full deity and emphasize the Trinity's unity. The procession of the Holy Spirit from both the Father and the Son expressed the inseparable relationship between the divine persons and the mutual indwelling of the Trinity. Despite attempts at theological dialogue and mutual understanding, the Filioque controversy remained contentious between East and West, exacerbating existing tensions and contributing to the broader theological, ecclesiastical, and cultural differences that culminated in the Great Schism of 1054.

Key Figures and Parties Involved

The Great Schism involved a complex array of figures and parties representing both the Eastern church and the Roman Catholic Church. Michael Cerularius served as patriarch of Constantinople during the turbulent period of the eleventh century, marked by heightened tensions between the Eastern and Western churches. He is best known for his role in the events leading to the Great Schism of 1054, which formalized the split between the Roman Catholic Church and the Byzantine church. Cerularius opposed Latin liturgical practices and doctrinal deviations, particularly the Western use of unleavened bread in the Eucharist and the insertion of the Filioque clause into the Nicene Creed. His confrontational stance toward the Latin church, culminating in the exchange of excommunications between himself and Pope Leo IX, contributed to the deepening rift between East and West and set the stage for the enduring division between these churches.

Cerularius resisted Roman innovations and assertions of papal authority in the East. He opposed practices such as unleavened bread in the Eucharist, which was common in the Latin church, but viewed as unacceptable by the Eastern church. Cerularius also contested the inclusion of the Filioque clause in the Nicene Creed, arguing that it constituted a departure from the ecumenical consensus established by the early church councils.

In addition to his theological disputes with the Latin church, Cerularius engaged in ecclesiastical and political maneuvering to assert the independence and authority of the Eastern church. Cerularius's tenure as patriarch of Constantinople coincided with an increasing estrangement between the Eastern and Western churches, culminating in the events of 1054. His resistance to Roman influence and his efforts to uphold Eastern Christian traditions deepened the divisions between East and West, ultimately contributing to the formal rupture of the Christian church. Though viewed by some as a divisive figure, Cerularius was an important symbol of Eastern resistance to external pressures, particularly from the Roman church.

In the Roman church, the central figure was Pope Leo IX. As pope from 1049 to 1054, Leo sought to assert papal primacy and authority in spiritual and temporal matters, including appointing bishops and enforcing Roman Catholic doctrine in the East. Cardinal Humbert of Silva Candida was a papal legate sent by Pope Leo IX to Constantinople in 1054. His responsibility was to address the theological and ecclesiastical issues between the Eastern and Western churches. Humbert was known for his strong stance against perceived deviations from Roman Catholic doctrine and practices in the East. He was particularly critical of Eastern practices, such as using leavened bread in the Eucharist and omitting the Filioque clause from the Nicene Creed. Pope Leo IX and Cardinal Humbert's efforts to assert Roman Catholic authority in the East ultimately backfired, leading to the formal division of the Christian church. Their actions during the Great Schism underscored the complex interplay of theological, ecclesiastical, and political factors that shaped Christian history.

Besides the ecclesiastical figures, political figures also participated in the controversy and attempted to avoid schism. Byzantine Emperor Constantine IX Monomachos was crucial in navigating the political and religious dynamics between East and West. However, his diplomatic efforts to mediate between the Eastern and Western churches ultimately proved unsuccessful in preventing the schism. During the time leading up to the Great Schism, Byzantine Emperor Alexios I Komnenos and various Western rulers were critical in the ecclesiastical and political dynamics between the Eastern and Western churches. Their interactions and decisions escalated tensions that led to the formal rupture between East and West.

Alexios I Komnenos ascended to the Byzantine throne in 1081 and reigned until 1118. His reign coincided with geopolitical and religious upheaval in the Byzantine Empire, including the aftermath of the Byzantine defeat at the Battle of Manzikert in 1071 and the onset of the First Crusade in 1096. Alexios I faced numerous challenges during his reign, including external threats from the Seljuk Turks in Anatolia and internal turmoil within the Byzantine aristocracy. In response to these challenges, he pursued diplomatic and military strategies to consolidate Byzantine power and defend the empire's territories. In the context of the Great Schism, Alexios I navigated the complex relationship between the Byzantine church and the Roman Catholic Church. While he sought to maintain the independence and autonomy of the Byzantine church, he also faced pressure from Western rulers, particularly during the Crusades, to reconcile with the Roman Catholic Church.

The Rise of the Normans

In the eleventh century, a group of Normans, originally of Viking descent who settled in Normandy, France, embarked on a campaign to conquer Southern Italy and Sicily. Led by figures such as Robert Guiscard and his brother Roger I of Sicily, the Normans gradually gained control over the region through military campaigns and alliances. A blend of military prowess, political maneuvering, and cultural assimilation characterized the Norman conquest of Southern Italy. The Normans established themselves as powerful rulers in the region, establishing the Norman Kingdom of Sicily and exerting influence over neighboring territories. The Norman conquest changed the balance of power in the Mediterranean region and contributed to the fragmentation of Byzantine authority in Southern Italy. The Normans effectively challenged Byzantine control over the area and established their independent realm, which would become a key player in Mediterranean politics.

Before the Norman conquest, Southern Italy and Sicily had been part of the Byzantine Empire. Byzantine influence in the region was enormous, with Greek culture, language, and religious practices ever present among the local population. The Byzantine presence in Southern Italy and Sicily contributed to the region's economic prosperity, cultural diversity, and religious pluralism. Byzantine cities such as Bari and Reggio Calabria were important centers of trade, administration, and religious activity, with Greek Christianity coexisting alongside Latin Christianity and Islam. The Norman conquest gradually eroded Byzantine influence in Southern Italy and Sicily despite Byzantine efforts to maintain control over the region. The Normans established their political institutions, promoted Latin Christianity, and assimilated Greek-speaking populations into their realm, transforming the cultural and religious landscape of the region.

Building on their successes in Southern Italy and Sicily, the Normans expanded their territorial ambitions into the Balkans, particularly in modern-day Greece and the southern Balkan Peninsula. The Normans launched military campaigns, led by figures like Robert Guiscard and his son Bohemond of Taranto, to capture strategic cities and territories from the Byzantine Empire. The Norman conquests in the Balkans posed a direct challenge to Byzantine authority in the region and intensified tensions between the Normans and the Byzantine Empire.

The Byzantine Empire had maintained a longstanding presence in the Eastern Mediterranean, controlling key territories, such as Constantinople, Anatolia, and parts of the Levant. Byzantine interests in the region were multifaceted, encompassing trade, diplomacy, and military defense against external threats, including Islamic powers, such as the Seljuk Turks and the Fatimid Caliphate. Byzantine efforts to maintain control over the Eastern Mediterranean often brought them into conflict with Norman expansionism, particularly in areas where Byzantine and Norman interests overlapped.

Events Leading to the Schism

In the years preceding the Great Schism of 1054, there were various exchanges of letters and diplomatic efforts between the Eastern and Western church leaders to address the growing tensions and differences between them. Though initially aimed at reconciliation, these efforts failed to bridge the widening gap between the Eastern and Roman churches. Patriarch Michael Cerularius of Constantinople and Pope Leo IX corresponded in the mid-eleventh century, addressing theological and liturgical differences between the Eastern and Western churches. The exchange of letters between the patriarch and the pope reflected attempts at diplomatic dialogue, but underlying theological disagreements and ecclesiastical grievances hindered meaningful reconciliation. Despite their efforts to find common ground, the letters often highlighted the deep-seated divisions and mutual suspicions between the two churches.

Pope Leo IX sent a group of representatives to engage with Patriarch Michael Cerularius and other Eastern church leaders. Upon their arrival, these representatives, led by Cardinal Humbert of Silva Candida, delivered a letter from the pope to the patriarch. However, the patriarch refused to meet them, citing procedural grievances and accusing the legates of overstepping their authority. In a dramatic gesture, Cardinal Humbert and his entourage entered Hagia Sophia on July 16, 1054, and placed a letter from the pope on the altar, formally excommunicating patriarch Cerularius. Excommunication severed Cerularius and the Eastern church from communion with the Roman Catholic church, representing the culmination of years of theological and ecclesiastical tensions between East and West. Patriarch Cerularius reciprocated the excommunication by condemning and excommunicating Cardinal Humbert, the pope's representatives, and Pope Leo himself. The mutual excommunication was dramatic and unprecedented, formalizing the rupture between the two churches.

The schism reinforced cultural divisions between Eastern and Western Europe, with the Eastern Orthodox Church preserving Byzantine and Slavic cultural traditions while the Roman Catholic Church fostered Latin and Western European cultural identities.

In the East, the Byzantine Empire maintained its influence over the church, asserting its political and cultural hegemony over the Balkans, Anatolia, and the Eastern Mediterranean. In the West, the Roman Catholic Church became increasingly intertwined with emerging European nation-states, such as the Holy Roman Empire, France, and England, shaping the political landscape of Western Europe.

The division between the Eastern church and the Roman Catholic Church disrupted missionary coordination and cooperation, hindering efforts to evangelize non-Christian populations. Missionary activities, which had previously been undertaken jointly by Eastern and Western Christians, became increasingly fragmented as each branch of Christianity focused on its territories and theological priorities. Eastern-church and Roman Catholic missionaries adopted different approaches to evangelization, reflecting their distinct theological emphases and ecclesiastical structures. Eastern-church missionaries focused on preserving traditional liturgical practices and spiritual disciplines, while Roman Catholic missionaries emphasized theological education, institutional development, and conversion efforts.

In addition to the fracture within Christianity, the Great Schism exacerbated tensions between Christians and non-Christian communities, complicating efforts at meaningful dialogue with adherents of other faiths, such as Judaism, Islam, and indigenous religions. This interaction between Christianity and other religions happened particularly in the Middle East, where Eastern Christianity had historically been dominant.

Developments in the Eastern Church

Following the division between the churches of the East and the West, the church in the Byzantine Empire had its own theology and political controversies. These controversies often involved differences of theological opinions between bishops and theologians, as well as the bishops' resistance to undue influence from political leaders. When later efforts at discussing reunification arose, it was not just the original causes of the schism that prevented progress but the distinct ways the churches developed over the centuries that followed. In the East, those developments were significant.

Hesychasm and Mystical Tradition: Gregory Palamas

Hesychasm is a mystical tradition centered on contemplative prayer and inner stillness associated with foremost proponent, Gregory Palamas. Hesychasm advocated a life of inner calm or stillness. It emerged in the monastic communities of Byzantium during the late Byzantine period. Rooted in the teachings of the desert fathers and the ascetic tradition of early Christian monasticism, hesychasm emphasized the pursuit of divine union through unceasing prayer and the cultivation of inner peace.

Gregory Palamas (1296–1359), an ascetic monk and theologian, became the leading exponent of hesychasm and its theological defender against opposition. Born in Constantinople and educated in secular and theological studies, Palamas withdrew to Mount Athos, where he immersed himself in the ascetic practices of hesychasm under the guidance of experienced spiritual elders. Palamas's theological writings, particularly his *Triads in Defense of the Holy Hesychasts*, articulated the experiential knowledge of God attained through hesychastic prayer and defended the authenticity of mystical experiences against intellectual skepticism. Central to Palamas's theology was the distinction between God's essence (Greek: *ousia*) and energies (Greek: *energeiai*), which he developed as a response to theological debates surrounding the nature of divine revelation and the possibility of direct communion with God. According to Palamas, while God's essence remains inaccessible and unknowable to human beings, his energies are the means through which he reveals himself to humanity and communicates his divine life. Through hesychastic prayer, believers can directly participate in God's energies and experience his presence.

> He who applies himself to prayer must quiet the senses and entirely put to death the passionate part of the soul so that none of his powers may act; so too with all activity common to soul and body; for each of these activities is an obstacle to prayer.
>
> ---
>
> Gregory of Palamas,
> *Triads in Defense of the Holy Hesychasts*

Palamas's theological teachings sparked controversy within the Byzantine church, particularly among intellectuals and theologians who viewed hesychasm with suspicion and accused its practitioners of heresy. The dispute, known as the hesychast controversy, culminated in the hesychast councils of Constantinople in 1341 and 1351, where Palamas's teachings were vindicated and affirmed as orthodox doctrine. The Eastern Orthodox Church later canonized Palamas's theological insights, recognizing him as a saint and doctor of the church, with his feast day celebrated on November 14. Gregory Palamas contributed a theological synthesis of hesychasm and his defense of mystical prayer, shaping the understanding of prayer, divine grace, and the possibility of union with God in the Eastern tradition.

Caesaropapism vs. Conciliarism

From its earliest days, the Byzantine Empire grappled with the intricate relationship between church and state, manifesting in the ongoing theological debates surrounding the concepts of caesaropapism and conciliarism. Caesaropapism refers to the political theory in which the secular ruler, typically the emperor, possesses supreme authority over the state and the church, exerting control over ecclesiastical matters. In Byzantine political thought, caesaropapism found expression in the emperor's role as the "God-appointed" sovereign, responsible for maintaining the empire's temporal and spiritual welfare. Proponents of caesaropapism argued for the emperor's authority to intervene in ecclesiastical affairs, appointing bishops, convening councils, and influencing theological doctrine to serve the state's interests.

Conversely, conciliarism advocated for the supremacy of ecumenical councils in determining matters of faith and governance within the church, asserting the collective authority of bishops and clergy over secular rulers. Rooted in the tradition of conciliar decision-making, conciliarism emphasized the importance of synodical consensus and the autonomy of the church from undue secular interference. Supporters of conciliarism sought to limit imperial control over ecclesiastical affairs, safeguarding the church's independence and preserving its spiritual integrity.

The tension between caesaropapism and conciliarism often led to conflicts between the Byzantine emperors and the church hierarchy, particularly during theological controversy and ecclesiastical reform. Instances of imperial interference in church affairs, such as the appointment of patriarchs and the imposition of theological doctrines, provoked resistance from ecclesiastical authorities, fueling debates over the proper balance of power between church and state. Over time, Byzantine political and ecclesiastical thought evolved to accommodate elements of both caesaropapism and conciliarism, resulting in a complex synthesis of secular and religious authority. While the emperor retained influence over the church, particularly in ecclesiastical administration and imperial ideology, the church also maintained a degree of autonomy through synodical decision-making and ecclesiastical tradition. The theological conflicts surrounding caesaropapism and conciliarism reflect the Byzantine Empire's ongoing struggle to reconcile the competing claims of secular and spiritual authority. Despite tensions and disagreements, Byzantine political and ecclesiastical institutions ultimately navigated a path of compromise, forging a unique synthesis of church-state relations.

Expansion of Byzantine Christianity

The influence of Byzantine Christianity extended far beyond the borders of the Byzantine Empire, playing a pivotal role in the spread and consolidation of Orthodox Christianity in eastern Europe and the Balkans. Byzantine missionaries, clergy, and theologians undertook extensive missionary efforts to evangelize neighboring regions and propagate Orthodox Christianity. Amidst the rich tapestry of Byzantine history, missionary endeavors emerged as a vital component in the expansion and consolidation of Christianity within and beyond the borders of the Byzantine Empire. Byzantine Christians desired to spread the gospel to new lands and leave an enduring legacy in language, culture, and ecclesiastical organization. Byzantine missionaries were pivotal in bringing the Christian faith to the Slavic peoples inhabiting the vast territories to the north and east of the Byzantine Empire. Led by luminaries, such as Saints Cyril and Methodius, these missionaries undertook arduous journeys into the heartlands of Slavic tribes, preaching the gospel in their native tongues and adapting Christian teachings to local customs and traditions.

The missionaries contributed the Cyrillic alphabet to the Slavs. Named after Saint Cyril, this script was devised to translate the sacred texts and liturgical rites of Christianity into Slavic languages, facilitating the spread of literacy and the preservation of Christian teachings among Slavic communities. As Christianity took root among the Slavic peoples, Byzantine missionaries established new ecclesiastical centers to oversee the spiritual needs of these burgeoning Christian communities. Notable among these was the church at Kiev, established in the heart of the Slavic lands, which became a focal point for the dissemination of Byzantine Christianity and the cultivation of Slavic Christian culture. Through their tireless efforts, Byzantine missionaries not only converted vast swathes of pagan territories to Christianity but also laid the foundation for the emergence of distinct Slavic Christian traditions. Slavic rulers, such as Prince Vladimir of Kiev, converted to Christianity. Their conversions led to the widespread conversion of their subjects and the establishment of Orthodox Christian kingdoms and principalities throughout eastern Europe and the Balkans.

Attempt at Reconciliation and Reunion

The Council of Florence (1431–49), one of the most ambitious attempts to achieve reconciliation between the Eastern and Western churches, brought together prominent bishops and theologians from both traditions. These figures played pivotal roles in the theological debates and political negotiations that defined the council. Below are some of the most influential participants and their contributions.

The reigning pope, Eugenius IV (1383–1447), was a central figure in the Council of Florence. He convened the council and presided over its proceedings in an effort to heal the Great Schism between the Eastern Orthodox and Roman Catholic Churches. Eugenius saw the council as an opportunity to restore papal authority and unify Christendom, particularly in light of the growing Ottoman threat. His diplomatic efforts and financial support facilitated the attendance of the Eastern delegation, although his approach also faced criticism for being overly authoritative.

The Greek bishop and theologian John Bessarion (1403–72) was the metropolitan of Nicaea and later became a cardinal in the Roman church. He was one of the leading intellectuals of the Eastern delegation, renowned for his mastery of both Greek and Latin theology. Bessarion's arguments in favor of unity were rooted in his deep knowledge of Scholasticism and his belief in the compatibility of Eastern and Western traditions. He played a critical role in bridging linguistic and theological divides during the debates. After the council, Bessarion remained in the West and worked tirelessly to promote the reunification of the churches, earning him respect as a mediator between East and West.

Mark of Ephesus (c. 1392–1444) was one of the most outspoken members of the Eastern delegation. He vehemently opposed many of the doctrinal concessions required for union, particularly regarding the Filioque clause and papal supremacy. Mark refused to sign the decree of union and became a symbol of resistance to the council's decisions in the Eastern church.

Another key figure in the Eastern delegation was Isidore of Kiev (c. 1385–1463). He supported the union and played an active role in the negotiations. After the council, Isidore returned to eastern Europe to promote the union, but he faced significant opposition, particularly in Russia, where the union was rejected. He was eventually forced to flee to the West, where he continued to serve as a cardinal and advocate for unity.

A prominent representative of the Latin Church, Nicholas of Cusa (1401–64), was a cardinal, philosopher, and theologian. His expertise in ecclesiology and his vision of church unity informed many of the discussions at the council. Nicholas was instrumental in presenting the Western perspective on papal authority and the Filioque clause, emphasizing the importance of theological harmony for the defense of Christendom.

The patriarch of Constantinople Joseph II (1360–1439) led the Eastern delegation and was a staunch supporter of the union. He hoped that reconciliation with Rome would secure military and financial assistance against the encroaching Ottoman Empire. Joseph's death during the council in 1439 was a significant blow to the Eastern delegation and created uncertainty about the reception of the council's decisions in Constantinople.

These bishops and theologians represented a wide spectrum of views, reflecting the deep theological, cultural, and political complexities of the union efforts at the Council of Florence. While the council achieved a temporary decree of union in 1439, its decisions were never widely accepted in the East, highlighting the enduring challenges of reconciling the divided churches.

The hoped-for reunion between East and West ultimately proved short-lived, as the agreement reached at the Council of Florence failed to gain widespread acceptance and support among Eastern Christians. Political instability, religious tensions, and the fall of Constantinople to the Ottoman empire in 1453 all but ended future efforts at reconciliation.

Conclusion

At its core, the Great Schism was a culmination of longstanding tensions and disagreements between the Eastern and Western branches of Christianity. These divisions manifested in theological disputes, ecclesiastical controversies, and cultural differences that had been simmering beneath the surface for centuries. Key issues contributing to the schism included divergent understandings of papal authority, liturgical practices, doctrinal nuances, and linguistic and cultural disparities between the Latin West and the Greek East.

The significance of the Great Schism extends far beyond its immediate theological and ecclesiastical ramifications, representing a rupture in the unity of the Christian faith, dividing the church along geographical and cultural lines and setting the stage for centuries of estrangement and animosity between Eastern and Western Christians. The schism also had geopolitical implications, as it reshaped the balance of power in Europe and the Mediterranean world, leading to the emergence of distinct spheres of influence centered around Constantinople and Rome.

Recommended Reading

Brown, Peter. *The Rise of Western Christendom: Triumph and Diversity, A.D. 200–1000*. 10th anniversary rev. ed. Wiley-Blackwell, 2013.

Congar, Yves. *After Nine Hundred Years: The Background of the Schism Between the Eastern and Western Churches*. Fordham University Press, 1959.

Erickson, John H. *The Challenge of Our Past: Studies in Orthodox Canon Law and Church History*. St. Vladimir's Seminary Press, 1991.

Fortescue, Adrian. *The Orthodox Eastern Church*. Catholic Truth Society, 1908.

Gill, Joseph. *The Council of Florence*. Cambridge University Press, 1959.

Herrin, Judith. *Byzantium: The Surprising Life of a Medieval Empire*. Princeton University Press, 2009.

Hussey, J. M. *The Orthodox Church in the Byzantine Empire*. Oxford University Press, 1986.

Louth, Andrew. *Greek East and Latin West: The Church AD 681–1071*. St. Vladimir's Seminary Press, 2007.

Meyendorff, John. *Byzantine Theology: Historical Trends and Doctrinal Themes*. 2nd ed. Fordham University Press, 1983.

Meyendorff, John. *The Primacy of Peter: Essays in Ecclesiology and the Early Church*. St. Vladimir's Seminary Press, 1992.

Nichols, Aidan. *Rome and the Eastern Churches: A Study in Schism*. Ignatius, 2010.

Noble, Thomas F. X. *The Republic of St. Peter: The Birth of the Papal State, 680–825*. University of Pennsylvania Press, 1984.

Obolensky, Dimitri. *The Byzantine Commonwealth: Eastern Europe, 500–1453*. Weidenfeld & Nicolson, 1971.

Ostrogorsky, George. *History of the Byzantine State*. Translated by Joan Hussey. Rev. ed. New Rutgers University Press, 1969.

Papadakis, Aristeides, and John Meyendorff. *The Christian East and the Rise of the Papacy: The Church 1071–1453 A.D.* St. Vladimir's Seminary Press, 1994.

Runciman, Steven. *The Eastern Schism: A Study of the Papacy and the Eastern Churches During the XIth and XIIth Centuries*. Clarendon, 1955.

Siecienski, A. Edward. *The Filioque: History of a Doctrinal Controversy*. Oxford University Press, 2010.

Ware, Kallistos. *The Orthodox Church*. New ed. Penguin, 1997.

—— Chapter 20 ——

Scholasticism and Its Legacy

Amidst the Crusades, monastic reform, and papal drama and development discussed in previous chapters, there remains a slightly more positive thread through the eleventh to fourteenth centuries, namely the development of theological schools leading to the rise of universities and the emergence of Scholasticism. We have only touched on the corners of this story thus far, but now we seek to address this angle head-on. This story climaxes in the person and work of Thomas Aquinas, a theologian whose life and legacy, like that of Augustine of Hippo, serve as a watershed moment in the history of the church, demanding outsized attention relative to others who feature along the way.

This chapter thus considers the rise of Scholasticism from the beginning of the theological schools through Anselm and the Peters, focusing the bulk of attention on the life and thought of Thomas. The following chapter will then consider a few key thinkers after Aquinas, such as Dante and Duns Scotus, who further illustrate the height of medieval Scholastic thought and creativity, ending with Great Tradition reflections.

The Beginnings of Scholasticism

Cathedral Schools

Schools associated with monasteries emerged as early as the sixth century. But it was Charlemagne who in 789 decreed that every monastery have a school to ensure an educated clergy and nobility. Given that the cathedrals were the home of the bishops, the schools associated with these locations soon set the standard for medieval education. These schools were located in cities such as Chartres, Paris, Orleans, and Reims. The curriculum was a return to the classical subjects of the trivium and quadrivium—grammar, rhetoric, and logic (the trivium), as well as arithmetic, geometry, music, and astronomy (the quadrivium). While Charlemagne's renaissance attempt would be thwarted by the Norse invasions of the ninth century, his push toward an educated clergy would persist and pave the way for universities and the later medieval renaissance.

Anselm (1033–1109)

Anselm was born in 1033 in Aosta, Italy, where he was educated at a local Benedictine monastery. From an early age, he desired the monastic life, but he was refused by the local abbot when he was fifteen years old. He then headed to France, eventually landing in Bec in Normandy, where he studied under the famous Lanfranc. In 1060 Anselm officially entered the Benedictine monastic life at Bec, and by 1063, when Lanfranc was appointed the first abbot at St. Stephen's in Caen by William of Normandy, Anselm was chosen as prior of the monastery. In 1078 he was elected abbot, a position he would hold until 1093. Under Anselm's leadership, Bec became well-known for its excellence in scholarship.

This quick ascension to the rank of prior signaled the political dimension of the rest of Anselm's life. His father, Gundulf, desired for Anselm to pursue the high office of political leadership. But Anselm was drawn to the obscure life of the monastics, especially the life of mental and spiritual devotion. Even in the quiet monastic life, Anselm's extraordinary abilities could not remain hidden, hence his ascension to prior only three years into his monastic life. Despite Bec's growing reputation under Anslem's oversight, he desired to give himself to study rather than administrative responsibilities. While Anselm's greatest gifts to the church are found in his scholarship and theological insight, his trials amidst ecclesiastical leadership remain an important part of his legacy.

Father of Scholasticism

Anselm is often called the father of Scholasticism, though it is impossible to identify any one person as the source of such a variegated movement and method. In summary, Scholasticism is a method of inquiry and education that came to dominate the high Middle Ages. It is chiefly characterized by the dialectical approach of question and answer, cross-examining a question from multiple perspectives. Each perspective is then systematically disproven with reasons and evidence until the final answer offers what is believed to be the correct and authoritative ruling on the question. The Scholastic method relies heavily on the power of human reason to offer insight into the logical coherence and consistency of any doctrinal issue in light of the authorities of Scripture and the tradition of the church.

Anselm's influence on the Scholastic movement is due to his heavy reliance on the power of reason to penetrate matters of doctrine, but not to the exclusion of faith. Rather, Anselm believed his method to be in keeping with Augustine's "faith seeking understanding" approach by employing reason fueled by faith to yield theological insight. In his Epistle 136, Anselm wrote, "A Christian should progress through faith to understanding, not reach faith through understanding or, if he cannot understand, fall away from the faith. Indeed, someone who can attain understanding should rejoice, but someone who cannot understand should venerate what he is unable to comprehend."[1]

Classical Scholasticism is not always recognizable in Anselm but is rather identified in seed form. It flowers into mature form in the work of Peter Lombard, Peter Abelard, and most importantly Thomas Aquinas.

Theologian

Known as the "Second Augustine," Anselm is lauded as one of the greatest minds of the Middle Ages. After beginning his studies at Bec, he was quickly recognized for his unique abilities. He was unquestionably Lanfranc's greatest student. A few years into his teaching at Bec, Anselm's students insisted that he pen his thoughts rather than just teach. The encouragement led to the writing of his *Monologion* (c. 1077) and his *Proslogion* (c. 1078), hailed as some of his greatest and most creative works.

---

[1] Letter 136, Anselm to Fulk, bishop of Beauvais, in *The Letters of Saint Anselm of Canterbury*, trans. Walter Fröhlich, 3 vols. (Cistercian, 1990), 1:315

Monologion (meaning "soliloquy") is an extended meditation on the being of God employing especially the force of reason. His purpose is apologetic in nature, arguing for the triune God based on the nature of the good ascending in degrees ultimately to God, a less developed form of his later "cosmological argument." While not an exposition of Scripture, Anselm is careful to say nothing that is inconsistent with Scripture or with the tradition of the fathers, especially Augustine.

Proslogion (meaning "discourse") was penned soon after the *Monologion* and was originally titled *Faith Seeking Understanding* as, in Anselm's words, "I have written the following treatise, in the person of one who strives to lift his mind to the contemplation of God, and seeks to understand what he believes."[2] Whereas the *Monologion* linked together many arguments toward proofs for the existence of God, the *Proslogion* aims to put forward a single argument that "alone would suffice to demonstrate that God truly exists."[3]

In chapter 2 of *Proslogion*, Anselm introduces the "ontological argument," for which he is arguably most famous. In sum, the argument suggests that *God is that than which nothing greater can be conceived* (i.e., the greatest conceivable being). He writes at the end of chapter 2,

> Therefore, if that, than which nothing greater can be conceived, exists in the understanding alone, the very being than which nothing greater can be conceived, is one, than which a greater can be conceived. But obviously this is impossible. Hence, there is no doubt that there exists a being, than which nothing greater can be conceived, and it exists both in the understanding and in reality.[4]

Chapters 2–4 serve as the heart of the argument. Chapter 2 argues positively for God as that than which nothing greater can be conceived, while chapter 3 argues in the other direction, that if the positive assertion is true, the negative assertion must not be true, namely that God cannot be conceived not to exist. For that which can be conceived not to exist is not God. The remaining twenty-two chapters carry forward from the initial argument of the greatest conceivable being toward extended reflection on the single and

---

[2] Sidney Norton Deane with Saint Anselm, *Proslogium; Monologium; An Appendix, In Behalf of the Fool, by Gaunilon; and Cur Deus Homo* (Open Court, 1939), 2.

[3] Deane with Anselm, *Proslogium*, 1.

[4] Deane with Anselm, *Proslogium*, 8.

simple nature and yet the manifold attributes of the Christian God as articulated in the faith catholic.

Anselm's "ontological argument," as it was called by Immanuel Kant, who was critical of Anselm's approach, continues to influence the philosophical and theological schools of thought. Despite both its many defenders and opponents across the centuries, Anselm's contribution is undeniable. Perhaps most notable in the last century is Anselm's influence on Karl Barth, who credited Anselm's *Proslogion*, chapters 2–4, with teaching him the proper attitude toward the knowledge and existence of God.

Anslem's *Cur Deus Homo* (*Why God Became Man*, c. 1092) provided another important contribution in theology, especially concerning understanding the atonement of Christ. It is safe to say that any subsequent work on the atonement from the past millennium since Anslem's writing has engaged with his thought on the atonement of Christ. As the title of the work suggests, the question undertaken in the work is, Why did God become man? Anselm begins by acknowledging the objections of those who oppose the Christian faith, especially concerning why it was necessary for God to become man and to die to redeem the world. Anselm takes up the task of answering this in a dialogue form. The two characters of the dialogue are Anselm himself and Boso, a self-proclaimed Christian though critical and unlearned in the faith.

> If it be necessary, therefore, as it appears, that the heavenly kingdom be made up of men, and this cannot be effected unless the aforesaid satisfaction be made, which none but God can make and none but man ought to make, it is necessary for the God-man to make it.
>
> ———
>
> Anselm of Canterbury,
> *Cur Deus Homo*

Embedded in a hierarchical society rich with relational and legal obligations, Anselm's approach is contextualized by his feudalistic and legal-minded culture. This is not to reduce his thought, however, to mere feudalism and rationalism. While optimistic and intentional with respect to human reason, Anselm proves to be a sophisticated, historically informed faith-first theologian with multifaceted insights that have stood the test of time. Anselm's view of the atonement is often labeled the "satisfaction" view, referring to the work of Christ as a payment for sin. After his ontological argument for God's existence, his view of the atonement is his greatest contribution to the development of doctrine. The heart of Anselm's view is summarized in book 2.6:

Anselm. But this cannot be effected, except the price paid to God for the sin of man be something greater than all the universe besides God.

Boso. So it appears.

Anselm. Moreover, it is necessary that he who can give God anything of his own which is more valuable than all things in the possession of God, must be greater than all else but God himself.

Boso. I cannot deny it.

Anselm. Therefore none but God can make this satisfaction.

Boso. So it appears.

Anselm. But none but a man ought to do this, other wise man does not make the satisfaction.

Boso. Nothing seems more just.

Anselm. If it be necessary, therefore, as it appears, that the heavenly kingdom be made up of men, and this cannot be effected unless the aforesaid satisfaction be made, which none but God can make and none but man ought to make, it is necessary for the God-man to make it.

Boso. Now blessed be God! we have made a great discovery with regard to our question. Go on, therefore, as you have begun. For I hope that God will assist you.

Anselm. Now must we inquire how God can become man.[5]

Archbishop

Lanfranc held the post of archbishop of Canterbury from 1070 until his death in 1089. Following his death, King William Rufus left the post vacant for four years, as he hoped to ensure the next archbishop would not oppose royal control of the English church. Anselm was reluctantly appointed to the position on December 4, 1093. Stories are told of Anslem clinching his fist, refusing to embrace the episcopal staff. Such protests by new bishops were

[5] St. Anselm, *Basic Writings*, trans. S. N. Deane (Open Court), 258–59.

common as demonstrations of modesty, but for Anselm it was sincere. He desired study, not administration.

Legacy

Anselm's legacy is a mixed one. Politically, Anselm may be viewed as a disappointment, and this would not be altogether inaccurate. It is worth bearing in mind, however, that Anselm never sought political or ecclesial position, preferring instead the life of contemplation and study. But, regarding theological contributions, Anselm achieved remarkable success.

Anselm also signals an important development, particularly concerning theological method. While Scholasticism was only just emerging with Anselm's work, the level of optimism toward and reliance upon human reason is new in the development of doctrine up to this point. It is not without philosophical precedent in the ancient work of Plato and Aristotle or in Boethius's sixth-century work. Even Anselm's forebearer, Augustine, demonstrated strong reliance on human reason, though the time, place, and motivation for his work yields a different tone and flavor of writing. Anselm's apologetic arguments for God's existence and defense for the necessity of the Incarnation against both believing and unbelieving critics signals his increasingly pluralistic context forcing the common ground of human reason as a necessary starting place.

Peter Abelard (1079–1142)

Born only a few decades after Anselm, the Frenchman Peter Abelard developed his own reputation for philosophical and theological insight, besides being an accomplished musician and poet. Abelard is also remembered for a love affair with Heloise d'Argenteuil, from which a son was conceived and for which Abelard was castrated by Heloise's uncle. Subsequently he entered the Benedictine monastery in Saint Denis on the north side of Paris.

Abelard's contributions include advancement in philosophy, theology, logic, and ethics. Of note is his formulation of nominalism. This is the metaphysical view that universals do not exist in reality but rather are simply words (*nomina*) used as labels for the idea of universals. For example, there is no material reality of "horseness," only actual horses. For Abelard, "horseness" is accounted for by the word "horse," but this is not a reference to a universal form of "horse." This view was original to Abelard, and it would continue to be influential as it was developed in the years that followed, eventually becoming the center of a controversy in the early fourteenth century between Duns Scotus and William of Ockham.

Abelard's approach was heavily rational. While he differed with Anselm's view of the atonement, Abelard can be viewed as the next step toward rationalism in his theological method. While a proponent of faith seeking understanding, his heavy use of logic stresses the balance of faith and reason. His work *Sic et Non* (*Yes and No*) is representative of his dialectical method, with a list of 158 questions with seemingly contradictory answers and the logical principles for resolving them.

Peter Lombard (c. 1100–1160)

Peter from Lombardy studied at Reims then Paris and began teaching at the cathedral school at Notre Dame by 1136. In 1159, on the feast days of Saints Peter and Paul, he was made bishop of Paris, a post he held only a short time before his death.

Lombard is remembered less for his contribution of original thought than for his systematization of theology, especially in his *Sentences*. Despite some opposition, Lombard's *Sentences* was affirmed by the Fourth Lateran Council in 1215 and served as the textbook for theology throughout the Middle Ages.

> If it is asked, "For what is the rational creature created?" Answer: to praise God, to serve him, to enjoy him. By these things the creature profits, not God.
>
> ———
>
> Peter Lombard, *Sentences*, book 2

The spirit of Lombard's works may be recognized as a blend of Augustine, John of Damascus, and his contemporaries Peter Abelard and Hugh of St. Victor. While he authored other notable works, such as glosses on the Psalms and Paul's Epistles that were widely commented on, his *Sentences* had the greatest impact across the centuries, including the first authoritative affirmation of the seven sacraments of the church, listed as baptism, confirmation, penance, Eucharist, marriage, ordination, and extreme unction. The work is organized in four books:

- Book 1: The Mystery of the Trinity
- Book 2: On Creation
- Book 3: On the Incarnation of the Word
- Book 4: On the Doctrine of Signs

Lombard's work thus served to structure, direct, and even limit theological conversations. As university masters were required to lecture on Lombard's sentences beginning in the early thirteenth century, students were catechized in the synthesized and organized thought of Lombard infused with the mature late patristic thought of Augustine, the early medieval eastern thought of John of Damascus, the Scholastic thought of Abelard, and the mystic thought of Hugh.

Aristotelian Revival

By the early to mid-twelfth century, portions of Aristotle's works made their way to Paris from translation centers in Spain and Sicily. The preservation of Aristotle's works was largely due to the efforts of Arabs, but the translation work was mostly conducted by Christian monastics. This led to a revival of interest in Aristotle's thought and its integration into the burgeoning academy of the day. Since the lead educators were rooted in cathedral schools, the biblical and theological disciplines were first in line for Aristotelian synthesis.

The work of both Peter Abelard and Peter Lombard illustrates the growing influence of Aristotle, and especially of the high view of reason, that was gaining momentum in the eleventh century. Even pedagogy was affected by this as the lecture was being replaced by the *disputatio* (debate) as the skill of argumentation was deemed more valuable than the mere recitation of ancient authorities. While the tradition of the church remained an integral part of one's education, the role of reason challenged its uncritical reception.

The Aristotelian revival was well under way by the time of Thomas Aquinas, though he is rightly credited as the most influential synthesizer of Aristotle's thought. What Plato was to Augustine, Aristotle was to Aquinas. And while Aquinas creatively explored the sacred science of doctrine with an Aristotelian ethic and metaphysic, he was careful to tether his thought to the Nicene and Chalcedonian tradition of the church and to tip his hat frequently to Augustine.

Universities

Where Charlemagne's efforts were stalled in the early ninth century, Pope Gregory VII reignited these efforts in 1079 with a papal decree ordering the establishment of schools in all cathedrals and monasteries. As a result, many new schools were formed, and the influence of established schools expanded. This was especially true in Paris.

Moreover, in addition to Gregory VII's decree, because of renewed vigor for learning among the new mendicant orders of the late twelfth and thirteenth centuries, and the Aristotelian revival, the move to formalize institutions of higher learning was inevitable. The first university to officialize was the University of Bologna in northern Italy, chartered in 1158. This was quickly followed by the Universities of Paris and Oxford, chartered in 1200 and 1248, respectively, though teaching had begun in both decades before they were chartered. In fact, the University of Cambridge, founded by scholars who left Oxford following a dispute, received its official charter some seventeen years before the University of Oxford, though higher education was offered in Oxford for more than 100 years longer than Cambridge.

By the year 1400, more than forty universities had been founded across Europe. The European continent had become the educational beacon of the world, for better or worse. Once a student completed foundational work in the classical trivium and quadrivium subjects, the student could choose to continue studies in one of the "higher faculties" of theology, medicine, or law (either canon law or civil law). While the disciplines are far broader today than in the thirteenth century, the basic programmatic footprint of the medieval university continues to shape universities around the world today.

With the rise of the university also arose a third kind of social elite. Now, though neither royalty nor high-ranking clergy, university professors carried a cultural authority that influenced ideas and societal development. Scholars of various stripes had been around for millennia, so a class of intelligentsia was nothing new. But this new institution called "university" immediately assumed an elevated social platform, and those installed as the intellectual custodians were platformed along with it. This is why most intellectual history from the past thousand years in the West has pivoted around students and scholars from Paris, Oxford, Cambridge, and the like.

Bonaventure (c. 1221–1274)

Giovanni di Fidanza, better known to history as Bonaventure, represents a more traditional Augustinian approach to life and doctrine with a spiritualist flare amidst the rising Scholastic thought and Aristotelian revival of the thirteenth century. Born in Bagnoregio, Tuscany, around 1221, Bonaventure was struck with severe illness as a child but was healed through the intervention of Francis of Assisi. Unsurprisingly, Bonaventure joined the Franciscan

Order in 1243, when he officially took the name "Bona Ventura" (meaning "happy voyage") and then studied at the University of Paris under the well-known Franciscan Alexander of Hales. Bonaventure received his doctorate and license to teach around 1253–54 from the University of Paris, where he sought to resolve factions that emerged among the Franciscan Order following Francis's death. Pope Gregory X (1271–76) made him the cardinal bishop of Albano and summoned him to the Second Council of Lyon in 1274 to facilitate reunification attempts between the Eastern and Western churches. He died in Lyon on July 15, 1274. As is common with church leaders, Bonaventure's life and legacy may be divided into a tale of politics and administration and a tale of theological and spiritual influence. For our purposes, we will attend closer to the latter.

Bonaventure is best remembered for his attempt to synthesize Augustinian thought with the Scholastic method of the day. His writings include a *Commentary on the Sentences of Lombard*, *Commentary on the Gospel of Luke*, more famously *The Journey of the Mind to God*, *Breviloquium* (or *Brief Reading*, an outline of a fuller theological treatise that was never written), *The Tree of Life*, and *The Triple Way*.

Bonaventure's legacy includes a renewed Augustinian spirituality that moved from the outside, created realm, to the interior of the human person, then upward toward God in contemplation. He writes in *The Journey of the Mind to God*,

> By praying in this way, we receive light to discern the steps of the ascent into God. In relation to our position in creation, the universe itself is a ladder by which we can ascend into God. Some created things are vestiges, others images; some are material, others spiritual; some are temporal, others everlasting; some are outside us, others within us. In order to contemplate the First Principle, who is most spiritual, eternal and above us, we must pass through his vestiges, which are material, temporal and outside us. This means to be led in the path of God. We must also enter into our soul, which is God's image, everlasting, spiritual and within us. This means to enter in the truth of God. We must go beyond to what is eternal, most spiritual and above us, by gazing upon the First Principle. This means to rejoice in the knowledge of God and in reverent fear of his majesty (cf. Ps. 85:11).[6]

---

[6] Bonaventure, *Bonaventure: The Soul's Journey into God; The Tree of Life; The Life of St. Francis*, ed. Richard J. Payne, trans. Ewert Cousins, Classics of Western Spirituality (Paulist Press, 1978), 60.

Bonaventure is also remembered for his theology of history and anti-Aristotelianism.[7] Given that the Aristotelian revival was well underway during the life of Bonaventure, his intent to promote a classical Augustinianism signals an important resistance to the philosophical headwinds of the day.

Thomas Aquinas and Scholasticism

It is no exaggeration to declare Thomas Aquinas (1225–74) the greatest theological figure of the medieval era. Like Augustine, Thomas represents a watershed in the history of the church, especially for his contributions in theology, philosophy, and ethics. The depth and influence of his work demands serious reflection and consideration by all subsequent theological traditions. Thomas represents the height of medieval theological development and Aristotelian synthesis, and he serves as the quintessential Scholastic theologian.

Who Was Thomas?

Thomas was born in 1225 to a noble family in Roccasecca, Italy, halfway between Rome and Naples. Thomas's father was the count of Aquino, some five miles south of Roccasecca, hence the "Aquinas" association. Thomas's parents expected him to pursue a life of nobility beginning with the well-known and prestigious Benedictines. His uncle Sinibald was abbot of Monte Cassino, the original Benedictine monastery. But local conflicts eventually compelled Thomas's father to send the young man to Naples, where Thomas was exposed to the newly founded Dominican order, the "begging preachers" (see chapter 15), who were vigorously committed to the intellectual life as well as to preaching and meeting the needs of the people. He joined the order in 1244.

Thomas's parents were sorely disappointed in his decision to join the Dominicans rather than the Benedictines and thus imprisoned the nineteen-year-old at home. They even tempted him with prostitutes, whom he resolutely chased out of his room with a firebrand, with which he then burned a cross in the door. Eventually, Thomas's mother saw fit to leave his window open, allowing him to escape. Reconnecting with his Dominican friends in Naples, he was then sent to Paris to study with the venerable Albert the Great (c. 1200–c. 1280), known for his contributions to science and to the integration of Aristotelian thought in

---

[7] Cf. Joseph Ratzinger, *The Theology of History in Saint Bonaventure* (Cluny, 2020).

theology. Thomas's personality did not give off the immediate impression of brilliance. But as Albert famously said, "We call this young man a dumb ox, but his bellowing in doctrine will one day resound throughout the world."[8]

From there he spent time in Cologne and Lyons, then was named master of theology at Paris in 1256, though he was sent to Italy to teach in various places, including Rome. Thomas was called back to Paris in 1269 to combat Averroist philosophers, such as Siger of Brabant. The Averroists followed the Muslim philosopher Averroes (1126–98), who integrated Aristotle's thought with Islam, leading to ideological conflict with both Christian and Muslim doctrine.

The decade of the 1260s through the early 1270s is recognized as the period of Thomas's most influential work. During this time, he penned his *Summa contra gentiles* (*Summary Against the Gentiles*) followed by his unfinished but most famous *Summa theologica* (*Summary of Theology*). Thomas began the *Summa theologica* around 1265 but stopped writing in 1273 after a mystical experience. Following this experience, he said, "I can write no more. I have seen things which make all my writings like straw."[9] He died the following year at age forty-nine, en route to the Second Council of Lyon. Thomas's teachings were required reading by Dominicans in 1278—only four years after his death—and he was canonized less than fifty years later in 1323.

Contours of Aquinas's Thought

As with the legacy of Augustine, Aquinas scholars debate the degree to which Thomas was first a philosopher, a theologian, or something else altogether. Our view, following the work of Frederick Christian Bauerschmidt, is that Aquinas's overall project was "consistently and without deviation, holy teaching as a way of life."[10] Bauerschmidt suggests that to speak of Thomas's work as an "intellectual project" may be misleading. More accurately, we may refer to it as "an intellectual ministry, the ministerial role of the teacher of divine wisdom."[11] Aquinas, as a pastor-theologian and an ordained Dominican, wholly committed himself

[8] G. K. Chesterton, *St. Thomas Aquinas: The Dumb Ox* (Doubleday, 1956), 50.

[9] Alban Butler, *Butler's Lives of the Saints*, ed. David Hugh Farmer and Paul Burns, new ed. (Burns & Oates, 2000), 511.

[10] F. C. Bauerschmidt, *Thomas Aquinas: Faith, Reason, and Following Christ* (Oxford University Press, 2013), 80.

[11] Bauerschmidt, *Thomas Aquinas*, 41.

to the most rigorous reflection on God and his world using the best classical sources at his disposal to aid him toward this end of truth and wisdom. In the space remaining, we merely introduce a few important areas of Thomas's thought.

Faith and Reason

One of Thomas's chief aims was to resolve the tension between faith and reason. While optimistic about the role of human reason, Thomas did not believe that reason alone could plumb the depths of God apart from faith. It could only consider the preliminary matters. Faith remained essential to enable one's reason to align properly with God and thus to explore the deep things of God and nature. Thomas explains the relationship between faith and reason in Question 1, saying, "sacred doctrine makes use even of human reason, not, indeed, to prove faith (for thereby the merit of faith would come to an end), but to make clear other things that are put forward in this doctrine. Since therefore grace does not destroy nature but perfects it, natural reason should minister to faith as the natural bent of the will ministers to charity."[12]

Grace Perfects Nature

Like Augustine before him, Aquinas also affirmed a hierarchical shape of reality. Aquinas held to a two-story shape for all things, an upper realm of the spiritual dimension and a lower realm of nature. Grace and divine revelation relate to the upper realm while nature is associated with the lower realm, leading Thomas to distinguish between the natural and the supernatural in accord with the upper and lower realms. He believed these realms to be fundamentally congruent and in no way at odds with one another when understood correctly. Right reason is sure to interpret the natural world in a way that accords with the upper realm, and where there appear to be inconsistencies between reason (lower realm) and divine revelation (upper realm), faith must remain firm and active, confessing that reason only carries us so far. For example, reason may account for the existence of God, but it cannot arrive at the Trinity or the incarnation without the aid of divine revelation. "In this synthesis grace *perfects and completes* nature but does not

---

[12] Thomas Aquinas, *Summa Theologica*, trans. by the Fathers of the English Dominican Province (Benziger Bros., 1947), 9.

destroy it. . . . Philosophy can take you so far up the ladder of truth, but theology takes you the rest of the way."[13]

Five Ways

Aquinas's Five Ways, or Proofs, for the existence of God are among his best-known contributions to Christian thought. While Thomas believed these to be the best rational arguments for the existence of God, Edward Feser insists that "it is crucial to understand that they are *summaries*. Aquinas never intended for them to stand alone and would probably have reacted with horror if told that future generations of students would be studying them in isolation, removed from their original immediate context in the *Summa Theologiae*."[14] Aquinas's Five Ways are found in book 1 of his *Summa* and may be summarized as follows:[15]

1. Unmoved mover: Motion in the world can only be explained if there is first an unmoved mover
2. First cause: The series of efficient causes in the world must lead to a first cause, an uncaused cause
3. Contingency and corruptibility: Contingent and corruptible beings depend on an independent and incorruptible being
4. Gradation: Varying degrees of reality and goodness in the world must be approximations of a greatest, maximum good
5. Goal-oriented design: The innate teleology (or goal-oriented nature) of non-conscious agents suggests the existence of an intelligent designer to the universe

Four Causes

Concerning ontology, or the nature of being, Aquinas affirmed the Aristotelian commitment to the four causes. These include (1) material, (2) formal, (3) efficient, and (4) final causes. Edward Feser succinctly and creatively explains:

---

[13] Craig G. Bartholomew, Michael W. Goheen, *Christian Philosophy: A Systematic and Narrative Introduction* (Baker Academic, 2013), 86.

[14] Bartholomew and Goheen, *Christian Philosophy*, 62.

[15] Articulation of the Five Ways adapted from Anthony Kenny, *Medieval Philosophy; A New History of Western Philosophy*, vol. 2 (Oxford University Press, 2005), 303.

> The *material cause* or underlying stuff the ball is made out of is rubber; its *formal cause*, or the form, pattern, or structure it exhibits, comprises such features as its sphericity, solidity, and bounciness . . . the *efficient cause*, that which actualizes a potency and thereby brings something into being. In this case that would be the actions of the workers and/or machines in the factory in which the ball was made. . . . Lastly we have the *final cause* or the end, goal, or purpose of a thing, which in the case of the ball might be to provide amusement to a child.[16]

For Aquinas, Aristotle's four causes offer an account of the beginning, end, and nature of all things that complements, if not accentuates, the biblical account of creation.

Anthropology

Thomas's view of the human person is among the most relevant aspects of his thought for contemporary Christians. In recent decades, especially amidst cultural battles over gender, sexuality, beginning- and end-of-life questions, transhumanism, and the like, Thomas has proven a fount of insight into these important discussions. At the most basic level, Thomas remains dualistic in his anthropology, meaning that he affirms that people are essentially both body and soul. His approach is quite nuanced, however, so as not to align too closely with Plato on one side or Descartes on the other, leading followers of Thomas to label his view "hylomorphic dualism."

Jason Eberl has described Thomas's hylomorphism by stating that human beings are "metaphysical hybrids," an integrated body and soul. Simply put, Eberl summarizes Aquinas's view "that a human being exists as a unified substance composed of a rational soul informing—that is, serving as the specific organizing principle of—a material human body."[17] This view thus avoids too much division between body and soul, "for a living organic human body could not exist without being informed by a rational soul."[18]

---

[16] Edward Feser, *Aquinas: A Beginner's Guide* (Oneworld, 2009), 16.

[17] Jason T. Eberl, *The Nature of Human Persons: Metaphysics and Bioethics* (University of Notre Dame Press, 2020), 19.

[18] Eberl, *Nature of Human Persons*, 21.

Ethics

Aquinas's approach to ethics begins with his commitment to the classical notion of virtue. Thomas recognized at least three categories of virtue, including intellectual virtues, moral virtues, and theological virtues. The first two align with Aristotle's thought, but the third is new. Aquinas believed the intellectual virtues of knowledge, understanding, and wisdom to be superior to the moral virtues of prudence, justice, temperance, and courage more traditionally referred to as the cardinal virtues. Prudence (or wisdom) is first on the list, as it properly belongs both to the intellectual and moral virtues.

For the intellectual virtues, knowledge (*scientia*) and understanding work together toward grasping both the "what" and "why" of a topic or field of study. It is one thing to know facts about something, but another thing to understand "why." Further, it is yet another thing to understand how the "what" and "why" of a particular field of study relates to the whole of reality. To arrive at an understanding of the part in light of the whole is wisdom (*sapientia*) for Aquinas.

The theological virtues distinguish Thomas in the history of moral thought, as he grounds his approach in a proper theological framework of faith, hope, and love (charity). By identifying these three virtues, Thomas clarifies that by nature a person can only get so far in his journey toward perfection. Rather, "Man is perfected by virtue for those actions by which he is directed to happiness," and this happiness to which we are called is beyond our natural ability. Supernatural intervention is required. Thomas addresses this beautifully in Question 62 of his *Summa theologica:*

> Now man's happiness or felicity is twofold. . . . One is proportioned to human nature, a happiness, namely, which man can obtain by means of the principles of his nature. The other is a happiness surpassing man's nature, and which man can obtain by the power of God alone, by a kind of participation of the Godhead; and thus it is written (2 Pet. 1:4) that by Christ we are made *partakers of the divine nature.* And because such happiness surpasses the power of human nature, man's natural principles, which enable him to act well according to his power, do not suffice to direct man to this same happiness. Hence it is necessary for man to receive from God some additional principles, albeit not without divine assistance. Such principles are called *theological virtues.* They are so called, first, because their object is God, inasmuch as they direct us rightly to God; secondly, because they are infused in us by

> God alone; thirdly, because these virtues are not made known to us, save by divine revelation, contained in Holy Scripture.[19]

Moreover, Aquinas's teleological (or goal-oriented) view of reality placed happiness (*eudaimonia*, or blessedness) as the ultimate end goal of life. The virtues serve as the means toward true happiness, which is only found in God and will ultimately be experienced only through perfect union with God through Christ in the life to come.

Finally, Thomas argued for the existence of four types of laws: eternal, divine, natural, and human. The ethicist Daniel R. Heimbach explains,

> Aquinas viewed ethical life as set in a well-ordered universe governed by four kinds of law, of which two came from Aristotle (natural and human) and two from Scripture (eternal and divine). The ultimate pattern for right and wrong located in the mind of God, where It is in Itself beyond knowing, he identified as "eternal law." The expression of eternal law reflected in creation Aquinas defined as "natural law," and this, he claimed, is open to the reason of all, whether they be regenerate or not. "Human law" he viewed to be applications of natural law made by men to particular situations and communities, and "divine law" referred to standards revealed in the Bible, part of which overlaps natural law and regards material life and part of which goes beyond natural law and regards spiritual life.[20]

Aquinas and the Great Tradition

In each category of the Great Tradition—Scripture, doctrine, liturgy, and ethics—Thomas leaves an indelible fingerprint. His fresh philosophical synthesis mixed with penetrating insight and concern both to defend and promote the Catholic faith in an increasingly pluralistic context yielded a figure in the person of Thomas that Christians of all traditions do well to revisit time and again.

In the next chapter, we will consider additional ecclesial and cultural developments of the Middle Ages, as well as theological developments in the wake of Thomas's influence.

---

[19] Thomas Aquinas, *Basic Writings of Saint Thomas Aquinas*, ed. Anton C. Pegis, vol. 2 (Random House, 1945), Q.62.1 (p. 475).

[20] Daniel R. Heimbach, *Fundamental Christian Ethics* (B&H Academic, 2022), 165–66. See also Christopher Shields and Robert Pasnau, *The Philosophy of Aquinas* (Oxford University Press, 2016), 270–98, for a fuller treatment of Aquinas's ethics in relation to his overall cognitive framework.

Recommended Reading

Anselm. *Basic Writings*. Translated by S. N. Deane. Open Court, 1962.

Anselm. *The Letters of Saint Anselm of Canterbury*. Translated by Walter Fröhlich. 3 Vols. Cistercian, 1990.

Bartholomew, Craig G., and Michael W. Goheen. *Christian Philosophy: A Systematic and Narrative Introduction*. Baker Academic, 2013.

Bauershmidt, F. C. *Thomas Aquinas: Faith, Reason, and Following Christ*. Oxford University Press, 2013.

Bonaventure. *Bonaventure: The Soul's Journey into God; The Tree of Life; The Life of St. Francis*. Edited by Richard J. Payne. Translated by Ewert Cousins. Paulist Press, 1978.

Chesterton, G. K. *St. Thomas Aquinas: The Dumb Ox*. Doubleday, 1956.

Eberl, Jason T. *The Nature of Human Persons: Metaphysics and Bioethics*. University of Notre Dame Press, 2020.

Feser, Edward. *Aquinas: A Beginner's Guide*. Oneworld, 2009.

Heimbach, Daniel. *Fundamental Christian Ethics*. B&H Academic, 2022.

Kenny, Anthony. *Medieval Philosophy*. Vol. 2 of *A New History of Western Philosophy*. Oxford University Press, 2005.

Ratzinger, Joseph. *The Theology of History in Saint Bonaventure*. Cluny, 2020.

Shields, Christopher, and Robert Pasnau. *The Philosophy of Aquinas*. Oxford University Press, 2016.

—— Chapter 21 ——

Church, Culture, and Theology After Aquinas

The thirteenth century was home not only to major theological decisions and influencers, new monastic communities, and ongoing struggles with Islam and the Holy Land in the Crusades; along with the fourteenth century, it produced some of the greatest literature known to the West, including Chaucer's *The Canterbury Tales*, Boccaccio's *Decameron*, and Dante's *Divine Comedy*.

This chapter aims to zoom out and capture various developments and movements representative of the thirteenth and fourteenth centuries, including literary development like that seen in Dante, theological developments following from Thomas as seen in figures such as Duns Scotus and William of Ockham, the impact of the Black Death, and Jewish-Christian relations in light of the Plague and the Crusades.

Dante (1265–1321)

Dante occupies a unique place in the literature of the late Middle Ages. Dante captured the worldview of thirteenth- and fourteenth-century Italians and presented it as a microcosm of the theological framework and imagination of the entire West. In *The Divine Comedy*, Dante's poetic skill was used in the service of political polemic, yet its theological sophistication and literary creativity captured readers of his day. It was relevant for every citizen regardless of social status, as each had to deal with the realities of both church and empire and the endless associated drama. As Christian Blauvelt of the BBC aptly states, "The entire history of Western literature and theology is Dante's fodder to sample and mash up like some kind of 14th century hip-hop artist."[1]

The Italian Dante Alighieri was born in Florence in 1265 to a modestly wealthy and notable family. Dante reports having met Beatrice Portinari around the age of nine, when she was only eight years old. Dante was spellbound by her from that early age, a fascination that would return in his work. Central to Dante's legacy is the political circumstances of his time. In the early thirteenth century, Florence was divided between two factions, the Guelfs and the Ghibellines. Dante aligned with the Guelfs, who may be generally described as desiring political autonomy and supporting the papacy. At the time of Dante's birth, the Guelfs were the dominant faction in Florence, though they were quickly headed toward a fracturing of their own regarding economic issues and differences concerning papal support.

This division within the Guelfs eventually resulted in two parties known as the "Blacks" (pro-Papal party) and the "Whites" (pro-merchant party desiring less church control), the latter of which Dante was a member. Dante travelled to Rome in 1300 as part of a delegation from Florence to the pope. He would never return to his hometown. In 1302 his association with the Whites ultimately led to his banishment from Florence and his exclusion from public office. His remaining nineteen years were spent in various Italian cities, including lengthy periods in both Verona (c. 1315–19) and Ravenna (c. 1319 until his death in 1321).

While Dante wrote many other works—such as *The New Life*, written before exile, and *De monarchia*—his greatest work is undoubtably *The Divine Comedy*. Dante's sordid political past doubtless contributed both to the tone and imagination that bears itself out against political and religious figures in his *Divine Comedy*. Dante began work on *The Divine Comedy* in 1308. It is divided into three major parts, *Inferno*, first published in 1314, followed by *Purgatorio* and *Paradiso*, completed and published in 1320, about a year before his death. The work begins with Dante undertaking a journey on Good Friday of the year

[1] Christian Blauvelt, "Dante and The Divine Comedy: He Took Us on a Tour of Hell," BBC, June 5, 2018, https://www.bbc.com/culture/article/20180604–dante-and-the-divine-comedy-he-took-us-on-a-tour-of-hell.

1300—the same year he left Florence for Rome. In the first two parts of his journey, *Inferno* and *Purgatorio*, Dante is guided by the ancient Roman poet Virgil. Though Beatrice died in her early twenties in the year 1290, Dante included her as a figure full of beauty and virtue who takes over from the poet Virgil to lead Dante into paradise. She is the object of Dante's love throughout the story and the spark of his renewed Christian faith. In the story, Beatrice looking down from heaven, sees that Dante is lost, and sends Virgil to guide him through hell to set Dante free.

Beatrice guides him through the first part of paradise, and in the final part, Bernard of Clairvaux leads him to a brief but powerful vision of God. The first part of the work is a descent down into hell. Virgil leads him through nine concentric circles, and the deeper he goes, the more severe the punishments meted out to the damned. In the deepest circle, in the heart of a frozen lake, Dante sees the prison of Satan, the greatest betrayer, who possesses three heads in a grotesque parody of the Holy Trinity, with each head chewing on the three most infamous betrayers in history: Judas, Cassius, and Brutus.

The complete absence of the light of God is the very essence of hell in Dante's cosmology. Dante begins his journey "within a forest dark," and from there, his journey only gets darker. In fact, there is not a single mention of light in the entire *Inferno* until the very last section, when Dante climbs out of the pit and sees the stars above his head. Once he begins the ascent on the seven-terraced mountain of purgatory, daylight becomes a motif by which Virgil explains this world to Dante. Virgil guides Dante to the summit of purgatory (the place after death where souls are held for purification before heaven in Roman Catholic thought) and no further—as one of the virtuous pagans, he cannot enter heaven. Beatrice is his guide through the nine spheres of paradise, which ascend in blessedness from the moon through the planets and the sun, to the *primum mobile*, the realm of the angels. At the highest point, Dante has passed beyond the ability of human comprehension into the realm of mystical contemplation. As such, Bernard of Clairvaux guides him through these final steps. Dante glimpses the empyrean heavens, and his mind perceives that which is the source of all love: the triune God in whose holy light all the blessed live.

To read the *Divine Comedy* as a mere miscellany of sin or a geography of heaven would be a severe misunderstanding. The assimilation and layering of Aristotelian ethics, Ptolemaic cosmology, Thomistic theology, political commentary, and incisive social critique is too deeply embedded in the story for the reader to get the impression Dante believes that purgatory is a literal mountain with seven terraces or that hell has a fire escape in the southern hemisphere. As G. R. Evans has pointed out, the common understanding of the Middle

Ages is that heaven and hell were outside of space and time.[2] Dante is instead presenting the "hierarchical and moral structure" of the universe in vivid poetic imagery,[3] providing a window into the imagination of medieval Christianity—indeed, of any Westerner of that era. Like the great Gothic cathedrals, which begin on the ground but draw our gaze up toward heaven, or the monumental theology of Thomas Aquinas, which begins with what we can feel and takes us to the pure realm of reason, Dante Alighieri takes us on a journey into the darkness of sin and despair and up into the light of blessed holiness. Though Aristotelianism was slowly tilting the intellectual gaze of society more toward the horizontal dimension, the vertical gaze was still present and active in the moral and theological muscle memory of the people. No author from this era captures this more vividly than Dante.

> "Consider your origin. You were not formed to live like brutes but to follow virtue and knowledge."
>
> ———
>
> Dante Alighieri,
> *The Divine Comedy*

Dante, Francesco Petrarca (Petrarch), and Giovanni Boccaccio together serve as forerunners to the movement known as Renaissance humanism (further discussed in chapter 24). The reliance upon and retrieval of ancient sources incorporated into their writings served to light the way for the movement that inspired such figures as Erasmus of Rotterdam (c. 1469–1536) and Sir Thomas More (1478–1535), paving the way for the Protestant Reformation when combined with new technologies, such as the printing press, to spread ideas rapidly. We return to this important part of the story in chapter 23.

Scotus and Ockham—Voluntarism and Nominalism

While Aquinas's influence and legacy are hardly rivaled by any of his contemporaries or any after him before the Protestant Reformation, his approach to theology and philosophy was not the only one. Bonaventure, discussed in the previous chapter, represents a noteworthy alternative while also an immediate contemporary to Aquinas. Further north and west, leading thinkers at the new British universities were advancing Aristotelian thought further even than Thomas. Among these were Robert Grosseteste (c. 1175–1253)

---

[2] G. R. Evans, *Faith in the Medieval World* (InterVarsity, 2002), 25.

[3] Evans, *Faith in the Medieval World*, 25.

and the better-known Roger Bacon (c. 1214–92). Bacon, the Franciscan, is arguably best remembered for his advancements in philosophy and science, but Bacon believed both to be inferior to theology. Bacon recognized three forms of knowledge, including authority, reason, and experience, with the latter divided into internal and external. The external was associated with the senses, while the interior was the superior form, associated with mystical knowledge of God. But Bacon is not the only influential thinker from the British Isles.

Among the more notable turns in the late medieval period is the intertwined legacies of Duns Scotus and William of Ockham. Scotus (c. 1265/66–1308) is lauded as one of the greatest philosophical minds of the late medieval era. Born in Scotland, Scotus began his studies in theology and philosophy at Oxford before being ordained a priest in the Franciscan Order in 1291. His studies continued late into the 1290s until he left for Paris near the turn of the century to serve as a lecturer and was recognized as a doctor of theology in 1305, only three years before his untimely death.

Duns Scotus (c. 1265/66–1308)

Scotus, dubbed "the Subtle Doctor," is perhaps best remembered for his heavily intellectual and speculative approach to philosophical and theological inquiry. Rik Van Nieuwenhove argues that Scotus serves as the "last major thinker of the golden age of thirteenth-century scholasticism. In many ways, he is a pivotal figure, reflecting both the end of the classic age of scholasticism and inaugurating some of the new trends that were to come to fruition in the thought of his fellow Franciscan, William of Ockham."[4]

Scotus's arguments for the existence of God are among the most sophisticated of the late Middle Ages, often leaving readers vexed by apparent paradoxes. Though he leaned heavily on reason, Scotus did not believe speculation to be an end in itself but valuable only insofar as it assists the soul in loving contemplation of God.[5] Moreover, Scotus insisted that divine revelation was essential for proper knowledge of God and not natural knowledge alone.[6]

[4] Rik Van Nieuwenhove, *An Introduction to Medieval Theology* (Cambridge University Press, 2012), 229.

[5] C. Brown, *Christianity & Western Thought*, vol. 1 (InterVarsity, 1990), 136.

[6] Brown, *Christianity & Western Thought*, 136.

Scotus separates the distinctions between philosophy and theology more drastically than did his predecessors. While keen to maintain the primacy of divine revelation, Scotus understood theology and metaphysics to have different subjects. For theology, the subject is God. For metaphysics, the subject is being. Moreover, while divine revelation serves as theology's source of authority, metaphysics draws from natural reason, a distinct difference from Thomas's participatory approach.[7]

Univocity and voluntarism are two additional key features in Scotus's thought, the latter of which is picked up by Ockham. Scotus's univocity theory suggests that the words used to describe God are univocal, meaning they are precise and exact in their descriptions of God rather than analogous, as in Thomas's view. Van Nieuwenhove clarifies: "Thus, for Scotus, we have univocity when to affirm and to deny something of the same subject amounts to a contradiction. If 'God is being' and 'God is not-being' are contradictory statements then 'God' is used in a univocal manner. In short, words are univocal when they have the same meaning."[8] This approach to God talk offers the allure of precision of language rather than the "sloppiness" and imprecision of analogy. Univocity protects against the fallacy of equivocation (or ambiguity) when speaking of God and his attributes. But is such an approach true and necessary? Or is it the consequence of separating theology from philosophy?

> If a being is perfectly necessary of itself, that is, as necessary as we can conceive that a being may be, it cannot fail to exist, even if no other being than it exists.
>
> ———
>
> John Duns Scotus,
> *Opus Oxoniense*

Scotus's view of divine freedom, called "voluntarism," may have developed in response to the Condemnations of 1277, a list of statements enacted in the University of Paris to prohibit certain topics, books, and even beliefs on pain of excommunication. Condemnation 20 decried the notion that whatever God does is done of necessity. This, it was argued, is a violation of God's freedom. To protect such freedom in God, Scotus's view is that "God freely decides what is morally good without submitting himself to external standards."[9] Sometimes referred to as "facticity," this view implies that "things simply are the way they

---

[7] Nieuwenhove, *Introduction to Medieval Theology*, 231.

[8] Nieuwenhove, 233.

[9] Nieuwenhove, 239.

are, and we can't give any further reasons for the way they are (apart from God's will)."[10] The question at the heart of this issue may be simplified thus: Are good things good because God does them, or does God do them because they are good? For Scotus, this voluntarism extends to human action as well, leaning away from a Thomistic virtue ethic and toward a Kantian view of morality. "Incidentally, the divine command ethic, when secularized, results in a subjectivist ethics, in which we effectively *construe* values rather than recognize them."[11]

William of Ockham (c. 1280–1349)

William of Ockham, perhaps best known for "Ockham's razor," which may be summarized as "the simplest explanation is the best explanation," was likely born in or near Ockham village, just outside of London. Ockham studied at Oxford, where he is believed to have studied under Duns Scotus and may also have sat under his teaching while in Paris. Ockham, like Scotus, also joined the Franciscans at an early age. Though certainly influenced by Scotus, Ockham advanced Scotus's thought in some respects, while taking a different metaphysical turn in others.

It may be said that Ockham was a theologian with a passion for logical precision. He held firmly to Scotus's voluntarism concerning God's freedom, but Ockham departed from Scotus with his own promotion of nominalism. Nominalism, the view that universals do not exist independently but are simply accounted for with words/language (*nomina*), was not new (see chapter 20), though it struck a chord with those critical of the *via antiqua* (old way) of Magnus, Aquinas, and Scotus and sympathetic to the burgeoning school of the *via moderna* (new way). While Scotus found sympathies with Aristotle's horizontal approach, which rejected Plato's vertical approach of transcendent universals in favor of the view that understood universals to be located (instantiated) in the concrete world, Ockham took this further by arguing against universals entirely. For Ockham, universals simply do not exist. Rather, they are words designated to describe the phenomenon of similarity between things.

Ockham's promotion of nominalism and full rejection of universals (thus a rejection of realism) led to a disconnected view of reality, distancing him from his predecessors, while setting up his followers for the truly modern turn. It may be said that Ockham's thought leads to a two-worlds approach. One is the empirical world, informed by reason and

---

[10] Nieuwenhove, 240.

[11] Nieuwenhove, 241. Emphasis added.

experience, while the other is the world of faith, informed by divine revelation.[12] Thus with Ockham we observe the separation of theology and philosophy.

The Scholastic approach of Thomas offered a sophisticated synthesis of faith and reason. Scotus was sympathetic but applied stress to the connective tissue between the two, and Ockham detached the connective tissue altogether. Ockham sought to maintain Christian orthodoxy and confessed that some things must be accepted by faith (i.e., the Holy Trinity). But the separation of faith and reason was official, and in time modernity would finalize the divorce.

> It is futile to do with more what can be done with fewer.
>
> ———
>
> William of Ockham,
> *Summa logicae*

Spread of the Church—Global Perspective

It is impossible to quantify with any precision the number of Christians in the late Middle Ages. Thus, we will zoom out to provide a regional perspective of where Christianity was present around the world by the late Middle Ages.

East Asia (China/India)

The status of the church in the high to late Middle Ages was unique. It is said that Thomas the apostle was the first to take the faith to India in the first century. Then, as the early church spread, Nestorianism (see chapter 9) made its way into eastern parts of Asia. While Western Christendom lived on in the early medieval period, these Christians in Asia persisted, though separated from their Western cousins. One source estimates that there were at least several hundred thousand Christians in Asia in the thirteenth century.[13]

In the thirteenth and fourteenth centuries, the Roman church reestablished connection with the Christian populations in East Asia. Seven or eight missionary efforts "were dispatched on the long and difficult journey across Asia. Most of the missionaries were Franciscan, with a scattering of Dominicans."[14] Searching to convert people from other

---

[12] Nieuwenhove, 262.

[13] Paul R. Spickard and Kevin M. Cragg, *A Global History of Christians* (Baker, 1994), 138.

[14] Samuel Hugh Moffett, *A History of Christianity in Asia*, vol. 1 (Orbis, 1998), 407.

religions, the Western missionaries encountered their Nestorian cousins, largely in the Turko-Mongolian tribal people known as the Keraits: "In the early twelfth century the Keraits, who numbered about 200,000, began to convert to Nestorian Christianity, and by the thirteenth century were virtually entirely Christian."[15] The Mongols were a particularly accepting people of the Christian faith brought to them from the West.[16] In fourteenth-century Asia, as Daniel Bays argues, "both varieties of Christianity persevered, but without signal success."[17]

Africa

While North Africa had served as one of the epicenters of early Christianity, the Islamic world all but eradicated Christian practice and presence in North Africa by the eighth century, save the church in Ethiopia. The rise and fall of the church in Egypt and Ethiopia during the early to high Middle Ages is disputed, but the social, economic, and religious tensions brought on by the rise of Islam are undeniable. Concerning the state of the African church during this time, Mark Shaw notes that "African Christianity was by no means in universal retreat. Nubian Christianity grew for much of the middle period until its demise in the fifteenth century. Ethiopia underwent several cycles of renewal and emerged from the Middle Ages as the most vital of all the expressions of African Christianity."[18] Regarding the Nubian Kingdom, which stretched roughly from Egypt down to northern Sudan, Shaw also notes that Christianity was described by Arab observers as "still strong" in the 1360s.[19]

Christianity came to sub-Saharan Africa in the fifteenth century with the settlement of the Portuguese, with Dutch Christians following less than two centuries later. The Christian faith found some familiar parallels with various African religious practices, such as appreciation for creation, belief in the spiritual realm, and the notion of sacrifice. But there were also cultural contrasts, such as polygamy, which was commonplace in much of African culture. Such contrasts gave opportunity for Christians to promote and model the way of Christ in new cultural settings.

---

[15] Daniel H. Bays, *A New History of China* (Wiley-Blackwell, 2011), 12.

[16] Edward L. Smither, *Christian Misson: A Concise, Global History* (Lexham, 2019), 66.

[17] Bays, *New History of China*, 13.

[18] Mark Shaw, *The Kingdom of God in Africa: A Short History of African Christianity* (Baker, 1997), 81.

[19] Shaw, *Kingdom of God*, 96.

Balto-Slavic Region

The early history of the Baltics is notoriously difficult due to the lack of records before the sixth century. The Balto-Slavic region is characterized by its geographical location in central to eastern Europe, as well as by languages originating in the Indo-European family. This region begins with the Czech Republic, moving east through Ukraine into Russia as far east as Siberia, though Austria, Hungary, and Romania are not included due to different language families.

Concerning the Slavic regions in the Middle Ages, A. P. Vlasto argues that the development of the Slavic regions in the Middle Ages occurred due to pressure from either the West or East, as directed by the stronger civilizations from either side. He writes, "Each Slav people had to opt or accept either Eastern or Western Christianity; only Russia perhaps was exposed to the remoter possibility of being drawn into the Islamic world."[20]

It is clear that at least by the ninth century there was a Christian presence in the Balkans. The first major mission effort to the region was carried out by the brothers Cyril and Methodius to the Slavs in 863, who subsequently created the Cyrillic script and used it to translate the Bible. The ensuing centuries were characterized by a struggle of religious sway between the Western church, the Eastern church, and the Slavic and Russian peoples. The Eastern influence in Constantinople and the Western influence from Rome vied for influence in the Balkans. One example of the tension felt in the Balkans was the king of Serbia, Stefan, in the early thirteenth century. While the pope in the West had crowned him king, Stefan's brother, Sava, worked to strengthen the ties of Serbia with the church in the East. The Balkan people were not always content with far-away authorities, however. While the strongest influence in the Balkans was from the Eastern church in the fourteenth century, "Constantinople struggled with the growing power of the Slavic kingdoms and their drive for political and religious autonomy."[21]

Another characteristic of late medieval Christianity in the Balkans, especially in Russia, was danger and constant pressure from Mongolian invaders. And this was shared with their Christian counterparts in Asia. The Russian prince Alexander Nevsky struck a deal with the Mongolians and in doing so "is credited with preserving and uniting much of

---

[20] A. P. Vlasto, *The Entry of the Slavs into Christendom: An Introduction to the Medieval History of the Slavs* (Cambridge University Press, 1970), 314.

[21] Stephen Backhouse, *Essential Companion to Christian History* (Zondervan, 2019), 126.

Russian culture that otherwise would have been decimated."[22] This culture was largely represented by the church. Nevsky also defeated invaders from the West, preserving the influence of Eastern Christianity in greater Russia. These years served as a time of resurgence for Orthodoxy, especially under the leadership of Kirill III, and as Backhouse notes, "the institution of the church grew in wealth and power."[23]

It is difficult to number the Christian population of this region during the medieval centuries, though there is ample evidence of an ever-growing Christian imagination across the centuries, complete with symbols and recognition of saints.[24]

Black Death

The Black Death, also known as the Bubonic Plague, killed between 25 million people in Europe between 1348 and 1351 as it moved south to north, taking the lives of some 30 percent of the entire continent of Europe by moderate to low estimates.[25] The devastation was simply unimaginable.

While plagues were not new to human history (for example, in the Roman Empire from 165 to 180), the Black Plague of the fourteenth century was particularly significant both for its sheer impact by number of deaths in Europe and because of Europe's economic, intellectual, and imperial prominence at that point in world history. The plague is believed to have originated in Asia and then travelled into Europe by ship from Russia or the Middle East, spreading from rodents (likely from fleas on the rodents) to humans.

Well before germ theory and the rise of modern medicine, the general populace interpreted the phenomenon of disease in various ways. Concerning how Christians responded, Rodney Stark urges that church attendance was low in medieval times before the Plague, even in Italy. Thus, he suggests that the "only reliable evidence of a widespread religious reaction to the Black Death concerns an intense, if somewhat grotesque, deepening of faith."[26]

The Plague also inspired writers from Petrarch to Boccaccio to describe the conditions as they experienced them. Joseph Lynch argues that the population boom of the

[22] Backhouse, *Essential Companion*, 117.

[23] Backhouse, 118.

[24] Jean W. Sedlar, *East Central Europe in the Middle Ages, 1000–1500: A History of East Central Europe* (University of Washington Press, 1994), 140–96.

[25] Rodney Stark, *How the West Won* (ISI, 2014), 149.

[26] Stark, *How the West Won*, 150.

high Middle Ages placed great strain on the social and economic infrastructure. He writes that "the imbalance between land and people had begun in the thirteenth century, but the signs of distress were increasingly visible around 1300, including more frequent and severe famines."[27] Lynch references Thomas Malthus's well-known description of the 1330s and 1340s in Europe as general misery for the poor, resulting in a "Malthusian crisis" for that period due to the imbalance of food and opportunity relative to the population. This crisis, Lynch argues, "was resolved brutally in a short time by an epidemic disease to which Europeans had little resistance."[28] The population levels lost in the fourteenth century were not regained for some two hundred years.

Jewish-Christian Relations

Many questioned why the Plague struck in the first place. While various answers were given, one response was to blame the Jews; this only served to deepen the already broad divide between Jews and Christians of the medieval era.

Christians generally did not trust Jews. Since before the Crusades began in the late eleventh century, cultural attitudes toward Jews in the West were generally negative. Many believed the Jews colluded with the Muslims in Jerusalem in 1009 to destroy the Holy Sepulcher. The Crusades exacerbated this already adversarial view of the Jews, which was further complicated by the fact that Jews were common among the financial lenders of the time. It was also commonly believed that Jews practiced ritual killings of Christian children, sometimes referred to as "blood libel." While untrue, such myths lived on in the Western imagination for centuries, perhaps sustained in part by popular literature, such as Geoffrey Chaucer's "The Prioress's Tale," promoting distrust and often provoking violence against Jews. As rumors about Jewish beliefs and behavior abounded, the Fourth Lateran Council of 1215 declared that both Jews and Muslims were required to wear clothing that distinguished them from other citizens. They were also forbidden from recruiting converts to their faiths.[29]

---

[27] Joseph H. Lynch, *The Medieval Church: A Brief History* (Longman, 1992), 305.

[28] Lynch, *Medieval Church*, 306. This is not to affirm Malthus's broader thesis of natural "checks" by nature to control population growth. Rather, this simply acknowledges the economic effect of the Plague on the strained European economy of the time.

[29] Everett Ferguson, *Church History*, vol. 1, *From Christ to Pre-Reformation* (Zondervan, 2005), 511–12.

As the Black Death swept across the continent in the mid-fourteenth century, suspicion turned against the Jews. Rumors of Jews poisoning the wells with the Plague took hold, beginning in Spain. Isolated incidents of violence broke out but were quickly rebutted by Pope Clement VI, who decried the rumors and insisted that bishops urge their priests and people to not act in violence against the Jews lest they be excommunicated. Still, some 20,000 Jews may have been killed in total due to these false accusations, especially in areas where anti-Semitism had persisted since the beginning of the Crusades.[30]

Recommended Reading

Backhouse, Stephen. *Essential Companion to Christian History*. Zondervan, 2019.

Bays, Daniel H. *A New History of Christianity in China*. Wiley Blackwell, 2011.

Brown, Colin. *Christianity and Western Thought*. Vol. 1. InterVarsity, 1990.

Evans, G. R. *Faith in the Medieval World*. InterVarsity, 2002.

Lynch, Joseph H. *The Medieval Church: A Brief History*. Longman, 1992.

Moffett, Samuel Hugh. *A History of Christianity in Asia*. Vol. 1. Orbis, 1998.

Sedlar, Jean. *East Central Europe in the Middle Ages, 1000–1500: A History of East Central Europe*. University of Washington Press, 1994.

Shaw, Mark. *The Kingdom of God in Africa: A Short History of African Christianity*. Baker, 1997.

Smither, Edward L. *Christian Mission: A Concise, Global History*. Lexham, 2019.

Spickard, Paul R., and Kevin M. Cragg. *A Global History of Christians*. Baker, 1994.

Stark, Rodney. *How the West Won*. ISI, 2014.

Van Nieuwenhove, Rik. *An Introduction to Medieval Theology*. Cambridge University Press, 2012.

Vlasto, A. P. *The Entry of the Slavs into Christendom: An Introduction to the Medieval History of the Slavs*. Cambridge University Press, 1970.

---

[30] Stark, *How the West Won*, 152.

—— Chapter 22 ——

The Great Western Schism

Following the split between the Eastern and Western churches in 1054, the papacy in the West established itself with considerable temporal power. Besides marshaling armies throughout medieval Europe, the Roman church exerted influence over the Holy Roman emperor, established universities and other schools to consolidate intellectual power, and employed legions of monastic orders to help extend power throughout the Christian West. The papacy would eventually triumph over conciliarism, giving the bishop of Rome unrivaled power in church and politics. Kings and princes would find themselves in submission to the church while attempting to share power with it.

The Great Western Schism, also known as the Papal Schism or the Western Schism, was a tumultuous period in medieval Christianity marked by the divide of the Catholic church into two or even three rival papal claimants. It lasted from 1378 to 1417, resulting in confusion, discord, and political turmoil within the church and throughout Europe. Rival popes and antipopes were elected, each claiming legitimacy and authority over the Catholic church. This fractured the unity of the church, led to schisms within local communities, and undermined the credibility and moral authority of the papacy as the supreme spiritual authority in Western Christendom. The division also exacerbated existing political tensions, as secular rulers often aligned themselves with one pope or another, further complicating matters.

Political, Religious, and Ecclesiastical Climate in Medieval Europe

The context of the Great Western Schism is multifaceted, encompassing the political, religious, and ecclesiastical dynamics that shaped medieval Europe. At the heart of this context was the intricate interplay between secular power and spiritual authority and the time's broader social and cultural landscape. Politically, Europe in the late Middle Ages was fragmented and decentralized, with competing kingdoms, principalities, and city-states vying for power and influence. This fragmentation extended to the church, where the papacy wielded considerable political authority alongside secular rulers. The rivalry between European powers often spilled into ecclesiastical affairs as kings and princes sought to influence papal elections and appointments to further their interests. Religiously, medieval Europe was dominated by Catholic Christianity, with the church serving as the primary institution of spiritual and moral guidance. However, the church was not immune to internal tensions and disputes. The Great Western Schism occurred against a background of theological debates, religious fervor, and challenges to ecclesiastical authority. Issues such as clerical corruption, theological dissent, and the role of the laity in church governance simmered beneath the surface, contributing to a climate of uncertainty and unrest.

Ecclesiastically, the papacy was the focal point of religious authority, with the pope regarded as the supreme head of the church among Roman Catholics. However, the papacy faced challenges to its authority from within and without. The Avignon papacy, during which the papal court was relocated to Avignon, France, had already weakened its prestige and raised questions about its independence from secular influence. The papacy's return to Rome under Gregory XI did little to resolve these underlying tensions, setting the stage for a great division in the Western church, shaping the course of both ecclesiastical and secular history in medieval Europe.

Background and Causes of the Great Western Schism

The Avignon papacy, also known as the "Babylonian captivity of the church," refers to the period from 1309 to 1377 when the papal seat was located in Avignon, France, rather than Rome. This relocation was initiated by Pope Clement V, who was heavily influenced by the French monarchy, particularly King Philip IV of France. The Avignon papacy marked a departure from the traditional seat of the papacy in Rome and raised concerns about the independence and integrity of the papal office.

The move to Avignon also raised concerns about the influence of the French monarchy over the papacy. The relocation of the papal seat was seen as a concession to French influence, leading to accusations of undue political interference in ecclesiastical affairs. King Philip IV of France exerted pressure on the papacy, seeking to control papal elections and appointments to further his political agenda. The Avignon papacy was characterized by a close relationship between the papacy and the French monarchy, with successive popes often aligning with French interests. This close association eroded the perceived independence and impartiality of the papacy, undermining its spiritual authority and legitimacy in the eyes of many. However, despite the apparent closeness of their relationship, tension remained between the ecclesiastical and secular authorities.

The conflict between the papacy and the French monarchy during the Avignon papacy era was primarily rooted in the struggle for power and influence over ecclesiastical affairs. The French monarchy, particularly under King Philip IV of France, sought to assert control over the church within its territories, using various means to manipulate papal elections and appointments to advance its political interests.

King Philip IV also levied heavy taxes on the clergy and church property within France, seeking to bolster royal revenues and fund his military campaigns. However, the papacy resisted these attempts, asserting its right to manage ecclesiastical finances independently of secular authorities. This resistance led to clashes between the papacy and the French monarchy, as the latter sought to assert its control over church wealth and resources.

Papal elections leading up to the Great Western Schism were marked by allegations of simony, contributing to the erosion of trust in the papal office, and exacerbating tensions within the church. Simony, the buying or selling of ecclesiastical offices, was a particularly contentious issue, as it undermined the spiritual integrity of the church and raised concerns about the legitimacy of papal authority.

One of the primary manifestations of simony in papal elections was the influence of secular rulers and powerful noble families in determining the outcome of the election. Kings, emperors, and princes often sought to manipulate papal elections to install candidates favorable to their interests, offering bribes or exerting pressure on cardinals to secure their support. This practice compromised the independence and impartiality of the papal election process, leading to accusations of undue political interference and corruption.

Moreover, the growing influence of wealthy Italian families, such as the Colonna and Orsini, further complicated papal elections, as these factions vied for control over the papacy and sought to advance their agendas within the church. The rivalry between these factions often degenerated into open conflict, with armed clashes occurring within Rome during papal elections.

The allegations of corruption and simony surrounding papal elections laid the groundwork for the schism that would divide the church in the late fourteenth and early twentieth centuries. The perceived illegitimacy of certain popes and the rival claims to the papal throne further destabilized the church and contributed to a crisis of authority that would take decades to resolve.

Pope Gregory XI and the Return of the Papacy to Rome

Pope Gregory XI's return to Rome in 1377 marked the end of the Avignon papacy. Gregory XI (r. 1370–78), the last of the Avignon popes, decided to relocate the papal court to Rome in response to growing calls for the papacy to return to its traditional seat and amid increasing political and spiritual pressures.

The Avignon papacy had come under criticism for its perceived subservience to French interests and its distance from the historical and spiritual center of Christendom in Rome. Gregory XI's predecessors had considered returning to Rome but were deterred by the political instability in Italy, particularly the factional conflicts within the city of Rome and the broader challenges posed by the Italian city-states.

Gregory's decision was influenced by several factors. The spiritual pressure came from figures like Catherine of Siena, a Dominican mystic and influential reformer, who urged Gregory to return to Rome to restore the credibility and unity of the church. Catherine, in her letters and personal visits, emphasized the importance of the pope's presence in Rome for the spiritual renewal of Christendom and for reasserting the papacy's universal authority. Gregory was also influenced by Bridget of Sweden, another prominent mystic, who had similarly called for the papal return.

Political concerns also played a role. The Papal States, under nominal papal control, had become increasingly unstable, with various local rulers asserting independence and resistance to papal authority. Gregory XI hoped that his presence in Rome would help stabilize the situation and reestablish papal governance over the region.

The return was not without its challenges. Gregory XI left Avignon in September 1376 and arrived in Rome in January 1377. His journey was marked by hesitation, as he faced the prospect of navigating a politically volatile and divided Rome. The city itself was in a state of disrepair and factional strife, reflecting years of neglect during the papacy's absence. Gregory was also aware of the risks to his personal safety and the potential for failure in reestablishing papal authority.

Despite these challenges, Gregory XI's return to Rome was a significant moment in church history, symbolizing the restoration of the papacy to its traditional seat. However, his efforts to stabilize the church and the Papal States were short-lived. Gregory died in March 1378, only a year after his return, leaving the church on the verge of the Western Schism (1378–1417), a period of division in which multiple claimants to the papacy competed for legitimacy.

Urban VI and Election Controversy

Following Gregory's death, Urban VI (1318–89) was elected pope in 1378. Urban became pope during a period of extreme conflict among the cardinals. His election was initially met with enthusiasm, as he was seen as a reformer who would address the corruption and abuses that had plagued the papacy in previous years. However, his behavior quickly soured relations with the College of Cardinals and other influential figures within the church. Urban's fiery temper, arbitrary decision-making, and harsh treatment of dissenters led to widespread disillusionment and resentment among the clergy.

This disillusionment led to a revaluation of the election of Urban VI and sparked a bitter dispute over the legitimacy of his papacy. Rumors circulated, questioning the validity of the conclave that had chosen him as pope. Some cardinals alleged that they had been coerced or intimidated into voting for Urban and argued that the election was, therefore, invalid. This dispute over the legitimacy of Urban's papacy would ultimately lead to a schism within the church.

As pope, Urban sought to root out corruption within the church, reflecting his commitment to reform and moral rigor. However, these efforts, while earnest, were often undermined by his abrasive personality and authoritarian methods, which alienated many clergy and political allies. His reform initiatives were particularly aimed at addressing the excesses of the papal court, the lifestyle of the clergy, and the widespread nepotism and simony that had eroded the church's moral credibility.

Urban VI sought to eliminate the perceived decadence and corruption of the papal court, which had been criticized for its opulence and inefficiency. He took steps to curtail the extravagant lifestyles of cardinals and high-ranking officials, calling for simplicity, austerity, and greater devotion to spiritual duties. Urban demanded that cardinals reside in their dioceses and actively engage in pastoral care rather than enjoying the privileges and wealth associated with their positions in the hierarchy.

Urban VI was outspoken in his condemnation of nepotism, a practice that had flourished during the Avignon papacy and earlier periods. Nepotism often resulted in the appointment of unqualified relatives of church officials to lucrative positions, undermining the effectiveness of ecclesiastical governance. Urban's opposition to nepotism extended to his own administration, as he sought to distance himself from practices that prioritized family connections over merit and piety.

Urban VI called for moral reform among the clergy, emphasizing the importance of piety, discipline, and pastoral care. He condemned lax behavior among priests and bishops, insisting on higher standards of conduct. His efforts aimed to restore the clergy's reputation and renew the church's spiritual mission in the face of widespread public disillusionment with clerical corruption.

Urban's harsh and uncompromising methods provoked significant backlash. His confrontational style alienated many cardinals, leading to the election of Clement VII in Avignon and the beginning of the Great Western Schism (1378–1417). Urban's efforts to enforce discipline were often seen as excessively severe, and his lack of diplomatic finesse created divisions that weakened the effectiveness of his reforms.

Election of Clement VII and Division Within the Church

In September 1378, a group of dissident cardinals declared Urban's election invalid, claiming it had been made under duress, and convened at Fondi, a town outside Rome. There, they elected Robert of Geneva as pope, who took the name Clement VII. Clement was an experienced churchman and a former bishop with a reputation for decisive action. His election was intended to depose Urban and restore unity, but instead, it created a dual papacy. Clement established his court in Avignon, reactivating the Avignon papacy, while Urban remained in Rome, with both claiming legitimacy.

Upon his election, Clement VII initially sought to assert his authority and legitimacy as pope by appealing to the Catholic faithful and rallying support from European monarchs.

This move was intended to distance Clement from the tumultuous atmosphere in Rome and strengthen his position as the rightful successor to the papal throne. However, despite his efforts to consolidate his position and maintain unity within the church, Clement VII faced numerous obstacles during his pontificate. He struggled to assert his authority over the Avignon papacy while also seeking to reconcile with the supporters of Urban VI, who refused to acknowledge his legitimacy. Additionally, Clement's attempts to broker a resolution to the schism through diplomatic means were largely unsuccessful, further exacerbating the divisions within the church.

Clement VII's papacy in Avignon received support primarily from France and its allies, while Urban VI's papacy in Rome garnered backing from other European powers, particularly those outside the French sphere of influence. The schism led to political and diplomatic tensions between the factions supporting the rival popes, further complicating efforts to resolve the crisis.

Consequences and Effects of the Schism

The uncertainty surrounding the papal legitimacy raised theological and spiritual concerns. Questions arose about the validity of sacraments administered by priests aligned with one pope or the other. For example, were marriages conducted by a priest loyal to Clement VII valid in the eyes of Urban VI, and vice versa? This uncertainty caused anxiety and distress among believers, who feared the spiritual consequences of aligning with the "wrong" pope. The schism led to the emergence of factions within Christendom, with different regions and groups pledging allegiance to various popes based on political, national, or personal loyalties. This fractured the unity of the church along geographic and ideological lines, as bishops, clergy, and laypeople took sides in the dispute. This internal division weakened the church's fabric and hindered reconciliation and unity efforts. The spectacle of rival popes anathematizing each other as antipopes undermined the authority and prestige of the papacy itself. Traditionally viewed as the supreme spiritual authority in Christendom, the papal office lost credibility as its leaders engaged in bitter power struggles and mutual denunciations. This erosion of papal authority contributed to a broader crisis of faith and identity within the church.

The schism had far-reaching implications for the unity of Christianity in Europe. The split within the church not only fostered division and discord among Christians but also fueled political and social unrest across Europe. The inability of the church to resolve its internal disputes undermined its moral authority and weakened its ability to mediate conflicts and promote peace. The fragmentation of Christianity into rival camps cut the sense of shared identity and purpose among believers, hindering efforts to foster a unified Christian community.

Furthermore, the schism highlighted the church's theological and institutional challenges. Questions surrounding papal authority, conciliarism, and the nature of church governance came to the fore, sparking debates reverberating throughout the remainder of the Middle Ages and beyond. The crisis of the schism forced the church to confront issues of accountability, transparency, and legitimacy, prompting calls for reform and renewal within the ecclesiastical hierarchy.

Council of Pisa (1409) and Failed Attempts at Resolution

The Council of Pisa (1409) was an attempt to resolve the Great Western Schism. During the divide, two lines of popes existed, one centered in Rome and the other in Avignon. In the early fifteenth century, Gregory XII represented the Roman papacy, while Benedict XIII occupied the Avignon throne. Efforts to negotiate an end to the division, including proposed resignations by both popes or arbitration by a council, consistently failed. Both Gregory XII and Benedict XIII clung stubbornly to their claims, prioritizing their legitimacy over the unity of the church. The inability of either camp to resolve the schism bred disillusionment among clergy, laity, and secular rulers, undermining the credibility of the papacy and fostering broader calls for reform.

This climate of frustration and urgency gave rise to the conciliarist movement, which argued that a general council of the church could act with supreme authority in times of crisis, even overriding the authority of the pope. Key figures, such as Pierre d'Ailly and Jean Gerson, theologians from the University of Paris, were prominent proponents of conciliarism. They contended that the unity of the church was paramount and that extraordinary measures were necessary to restore its spiritual and administrative coherence. The movement drew on theological and canonical precedents, including the idea that councils had historically been used to address heresies and disputes, as seen in the early ecumenical councils.

In this context, a group of disaffected cardinals from both Rome and Avignon took matters into their own hands. Gathering in Livorno in 1408, they declared their intention to convene an independent general council at Pisa to resolve the schism. Their plan was bold: to depose both Gregory XII and Benedict XIII as illegitimate claimants and elect a new pope who would be universally recognized. By bypassing the entrenched papal lines, these cardinals sought to assert the church's collective authority over its leadership, embodying the principles of conciliarism. The initiative reflected growing dissatisfaction with papal intransigence and a widespread belief that the institutional integrity of the church was at stake.

The stakes for the Council of Pisa were immense, not only for the church but for Christendom as a whole. The schism had fractured religious unity, with devastating consequences for governance, diplomacy, and the spiritual life of the faithful. Secular rulers, including the kings of France and England and the Holy Roman emperor, played significant roles in supporting or opposing the rival papal factions, further entangling the church's crisis with the political conflicts of the time, such as the Hundred Years' War. The council's organizers hoped that resolving the schism would restore the church's moral authority, reestablish its administrative coherence, and heal the divisions that had plagued Christendom for over three decades.

Despite these lofty aims, the Council of Pisa faced significant challenges. Both Gregory XII and Benedict XIII refused to recognize its legitimacy, denouncing the gathering as an unlawful assembly. Furthermore, while many clergy and secular leaders supported the idea of a council, the question of whether it could override papal authority remained contentious. The council convened in March 1409, attracting widespread attendance from across Europe, but its ultimate decisions—deposing both Gregory and Benedict and electing Alexander V as pope—would paradoxically deepen the schism by creating a third papal claimant.

The Council of Pisa's failure underscored the schism's complexity and inherent challenges in achieving reconciliation among the rival factions. It highlighted the deep-seated disagreements and divisions within the church and the political interests and ambitions that perpetuated the conflict. Ultimately, the council's inability to resolve the schism set the stage for further efforts at reconciliation and the eventual resolution of the crisis through the Council of Constance.

Council of Constance (1414–18) and Deposition of Multiple Claimants

Five years after the failure of the Council of Pisa, bishops at the Council of Constance convened in an effort to achieve unity and resolve the papal crisis. At this time there were three rivals who all claimed to be the rightful pope: Gregory XII in Rome, Benedict XIII in Avignon, and John XXIII, who had replaced Alexander V, the man elected at the Council of Pisa in 1409. The primary goal of the Council of Constance was to heal the schism by securing the resignation or deposition of the existing claimants and electing a single, universally recognized pope. The council brought together a diverse assembly of ecclesiastical dignitaries, including bishops, abbots, theologians, and representatives of secular powers. Notable attendees included the Holy Roman emperor Sigismund (1368–1437), who was crucial in facilitating the council's proceedings, and delegates from across Europe.

The Council of Constance achieved its primary objective by deposing all three claimants to the papal throne—Gregory XII, Benedict XIII, and John XXIII. Through skillful diplomacy and political maneuvering, Emperor Sigismund helped secure the resignations of Gregory XII and Benedict XIII, while John XXIII was deposed for various charges, including simony and immorality. Subsequently, the council elected Pope Martin V, who was universally recognized as the legitimate pope and selected Rome as the rightful seat of the papacy.

Election of Martin V and Restoration of Papal Unity

Upon his election, Martin V accepted the papal office and was ceremonially enthroned as the bishop of Rome, signaling the end of the Great Western Schism and the restoration of papal unity within the Catholic Church. As Martin V assumed the papal office, he faced numerous challenges in consolidating his authority and restoring order to the church. He worked diligently to address the lingering effects of the schism, reconcile factions within the clergy, and implement reforms to strengthen ecclesiastical governance. Despite the formidable obstacles he encountered, Martin V's leadership helped stabilize the papacy and fostered a renewed sense of unity and purpose within the church. The election of Martin V and the subsequent restoration of papal unity represented a watershed moment in the history of the Catholic Church. Martin V's pontificate began a new era of stability and continuity within the papacy, laying the groundwork for the church's resurgence and reaffirming its central role in medieval European society.

Theological and Ecclesiastical Implications

The Great Western Schism, with its rival papal claimants and confusion among Christians, prompted theologians and church leaders to reassess the sources and exercise of ecclesiastical authority. As we have seen, conciliarism emerged as a pragmatic solution to the crisis, offering a mechanism for resolving disputes and effectuating reforms within the church. According to conciliarists, ecumenical councils held supreme authority within the church, superior even to the papacy. They argued that councils, representing the collective wisdom and discernment of the church, could depose or elect popes, enact doctrinal reforms, and address matters of ecclesiastical discipline.

Conciliarists contended that councils, as manifestations of the church's universality and unity, held the divine mandate to guide and govern the church, particularly in times of crisis or doctrinal dispute. This challenged the traditional understanding of papal primacy and raised questions about the limits of papal authority. The Council of Constance (1414–18) represented the apex of the conciliarist movement. Convened to address the Great Western Schism and effectuate reforms within the church, the council asserted its authority to depose the rival claimants to the papal throne and elect a new pope. The election of Pope Martin V under the auspices of the council reaffirmed the conciliarist principle that ecumenical councils possess supreme authority in matters of faith and discipline.

While conciliarism enjoyed a resurgence during the schism era, its influence waned in subsequent centuries. Opposition from popes, particularly during the Renaissance and Counter-Reformation periods, contributed to its decline. However, the conciliarist legacy endured as a reminder of the church's capacity for self-correction and reform. Moreover, the conciliarist emphasis on the authority of councils contributed to ongoing debates over the nature of ecclesiastical authority and the proper balance of power within the Catholic church.

Reflections on the Authority and Unity of the Papacy

Following the Great Western Schism, reflections on the role of the papacy emphasized the need for a strong and authoritative pontiff to preserve the unity and cohesion of the church, but the schism era also prompted reflections on the need for reform and renewal within the papacy itself. The abuses and corruption exposed during the schism highlighted the importance of moral integrity, transparency, and accountability in papal leadership. Efforts were made to address these issues through institutional reforms, disciplinary measures, and a renewed commitment to ethical governance.

The schism era also sparked debates over the balance of power between the papacy and ecumenical councils. The conciliarist movement, which advocated for greater authority for general councils of the church, emerged as a response to the perceived abuses of papal power during the schism and led to a reevaluation of the proper relationship between papal primacy and conciliar authority within the church's governance structure. Reflections on the papacy's role also encompassed the church's mission of evangelization and outreach to the world. The pope was viewed as the universal pastor of the church, charged with leading Christians in spreading the gospel message to all nations. Ultimately, the resolution of the Great Western Schism served to emphasize a new perspective of the papacy which highlighted its role in promoting unity, defending truth, and advancing the church's mission of salvation.

Recommended Reading

Barraclough, Geoffrey. *The Medieval Papacy*. Thames and Hudson, 1968.

Broderick, James. *The Avignon Papacy: The Popes in Exile, 1305–1378*. Harper, 1970.

Duffy, Eamon. *Saints and Sinners: A History of the Popes*. 4th ed. Yale University Press, 2014.

Gerson, Jean. *On Church Unity: A Fifteenth-Century View of the Great Schism*. Edited by Robert E. McNally. Cistercian, 1998.

Grant, Raymond E. *The Politics of Papal Elections: Reform, Rebellion, and the Great Schism of 1378*. Cambridge University Press, 2011.

Housley, Norman. *Avignon: An Historical Guide*. Sutton, 2000.

Kaminsky, Howard. *The Great Schism of the West*. Holt, Rinehart, and Winston, 1967.

Renouard, Yves. *The Avignon Papacy, 1305–1403*. Translated by Denis Bethell. Archon, 1970.

Rollo-Koster, Joëlle. *Avignon and Its Papacy, 1309–1417: Popes, Institutions, and Society*. Rowman & Littlefield, 2015.

Tierney, Brian. *Foundations of the Conciliar Theory: The Contribution of the Medieval Canonists from Gratian to the Great Schism*. Brill, 1998.

Ullmann, Walter. *The Origins of the Great Schism: A Study in Fourteenth-Century Ecclesiastical History*. Methuen, 1948.

Chapter 23

The Road to the European Reformations

As we saw in the pervious chapter, the church of the late Middle Ages (AD 1300–1500) endured a period of political, social, and religious upheaval. The church itself suffered from widespread corruption when church leaders—from priests to bishops—adopted worldly lifestyles exploiting the people for selfish gain. The chaos and corruption in the church was fertile ground for dissent and reformist ideas to take root. Against ecclesiastical corruption, clerical abuses, and theological controversies, some notable figures sought to address perceived problems in the church. In addition to prominent figures like John Wycliffe (1328–84) and Jan Hus (1370–1415), other leaders emerged as outspoken critics of the church's hierarchy and practices. Their writings, sermons, and advocacy for reform challenged prevailing orthodoxy and inspired a wave of dissent that would shape the course of European Christianity. To lesser or greater degrees, these early reformers sought to promote Scripture and liturgy in the common language, advocated for lay participation in religious life, and confronted ecclesiastical corruption and excess.

The rise of nationalism challenged the universal claims of the church, which sought to assert its authority over all Christians regardless of nationality. As nations increasingly asserted their sovereignty and independence, they resisted external interference in their internal affairs, including religious matters. This tension between national autonomy and ecclesiastical authority led to conflicts between secular rulers and the church hierarchy and debates over the proper relationship between church and state.

The development of universities played a pivotal role in fostering intellectual inquiry and challenging established doctrines within the church. As centers of learning and scholarship, universities became hubs for exchanging ideas, studying classical texts, and developing new Scholastic philosophies that encouraged critical thinking and questioning traditional beliefs. The late medieval period witnessed the establishment and proliferation of universities across Europe, including notable institutions, such as the University of Paris (founded 1150), Oxford University (founded 1096), and the University of Bologna (founded 1088). These universities emerged as independent institutions of higher learning, providing education in various disciplines, including theology, philosophy, law, medicine, and the natural sciences. The university curriculum emphasized the study of classical texts, logic, rhetoric, and dialectics, laying the foundation for intellectual inquiry and debate. The University of Paris, in particular, became a center of theological controversy and debate, with scholars discussing the nature of God, the relationship between faith and reason, and the authority of church and state. The growth of universities and the spread of Scholasticism (see chapter 21) encouraged scholars to question established doctrines and challenge traditional beliefs within the church.

John Wycliffe: Morning Star of the Reformation (c. 1330s–1384)

Intellectuals such as John Wycliffe and William of Ockham critiqued the papacy's authority, questioned the church's infallibility, and advocated for theological reform based on scriptural authority. John Wycliffe, often hailed as the "Morning Star of the Reformation," was born in the early 1330s in Yorkshire, England. He received his education at Oxford University, where he excelled in his studies and earned a reputation as a brilliant scholar. While at Oxford, Wycliffe's intellectual curiosity led him to engage deeply with theological and philosophical questions. He became known for his sharp intellect, keen insights, and commitment to rigorous academic inquiry. His academic prowess earned him prestigious positions within the university hierarchy, eventually leading to his appointment as master of Balliol College, Oxford, in 1361. As a theologian and philosopher, Wycliffe delved into various areas of inquiry, including metaphysics, ethics, and political theory. His academic pursuits brought him into contact with the writings of prominent medieval thinkers, such as Thomas Aquinas and William of Ockham, whose ideas would influence his theological development.

Throughout his career at Oxford, Wycliffe's scholarly interests increasingly turned toward ecclesiastical reform and the study of Scripture. He became increasingly critical of the medieval Catholic Church, particularly its hierarchical structure, doctrinal teachings, and perceived moral corruption. Wycliffe's academic career laid the foundation for his later role as a reformer and biblical translator. His deep knowledge of theology and philosophy, coupled with his commitment to academic rigor and intellectual honesty, would shape his contributions to medieval England's religious and intellectual landscape.

Wycliffe challenged the authority of the medieval Roman Catholic Church, laying the groundwork for future reform efforts. He criticized the hierarchical structure of the Catholic Church, arguing that it had strayed from the simplicity and purity of the early Christian church. He advocated for a return to apostolic poverty and a rejection of the wealth and temporal power wielded by the clergy. Wycliffe called for abolishing papal authority, eliminating clerical wealth and privilege, and restoring simplicity and purity to Christian worship and life. He believed that the church had strayed from its original mission and needed reform according to the teachings of Scripture. Wycliffe questioned the efficacy of certain sacraments, particularly those administered by corrupt clergy. He rejected the doctrine of transubstantiation, instead advocating for a symbolic interpretation of the Eucharist.

Regarding ecclesiastical corruption, Wycliffe denounced the accumulation of wealth and material possessions by the clergy, particularly higher-ranking church officials, such as bishops and cardinals. He saw their opulent lifestyles as incompatible with the teachings of Jesus Christ, who preached simplicity and humility. Wycliffe argued that the church's pursuit of temporal power and riches had led to a departure from its spiritual mission. In his work, *On the Prelates*, he excoriates the religious leaders of his day, whom he calls "Antichrists, forbidding Christian men to know their belief, and to speak of Holy Writ. For they say openly that secular men should not intermeddle themselves with the Gospel to read it in the mother tongue, but attend to a holy father's preaching." Wycliffe says this practice of the Roman Catholic Church is

> We should believe that no pope is necessary by Christ's ordering, but has been introduced by the Devil. Given this, the faithful have no other such authority in the church militant through Scripture's law, save the bishop of souls who is above in the church triumphant.
>
> ———
>
> John Wycliffe,
> *Trialogus*

expressly forbidden in the Bible because, "God commandeth generally to each layman, that he should have God's commandments before him, and teach them to his children."

Wycliffe also condemned the practice of simony, whereby ecclesiastical offices and positions were bought and sold for financial gain. He viewed simony as a form of corruption that compromised the church's leadership's integrity and undermined its ministries' sacred nature. Wycliffe believed church offices should be conferred based on merit and spiritual qualifications rather than monetary considerations.

Like later reformers, such as Martin Luther, Wycliffe criticized the sale of indulgences, whereby individuals could purchase remission from sin or punishment. He saw indulgences as a form of spiritual manipulation and exploitation, preying on the fears and ignorance of the laity. Wycliffe argued that true repentance and contrition, rather than monetary payments to the church, were necessary to forgive sins. Wycliffe referred to those who sold indulgences as a "pack of apes" and said that priests who granted indulgences were guilty of blasphemy!

Wycliffe challenged the special privileges and exemptions enjoyed by the clergy, including immunity from secular law and taxation. He believed the clergy should be subject to the same moral and legal standards as the rest of society and should not be above reproach. Wycliffe advocated for greater accountability and transparency within the church hierarchy.

Wycliffe emphasized the primacy of Scripture as the ultimate authority for Christian belief and practice. He advocated for translating the Bible into the vernacular language so that ordinary people could read and understand God's Word for themselves. This emphasis on Scripture anticipated the later Protestant principle of *sola scriptura*. John Wycliffe gathered a team of followers to help with the translation of the Bible into English. There had been prior English translations of parts of the Bible, but Wycliffe's translation was monumental and foundational for future English translations. Before Wycliffe's translation, the Bible was primarily available in Latin, accessible only to clergy and educated elites. English translations before Wycliffe were either abridgements of the Bible or translations of smaller sections. The Venerable Bede, for example, translated the Gospel of John in the eighth century. By translating the Bible into English, Wycliffe made the Scriptures accessible to a much wider audience, including laypeople who could now read and understand the Word of God in their native language. This democratization of access to Scripture was crucial in shaping vernacular Christianity. In his work *On the Truth of Holy Scripture*, Wycliffe claimed, "the certitude and authority of Scripture should be given preference over human reason." Only the Bible is "true in all of its parts."

By affording the laity direct access to the Bible in the vernacular, Wycliffe empowered the people to approach the teachings of Christianity without the need for intermediaries, such as priests or scholars. Laypeople could now read and interpret the Bible for themselves, leading to greater individual engagement with religious texts and ideas. The practice of reading Scripture helped foster a sense of personal piety and religious independence among ordinary believers.

The translation of the Bible into English contributed to the growing religious reform momentum in England and Europe. By providing an English version of Scripture, Wycliffe challenged the authority of the medieval church and its monopoly on interpreting the Word of God. His translation opened the door for contemporary and later reformers who sought to reform the church based on the authority of Scripture alone.

The widespread dissemination of the Bible in English contributed to the growth of literacy and education among the general populace. As people had access to the Bible in the vernacular, they desired education to be able to read Scripture. A positive yet unintended consequence of translating the Bible into English was to help standardize and popularize certain linguistic forms and expressions, contributing to the evolution of the English language. For example, Wycliffe found the Latin words *sexus* and *femella* in the Vulgate's edition of Genesis. He turned those terms in the new English words "sex" and "female." He also coined the English words "glory," "ministry," "contradiction," "grasp," "treasure," and others.

In addition to translating the Bible, Wycliffe encouraged using English in preaching and worship services. He believed that sermons and liturgical texts should be in the vernacular to ensure that the congregation could understand the message for its own spiritual edification. By promoting vernacular preaching and worship, Wycliffe sought to break down the linguistic barriers that separated the clergy from the laity and to foster a more direct and personal encounter with the Christian message.

John Wycliffe's Eucharistic theology and his doctrine of consubstantiation reflected his broader reform agenda and tendency to challenge prevailing doctrines within the medieval church. He offered a radical critique of the doctrine of transubstantiation, which held that the bread and wine of the Eucharist become the literal body and blood of Christ while retaining their outward appearances. Wycliffe's writings, particularly in his treatise *De Eucharistia*, reflect his belief that the church's teaching on the Eucharist was a later innovation that deviated from the simplicity of Scripture and early Christian tradition. Central to his critique was the argument that the bread and wine remain materially bread and wine while Christ is spiritually present in the sacrament. He asserted, "The bread while becoming by virtue of Christ's words the body of Christ, does not cease to be bread," highlighting his rejection of the metaphysical transformation posited by transubstantiation.

Wycliffe grounded his arguments in a literal and straightforward interpretation of Scripture, emphasizing passages such as Matt 26:26–28, where Christ institutes the Eucharist: "Take, eat; this is my body" (NIV). For Wycliffe, these words affirmed Christ's presence in the sacrament but did not necessitate a transformation of substance. Instead, he viewed the bread and wine as symbols of Christ's body and blood. He argued that this understanding was consistent with the gospel accounts and the practices of the early church. In rejecting transubstantiation, he stated, "It is impossible that the bread and wine should cease to exist while the accidents of the bread and wine remain, as this destroys the principles of natural philosophy and divine revelation." Here, Wycliffe critiqued the Aristotelian metaphysics underlying transubstantiation, asserting that it contradicted both reason and biblical teaching.

Wycliffe further condemned transubstantiation as a source of idolatry within the church. He believed that worshiping the consecrated elements as the literal body and blood of Christ led believers to venerate the physical substance rather than focusing on Christ's spiritual presence and redemptive work. He declared, "This heresy [transubstantiation] robs the Church of the reality of Christ's body and multiplies manifold idolatries." This critique reflected his broader concern with the church's reliance on elaborate rituals and theological constructs that, in his view, distracted from the simplicity of the gospel message.

Wycliffe also appealed to the practices of the early church, arguing that transubstantiation was a doctrinal innovation that lacked support in the apostolic tradition. Drawing on 1 Cor 11:23–26, where Paul recounts the institution of the Lord's Supper, Wycliffe emphasized the memorial nature of the Eucharist: "For as often as you eat this bread and drink the cup, you proclaim the Lord's death until he comes." For Wycliffe, Paul's words affirmed that the Eucharist was a spiritual act of remembrance and proclamation rather than a literal transformation of substances.

Wycliffe's critique of the Eucharist was also part of his broader call for ecclesiastical reform. He rejected the notion that the efficacy of the sacrament depended on the actions of the priest, asserting instead that "the Eucharist is made not by man's work but by Christ's words, not for display but for spiritual strengthening." This emphasis on Christ's role and the spiritual purpose of the sacrament reflected his concern with the church's focus on ritualistic practices over genuine faith and devotion.

Wycliffe's challenges to the doctrine of transubstantiation were deeply controversial and were ultimately condemned by the Catholic Church as heretical. The Council of Constance (1414–18) declared Wycliffe a heretic, and his remains were exhumed and burned in 1428 as a posthumous punishment. Despite this condemnation, his writings on the Eucharist laid the intellectual groundwork for later reformers, like Jan Hus and Martin Luther. By returning to Scripture and emphasizing the spiritual significance of the sacrament, Wycliffe contributed to a broader movement of questioning church authority and doctrine, shaping the theological debates that would emerge during the Reformation.

John Wycliffe's Political Patron

In nearly every reform effort in the Western church, ecclesiastical figures needed a political patron who offered protection, funding, or support to change the church. Wycliffe was no different. His primary political patron was John of Gaunt, the Duke of Lancaster. John of Gaunt was one of England's most powerful and influential figures during the late fourteenth and early fifteenth centuries. As King Edward III's third son and King Richard II's uncle, he held considerable political sway and wielded significant influence at court. He was sympathetic to the reformist ideas espoused by John Wycliffe and patronized and protected Wycliffe and his followers, allowing them to disseminate their teachings and writings without fear of immediate reprisal from the ecclesiastical authorities.

His support for Wycliffe was part of his broader agenda to challenge the authority of the established church and assert more control over religious and political affairs. He saw in Wycliffe's teachings an opportunity to advance his political interests and weaken the influence of the church hierarchy. John also provided financial support to Wycliffe and his followers, enabling them to produce and distribute vernacular translations of the Bible and other religious texts. This support helped spread Wycliffe's ideas among the English populace, particularly in the lower social strata. John's political influence also protected Wycliffe and his followers from persecution by the ecclesiastical authorities. While Wycliffe faced opposition and condemnation from many church officials, his association with John of Gaunt provided a measure of security that allowed him to continue his work relatively unhindered for a time. Although John of Gaunt's support for Wycliffe was not without self-interest, his patronage contributed to the dissemination of Wycliffe's ideas and the advancement of religious reform in England, and as a political ally and protector of Wycliffe, he helped shape the landscape of late medieval English Christianity and set the stage for later reform movements.

John Wycliffe's Posthumous Condemnation

The Council of Constance dealt a posthumous blow to the legacy of John Wycliffe by officially condemning his teachings as heretical. Wycliffe's ideas, which had gained traction in Bohemia and other parts of Europe, were seen as a threat to the unity and orthodoxy of the Catholic Church. The council condemned Wycliffe's teachings as heretical and ordered his works to be burned. This condemnation was largely symbolic, as Wycliffe died four decades earlier in 1384. Nevertheless, it communicated that the church rejected his theological positions and sought to suppress his influence.

Ecclesiastical authorities intended this posthumous condemnation to dishonor Wycliffe and serve as a warning to others who might dare to challenge the authority of the church. Wycliffe's remains were then purportedly burned and scattered, further emphasizing the severity of the church's judgment against him. The burning of Wycliffe's works and the exhumation of his remains were intended to suppress his influence and deter others from adopting his ideas. However, these actions had limited success in extinguishing Wycliffe's legacy. Despite the church's efforts to eradicate his teachings, Wycliffe's ideas continued to resonate, particularly among his followers, known as the Lollards, who persisted in their calls for church reform and vernacular Bible translation.

The condemnation of Wycliffe's teachings had immediate repercussions for his followers. Lollardy had been gaining momentum as a religious and social movement advocating for church reform and vernacular Bible translation. The council's actions led to increased persecution of Lollards in England, as authorities sought to stamp out what they perceived as heretical beliefs and practices. Despite the council's efforts to suppress Wycliffe's teachings, his ideas continued to resonate and inspire reform-minded individuals throughout Europe. The translation of the Bible into vernacular languages, a central aspect of Wycliffe's legacy, persisted and contributed to the spread of literacy and religious dissent.

The Lollards: Followers of Wycliffe's Reformation

The Lollards emerged as fervent adherents to the theological and ecclesiastical reforms advocated by the English theologian John Wycliffe during the late fourteenth and early fifteenth centuries. Their significance to church history lies in their role as pioneers of religious dissent, champions of vernacular Bible translation, and catalysts for the English Reformation. As advocates for reform, they embraced Wycliffe's critique of the medieval

Catholic Church's hierarchy, rituals, and doctrines. They rejected papal authority, the doctrine of transubstantiation, the veneration of saints and relics, and the sale of indulgences. Instead, they emphasized the primacy of Scripture and the priesthood of all believers, calling for a return to the simplicity and purity of early Christianity.

Central to the Lollard movement was translating the Bible into English, a groundbreaking endeavor that aimed to make the Word of God accessible to ordinary people. By translating the Scriptures into the vernacular, Lollards sought to empower individuals to read and interpret the Bible for themselves, bypassing the traditional authority of the clergy and fostering a more direct relationship with God. The Lollards' message resonated with a wide range of English society, including peasants, artisans, and members of the emerging middle class. Their advocacy for Christian charity, moral reform, and religious freedom challenged the established order and inspired calls for greater equality and accountability within both church and state. Both ecclesiastical and secular authorities persecuted the Lollards and attempted to suppress their practice of the faith. Authorities arrested, imprisoned, or executed many reform-minded Christians for their beliefs, yet their movement persisted, fueled by a deep commitment to their vision of a reformed church and society.

Jan Hus and the Hussite Movement: Continuing the Legacy of Wycliffe

Jan Hus, a seminal figure in late medieval Christianity, was influenced by the ideas and teachings of John Wycliffe. Hus rose to prominence as a priest, theologian, and reformer, advocating for church reform and challenging the authority of the Roman Catholic Church. Hus was born in Bohemia—now in the Czech Republic—around 1372. He studied at the University of Prague, where he discovered the writings of John Wycliffe and his followers. Hus distinguished himself as a scholar and became a priest in 1401.

Like Wycliffe, Hus was deeply critical of the moral and institutional corruption within the church, advocating for reforms that aligned with Wycliffe's teachings. He condemned the sale of indulgences, the wealth and worldliness of the clergy, and the excessive power wielded by the papacy. Hus also embraced Wycliffe's emphasis on the authority of Scripture and the priesthood of all believers. As a preacher at Bethlehem Chapel in Prague, Hus attracted a large following among the Bohemian people. His sermons, delivered in the vernacular, resonated with the common people, who found his message of moral renewal and religious reform appealing. The Hussite movement gained momentum, fueled by Hus's impassioned advocacy for a return to the simplicity and purity of early Christianity.

Hus embraced many of John Wycliffe's theological teachings, which challenged the prevailing doctrines and practices of the Roman Catholic Church. Like Wycliffe, Hus emphasized the authority of Scripture as the ultimate source of religious truth and rejected certain tenets of Catholic doctrine, such as the doctrine of transubstantiation and the infallibility of the papacy. Hus's sermons and writings echoed Wycliffe's calls for church reform. For example, in *De ecclesia* (*On the Church*), Hus called for a moral and structural renewal of the church, addressing issues such as clerical immorality, simony, indulgences, and the misuse of ecclesiastical authority. He was particularly critical of the moral failures of the clergy, asserting that their behavior undermined the church's spiritual mission. He wrote, "As Christ's disciples must follow Christ in humility, poverty, patience, and toil, so priests must do the same, that they may not be the downfall of the people," emphasizing the responsibility of priests to lead virtuous lives reflecting Christ's example. Hus rejected the idea that the church's hierarchical structure or the pope was above the moral demands of Scripture, declaring, "The papal dignity is not greater than the Gospel."

> As for antichrist occupying the papal chair, it is evident that a pope living contrary to Christ, like any other perverted person, is called, by common consent, antichrist.
>
> ———
>
> Jan Hus,
> *De Ecclesia*

Hus's critique extended to the practice of simony, which he denounced as a corrupting influence that prioritized wealth over spiritual integrity. He lamented, "The Church has long ago strayed from the path of Christ by seeking wealth and temporal power, rather than humility and service," highlighting the gap between the church's worldly ambitions and its spiritual responsibilities. He also rejected indulgences as a distortion of Christian doctrine, stating, "No one can be absolved of sins by human power, for God alone forgives sins." For Hus, such practices not only mislead the faithful but also exploit them for material gain, undermining the core Christian principles of grace and repentance.

At the heart of Hus's reformist vision was his belief in the supreme authority of Scripture, which he regarded as the ultimate guide for faith and practice. In *De ecclesia*, he wrote, "The Holy Scriptures are the infallible authority and the standard by which every Christian should regulate their faith and conduct." This view challenged the institutional church's reliance on tradition and papal decrees, advocating instead for a return to biblical principles. Hus emphasized that reform must involve not only the clergy but also the laity, asserting, "Let every faithful Christian, whether priest or layman, follow the truth in love, so that Christ may reign as Head of the Church." His vision of the church as a spiritual community was encapsulated in his assertion "The true Church is the assembly of all those who are predestined to salvation," shifting focus from the visible hierarchy to the spiritual integrity of believers.

Inspired by Wycliffe's translation work, Hus sought to replicate this initiative in Bohemia by translating the Bible into Czech. This endeavor was pivotal in spreading Wycliffe's theological ideas and fostering a sense of national identity among the Czech-speaking populace. In addition to translating the Bible, Jan Hus and his followers actively circulated John Wycliffe's writings throughout Bohemia, further disseminating his theological ideas and reformist agenda. Wycliffe's works, including his theological treatises, sermons, and polemical writings against papal authority and ecclesiastical corruption, informed the burgeoning Hussite movement. Hus's advocacy for church reform and his critique of the papacy were deeply informed by Wycliffe's ideas, contributing to the growing discontent with the Roman Catholic Church in Bohemia.

Jan Hus's critique of ecclesiastical authority and his denunciation of the corrupt practices of the clergy struck a chord with the Bohemian laity, long disillusioned with the opulence and moral laxity of the church hierarchy. Hus challenged the papacy's authority and the church's hierarchical structure, advocating for a more egalitarian and spiritually focused form of Christianity. His bold stance against the excesses of the ecclesiastical establishment garnered him a dedicated following among the common people and the nobility alike. In addition to his preaching, Jan Hus actively pursued reforms within the Bohemian church, seeking to align its practices with the teachings of Scripture and the principles of simplicity and piety. He advocated for the administration of the Eucharist in both bread and wine to the laity, in opposition to the doctrine of transubstantiation upheld by the Catholic Church. Hus also called for an end to the sale of indulgences and the secularization of church property, aiming to combat the financial exploitation and moral decadence prevalent within the church.

The Hussite Wars erupted in the early fifteenth century as a response to attempts by the Catholic Church and the Holy Roman Empire to suppress the Hussite movement and enforce religious conformity. After the death of Hus, the Hussites organized into various factions, including the Utraquists, Taborites, and Orebites, and engaged in armed resistance against external forces and launched raids against Catholic strongholds.

The Hussite Wars exacerbated political instability and factionalism within Bohemia as rival Hussite factions vied for dominance and pursued divergent agendas. The conflict also sparked tensions between Bohemia and neighboring regions, leading to diplomatic and territorial conflicts. Efforts to resolve the Hussite Wars through diplomatic negotiations and ecumenical councils, such as the Council of Basel, proved largely unsuccessful, as deep-seated religious and political differences persisted. Despite intermittent truces and agreements, sporadic outbreaks of violence continued to plague Bohemia for several decades. The Hussite Wars contributed to the erosion of Catholic hegemony in central Europe and fostered a spirit of religious independence and national identity among the Czech people. Although the conflict ultimately subsided, the memory of the Hussite movement endured as a symbol of resistance against oppression and tyranny and advocacy for religious freedom.

John Hus and the Hussites were outspoken critics of clerical corruption and wealth accumulation within the Catholic church. Speaking of the corrupt priests and bishops, Huss remarked, "No one does more injury in the church that he who acts perversely and yet has the name and order of sanctity." The pervasive materialism and worldliness among the clergy was one of the central grievances of Hus and the Hussites. They condemned the opulent lifestyles of bishops, abbots, and other church officials who amassed vast fortunes and wielded political influence, often at the expense of their spiritual duties and moral integrity. Like Wycliffe before him, Hus opposed the sale of indulgences and the practice of simony, whereby ecclesiastical positions and privileges were bought and sold for personal gain. He denounced the commercialization of religious rites and sacraments, arguing that true repentance and salvation were not for sale. Monetary payments or material offerings in exchange for ecclesiastical offices offended Hus.

Hus and his followers criticized the moral laxity and ethical compromises among the clergy, including nepotism, concubinage, and moral turpitude. They called for a renewal of clerical discipline and accountability, advocating for greater transparency and accountability within the church hierarchy. In response to these concerns, Hus proposed a series of ecclesiastical reforms to purify the church and restore its moral authority. He called for eliminating corrupt practices, the equitable distribution of church wealth, and piety and humility among the clergy. Attacking the perceived hypocrisy of the pope, Hus wrote, "As for antichrist occupying the papal chair, it is evident that a pope living contrary to Christ, like any other perverted person, is called, by common consent, antichrist."

Hus's conflict with the Roman Catholic Church culminated in his trial and eventual condemnation by the ecclesiastical authorities. In 1414, he was summoned to the Council of Constance to address theological disputes and church reform. Promised safe conduct to and from the council by Emperor Sigismund, Hus attended the council, hoping to defend his teachings and clarify any misunderstandings. However, the council authorities immediately arrested and imprisoned him upon his arrival. Procedural irregularities and biases marked the trial of John Hus, and the council denied him the opportunity to present a proper defense, accusing him of heresy. Despite his insistence on the primacy of Scripture and his commitment to theological dialogue, Hus's refusal to recant his beliefs led to his formal condemnation by the council. On July 6, 1415, the Council of Constance officially pronounced Hus guilty of heresy and schism. Despite appeals for clemency and intervention from various quarters, including some members of the council, the council sentenced him to death by burning at the stake. On July 6, 1415, he was led to the stake and martyred for his beliefs, becoming a symbol of resistance against ecclesiastical tyranny and a martyr for the cause of church reform. Before the flames engulfed him, he reportedly declared, "You are going to burn a goose today, but in one hundred years, you will have a swan which you can neither roast nor boil."

Hus's martyrdom galvanized his followers and sparked a series of religious and political upheavals known as the Hussite Wars. Although his life was cut short, his legacy lived on in the Hussite movement, which continued to advocate for religious reform and national independence in Bohemia. The Hussites rejected the authority of the papacy and the Roman Catholic Church, asserting the right of the Bohemian people to determine their religious practices and governance. While the Hussite Wars ultimately ended in compromise, and the Hussite movement fragmented, Hus's ideas inspired subsequent generations of reformers.

The subsequent Hussite Christians sought to further Hus's reforms and honor his memory. One group of Hussites, the Utraquists, advocated communion "in both kinds" for the laity. While it was typical for Roman churches to offer only the communion bread to the people, the Hussites offered both the bread and the wine. They secured the right to practice their faith in this manner in the 1436 Compacts of Basel. This distinct practice within the Roman church persisted for some time. Another group, the Taborites, challenged the practice of feudalism, advocating for social and religious reforms. While the Roman Catholics eventually defeated the Taborites in the Hussite Wars, their ideas resonated with later Radical Reformers of the sixteenth century. The Hussites established new schools promoting education and intellectual discourse. This emphasis on learning contributed to Czech culture and scholarship flourishing in the following centuries.

Despite internal conflicts, Bohemia became known for its relative tolerance toward different religious views, compared to the religiously repressive atmosphere elsewhere in Europe. This legacy attracted later persecuted groups like the Unity of the Brethren, creating a haven for diverse religious expression. Hus's ideas about Scripture, authority, and communion resonated with later reformers, making Bohemia fertile ground for the Protestant movements of the next century.

Other Early Reformers

Contrary to any idea that the late medieval Roman Catholic Church was monolithic, there were early reformers throughout Europe who sought to end corruption, focus on the biblical faith, and inspire Christians to faithful living. Peter Waldo (1140–1205), a wealthy merchant from Lyon, France, led a reform movement during the twelfth century. His life and reform efforts played a crucial role in the emergence of the Waldensian movement, a precursor to the Protestant Reformation. He was born around the late twelfth century and was a successful merchant in the cloth trade. He experienced a spiritual awakening after a personal crisis and began to devote himself to a life of Christian piety and simplicity. One of the most notable aspects of Waldo's life is his decision to divest himself of his wealth and possessions, following the example of Jesus's instructions to the rich young ruler in the Gospels. Inspired by the teachings of Jesus and the apostles, Waldo embraced a life of poverty, humility, and preaching, distributing his wealth to the poor and focusing on spiritual matters.

Waldo's reform efforts centered on translating Scripture into the vernacular language and disseminating biblical teachings to the common people. Along with other reformers, Waldo believed every Christian should have access to the Word of God and sought to empower laypeople to read and interpret the Bible for themselves. In addition to promoting Bible reading and study, Waldo and his followers engaged in itinerant preaching and evangelism, traveling throughout France and beyond to spread their message of repentance, faith, and holy living. They emphasized the importance of living according to the teachings of Jesus, renouncing worldly wealth and power, and following Christ in humility and obedience.

Waldo's reform movement faced opposition from the established church hierarchy, which viewed his teachings as heretical and subversive. In 1184, Pope Lucius III condemned Waldo and his followers as heretics at the Council of Verona, leading to their excommunication and persecution by ecclesiastical authorities. Despite facing persecution and suppression, the Waldensian movement persisted and influenced Christian thought and practice in Europe. The Waldensians committed themselves to biblical authority, simplicity of life, and evangelistic zeal, seeking to advance the kingdom of God.

Marsilius of Padua (1275–1343) offered political theories that challenged the authority of the medieval church and laid the groundwork for later developments in secular governance and religious freedom. Marsilius was born in Padua, Italy, around the early fourteenth century. He was a prominent scholar, philosopher, and political theorist, educated at the University of Paris. He became known for his critical views on the relationship between church and state, advocating for the primacy of secular authority over ecclesiastical power. One of his most influential works is *Defender of the Peace*, written around 1324 in collaboration with John of Jandun. In this treatise, Marsilius articulated a radical political theory that challenged the medieval concept of papal supremacy and advocated for a secular republic governed by elected representatives. Marsilius argued that the church should be subordinate to the state and that temporal rulers, rather than the pope or clergy, should have ultimate authority over civil affairs. He rejected the idea of papal infallibility and insisted on the separation of church and state, advocating for the secularization of government and the elimination of ecclesiastical interference in political matters.

In addition to his political theories, Marsilius also critiqued the hierarchical structure of the medieval church, denouncing wealth, corruption, and abuses of power among the clergy. He called for the abolition of ecclesiastical privileges and the redistribution of church property to benefit the common people. Marsilius's ideas were considered radical and heretical by the medieval church, and he faced condemnation and persecution for his writings. The ecclesiastical authorities banned his writings, and Marsilius fled Paris to escape persecution. Despite facing opposition during his lifetime, Marsilius's ideas would later influence the development of secular governance and religious freedom in Europe. His advocacy for the supremacy of secular authority, the separation of church and state, and the individual's rights laid the groundwork for later movements for political reform and the emergence of modern democratic principles.

Jan Žižka, born around 1360 in the Kingdom of Bohemia, was a military leader and a key figure in the Hussite movement during the early fifteenth century, playing a pivotal role in the Hussite Wars and the broader context of religious reform in Bohemia. His involvement in the Hussite movement stemmed from his discontent with the corruption and abuses within the Catholic Church and his sympathy for the reformist ideas of figures like John Hus. As a military leader, Žižka organized and led the Hussite forces, which included peasants, nobles, and townspeople, in numerous battles against the combined forces of the Holy Roman Empire, the papacy, and other opponents. Žižka led the Hussites to several critical victories, including the Battle of Vítkov Hill in 1420 and the Battle of Kutná Hora in 1421. His success against much larger and better-equipped armies demonstrated the strength and resilience of the Hussite movement and its demands for religious reform and national autonomy.

Girolamo Savonarola, born in 1452 in Ferrara, Italy, was a Dominican friar, preacher, and reformer who led a reform effort during the late fifteenth century. He offered an uncompromising critique of the corruption and moral decay within the Catholic Church and called for spiritual renewal and moral reform. Savonarola entered the Dominican Order at a young age and pursued theological studies, eventually becoming known for his eloquent preaching and devotion to God. He became a prominent preacher in Florence, where his impassioned sermons attracted large crowds and stirred public consciousness.

One of Savonarola's key reforms was his condemnation of the secular excesses and moral laxity prevalent in Florence during the Renaissance. He denounced the city's ruling elite for their extravagance, corruption, and immorality, calling on them to repent and lead virtuous lives. His preaching emphasized the need for personal piety, humility, and devotion to God, rejecting the materialism and hedonism of the times. Savonarola's reform efforts extended to the church, where he criticized the papacy and clergy for their worldliness and neglect of spiritual duties. He called for a return to the simplicity and purity of early Christianity, advocating for reforms within the church hierarchy and the eradication of abuses, such as simony and nepotism. Savonarola's sermons resonated with Florentines yearning for change. He was crucial in overthrowing the Medici family and establishing a short-lived republic in 1494. He envisioned Florence as a "New Jerusalem," a model city guided by Christian principles.

One of the most famous episodes of Savonarola's life was his role in the "Bonfire of the Vanities" in 1497, where he and his followers gathered and burned a vast array of secular and sinful objects, including books, artworks, and luxury items deemed immoral or idolatrous. This event symbolized Savonarola's uncompromising stance against the excesses of secular culture and his commitment to spiritual renewal. Ultimately, Savonarola's reform efforts led to his downfall. He faced increasing opposition from political and religious authorities, culminating in his excommunication by Pope Alexander VI in 1497 and his subsequent arrest, trial, and execution for heresy in 1498. Despite his tragic end, Savonarola's legacy as a reformer and preacher of moral renewal endures, inspiring subsequent generations to strive for spiritual authenticity and Christian charity within the church.

Conclusion

Several theologians in the late medieval church opposed the Roman Catholic hierarchy for practical and theological reasons, believing the church of Rome had abandoned the faith and practice of the ancient church. The Great Tradition was a consensus of the apostolic teaching. The papacy against which these reformers contended, however, was a corruption of that faith and practice. Practically, these reformers considered the clergy to be irreparably corrupt. They proposed ending practices such as simony to prevent priests from becoming wealthy. Theologically, Wycliffe, Hus, and other early reformers sought a retrieval of the early church's emphasis on the biblical faith. They encouraged people to read the Bible in the vernacular and urged priests to teach the Bible rather than the man-made teaching of the Roman church. They opposed both the sale of indulgences and their use in churches, preaching a gospel of salvation by grace through faith instead. Each of these efforts, and others, anticipated the Protestant Reformation, which would come to Europe in the sixteenth century.

Recommended Reading

Betts, Robert R. *Jan Hus: Courageous Rebel*. Harper & Row, 1969.

Betts, Robert R. *John Wyclif: Man of Courage, Reformer for the Ages*. Eerdmans, 1965.

Deansly, Margaret. *The Lollard Bible and Other Medieval Biblical Versions*. Cambridge University Press, 1920.

Fudge, Thomas A. *The Magnificent Ride: The First Reformation in Hussite Bohemia*. Ashgate, 1998.

Hudson, Anne. *The Premature Reformation: Wycliffite Texts and Lollard History*. Clarendon, 1988.

Kaminsky, Howard. *A History of the Hussite Revolution*. University of California Press, 1967.

Kenny, Anthony. *Wycliffe*. Oxford University Press, 1985.

Lambert, Malcolm. *Medieval Heresy: Popular Movements from the Gregorian Reform to the Reformation*. 3rd ed. Blackwell, 2002.

Levy, Ian Christopher. *Holy Scripture and the Quest for Authority at the End of the Middle Ages*. University of Notre Dame Press, 2012.

Loserth, Johann. *Wyclif and Hus*. Hodder and Stoughton, 1889.

McFarlane, Kenneth B. *John Wycliffe and the Beginnings of English Nonconformity*. English Universities Press, 1952.

Molnár, Amedeo. *Jan Hus: Church Reformer*. Kalich, 1965.

Oberman, Heiko A. *Forerunners of the Reformation: The Shape of Late Medieval Thought*. Fortress, 1981.

Schaff, Philip. *History of the Christian Church*. Vol. 6, *The Middle Ages, A.D. 1294–1517*. Eerdmans, 1910.

Spinka, Matthew. *Hussite Theology and the Reformation*. Princeton University Press, 1953.

Spinka, Matthew. *John Hus and the Czech Reform*. University of Chicago Press, 1941.

Spinka, Matthew. *The Letters of John Hus*. Manchester University Press, 1972.

Thomson, Samuel Harrison. *The Wycliffite Heresy: A Study of Medieval Religious Dissent*. Cambridge University Press, 1965.

Wilks, Michael. *Wyclif: Political Ideas and Practice*. Oxford University Press, 2000.

Workman, Herbert B. *John Wyclif: A Study of the English Medieval Church*. Clarendon, 1926.

—— Chapter 24 ——

The Renaissance and the Prelude to the Protestant Reformation

The Renaissance was a multifaceted cultural movement that affected almost every aspect of Western thought and life. It is hard to define but easy to identify. The movement began in Italy sometime in the 1300s among students of rhetoric who were preparing for civil service and quickly spread to every corner of Europe. It was a movement back to an idealized classical Roman antiquity, but this return to the past brought about a change so profound that it seemed like the world had been reborn. In fact, that is what they called it: a *renaissance*, a rebirth. In this chapter, we will highlight several key features of this important movement that directly impacted the church in the days leading up to the sixteenth century.

Humanism: Back to the Sources

For as long as thinkers in the Western world have contemplated the distinction between *knowing* what is good and *communicating* what is good—content and form—they have struggled to determine which should take priority. Philosophers and theologians tend to suggest that knowledge is more important, and so we should devote our energies to expanding the content of our knowing. Orators and rhetoricians, however, suggest that *how* we communicate knowledge takes priority, and thus our energies should be devoted to honing communication skills.

The church in the West has not avoided choosing sides in this struggle. While it is certainly a broad generalization, medieval Scholasticism represented an emphasis of content over form. For the Scholastics, theology was the queen of the sciences. Renaissance humanism arose in the latter days of the Middle Ages in reaction to Scholasticism. Humanists tended toward a primacy of rhetoric over theology, form over content. They fiercely defended the conviction that rhetoric is the highest and most admirable discipline, arguably to the demise of philosophical and theological precision.

The centrality of rhetoric in humanist thought was not merely a desire for flowery speeches and entertaining letters. Rather, it was an elevation of rhetoric to first priority in the hierarchy of disciplines. This elevation of rhetoric brought to prominence a cluster of related disciplines that gave humanism its name (the humanities, i.e., history, literature, philology, moral philosophy, and the arts) and distinguished it from medieval Scholasticism. Implicit in this rejection of Scholasticism was a conviction that this form of Christianity had failed to make the world a better place. The church was supposed to be the means of salvation, but for many, it was not much more than a means for enriching bishops and popes and merchant kings. Humanists began to wonder if perhaps there was another way of becoming good, another view of the good, true, and beautiful life promised by Christianity though seemingly missing from the medieval church up to this time.

The motto of the humanists was *ad fontes*—back to the ancient sources. Among these sources, pride of place went to the Roman statesman Marcus Tullius Cicero (106–43 BC). Cicero was a model of the best form of Latin to be imitated, which was very different from what Latin had become in the medieval theological faculties. Not only that, but Cicero was the model of "man in society": a person whose basic identity was that of the *orator*.[1] The Renaissance humanist was not a lover of wisdom contemplated, but a lover of wisdom communicated, and there was no greater communicator than Cicero.

According to Cicero, the orator has three tasks: *docere*, *delectare*, *movere*—teach, delight, and move the heart. Cicero's genius was not in emphasizing rhetoric against philosophy, but in his eloquent vision for the balance between them. He insisted that "no man has ever succeeded in achieving splendour and excellence in oratory, I will not say merely without

---

[1] Jerrold Seigel, *Rhetoric and Philosophy in Renaissance Humanism* (Princeton University Press, 1968), 5.

training in speaking, but *without taking all knowledge for his province as well.*"[2] This ideal of subjecting deep and wide knowledge to the rigors of rhetoric meant that humanism was first a pedagogy, a way of learning.

In fact, the movement emerged in the universities where rhetoric was relegated to the *ars dictaminis*, the art of letter-writing, and it was from among these *dictamen*—who worked as secretaries and notaries to powerful people—that the very earliest humanists arose. One such student was Francesco Petrarca (1304–74), known to us as Petrarch, who in 1345 discovered a collection of Cicero's letters and was so captivated by what he found that he dedicated the rest of his life to searching out ancient Roman works forgotten in European libraries. Petrarch's commitment to restoring the glory of Roman antiquity was such that he began to speak of the period between his own and Cicero's as a time of darkness or, as they came to be known, the Dark Ages. As important as romanticizing the Roman past was to Petrarch, it was his discoveries of Cicero and his assimilation and emulation of him that earned him the title of being the first Renaissance humanist. While what we know as Renaissance humanism would not be recognizable for another few decades, Petrarch's discovery of Cicero's letters in 1345 may be viewed as the beginning of the movement.[3]

Out of sheer necessity, Petrarch developed a process of identifying manuscripts, copying them, and sharing his findings in letters and other writings. These letters were often modelled after the very manuscripts he was writing about. This process became identified with what it meant to be a humanist. The commitments of Renaissance humanism all centered around texts that modelled an ideal union of rhetoric and knowledge. Some of these texts were exceedingly rare, some of them were only known by reputation or rumor, and all of them represented varying degrees of antiquity and quality. The intellectual appetite of the humanists was insatiable. They became travelers and searchers, going from library to library, abbey to abbey, and from one city to another chasing down elusive manuscripts and codices.

---

[2] Cicero, *De oratore* 2.1.5, trans. E. W. Sutton, Loeb Classical Library 343 (Harvard University Press, 1948), 201. Emphasis added.

[3] See, for instance, Paul Oskar Kristeller's seminal lecture from 1954, "The Humanist Movement," in *The Classics and Renaissance Thought* (Harvard University, 1955). More recently, Nicholas Mann, "The Origins of Humanism," in *The Cambridge Companion to Renaissance Humanism*, ed. Jill Kraye (Cambridge University Press, 1996); and Martin McLaughlin, "Petrarch and Cicero: Adulation and Critical Distance," in *Brill's Companion to the Reception of Cicero*, ed. William H. F. Altman (Brill, 2015). These works trace the origins of Renaissance humanism to Petrarch's discovery of Cicero's *Epistulae ad Atticum*.

Their international reputation was due as much to their extensive letter writing as it was to their indefatigable travels.

Humanism was a text-centered movement, and it gave rise to a process of ascertaining authorship, authenticity, and quality that continued to be developed for centuries. It is with good reason that this process echoes the contemporary practice of textual criticism. But the road from this early humanistic discipline to modern textual criticism is not a straight one. As the earliest students of rhetoric were not training for professorships in theology or positions within the hierarchy of the church, it meant that humanism arose outside of the more ordinary structures of the church. Many of the first humanists were part of a rising class of highly educated laypeople who did not approach texts with the same agenda as Scholastic theologians. In fact, because they were not interacting with Scripture at all, they had freedom to ask questions about the integrity of texts that would have been considered inappropriate to ask of the Scriptures. This freedom to question and ascertain the integrity and quality of the sources developed into a discipline known today as *philology*. Eventually, their efforts turned toward the church fathers and even the Bible itself. As we will see below, this impulse within humanism reached its zenith with Erasmus of Rotterdam, who in 1516 would publish the world's first critical edition of the New Testament.

These changes in educational methods created opportunities for new investigations of old documents. This also meant fresh challenges to old assumptions. Among these was the Donation of Constantine, purported to have been drafted by the emperor Constantine himself and given to the bishop of Rome in the fourth century, granting him authority over Rome. With new approaches to philology and grammar emerging during the renaissance, the Italian scholar and rhetorician Lorenzo Valla took a fresh look at the Donation of Constantine. In 1440 Valla published a treatise entitled *On the Donation of Constantine*, in which he used the methods of his day to demonstrate that the document was certainly not of fourth-century origin. Rather, given the grammar and style, it was more likely a mid-eighth-century document. This proved deeply disruptive for the Roman Catholic Church, especially for papal authority, further setting the stage for the inevitable—a reformation.

While we often associate the Renaissance with paintings, frescoes, sculptures, fashion, architecture, and many other artistic endeavors, it was the written works of the humanists (such as Dante, discussed in chapter 21) that gave the Renaissance its center of gravity. As Martin Davies asserts, the central conviction of humanism was "that good letters lead, under

God's guidance, to good men."[4] The foundation of the Renaissance movement was the quest to capture the spirit of classical antiquity to live well in the present. But the impact of the Renaissance was not limited to living well. It also motivated innovation in architecture and technology.

Architecture

While Renaissance humanists searched libraries and monasteries for glimpses into the literary glory of the Roman past, Renaissance architects, motivated by the same *ad fontes* spirit, carefully studied the many ruins of ancient Roman buildings that remained in northern Italy. The complex systems and irregular patterns of medieval Gothic architecture stood in stark contrast to the orderly symmetry of Roman columns, domes, and arches. Much like Petrarch and the humanists, Renaissance architects allowed their study and admiration to become imitation. Their use of symmetry, space, and geometrical features quickly developed into a style that would mark the most impressive buildings in Europe. While humanism was largely confined to a portion of the literate class, architecture brought the Renaissance to the masses. Its most spectacular accomplishments were chapels and churches in which every pilgrim could worship.

After Europe began to recover economically from the toll taken by the plague-riddled fourteenth century, rich banking families in northern Italy, such as the Medici and the Pazzi, began to invest heavily in patronage of artists who had been exploring classical principles in their paintings and sculptures. This allowed them to take on architectural projects that required greater financial resources. Further, the return of the papacy to Rome brought an economic boom in Italy. As discussed previously, throughout most of the fourteenth century (1309–76), seven consecutive popes ruled from Avignon rather than Rome. When Gregory XI moved the papal courts back to Rome, it restored the city's economic fortunes and cultural importance. Additionally, the temporal power of the pope continued to grow, especially as the Council of Constance (1417) sought to undo the damage of the Avignon papacy. The continued succession of popes with unsatiable appetites for grand building programs and lavish displays of wealth translated into an unprecedented tidal wave of financing for sculptors, painters, and architects.

---

[4] Martin Davies, "Humanism in Script and Print," in *The Cambridge Companion to Renaissance Humanism*, ed. Jill Kraye (University Press, 1996), 60.

The Florentine sculptor Filippo Brunelleschi (1377–1446) is considered the first Renaissance architect. His design of the Ospedale degli Innocenti (Hospital of the Innocents) in Florence in 1419 reintroduced Europe to the simplicity and elegance of classical construction principles. It is easily recognizable by an arcade of high arches supported by simple columns with Corinthian capitals. At the time, there was nothing in Florence like it. Brunelleschi would continue to explore and develop classical principles in many subsequent projects, primarily chapels and churches. He was the first to employ many of the principles that became Renaissance mainstays, such as linear perspective, geometric proportions in

Image 24.1. *Santa Maria del Fiore*

space, and mathematical harmony. His design and construction of the dome of the cathedral of Santa Maria del Fiore (known as the Florence Cathedral and completed in 1434) is one of the greatest architectural feats in history. More importantly, it forever linked the highest expressions of Renaissance architecture with the Roman church.

After Brunelleschi, Renaissance architecture continued to flourish in tandem with developments in the arts. The building boom Rome was experiencing at the hands of increasingly wealthy and powerful popes helped bring about the period known as the High Renaissance. This is when Leonardo da Vinci painted *The Last Supper* (c. 1495), when Michelangelo painted his frescoes in the Sistine Chapel (c. 1508–12), and Raphael painted *The School of Athens* in the Vatican (1508). This time represents the most mature artistic attempts at uniting Renaissance principles to an explicitly Christian message.

Yet, this period also represents the height of the lavish and worldly spending programs that were funded by indulgences and the threat of war. While there is no doubt that many Renaissance works represent some of the highest peaks of human creativity, many of those who lived through those days found the attendant factors to be in opposition to the principles of Christ.

Perhaps in no other building is this tension more visible than in the quintessential achievement of Renaissance architecture: Saint Peter's Basilica in Rome. A vast, magnificent building at 352,800 square feet, it boasts the largest interior space of any church in the world. Its dome is the defining feature of the Roman skyline. Its portico overlooking St. Peter's square is synonymous with the papacy in the modern world. The entire building within and without is decorated with reliefs and sculptures, many of which are incredible works of art in their own right.

Michelangelo's *Pietà* (meaning "compassion," a sculpture of Mary holding the dead body of Jesus), completed in 1498/99, while he was in his early twenties, and considered by many to be Michaelangelo's greatest sculpture, resides within the walls of St. Peter's Basilica. Michelangelo himself was the chief designer and architect of the basilica. He took up the project in his seventies after the foundations and pillars for the dome had already been set on Donato Bramante's designs and Raphael's modifications. Michelangelo died in 1564, but the remainder of the work was carried out according to his designs. The engineering required for the massive scale of the building is as impressive as the artistic accomplishment that the building represents.

But for all its beauty and grand scale, the building also signified much of what ailed the church in the fifteenth and sixteenth centuries. When Julius II (1503–13) began to plan the building of his own tomb, he took the commission of Nicholas V (1447–55) to repair the original basilica built during Constantine's reign and reimagined it as an entirely new building, within which he would be entombed. The cost of this building project was astronomical. To help finance it, Julius authorized the selling of indulgences in exchange for contributions to its construction. One of his most controversial salesmen, Johan Tetzel, caught the disapproving attention of an Augustinian priest in Wittenberg, Germany, named Martin Luther. Luther's *Disputation on the Power and Efficacy of Indulgences*, otherwise known as the *Ninety-Five Theses*, was written in direct response to the papacy's efforts to build St. Peter's Basilica.

Gutenberg's Press

Europe in the fifteenth century was poised for an information revolution. Thanks to the "New Learning," as humanism was called, educated theologians were no longer the only literate people in society, and their libraries were no longer the reading material of choice for most people. The material prosperity of cities and dioceses was no longer in the hands of a few elites. A clear middle class was emerging. They were not recognized as equals to archbishops and emperors, but their prosperity afforded them access to an equal or sometimes superior education. This "prosperity seeking understanding" quickly exposed the struggle of older methods of disseminating information. Hand-copied manuscripts were simply inefficient.

In the late 1430s, a goldsmith by the name of Johannes Gutenberg invented the printing press. Details are scant, but what is clear is that Gutenberg's unique combination of devices in a single machine for printing books had never been done before. The screw press had been in existence for centuries, primarily in agricultural applications, such as olive oil presses. The process for making paper had arrived in Europe from China via Arab Muslims. The codex format of a book had replaced the scroll centuries prior. Printing itself—as opposed to handwriting—had been used in Egypt in more primitive ways. Gutenberg's genius was putting these together with a revolutionary invention of his own: movable type. Suffice it to say, Gutenberg didn't invent printing, just the printing press.

Gutenberg had the advantage of working with the Latin writing system, which allowed him to work from a smaller batch of characters. He himself created his own type pieces and the process for laying them out in a matrix that could be stamped onto a piece of paper repeatedly, a process referred to as "typesetting." Combined with the screw press and the book format of collating paper, this method enabled thousands of pages to be printed daily. Mass production of books was now possible at a scale never before seen. Famously, the Gutenberg Bible was the first major work published on Gutenberg's press.

Within a generation, every major city was home to several print shops, and even many small towns had at least one. Bibles represented the lion's share of a publisher's bread and butter, but the humanist desire for quality editions of the classics and the church fathers sometimes turned a profit, as did the published letters of their luminaries. Lorenzo Valla's (1407–57) *Elegantiae linguae Latinae* (*Elegances of the Latin Language*) was reprinted some sixty times. Leon Battista Alberti's *De re aedificatoria* (*On the Art of Building*) was the first printed work on architecture (1470) and was immensely influential. Papal bulls and certificates of indulgence were also printed by the thousands. But perhaps the power of the printed press was best harnessed by Martin Luther and the Protestant Reformers.

Before Luther, the printer's art was still mainly an academic endeavor that was often unprofitable. Erasmus of Rotterdam was the closest thing to a sure profit, with nearly three-quarters of a million copies of his works sold in his lifetime. But coupled with the momentum of the Protestant Reformation, printing became a profitable industry, driving the spread of information, news, and knowledge with unprecedented volume and efficiency.[5] While we aim to avoid historical conjecture, it is difficult to imagine how the Protestant Reformation could have occurred without the printing press.

The great city of Constantinople fell on May 29, 1453, officially marking the end of the Byzantine Empire. The Ottoman forces of Mehmed II laid siege to it on April 6, after several years of preparation. Byzantine Emperor Constantine XI had attempted reconciliation with the West in an attempt to gather allies. Pope Nicholas V (1447–55), however, despite promises to send support, found Western European leaders unable or unwilling to answer his calls for military aid to Constantinople. Prior efforts to repair the breach between West and East had failed. The mutual excommunications of 1054 were neither forgotten nor forgiven, and they showed themselves in the form of ethnic hatred between the Greek East and the Latin West.

When the time came to offer support, both sides drug their feet but eventually cooperated. The Byzantine Empire was a shadow of its former self, having lost nearly half of its population in the Black Death. Other internal conflicts had reduced its actual land mass to

---

[5] See Andrew Pettegree, *Brand Luther: 1517, Printing, and the Making of the Reformation* (Penguin, 1015).

a few square kilometers. The "Byzantine Empire" had dwindled to little more than the city of Constantinople itself.

Erasmus and Christian Humanism (1466–1536)

Desiderius Erasmus was born in Rotterdam, Holland (now the Netherlands), on October 28, c. 1466. He was the illegitimate son of Gerhard and Margaret, a priest and a physician's daughter. Although unable to give Erasmus a legitimate pedigree, Gerhard provided for him an education in Deventer, where he was exposed to the classics and the Devotio Moderna (Modern Devotion movement, especially modeled by the likes of Thomas à Kempis).[6] His parents both died in a plague outbreak in 1483. In his early twenties, like many of illegitimate birth, he entered the monastic life, joining the cloister of the Canons Regular of St. Augustine at Steyn. He quickly developed a reputation as a gifted Latinist, so much so that while he was at the University of Paris for a time in the 1490s, he wrote to a friend, "I am trying with might and main to say nothing in good Latin, or elegantly, or wittily; and I seem to be making progress; so there is some hope that eventually they will acknowledge me [as a theologian]."[7] He became a secretary to the bishop of Cambrai, who gave him a great deal more freedom to write than he had in the monastery. In 1500, he published the *Adagia* (collection of Greek and Latin adages) and then in 1503 the *Enchiridion militis Christiani* (*Handbook of the Christian Soldier*), both of which helped establish his reputation as a learned and eloquent Christian humanist.

At this point, it may be helpful to distinguish between Renaissance humanism and Christian humanism. While there is much overlap between the two, they maintain different focuses and represent distinct eras. For example, most humanists would have insisted that high learning is an instrument to lead a person to genuine devotion to Christ and to avoid empty academic pursuits. But for the average Renaissance humanist, disciplines such as biblical textual criticism and theology seemed to have been less urgent concerns, whereas for a Christian humanist like Erasmus, they were central.

---

[6] The Devotio Moderna's most famous adherent was Thomas à Kempis. See his *The Imitation of Christ*, ed. Harold C. Gardiner, SJ (Image, 1989).

[7] Desiderius Erasmus, Epistle 64.90, in *The Erasmus Reader*, ed. Erika Rummel (University of Toronto Press, 1990), 4.

There is a difference in eras as well. The best representatives of Renaissance humanism are found in the mid-fifteenth century. This form of humanism was not concerned only with ancient texts, but also with architecture, art, and science, as discussed above. Geographically, they were centered mainly in northern Italy. Erasmus, whose works were published in the sixteenth century, was the standout of a northern European brand of humanism that focused almost exclusively on the Bible and would be admired by later Protestant Reformers, such as Ulrich Zwingli, Phillip Melanchthon, William Tyndale, and John Calvin.

In 1499, Erasmus went to England to teach at the University of Oxford. There, he was introduced to the teaching of John Colet, whose hermeneutic focused on the history and literal meaning of the text. This encounter transformed the young Erasmus. In the following years, he mastered the Greek language and was unwavering in his commitment to studying the Bible in its original language and to sharing his findings with the world.

From England, Erasmus went to Italy, where he spent several years in the legendary publishing house of Aldus Manutius. The significance of Erasmus's relationship to the nascent art of printing is difficult to overstate. Until Martin Luther's own writings were to set Europe ablaze, there was no one who came close to Erasmus in terms of publishing power. Much of his traveling itinerary was determined by the various printing facilities available in cities across Europe, since Erasmus saw it as his life's work to disseminate not his own writings, but the writings of the church fathers. His editions of Augustine, Jerome, and the humanist Lorenzo Valla (1407–57) were landmarks in publishing history.

Erasmus was quite well-known in the early sixteenth century, being associated with reformations. His purpose, however, was not always consonant with that of the Reformers, as Erasmus sought to retrieve the Christian faith and practice of the ancient church. Despite his criticism of the Roman Catholicism, Erasmus never left the church.

Many of the Reformers were very open in their admiration of Erasmus and counted him as an ally. Regarding Erasmus's impact on the Reformers, a common quip during the period of the Reformation was that "Luther hatched the egg that Erasmus laid." Many within Catholicism sought to leverage his celebrity against the Reformation. Eventually, he entered the fray with a series of works against Luther in 1524–26 debating the freedom of the will. These pleased no one, for the Reformers were disappointed that the Erasmus who rejected much of the medieval church's practice in works such as *The Praise of Folly* did not join them in ultimately rejecting the Roman church outright. Roman Catholics were disappointed that the world's most famous son of Rome had nothing more than a polite discourse on an obscure theological matter with which to engage the ruinous reformer from Wittenberg.

Erasmus would continue to write and publish, but the displeasure from the belligerents of the Reformation followed him until he died in Basel on July 12, 1536. His last words were *O Jesu, misericordia, Domine libera me; Domine miserer mei* ("O Jesus, have mercy, Lord, deliver me, Lord have mercy upon me").[8]

Handbook of the Christian Soldier

One of the enigmas of Erasmus is his level of influence over so many different people. Before his skirmish with Luther cast a cloud over his name, Reformers and popes, bishops and kings, printers and readers all drank deeply from the well of Erasmus's thought. Even after the Reformation complicated his reputation, the immensity and quality of his work guaranteed his place in the pantheon of those whose influence and work would outlive them. This was due to Erasmus's role in bringing Renaissance humanism into Christendom. Humanism, as we have seen, was not as much a worldview as it was a method of learning, a pedagogy. Whether through painting, sculpture, or the written word, its intent was to capture the wisdom and spirit of classical antiquity to live well in the present. One of the reasons for Erasmus's popularity in his day was his unique ability to package the classics for popular consumption.

That popularizing instinct was also present in his criticism of the inaccessible dialectical method prevalent in theological schools and monasteries. He reacted to this by writing books in straightforward prose (albeit Latin) which encouraged simple piety and commonsense living. His most popular such work, the *Enchiridion militis Christiani*, or the *Handbook of the Christian Soldier*, published in 1503, was criticized for its simplicity. A Renaissance humanist to his core, Erasmus considered himself, above all, a communicator of ancient truths long neglected under the veneer of complexity posing as erudition.

No theme is more prominent and important in Erasmus's work than that of *pietas*, piety. From the time the *Enchiridion* was published in 1503 until his death in 1536, the conviction that piety was the true path to Christian virtue never departed from Erasmus's pen. One modern biography of Erasmus argued for a four-fold meaning to *pietas* in Erasmus's writings: First, piety is "the correct attitude of the individual toward God and society"; it is, second, an inwardness "independent of the external observance of rites," which leads, third, to a

[8] Ronald Bainton, *Erasmus of Christendom* (Hendrickson, 1969), 290.

"detachment from the world" and, fourth, "engenders intellectual humility and an awareness of the limits of human wisdom."[9] The concern for piety and simple godliness present in the *Enchiridion* remained Erasmus's chief concern whether in letter writing, catechisms, meditations, or commentaries on the Psalms.

One of the most quoted lines in the *Enchiridion* concerns a central doctrine in Roman Catholicism, and it perfectly captures Erasmus's notion of piety: "No veneration of Mary is more beautiful than the imitation of her humility. No devotion to the saints is more acceptable to God than the imitation of their virtues."[10] While the Reformation would later attack the Mass as an abominable idolatry, Erasmus encouraged his readers to seek its spiritual significance. "If you believe in what takes place at the altar but fail to enter into the spiritual meaning of it, God will despise your flabby display of religion."[11]

The Praise of Folly

The most controversial and celebrated of Erasmus's works is *The Praise of Folly* (1511), a satirical work confronting what he believed was the false piety of the Roman Catholic Church of his day. It was *The Praise of Folly* that established Erasmus's position as commentator on ecclesiastical matters. The work remains a classic of world literature. In his own day, its undercurrent of pessimism about the human condition and the irreverent criticism of those who thought they had the cure brought about questions regarding his character and even charges of heresy. Erasmus protested in a letter that many of his critics had a "religious sense" that was "so distorted that they find the most serious blasphemies against Christ more bearable than the slightest joke on pope or prince, especially if it touches their daily bread."[12] Eventually, *The Praise of Folly* was included in the *Index of Prohibited Books*, a list of heretical and dangerous writings established by Pope Paul IV to protect Roman Catholic readers.

But behind the satire and wit, the same concern for genuine piety runs throughout. The main character, Folly, drives home the point that only foolish abandon to Christ deserves to be called piety. "You will find some among the monks," says Folly, "who are so strictly religious and pious that they will wear no outer clothes other than those made of Cilician

---

[9] Erika Rummel, *Erasmus* (Continuum, 2004), 34.

[10] Erasmus, *Enchiridion*, in *Essential Erasmus*, ed. John P. Dolan (Mentor, 1964), 66.

[11] Erasmus, *Enchiridion*, 65.

[12] *Collected Works of Erasmus*, vol. 27, A.H.T. Levi, ed., (University of Toronto Press, 1986), 84.

goat's hair or inner garments other than the ones made of Milesian wool. . . . [it is not] so much their concern to be like Christ as it is to be unlike one another."[13] Those who do not embrace Folly are those who take themselves too seriously. Ultimately, those who reject Folly are the greatest fools. Only he who is fool enough to love the virtuous things in life can find true happiness:

> The more perfect the love, the greater the madness—and the happier. What, then, will life in heaven be like, to which all pious minds so eagerly aspire? . . . Although this perfect happiness can only be experienced when the soul has recovered its former body and been granted immortality, since the life of the pious is no more than a contemplation and foreshadowing of that other life, at times they are able to feel some foretaste and savour of the reward to come. . . . This is surely what the prophet promises: "Eye has not seen, no ear heard, nor have there entered into the heart of man the things which God has prepared for those that love him." And this is the part of folly which is not taken away by the transformation of life but is made perfect.[14]

In the above quote, one finds the quintessential Erasmus: deep concern for piety, sharp wit, reverence for the classics, and disdain for medieval monasticism and Scholasticism, all in a work of literary quality still easily recognized centuries later.

The 1516 New Testament

A final work that must be accounted for in any reckoning of Erasmus is his landmark critical edition of the Greek New Testament, published in 1516. Erasmus's discovery of a manuscript of Lorenzo Valla's *Annotations on the New Testament* in 1504 was a watershed moment for him. In these notes, Valla applied the philological principles long developed by Renaissance humanism to the Latin Vulgate of the New Testament. Erasmus set out to build on Valla's work, but after encountering John Colet, he saw the need to edit not only Jerome's Latin translation, but the Greek text itself, on which a reliable translation could then be based. In the sixteenth century, most vernacular translations were based on the Latin Vulgate, which was seen as authoritative. But even the Latin text was demonstrably unreliable. Erasmus insisted that a reliable Latin text could not be determined until a reliable Greek text was settled.

---

13 *Collected Works of Erasmus*, 27:149.

14 *Collected Works of Erasmus*, 27:152.

Ultimately, however, Erasmus's fight was not against the faulty manuscripts or the deficient Latin translations, but against the ignorance of theologians and divines who built and maintained their erroneous doctrine on the foundation of faulty biblical evidence acquired through dubious methodology:

> If they once become dictators, farewell to all the best authors! The world will be compelled to accept their brainless rubbish as oracles; and so little sound learning is there in it, that I would rather be a humble cobbler than the best of their tribe, if they can acquire nothing in the way of a liberal education. These are the men who do not like to see a text corrected, for it may look as though there were something they did not know. It is they who try to stop me with the authority of imaginary synods; they who build up this great threat to the Christian faith; they who cry "the church is in danger" (and no doubt support her with their own shoulders, which would be better employed in propping a dung-cart) and spread suchlike rumours among the ignorant and superstitious mob; for the said mob takes them for great divines, and they wish to lose none of this reputation. They are afraid that when they misquote Scripture, as they often do, the authority of the Greek or Hebrew text may be cast in their teeth, and it may soon become clear that what used to be quoted as an oracle is all a dream.[15]

For Erasmus, a clear and correct text is as vital to the well-being of the church as right doctrine. He insisted that the theologian could not exist apart from the grammarian and the scribe. After gathering manuscripts and mastering the Greek language, he settled in Basel in 1514 and began the massive undertaking of creating a critical edition of the Greek New Testament.

The work was divided into five parts: a section entitled the "Exhortation" (*Paraclesis*), an encouragement to read the New Testament as the way of Christ; the "Method" (*Methodus*), a series

> Transformation is a more important matter than intellectual comprehension. Only a very few can be learned, but all can be Christian, all can be devout, and—shall boldly add—all can be theologians.
>
> Desiderius Erasmus, *The Paraclesis*

[15] Desiderius Erasmus, *The Correspondence of Erasmus: Letters 298 to 445 (1514–1516)*, trans. R. A. B. Mynors and D. F. S. Thomson, annotated by James K. McConica, vol. 3 of *Collected Works of Erasmus* (University of Toronto Press, 1976), 337 (§136).

of admonitions on how to read the New Testament rightly; and the "Defense" [*Apologia*], an explanation of Erasmus's rationale for the present work. Next, Erasmus provided the text itself of the Greek New Testament, which was accompanied by a parallel column of Erasmus's own Latin translation, heavily dependent on Jerome's Vulgate. Finally, Erasmus included the annotations, which were his notes on the text of the Greek and Latin. This fifth section was almost as long as the New Testament text itself. Any one of these parts by itself would have been revolutionary in the history of the transmission of the Scriptures; together they represent the single greatest achievement of Christian humanism.

Recommended Reading

Bainton, Ronald. *Erasmus of Christendom*. Hendrickson, 1969.

Cicero. *De Oratore Books I–II*. Translated by E. W. Sutton. Loeb Classical Library 343. Harvard University Press, 1948.

Davies, Martin. "Humanism in Script and Print." In *The Cambridge Companion to Renaissance Humanism*. Edited by Jill Kraye. Cambridge University Press, 1996.

Desiderius Erasmus. *Enchiridion*. In *The Essential Erasmus*. Edited by John P. Dolan. Mentor, 1964.

Desiderius Erasmus. *The Erasmus Reader*. Edited by Erika Rummel. University of Toronto Press, 1990.

Desiderius Erasmus. "The Life of Erasmus." In *The Essential Erasmus*. Edited by John P. Dolan. Mentor, 1964.

Kempis, Thomas á. *The Imitation of Christ*. Edited by Harold C. Gardiner, S. J. Image, 1989.

Mann, Nicholas, "The Origins of Humanism." In *The Cambridge Companion to Renaissance Humanism*. Edited by Jill Kraye. Cambridge University Press, 1996.

McLaughlin, Martin, "Petrarch and Cicero: Adulation and Critical Distance." In *Brill's Companion to the Reception of Cicero*. Edited by William H. F. Altman. Brill, 2015.

Pettegree, Andrew. *Brand Luther: 1517, Printing, and the Making of the Reformation*. Penguin, 2015.

Seigel, Jerrold. *Rhetoric and Philosophy in Renaissance Humanism*. Princeton University Press, 1968.

EPILOGUE

Christians living in the late Middle Ages or during the period of the Renaissance obviously had no way of knowing what momentous events were to follow in the European Reformations. In most ways, life simply continued for everyday Christians, who gathered each week in worship. But the combination of economic, political, cultural, and theological developments in the late fifteenth and early sixteenth centuries would erupt in a series of conflicts in Europe and the British Isles that would shape all of Western civilization. In the volume that follows this one, the story of the continued development of Christian life and thought moves forward through the European Reformations and beyond. The Great Tradition of faithfulness to the gospel, which Jesus Christ delivered to the apostles and which the apostles handed down through their writings, persists throughout the world, being preached and practiced in diverse ways but always with a view to the Scriptures in which that tradition finds its genesis. Christians everywhere sought fidelity to the biblical faith of Jesus Christ according to Scripture. Where radical alternatives to that faith were present, theologians persisted in their efforts to articulate a gospel and live their faith through engagement with Scripture and those who came before them. Having received Christian belief and practice applicable in their present context, Christians insisted on fidelity to the message of Christ and the apostles found authoritatively in the Bible. In the next volume, the story of this continued effort follows. Here, on the eve of the Reformations, Christianity in Europe stood at a crossroads between insisting on the biblical faith of the ancient church or embracing a syncretism between Christianity and the culture of the medieval world.

ILLUSTRATION CREDITS

Image 1.1. Arch of Titus, Forum Romanum, Rome, Italy. Wikimedia Commons. Public domain.

Image 1.2. The maximum extent of the Roman Empire. Wikimedia Commons. Public domain.

Image 8.1. The Council of Nicaea. Wikimedia Commons. Public domain.

Image 17.1. The spread of Cistercian monasticism in Europe. Christian History Institute.

Image 24.1. The façade of *Santa Maria del Fiore*, the Florence Cathedral. Annotations for the three mosaics tympanums. Wikimedia Commons. Public domain.

INDEX

C

D

E

F

G

N

O

T